THE CATHOLIC GIRL'S GUIDE

COUNSELS AND DEVOTIONS

FOR

GIRLS IN THE ORDINARY WALKS OF LIFE

AND IN PARTICULAR FOR

THE CHILDREN OF MARY

ABRIDGED VERSION

BY

REVEREND FRANCIS X. LASANCE

2012
ST. AUGUSTINE ACADEMY PRESS
LISLE, ILLINOIS

This book is newly typeset based on the 1906 edition by Benziger Brothers. All editing strictly limited to the correction of errors in the original text, minor clarifications in punctuation or phrasing, and the addition of select footnotes. Any remaining oddities of spelling or phrasing are as found in the original.

This book is considered abridged due to the fact that most of the final section, consisting of prayers and devotions as well as the order of Mass, has been omitted. Those prayers which have been retained have been inserted at the end of each chapter, sometimes in a different translation than was found in the original text. All other text herein is unchanged as noted above.

Nihil Obstat
  Remigius Lafort
    Censor Librorum

Imprimatur
  ✠ John M. Farley
    Archbishop of New York

New York, December 18, 1905.

This book was originally published in 1906 by Benziger Brothers. This edition ©2012 by St. Augustine Academy Press. Editing by Theresa Kleck and Lisa Bergman.

ISBN: 978-1-936639-12-0
Library of Congress Control Number: 2012940967

The botanical engravings used to illustrate this book are taken from the 1640 reprint of the landmark 1616 *Hortus Eystettensis* by Basilius Besler. Unless otherwise noted, all other illustrations in this book, including the cover, are public domain images.
page 382: Illustration of St. Aloysius by Julie Streeter.

"**Father Lasance** displays excellent judgment in selecting the material for his books; he seems to understand just what the faithful want, so that there is scarcely a page which is not treasured."
—The Rosary Magazine, October, 1903

About Father Lasance:

Reverend Francis Xavier Lasance was born in Cincinnati, Ohio in 1860. He studied at St. Xavier College (Now known as Xavier University), then went on to St. Meinrad Seminary in Indiana. He was ordained a priest May 24, 1883, and for seven years he served as assistant and rector in several parishes of the Archdiocese of Cincinnati. Due to a physical breakdown he was forced to give up active parish work in 1890, and after a visit to Europe, he was appointed chaplain to the Sisters of Notre Dame in his native city. During this period, he wrote over three dozen devotional books, for which he received a special blessing from Pope Pius XI in 1927. He died in 1946 at the age of 86.

About *The Catholic Girl's Guide:*

Like many of Father Lasance's books, this volume is a compilation of meditations and prayers. In this case, he chose to translate and adapt a German work, *Mit ins Leben*, by Rev. P. Coelestin Muff, O.S.B., adding to it a treasury of prayers and a set of meditations on the Life of Mary by Rev. Richard Clarke, S.J.. This *Guide* begins by examining the ideal virtues of the Catholic young lady, with particular attention to maidenly purity and its safeguards. Much good advice can be found throughout the book, which even discusses family life and the education of children.

"The first part, the 'Maiden's Wreath,' contains a unique feature, perhaps suggested by the writings of St. Francis de Sales: the virtues proper to the Catholic girl are symbolized by flowers. Thus the sunflower is made the emblem of faith, the ivy of hope, the peony of love of God, etc. The counsels are comprehensive in scope and practical in application. They examine in a dispassionate way not only such matters as dress, dancing, and the theatre, but such vital topics as vocation, the religious life, and the responsibilities of motherhood. The book is valuable and timely."
—The Manhattan Quarterly, October 1906

To find more books like this one, visit our website at
www.staugustineacademypress.com

Jesus, Mary, and Joseph,
I give you my heart and my soul.
Jesus, Mary and Joseph,
may I breathe forth my soul in peace with you.

Editor's Note

The edition you hold in your hands is a faithful reproduction of the original in all ways but one: after much deliberation, we decided to exclude the final section of *The Catholic Girl's Guide*. However, we want to reassure the reader that the valuable content you will find in these pages was not changed in any way, except to correct errors of spelling or punctuation in the original.

The reasons for omitting the final section were many and compelling. First, the original book, like most prayer books of its day, was printed as a small leatherbound volume with the thin pages one would find in a missal, making its nearly 700 pages not only much more portable, but much more durable. To print so many pages in an affordable paperback format for today's Catholic families would have resulted in a much larger, heavier and less durable book.

We carefully examined the content of the final section and chose those prayers which every Catholic ought to be familiar with, and placed a selection of these at the end of each chapter of the first section of the book. We also retained the section on preparation for confession, which contained a very thorough examination of conscience, and the Devotions for the Month of May. However, the rest of the final section included such things as the order of Mass as it was said in 1906—that is, the Tridentine Mass (or Extraordinary form, as it is commonly known today). For those unfamiliar with it, this may have been of some interest or curiosity; however, for those who attend the Latin Mass, a true Missal would serve far better, since it would contain (again, in more durable form) not merely the order of Mass but also the readings and other propers.

Likewise, the other prayers and devotions, such as the Stations of the Cross, various Litanies, Morning and Evening Prayers, etc. could easily be found in any number of prayer books which would be much more portable than this one.

Another issue was the great deal of redundancy in this section, where, for example, three or four versions of the same prayer are given, differing only in verbosity or floridity of language. For this same reason, for the prayers we did retain, we sometimes substituted a more widely-known or well-translated version than the one found in the original book. (Though it should be noted that we preferred versions that used *thees* and *thous* rather than the more informal *you*.)

Above all, however, the knowledge that the unabridged version is available through other sources, for those who wish to have the entire book as it was originally published, reassured us that it made sense to provide this abridged version for families who wished to have the content of this unique book at the most affordable price possible. Therefore, we hope you will agree that the current volume is much easier to use without the addtional 300 pages and we hope that you will enjoy *The Catholic Girl's Guide* for many years to come.

In Christ,
Lisa Bergman
St. Augustine Academy Press
May 2012

Contents

To Today's Catholic Girl	xv
Foreword	xvii
Preface	xxi

Part First: THE MAIDEN'S WREATH

The Sunflower: Faith

I. How Great a Blessing Is the True Faith	1
II. Keep the Faith	5
III. Whose is this Image?	8
IV. Be Vigilant	12
Act of Faith	16
Act of Spiritual Communion	16
Adoro Te Devote	17

The Ivy: Hope

V. Hope in the Lord	19
VI. God Doeth All Things Well	22
VII. The Blessed Fruits of Patience	26
VIII. Weep Not!	30
Act of Hope	34
Memorare	34
Te Deum	35

The Peony: Love of God

IX. *Sursum Corda!*--Lift Up Your Hearts!	37
X. Let the Love of God Dwell in Your Heart	41
My God, I Love Thee	44
XI. The Miracle of Love	45
XII. Love upon the Altar	48
XIII. In the Bright Days of Youth	52
Act of Love	56
I Love Thee, O Thou Lord Most High	56
Jesus, my Lord, my God, my all	57

The Rose: Love of Our Neighbor

XIV. Kindheartedness	59
XV. Honor thy Father and thy Mother	63
XVI. An Earnest of Future Blessings	66
XVII. The Ambassadors of Christ	70
XVIII. What Friendship Ought to Be	74
XIX. It is Difficult Yet not Impossible	78
Alma Redemptoris Mater	82
Veni Creator Spiritus	83

The Carnation: Obedience

XX. Our Great Exemplar	85
XXI. A Careful Mother	89
XXII. Obedience: the Christian's Ornament	93
XXIII. Some Objections Which May Be Urged	96
The Angelus	100
Suscipe	101
Anima Christi	101

The Forget-me-not: Piety

XXIV. The Real Flower	103
XXV. "Remember Thy Last End"	107
XXVI. "One Thing is Necessary"	110
XXVII Do Not Imitate Eve	114
XXVIII. Imitate Mary	118
XXIX. A Ladder to Heaven	122
XXX. A Fount of Healing	126
XXXI. Is Confession Difficult?	130
XXXII. The Table of the Lord	134
XXXIII. The Robe of Piety	138
Sighs to Jesus in the Blessed Sacrament	143

The Violet: Humility

XXXIV. The Maiden's Ornament	145
XXXV. Humility is Essential to Salvation	149

XXXVI. The Fruits of Humility	153
Sub Tuum Praesidium	157
Prayer Before A Crucifix	157
Prayer to St. Michael	157

The Daffodil: Industry

XXXVII. The Value of Work	159
XXXVIII. Love of Work	163
XXXIX. Away from Home	166
Salve Regina	170
Ave Regina Coelorum	171
Regina Cæli	171

The Narcissus: Truthfulness

XL. False Prophets	173
XLI. Truth Before All	177
XLII. Let Your Speech Be Always with Charity	180
XLIII. There Is no Great Harm in It!	184
XLIV. Calumny and Contempt	187
XLV. Sins Committed by Hearing	191
XLVI. A Small, but Dangerous Member	195
Petitions of St. Augustine	199

Part Second: A WREATH OF LILIES

The Lily in Untarnished Splendor

XLVII. How Beautiful Is the Chaste Generation!	203
XLVIII. Blessed Are the Clean of Heart	207
XLIX. Fight and Conquer	210
L. Take Courage!	213
Prayer to St. Aloysius	217

The Lily and her Enemies

LI. The Enemy in Our Own Heart	219
LII. The Enemy in Human Shape	222
LIII. The Enemy in Finery and External Attractions	226

LIV. The Enemy in Our Eyes	229
LV. The Enemy in What We Hear and Read	232
LVI. The Enemy in the Ballroom	235
LVII. The Enemy in the Theatre	239
Prayer in Honor of St. Agnes	241

The Faded Lily

LVIII. What a Misfortune!	243
LIX. The Consequences of That Misfortune	246
LX. The Lily Fades! To What an End Does This Lead!	248
An Act of Reparation (The Divine Praises)	251

The Lily Protected and Cared For

LXI. The Sentinels Who Guard the Lily of Chastity	253
LXII. Sunshine	256
LXIII. Celestial Dew	260
LXIV. A Mother's Care	264
The Canticle of the Blessed Virgin Mary	267

Part Third:
AT THE PARTING OF THE WAYS

Which is My Path?

LXV. The Decision to Be Made	271
LXVI. Useful Advice	274
LXVII. The Means to Make a Wise Choice	278
Prayer to St. Lucy	282
Prayer for Youth to beg the Divine Direction in the Choice of a State of Life	283

The Married State

LXVIII. Ought I to Marry?	285
LXIX. Whom Should I Marry?	288
LXX. The Time of Courtship	292
LXXI. Marry a Catholic	295
LXXII. Are Mixed Marriages Happy?	298

LXXIII. The Conditions Under Which the Church Tolerates Mixed Marriages	302
To be said after the Hail Mary	305

The Religious State

LXXXIV. The Happiness of a Religious Vocation	307
LXXV. The Sacrifices of a Religious Vocation	311
All for Thee, O Heart of Jesus	315
LXXVI. The Signs of A Religious Vocation	315
The Road of Life	319
De Profundis (Psalm 129)	319

Unmarried Life in the World

LXXVII. The Value of Virginity	321
LXXVIII. The So-called "Old Maids"	324
Jesus, Master, Teach Me	328
A Morning Offering	329
Night Prayer	329
Confiteor	329

Part Fourth: FAMILY LIFE

Religion: The Foundation of Family Life

LXXIX. The Happiness of Family Life	333
LXXX. The Safeguard of Family Life	336
To The Holy Family	339
LXXXI. The Peace of Family Life	339
Prayer to St. Joseph as Patron	343
For His Safe-Conduct Through Life	343
Indulgenced Prayer for a Christian Family	344

The Religious Education of Children

LXXXII. Happiness or Misery	347
LXXXIII. Begin the Work Early	350
LXXXIV. The Principal Factors and Supports in the Training of a Child	353

LXXXV. Studies: Higher Education.	356
LXXXVI. The Blessing From Above	361
Prayer of Venerable Father Olier	365

The Housewife's Adorning

LXXXVII. Beautiful Apparel	367
LXXXVIII. Gold Ornaments	370
LXXXIX. Diamonds	373
XC. Precious Stones	376
Hymn to the Holy Family	380
Prayer to Saint Anne	381

Part Fifth:
A FEW CONCLUDING WORDS

A Few Concluding Words

XCI. Farewell!	385
A Rule of Life	390
Ejaculatory prayers to obtain a good death	392
The Art of Being Happy	393

Appendix

Devotions for The Month of May	401
Prayer of St. Alphonsus de Liguori	402
St. Aloysius' Act of Consecration	404
Prayer to our Queen of the Most Holy Rosary	404

Meditations on the Life of Mary

Introduction	405
Ave Maris Stella	411
1st Day: Mary's Immaculate Conception	412
2nd Day: Mary's First Graces	413
3rd Day: Mary's Earliest Gift	414
4th Day: God's Design in Beautifying Mary	415
5th Day: The Birth of Mary	416
6th Day: The Presentation of Mary in the Temple	417

7th Day: Mary's Life in the Temple	418
8th Day: Mary's Espousals	419
9th Day: The Marriage of Mary	419
10th Day: The Annunciation	420
11th Day: The Incarnation.	421
12th Day: The Visitation	422
13th Day: Mary's Time of Expectancy	423
14th Day: The Nativity	424
15th Day: Mary's Purification	425
16th Day: Simeon's Prophecy to Mary	426
17th Day: The Flight into Egypt	426
18th Day: Mary's Life at Nazareth	427
19th Day: Mary's Loss of Jesus for Three Days	428
20th Day: The Death of St. Joseph	429
21st Day: Mary at Cana	430
22nd Day: Mary During Our Lord's Public Life	431
23rd Day: Mary Meets Jesus Carrying the Cross	432
24th Day: Mary at the Foot of the Cross	432
25th Day: Jesus is Placed in His Mother's Arms	433
26th Day: Mary Sees Jesus Laid in the Sepulchre	434
27th Day: Jesus Appears to Mary after the Resurrection	435
28th Day: Mary the Mother of the Infant Church	436
29th Day: Mary's Death	437
30th Day: Mary's Assumption into Heaven	438
31st Day: Mary's Coronation as Queen of Heaven	439
Mary, thy Heart	440

Devotions for Confession

Examination of Conscience for Young Women	441
Prayer before Confession	441
Act of Contrition	448
Resolution of Amendment	449
Prayer for the Grace to Persevere	449
Clementissime Jesu	449

"The virgin thinketh on the things of the Lord:, that she may be holy both in body and in spirit."
—I Cor. iii. 34.

"Be thou an example of the faithful, in word, in conversation, in charity, in faith, in chastity."
—1 Tim. iv. 12.

"Listen attentively, my daughter, to the words of thy teacher, incline the ear of thy heart to them, receive with a good will the admonitions of a loving father, and strive earnestly to put them into practice."
—St. Benedict.

To Today's Catholic Girl

I HAVE good news and bad news for you.
First, the bad news: This book is so old, it was probably written when your great-grandmother was your age. The world of the author and his intended audience was vastly different from today. Society was divided by wealth and "station"; the automobile was still in its infancy, and the entire entertainment industry as we know it today—from movies and television to radio and the internet—were beyond the wildest imagination to conceive. How could a world of boarding school, balls and "women's work" possibly be relevant to you?

Well, here's where the good news comes in. It turns out that despite differences in culture, dress, language and custom, the human race—and its weaknesses—has changed very little since that distant day when a naiive young woman listened to a wily serpent and got us all kicked out of Eden. What's more, the wisdom of our Faith with regard to those same weaknesses—the same which has safeguarded the saints in their own journey toward heaven—is equally relevant in our modern age; and if relevant, then also more crucial than ever in dealing with the daily onslaught of nearly insuperable temptations.

So while the advice you will find in this book will seem at first quaint and outdated—the language especially—no Delphic oracle could offer you wiser counsel than Father Lasance will in this book. I promise you that if you will heed his advice and take it to heart, you will most certainly have cause to look back upon those periods of trial in your life with the comfort of knowing that God's will has guided your steps and has preserved you from the greatest dangers.

With this view in mind, I know that you will treasure this Guide in years to come, and—who knows—perhaps someday you will read it to *your* daughter...

>Yours in Jesus and Mary,
>LISA BERGMAN

Foreword

WE trust that this little book will appeal to Pastors, and Directors of sodalities, to the Children of Mary in particular and to all Catholic girls in general.

To Pastors this little guide will supply suggestive reading for exhortations; to Directors and Prefects of sodalities it will lend assistance by means of its *Conferences*; to the *Children of Mary* in particular and to all Catholic girls in general it will furnish helpful spiritual reading at home, and serve also as a complete Prayer-Book, specially adapted to their needs, in all their devotions at church.

The *Conferences*, in connection with other pious exercises, originally appeared in German under the title *Mit ins Leben*. Their author is the Rev. P. Coelestin Muff, O. S. B., of Einsiedeln, Switzerland. This good Religious speaks to young women from a heart that glows with charity, and is consumed with zeal for God's glory and the salvation of souls.

We see in him a man of God and a man of culture—one who is broad-minded and large-hearted, wise and sympathetic, with the experience of years as a Director of young girls in a Catholic Institute.

We revised the English translation of the Conferences, eliminated parts of the original matter that seemed to us undesirable, added a few new features, substituted portions of well-known hymns in place of some of the author's verses, and endeavored to bring the whole book into greater harmony with the views and customs of Catholics in our own country.

The latter part of this volume, consisting of Devotions, Prayers, and Pious Exercises, is mainly our own compilation and adaptation and was prepared with a view to making the book more generally useful. [*Editor's note*: selected prayers have been included at the end of each chapter, but the rest have been omitted. See note p. v.]

At the end are added Father Clarke's short but very excellent and practical Meditations on the Life of Mary for the Month of May.

May our dear *Lady of the Sacred Heart*, the *Queen of the Most Holy Rosary*, deign to accept this little volume, which we most humbly dedicate to her; may she from her heavenly throne bless this work, so that it may be a firm guide to her servants and her children in the way of perfection.

> F. X. Lasance.
> Notre Dame Convent,
> Walnut Hills,
> Cincinnati, Ohio.
> Feast of the Blessed Virgin Mary—
> "Help of Christians."

To the Holy Family

III. *Syringa flore lacteo.*   I. Buxus.   II. *Syringa flore cœruleo.*

Preface

In the joyous springtime the plain but fresh, sweet verdure of wood and meadow is almost as pleasing to the view as the more showy and brilliant hues of flower and blossoming shrub. May the youthful reader be affected in like manner by the perusal of this unpretentious little book.

The exhortations or instructions which constitute the principal part of this work were originally conferences which I, in my character of chaplain to a young ladies' Institute, gave to girls between fifteen and twenty years of age. The following are the reasons which led me to place them before the public. In the first place, I felt that the conferences would be of more permanent utility to the girls who heard them, if they could be read by them afterward in print. In the second place, I knew that if these instructions were published, whatever beneficial influence they might have would no longer be restricted to those who were present when they were delivered, since they would become to a greater or less extent the common property of a far wider circle of Catholic girls, in equal need of counsel and instruction. And my third reason was that amongst all the numerous and excellent instructive Manuals and Prayer-Books for Catholic girls there is not, to my knowledge, a single one that treats of the spiritual life of a young girl in so comprehensive and detailed a manner as is done in these pages.

Thus the little book now laid before the reader was written for the use of Catholic girls from the time of their leaving school until they embraced some calling or state of life; it is intended, as may be gathered from the title, to be their companion and guide amid the dangers and snares that beset the path of youth. I have made it my constant aim to give, as far as possible, counsels of practical use for daily life, and to avoid anything which would not apply to girls of the middle class, or which, being beyond their comprehension, would be of no profit to them.

My first and foremost wish is to inspire the maiden who stands on the threshold of womanhood with a love of virtue, and to encourage her in the pursuit of it. I wish to impress upon her the fact that virtue and piety are not inconsistent with the enjoyment of life, that they are not incompatible with mirth and high spirits, with sport and recreation; in fine, with a moderate participation in harmless amusements. On the other hand, I wish to show her that youth without virtue is like spring on a bleak, barren height where an icy blast nips every flower in the bud. Youth without virtue is destitute of the very thing that renders youth the springtide of life, which makes it truly a joyous period; I mean the supernatural atmosphere, the buoyancy of spirits, that is concomitant with innocence and peace of heart—heavenly gifts, which in their true beauty and bliss create a very paradise on earth.

That is also the motive which led me to devote in the present work especial care to depicting, besides the lily-crown of virginal purity, in considerable detail the maiden's garland composed of nine fair flowers—the virtues most becoming to the young—in their varied forms and colors.

And since this Manual is to accompany the maiden on her way through life until she comes to the cross-roads, when it is incumbent on her to make the definite choice of a state of life, the needful advice and useful points are given to aid her, at this most important epoch, on which so much depends, in determining her vocation—in making her choice between the married and unmarried state. Furthermore, as a young woman ought not to enter into holy matrimony—the state to which the majority are called—without some general knowledge of what family life is in the highest sense of the word, in its religious import, as well as of the training of children and the virtues essential to the mistress of a household, some brief admonitions are added on these points; though fuller instructions as to the duties of wedded life must naturally be sought in a Manual for mothers, not in one intended exclusively for the unmarried.

Finally, in order that this book may serve not only for spiritual reading, but also as a Prayer-Book for young girls, and may give them practical aid in approaching the throne of grace, some suitable devotions are added to the instructions. This part is compiled with especial reference to the Children of Mary, and with a view to making the book useful as a *Sodality-Manual*.

May God grant that through the blessed influence of His grace, this little book, in spite of its deficiencies, may prove to the maiden who has to encounter the dangers of the world, a powerful support, a sure guide, a wise counsellor, a faithful friend and loving comforter, a protecting angel and an unfailing defence.

A threefold word of warning addressed to the youthful reader yet remains to be added:

1. Do not, my dear child, select from the spiritual aliments here offered you only the dainty morsels, the attractive sweetmeats; that is to say, do not read merely the stories, anecdotes, or verses, but peruse the whole thoughtfully and attentively, each chapter, each instruction in turn, and apply what you have read to yourself, not to others.

2. In church, at Mass, do not spend more time in reading than in prayer, but follow the prayers of the Mass devoutly.

3. Both before and after reading your accustomed portion, pray fervently for help and blessing from above.

May God vouchsafe to bestow on you to the full His fatherly benediction is the heartfelt wish of the author.

To the Gentle Reader

The Child of Mary

O Maiden! let thy heart like a fragrant garden be;
Flowers fair of virtue thy Mother loves to see;
Then sweet thy prayer shall sound in that fond Mother's ear,
And when thou needest help, that Mother will be near.

She strengthens thee to conquer in the arduous strife;
And when thou standest at the crossways of thy life,
Thou shalt feel a heavenly breath to guide thee right;
The rough ways shall be smooth;
                    the dark ways be made light.

    O Child of Mary! in thy youth's springtide,
    Go to that Mother dear, and without fear
    To her thy joys, thy grief, thy hopes confide.

    In life, in death, whatever may betide—
    If foes assail, let not thy courage fail,
    Her arm will thee protect, her wisdom guide.

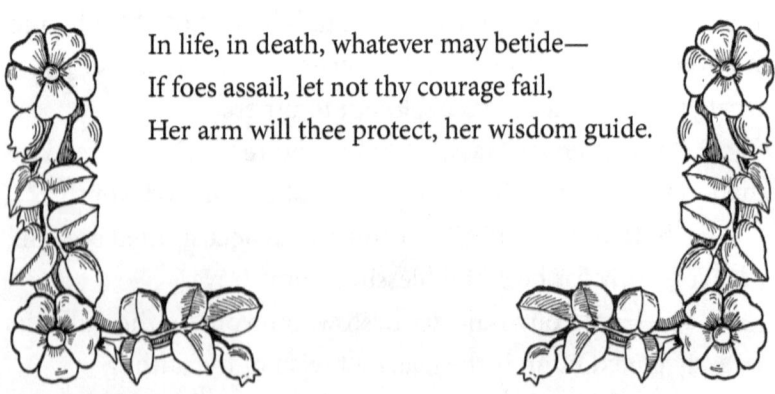

Part First
THE MAIDEN'S WREATH

‹ 1 ›

The Sunflower

Faith

I. How Great a Blessing Is the True Faith

THERE is a flower which possesses this peculiarity, that it turns constantly to the sun, following it in its course; on this account it is called the sunflower. Our faith may be compared to this flower, since its gaze is ever fixed above, and turned toward the glorious sun of divine truth. The first flower in the maiden's blooming garland of virtues is and ought to be the faith of which we speak. For this faith, a clear, living, steadfast, unalterable faith is supremely necessary and all important for the maiden, especially in the present day. Therefore make it the subject of your present meditation, my child, and consider first how great a blessing it is to possess the one true, Catholic faith.

Our Lord said upon one occasion: "Blessed are they that have not seen and have believed." Why did He thus speak? why are those blessed who possess the true faith?

The first reason is this: by faith we please God. The desire for happiness is deeply implanted in every human breast, and the history of mankind is merely the recital of a ceaseless search for happiness. But where is man to find happiness, and where alone? The following lines will tell you:

> Would you be happy, this is the way:
> Please God and do His will day by day;
> Saint-like your duty do; fervently pray.

Note well that we must strive to be pleasing to God, and it is only by believing in Him that we can please Him. This is so true that the Apostle Paul says expressly: "*Without faith it is impossible to please God.*" And if you wish to understand the matter more clearly, reflect upon the relation in which you stand to your earthly father. When do you please him best, when do you honor him most? Is it not when you believe in him most firmly, and show a childlike confidence in him? And how much more is this the case in regard to your heavenly Father, our Lord and God! For it is the will of the eternal Father that we should believe what He once taught and commanded us by the voice of His Son, and now continues to teach us by the voice of holy Church. And if St. Paul says: "*This is the will of God, your sanctification,*" it is also the will of God that we should believe in Him, for faith is the beginning, foundation, and root of all righteousness. Therefore when we believe in God we do His will, and by so doing we please Him, and are ourselves rendered happy.

Our holy Catholic faith is the source of our greatest happiness even while we are yet on earth. Simply reflect upon a few ordinary events of life. What is the brightest and happiest day of one's life? You know quite well; for you are reminded of it every year, when you see a procession of children entering the church, their heads adorned with wreaths, their faces beaming with joy. Do you not feel deeply, yet not without a certain tinge of melancholy, that the day of your First Communion was the brightest and happiest day of your life? Yet would the external solemnity, the magnificent ceremonial of Catholic worship alone make so deep an impression upon the heart? Is it not rather our holy Catholic faith, which enables us to appreciate the beauty, and understand the happiness of the pure and innocent soul of the girl, who is privileged to enter, for the first time, into the closest union with the Author of life, with the supreme Good, with the Source of all happiness, that is, with God Himself?

We will take another example. Have you perhaps beheld a pious and believing Catholic mother at the moment of her greatest happiness, her highest joy, a moment when her heart would adopt as its own the language of the *Magnificat*, and her eyes weep tears of joy? But when and where was this? Was it perhaps on the day when her child approached for the first time the table of the Lord with a pure and innocent soul, and a heart filled with the love of God? No, it was not then. Was it on the wedding-day of her son or daughter? It was not on this occasion either. There is yet another day which comprises in itself the happiness of both the others. The greatest joy, the highest happiness of the pious Catholic mother, is experienced on the day when the bells ring out from the church tower with gladsome yet solemn voice, calling the faithful to enter the sacred edifice, whither, a devout and expectant throng is hastening, and where her son, the most promising of all her children, is about to ascend the steps of the altar, in order to offer for the first time the spotless Lamb of God to the Eternal Father. What is the source of this happiness and joy? In the heart of a pious mother it can be nothing but the holy Catholic faith, which teaches her that her son is now the representative of Christ, and that he can win so many souls for heaven, and save so many poor sinners from hell.

But this happiness is vouchsafed only to a few mortals. If it is true that sorrow and suffering enter into the life of every child of man, and if it is equally true that the poor human heart needs some solid consolation amid grief and tribulation, in this case also it is the Catholic faith which is able to supply this consolation, and which can impart peace of mind under every form of sorrow and suffering.

You, my daughter, know as yet but little of sorrow and suffering. But ask those—and their number is large indeed—who have often and painfully felt that this world is a valley of tears, ask them what has sustained them in their darkest hours of sorrow and suffering, what has poured the healing balm of consolation into their wounded hearts, and even enabled them to rejoice in tribulation. Ask them, and they will tell you that it is faith which has done all this.

And what will faith do in the decisive moment, the supreme and terrible moment of death? When the mother of Melancthon[1] was lying on her deathbed, she suddenly opened her eyes and asked her son, who was standing beside her, whether she should keep to the ancient Catholic faith or embrace the new one, that of Martin Luther, as he had done. With deep emotion Melancthon, though himself an apostate, replied as follows: "Dear mother, keep to your ancient, Catholic faith. The new faith is indeed easier to live by, but the old faith is easier and happier to die by." Listen attentively to this, my daughter, and never forget that the Catholic faith renders death easier and happier. Cling therefore closely to this holy faith, never relinquish it, but prize it highly, prize it above everything else, as your happiness and consolation both in life and in death.

> Through faith will conscience wake
> In the human breast;
> Never therefore the path forsake
> Of present joy and future rest.

---

[1] Phillip Melancthon was perhaps the foremost theologian and collaborator in the Lutheran Reformation.

II. Keep the Faith

Let not the world, with promise fair,
Rob thee of faith—that good beyond compare;
'Tis thy soul's strength, and saves it from despair.

Faith is certainly so precious and supernatural a possession that no earthly good can be substituted for it. As innocence is the maiden's fairest ornament, so is faith her most precious possession. It resembles the glorious light of the sun, which cheers and animates all created nature. How sad and gloomy, how cold and unfruitful would the earth be without this light! But far more sad would our life be without the divine light of the true faith.

Therefore the first and most important affair of your life is to preserve this light, this precious treasure, with the utmost care. And this is no easy matter, especially in the present day, when unbelief is gaining ground with terribly rapid strides. Therefore mark well what you have to do in order to acquit yourself of your most important duty, in order to preserve your most precious possession—the holy faith.

The first thing is to attend diligently to religious instruction. In its origin, faith is a gift of grace, and this grace is imparted first of all in holy Baptism, for Baptism makes man a Christian. But faith is then only a germ, and if this germ is not to be nipped in the bud it must be developed. And it is the Church which develops this germ. This is why St. Paul says: "*Faith then cometh by hearing, and hearing by the word of Christ,*" and Our Lord Himself reminds us that: "*He that is of God, heareth the words of God.*"

Consequently you must set a high value on the word of God as announced to you in sermons and religious instructions, and not absent yourself from them on any frivolous pretext. Whenever you are about to listen to religious instructions be careful to recollect yourself, and invoke the aid of the Holy Spirit, in order that He may prepare your heart to receive the divine word. Afterwards apply what you have heard to yourself, *not to other persons*, and make it the guide of your life. In this manner you will not merely keep your faith, but be more and more confirmed in it.

The second means of keeping the faith is to live in accordance with its teaching. The more earnestly you strive to practise the precepts of the Gospel, the more will your faith be strengthened. The harder the blows dealt by the hammer, the more deeply the nail is driven in; similarly faith becomes all the deeper, firmer, and stronger, the more carefully its teaching is observed. The Japanese whom St. Francis Xavier converted in the sixteenth century grew and became strong in the faith in a manner which was nothing short of marvelous. But this was only the natural result of the extreme zeal they displayed in the performance of their Christian duties. For every kind of virtue was practised by these recent converts in great perfection. Their holy zeal was wonderful indeed, and so conscientious were they that it was not easy to soothe their distress whenever they fell into even trifling faults. Do you, my daughter, imitate their bright example, and be earnest in the fulfilment of your religious duties. As soon as you grow careless in this respect, in an equal degree will your firm, undoubting faith become weaker.

The third means, namely, the avoidance of sin, is inseparably connected with the second. In order to keep the faith it is indispensably necessary to avoid everything which is of the nature of sin, and to lead a life which is pleasing to God. For faith can never long dwell in a heart defiled by sin. And here listen to a parable. A wealthy Greek carefully selected a cask and filled it with the choicest wine. In order to protect himself against thieves he affixed his seal to the mouth of the cask. However, in spite of his precaution, a cunning slave bored a little hole in the bottom of the vessel, and thus succeeded in getting at the wine, being able to close the aperture without much difficulty. His master frequently broke the seal in order to partake of the wine, but he always replaced it. Ere long he perceived that the wine was rapidly diminishing, but, as the seal remained unbroken, he was at a loss to account for this. The mystery was solved by a friend, who said to him: "No doubt some one draws out the wine from beneath." However, the foolish man could not understand this and absurdly protested that the wine was not deficient at the bottom but at the top of the cask.

This is a very old story, for it is related by the heathen sage Hierocles. But it constantly repeats itself in regard to a widely different subject. Faith in God, in His divine love and saving doctrine, is the precious wine which renews, elevates, ennobles, gladdens and strengthens the life of man. Why has this faith so greatly diminished in the Christian world? The wine from above never diminishes; for "Every best gift and every good gift is from above, coming down from the Father of lights." No, it is from beneath that the decline of faith proceeds. It originates in the lower region of life, that, namely, of sensuality and the baser impulses. Guard against them, my child, and beware lest you become their slave, and thus your faith be endangered.

But the chief means of preserving a firm and enlightened faith is prayer. Faith is a gift of divine grace, as Isnard, a Frenchman who lived in the beginning of the last century, learned from experience. During the great French revolution he totally lost his faith, and became a so-called Freethinker. By a turn of fortune's wheel he lost his entire wealth, his life being also imperiled. At this juncture he applied himself with great ardor to the study of the truths of the Christian religion. Upon this point he expresses himself as follows in a work which he subsequently published: "I soon perceived that, in searching for the truth, everything depends on the disposition of the heart. Therefore I betook myself to prayer, and my mental horizon speedily cleared, so that I regained my faith."

Do you also pray diligently for faith, that most necessary virtue, and in seasons of temptations have recourse to God in the words which we find in the Gospel: "*I do believe; Lord, help my unbelief.*"

Christian maiden, on no account must you consider the Catholic faith to be a thing of little moment. For, as St. Augustine says: "There is no greater wealth, no more precious treasure, than the Catholic faith." Do everything in your power to keep it, so that one day you may be able to adopt the words of the Apostle: "*I have finished my course, I have kept the faith. As to the rest, there is laid up for me a crown of justice.*"

III. Whose is this Image?

In these days when faith has either grown cold or been lost altogether in so many instances, there are persons, and among their number girls of eighteen or twenty, who, when they are exhorted to reflect upon death and eternity merely reply: "I am no child to be frightened by nursery tales; who knows whether everything does not end at death!"

Such expressions in the mouths of young people fill us with horror and compassion. But how can it be possible to speak in this way? It is possible, because in the case of these individuals, faith in the fundamental truth of our holy religion no longer exists, because they either do not know, or refuse to know the true answer to the question: "*Whose is this image?*" or: "*In whose likeness was man created?*"

You, dear reader, know the answer, and are firmly convinced of the fundamental truth that man was created in the image and likeness of God. Yet, placed as you are amid the dangers of unbelief, it is of the very greatest importance that this conviction should be rooted as deeply as possible in your heart; therefore ponder well the chief reasons for this conviction.

Whose is this image? In whose image and likeness was man created? Holy Scripture tells us, clearly and distinctly, that he was created in the image of God. And the fact that we have a soul endowed with reason plainly proves that so it is and must be. But is it really true, we do indeed possess a soul? Does anything actually exist outside the sphere of our senses, besides the things which we see, hear, smell, taste or feel?

Once upon a time a simple peasant went to a priest who lived in Rome and laid before him a singular doubt. "Your Reverence," he said, "I cannot believe that I have a soul!" It is easy to imagine what was the astonishment of the priest on hearing this strange announcement. With all his might he tried to think how he could best convince the foolish man of his error, and the spirit of God at length suggested to him the means of doing this. "My good man," he inquired, "why cannot you believe that you have a soul?" "Because I cannot see it," was the reply. "Very well," continued the priest, "now think of something, anything you like." After the lapse of a few minutes he inquired again: "Have you thought of something?" "I have, your Reverence," said the peasant. "I don't believe you have thought of anything at all," rejoined the priest. "Why do you say this?" asked the other. "Because I cannot see your thought," was the reply.

In this summary fashion was the man delivered from his doubt. It would indeed be too unreasonable to doubt that man can think, will, and remember. In like manner it is utterly unreasonable to call in question the existence of a soul endowed with reason.

In the beginning of Holy Scripture we read that it was only in regard to the creation of man that God uttered the words, so full of meaning: "*Let us make man to our image and likeness.*" How sublime and how wondrous a thought is this! In regard to all other things which the Creator called into being, He merely said: "*Fiat*—be it done!" But in regard to the creation of man, the three Persons of the Most Holy Trinity took counsel as it were together. And then God formed the body of man out of the dust of the earth and breathed into him a living soul. And thus is this soul like unto God, a spirit like unto God, simple and immortal.

No one who intelligently considers the subject can deny the immortality of the soul. Would it be possible for you to deny this immortality when you stand beside the deathbed of any one who is dear to you, of a father, a mother, a brother, a sister, a friend? "It is difficult," an innocent person once remarked, "to believe that those whom we love not only die but sink into nothingness." And so it is; for all our feelings, all our convictions resist and struggle against the supposition that our existence ends with death. And Christ's own words clearly prove to us that death is not death but the entrance into life: "*The wicked shall go into everlasting punishment: but the just into life everlasting.*"

It is certain that the soul continues to live after the death of the body, and that we shall meet again those whom we love. Were no such future reunion possible, we might justly blame Heaven for having inspired us with affections which belie themselves. Then would the mother whom we loved so fondly have been taken from us forever! Then would everything be at an end at the close of this brief life which is often so full of sorrow and suffering, and nothingness alone would remain! Can love and friendship be mere empty words, can virtue and justice be but a delusion? No, it is impossible to entertain such ideas even for a moment, impossible at least for those in whose breast there beats a warm and affectionate heart. The soul was made in the image of God, and is therefore immortal.

Whose is this image? Man was created in the likeness of God, and we assert this, in the third place, because he has a soul destined to behold God, destined to enjoy everlasting happiness. Happiness! The mere mention of the word quickens our pulses, and stirs our being to its inmost depths. The desire for happiness is the strongest impulse in our nature. And this desire, this longing, must needs be satisfied somewhere. But where is this to be? Where is the happiness for which we so ardently long? Everything proves that it is not to be found on earth. Small as is our heart, the whole world would not suffice to fill it. Alexander the Great, who conquered the whole of the then known world, was not satisfied, but wept because there were no more worlds to conquer.

Therefore the words of St. Augustine will be true as long as the world shall last: "Thou didst make us for Thyself, O Lord, and our heart can find no rest until it rests in Thee!" Until it rests in God! This is indeed a true saying, for our hearts can find no permanent satisfaction, no lasting content, in temporal possessions, in health, friendship, honor, pleasure and renown. This earth is only a transitory abode; here we have no abiding dwelling-place, but we seek one which is to come, which awaits us in heaven. After a few days of exile in this valley of tears, we shall be admitted to the presence of God, we shall be privileged to behold the glories of the other world; there will all sorrow be at an end, all suffering cease, every tear be wiped away. Do you, my daughter, ever bear in mind that you have been made in the image of God, that your soul is like unto God, that it is immortal, and destined to behold Him one day in heaven.

> In His own image, child, God fashioned thee,
> Destined in realms of light His face to see.

IV. BE VIGILANT

IN the course of my long experience as a director of souls, I have often seen how young girls, even those who have been brought up by respectable parents and amid Catholic surroundings, on being introduced later on into an atmosphere where unbelief prevails, or where faith has grown cold, have not been able to keep straight, but have lost their faith, and with faith also their virtue and innocence. You will have to go out into society, and at some time or other will find yourself in company where danger threatens your holy faith. How important therefore, how necessary it is that you should be warned in time against this danger and should keep watch over yourself in regard to it.

St. Paul warned his disciple and friend St. Timothy against this danger in the following words: "*There shall be a time, when they will not endure the sound doctrine; but, according to their own desires, they will heap to themselves teachers, having itching ears: and will indeed turn away their hearing from the truth, but will be turned unto fables. But be thou vigilant.*" We are living in an age which resembles that here depicted by the Apostle. There are in our midst only too many men who, like those he portrays, cannot endure the sound doctrine of Jesus Christ, the Son of God, but decry, blaspheme, and ridicule it. Sometimes they express doubts as to particular doctrines of our holy religion, especially its mysteries, sometimes they scoff at abuses, sometimes they pour contempt on the external practises and ceremonies of our holy Church. They seek above all things to inoculate the minds of the young, and especially of young girls, with the germs of unbelief.

How grievous a misfortune would it be if your faith were shaken, or even lost, through the influence of such persons! And here I will quote the words of a lady who took a deep interest in young girls, and wrote for their benefit an admirable little book, in which she gives them a golden rule of life: "O that I had the tongue of an angel to warn them, and to bid them be on their guard against the poison of modern unbelief! . . . May your fate never resemble that which formerly overtook the city of Persepolis! It worshiped fire, and by fire it was destroyed." This means, beware of following the attraction of the brilliant light, which unbelief too often kindles in order to deceive men; it is as a delusion, a Will-o'-the-wisp, and, were you to follow it, it would destroy you and cast you into the fire of hell.

A father who was totally destitute of faith sent his children to be educated in Catholic establishments. A friend having remarked to him upon the inconsistency of his conduct, he replied: "I know only too well, by my own experience, the misery of unbelief, and I am not so cruel a parent as to permit my dear children to feel the same." So great, then, is the wretchedness of unbelief! Listen to these words, and mark them well, proceeding as they do from the lips of an unbeliever. Therefore guard against the dangers which may threaten your faith. Let me point out these dangers to you.

In the first place, doubts of the faith. If such doubts occur to you, do not dwell upon them, do not strive to solve them, but in all simplicity and humility say: "O my God, I believe this, because Thou hast said it, and because Thou art eternal Truth." If doubts which you cannot answer are brought before you by others, simply say: "I cannot explain this, but one thing I know: God and His holy Church can never err. You had better consult a priest; he will be able to answer you." And if you should yourself be troubled with doubts of the faith, tell them simply and frankly to your director or confessor, and he will advise you as to the best method of setting them at rest.

Avoid, as far as possible (and this is the second point), the society of those who deny the truths of religion and scoff at faith, the sacraments, and so on. If they are your equals and among the number of your acquaintances to whom you can speak plainly, cut them short with some such words as these; "May I ask you not to talk in this way, for, if you persist in doing so, this must be the last time I shall have anything to do with you." Do not argue with such persons, but say quite simply: "Are you wiser than the Catholic Church and almighty God Himself?" If they are persons to whom you cannot speak in this way, observe an expressive silence, and thus show your displeasure; or adroitly turn the conversation to a different subject. Under such circumstances it is a great advantage to possess a ready tongue, for those who have this gift can often, by some appropriate speech, silence the scoffer at once and forever. I formerly knew a witty Capuchin monk who frequently employed this method, as the following amusing incident may serve to show:

Upon one occasion a remarkably corpulent gentleman who was travelling in the same railway coach as the good Father, tried to make him angry by mocking at religion. Among other things he said: "How can there be a hell? Where could the Lord get the immense masses of fuel which would be required in order to heat it?" The Capuchin, who was very quick at repartee, instantly retorted: "My dear sir, pray set your mind at rest on this point, for as long as the Almighty has a store of such fat fellows, such 'blocks,' as you, He will be at no loss to find what he wants."

In the third place, beware of reading books and pamphlets hostile to the faith or which attack the Church. Above all things, guard against an inordinate craving in the matter of reading, and do not fancy that you must read everything which comes in your way. There are unfortunately many books, periodicals, newspapers, etc., in which the teachings of the Catholic Church, or faith in general, are more or less openly attacked, and in which shameless falsehoods, calumnies, and misrepresentations in regard to her ministers are given to the public. If once you harbor the thought that if there were no truth at all in such articles they would never have been printed, the most bewildering doubts of the faith might arise in your mind. Such doubts might be like poisonous seed, from which the accursed weeds of unbelief might spring up.

In conclusion, pay no heed to the false and foolish assertion that every religion is good, every system of beliefs can lead to heaven.

A pious mistress had a servant who very often talked in this way. The first time her wages were due the lady paid her in base coin or money which had been withdrawn from circulation. The girl objected, but her mistress replied: "But it's money just the same, and don't you think all money is equally good?" She then counted out genuine coins, saying as she did so: "Just as false money will not serve your purpose, so a false creed will never take you to heaven."

Therefore hold fast to your faith, as being the only true one and the only one which can take you to heaven. Christ established but one Church.

Be vigilant, and see that amid the numerous dangers and temptations by which you are surrounded the light of faith is not darkened within you, but shines with ever-increasing brightness, guiding you on your heavenward way.

> O blessed faith, thou gift divine,
>   Enlightener of the darksome heart,
> Cease not within my soul to shine,
>   And hope of heavenly joys impart.

Act of Faith

O MY GOD! I firmly believe that Thou art one God in three Divine persons, Father, Son, and Holy Ghost; I believe that Thy Divine Son became man, and died for our sins, and that he will come to judge the living and the dead. I believe these and all the truths which the Holy Catholic Church teaches, because Thou hast revealed them, who canst neither deceive nor be deceived.

Act of Spiritual Communion
by St. Alphonsus Liguori

MY JESUS, I believe that Thou art present in the Blessed Sacrament. I love Thee above all things and I desire Thee in my soul. Since I cannot now receive Thee sacramentally, come at least spiritually into my heart. As though thou wert already there, I embrace Thee and unite myself wholly to Thee; permit not that I should ever be separated from Thee.

Adoro Te Devote
(Hymn of St. Thomas Aquinas)

O Godhead hid, devoutly I adore Thee,
Who truly art within the forms before me;
To Thee my heart I bow with bended knee,
As failing quite in contemplating Thee.

Sight, touch, and taste in Thee are each deceived;
The ear alone most safely is believed.
I believe all the Son of God has spoken:
Than Truth's own word there is no truer token.

God only on the Cross lay hid from view,
But here lies hid at once the manhood too:
And I, in both professing my belief,
Make the same prayer as the repentant thief.

Thy wounds, as Thomas saw, I do not see;
Yet Thee confess my Lord and God to be.
Make me believe Thee ever more and more,
In Thee my hope, in Thee my love to store.

O Thou, memorial of our Lord's own dying!
O living bread, to mortals life supplying!
Make Thou my soul henceforth on Thee to live;
Ever a taste of heavenly sweetness give.

O loving Pelican! O Jesu Lord!
Unclean I am, but cleanse me in Thy Blood:
Of which a single drop, for sinners spilt,
Can purge the entire world from all its guilt.

Jesu! whom for the present veiled I see,
What I so thirst for, oh, vouchsafe to me:
That I may see Thy countenance unfolding,
And may be blest Thy glory in beholding. Amen.

‹ 2 ›

The Ivy

Hope

V. Hope in the Lord

A pious and pleasing legend runs as follows: When our first parents were driven out of paradise, they wandered about full of sadness, and weeping. Before them stretched the earth which was to be the scene of their toil, overgrown with thorns and thistles; in their ears the terrible sentence pronounced by their Judge sounded constantly: "In the sweat of thy face shalt thou eat bread." Then they sighed, exclaiming with tears: "Alas! why did not the angel with the flaming sword put an end to our existence!" Suddenly there breathed forth from paradise a gentle breeze; the shrubs bent their heads, and a tiny cloud, colored with the hues of the dawn, floated down from the hills. From this cloud a voice was heard to speak in accents of encouragement: "Though your eyes will not be able to behold me, yet unseen by you I will be your guide through life. I will dwell in your hearts and cheer your path. When thou, O Man, dost till the ground in the sweat of thy face, I will show thee in the hazy distance waving fields of golden grain and blooming gardens, and thou shalt fancy thyself in paradise. And when thou, O Woman, shalt be in pain on account of bearing children, thou shalt behold an angel from heaven in the person of thy child, and shalt weep tears of joy."

"Alas!" groaned the unhappy ones, "wilt thou forsake us when we come to die, O hidden messenger of consolation?" "No," sounded the voice from the cloud, "most certainly not, but after the darkness of night has passed away, a glorious morning shall dawn upon you. When the hour of your death is drawing near, my cheering light will illumine your soul, causing you to see the celestial portals open to admit you." "But who then art thou, celestial messenger of consolation?" queried they. "I am Hope," was the reply, "the daughter of Faith and Love." Then the cloud descended and encircled our first parents, so that they could not see their angelic visitant. But they were comforted and cheered.

My daughter, this heavenly being, this virtue of hope, must in like manner accompany you through life. Hope must encircle and cling to your heart like the climbing ivy. You must keep a firm hold on Christian hope, you must cling closely to it, and never let it go, for such is the will of God. God commands us to hope in Him, and indeed this injunction is embraced in the general precept: "Thou shalt love the Lord thy God with all thy heart." Hope therefore in the Lord! But wherefore ought we to do this? What is the basis of our hope?

Hope in the Lord: in the first place, because He is faithful and true, almighty and infinitely good; hence He is assuredly both able and willing to give us all that He has provided. Is it certain that He is *able* to do this? Yes, indeed! For how could He be almighty if He were not able to do everything, to pardon our sins, to give us His grace, and at length to receive us into heaven! He has only to will it, and His grace streams into our heart, causing it to burn with the fire of repentance, and our sins are blotted out, our debt is remitted. And He does will this, because He is infinitely good and merciful. He loves all men, and desires that all should dwell with Him in heaven. That this is true He has clearly proved by giving His only-begotten Son to suffer a cruel death upon the cross. And the words of St. John will remain forever true: "*God so loved the world as to give His only-begotten Son; that whosoever believeth in Him may not perish.*" Could God have given a more convincing proof that He loves us, that He desires our eternal happiness? Ought we not, must we not, on this account place our whole confidence in Him?

But to go still further, Hope in God, my daughter, because He has sealed His promises with the blood of His own Son. True it is that we could not of ourselves merit eternal happiness, or the grace which is necessary in order to obtain it, were we to strive through countless ages to do so; but what we could not merit, Jesus Christ has merited for us, through His bitter Passion and cruel death. Therefore we have, as the Apostle says: "*Such confidence, through Christ, toward God.*" And for the same reason St. Ambrose, in order to encourage us, writes as follows: "Behold what a judge thou hast! The Father hath committed all judgment to the Son. How then can He condemn thee, who redeemed thee with His blood, who gave Himself for thee?" This thought ought to fill us with bright hope and blessed confidence. When St. Augustine thought upon the sins of his youth, his heart grew heavy and full of fear, so that he would have been overwhelmed with sadness had he not rested his hopes upon the merits of Jesus Christ. "O Lord," he would exclaim at such times, "Thou art the Life through which I live, the Hope to which I cling, the Glory which I ardently desire to possess forever."

Therefore, my daughter, I once more repeat: hope in the Lord! Contemplate the merits of Jesus Christ, and whilst so doing never lose confidence in Him. Even if you have already fallen into grievous sin, or if at a subsequent period you should be so unhappy as to fall into mortal sin, do not despair, but continue to hope in the mercy and pardoning love of your Saviour! Even if the priest and Levite—that is, your fellow creatures—should pass you by, and give you up for lost, your Redeemer will never act thus; He will never abandon you as lost. No, your weakness and the wounds of your soul will cause Him to draw near to you, they will move His Sacred Heart to have compassion on you. He will show Himself to be a merciful Samaritan, for He has for you only oil and wine, mercy and charity—and furthermore a piece of precious gold, giving Himself to you in the Blessed Sacrament of the Altar, in order to pay all your debts, those which you have incurred by your sins. Hope in Him!

Hope in Him when all else seems hopeless; have in Him such firm and implicit confidence as Susanna had in her dreadful distress. Everything seemed to have conspired to compass her ruin; she could, humanly speaking, hope for no deliverance, yet her confidence in God remained unshaken, firm as a rock. As Holy Scripture tells us: "She, weeping, looked up to heaven, for her heart had confidence in God."

> God, who to us Thyself doth give,
>   On Thee our hopes must all rely;
> In this hope will the Christian live,
>   And also in this hope will die.

VI. God Doeth All Things Well

I KNOW full well, my dear daughter, that you who are about to embark on the stormy sea of life will encounter many a trial, many a conflict, many an affliction; I know that sorrow will come to you and to those who are near and dear to you; I also know how easy it is for an inexperienced young girl to grow fretful and disheartened in such hours of suffering, and to say within herself: "God is not treating me in a just or kind manner, but like a harsh stepfather!" You must be armed beforehand against so insidious a temptation, and by the help of God you must engrave upon your heart the words: God doeth all things well!

When Our Lord worked a stupendous miracle on behalf of the man who was deaf and dumb, restoring to him both speech and hearing, the assembled multitude exclaimed with admiration. *"He hath done all things well!"* This saying still holds good, and can be applied to all that God has created, both in general and in particular. No proof of this will be required by any one who reflects a little on the manner in which all things, both great and small, are ordered and arranged so as best to serve their ends. It is certain that the further the pious inquirer penetrates into the wonders of the heavenly bodies which move above our heads in the azure firmament, the more his mind dwells upon the mysterious forces which govern the earth, the more he notes the formation of even lifeless stones, the life of plants, the anatomy of man and of the lower animals, the more forcibly will he feel himself compelled to exclaim: *"How great and good art Thou, O Lord; how wisely and how well hast Thou ordained and ordered all things!"*

Listen therefore to the lesson which all creation teaches, for it proclaims that God is Himself the supreme Good, because He has so wisely ordered all things. If we had more faith and more love, we should feel that everything in nature has a voice—a voice which proclaims to the whole world the wisdom, power, and goodness of God. To the saints, whose hearts glowed with such pure and fervent love of God, the stars in their nightly courses seemed to say: "How good is God who made all so wisely and so well!" They heard the blades of grass which sparkled in the morning dew and the spring flowers arrayed in their bridal loveliness exclaiming aloud: "How good is God, who made all so wisely and so well!" And in their ears the humming of the bees, the twittering of the feathered songsters in field and forest, uttered the same joyous refrain: "How good is God, who made all so wisely and so well!"

But you may perhaps raise an objection by saying: "I am thoroughly convinced that the heavens and the earth and all things in them have been well and wisely made. But how about the misfortunes, the sorrows and sufferings, by which man is so frequently and so heavily afflicted? Is God equally good when He sends these visitations upon His creatures?"

This most important question must at all times be answered in the affirmative with full conviction and unwavering decision. For God is also good to us when He sends us afflictions; He acts thus in order to promote our spiritual advancement and His honor and glory. He teaches us this in the words of Holy Scripture: *"Thou lovest all things that are, and hatest none of the things that Thou hast made."* Again, St. Paul says: *"We know that to them that love God all things work together for good."*

Numerous indeed are the instances to be found in the pages of history, and in the experience of men, to prove the truth of this assertion. To take our illustrations from Scripture only: remember the story of Joseph. Who could be more unfortunate than he was? Sold into slavery by his own brothers, torn away from his native land, though perfectly innocent, accused of a shameful crime, and on account of this cast into prison! Yet from his prison he was raised to a throne second only to that of the king. Thus did his misfortune prove to be for his good, and not for his good alone, but for that of his country, of his beloved father, and of his brethren. God certainly ordered everything for the best, as far as he was concerned. Yet He brought this about by secret means, in ways unseen by human eyes. In order to become ruler over the land of Egypt, Joseph was first made a slave, loaded with fetters, and cast into prison.

Now take the case of the chaste Susanna. Why did God permit the diabolical scheme of the wicked old men so far to succeed that the innocent woman was publicly scorned, and branded as an adulteress, led forth in deep disgrace to suffer a shameful death? He allowed it in order that her innocence might shine forth all the more brightly in the sight of all the people, in order that her own joy and the universal exultation might be all the greater, in order that the scandalous deeds of the old men might appear to be even darker and more disgraceful. In this case also it was clearly proved that God doeth all things well. Or, as St. Jerome says: "What we take to be a poison is in reality a medicine." Afflictions are blessings in disguise.

St. Chrysostom also exhorts us thus: "When any event is beyond our comprehension, it does not follow that on this account it is not for the best; but as we recognize, in part at least, the hand of divine Providence in ordering and governing the world, we must, in regard to events which we fail to understand, adore the unsearchable wisdom of God." Wonderful indeed are His ways; who is able to search them out?

What then should be your resolution, Christian maiden? It ought to be none other than the following: Never for one single moment to murmur or complain, as if God had not done all things wisely and for the best, but always to cling closely to that gift of Heaven, Christian hope. My dear daughter, if sometimes as you go on in life, waves of trouble and sorrow break upon your poor forlorn heart; if those whom you love most dearly are torn from your side and consigned to the grave; if poverty and painful family circumstances weigh upon you like lead; if anxiety, if the contempt of those around you, and strange misunderstandings, secretly torture you like some gnawing worm; if wearisome illness confines you to a sick-bed for weeks, or even months; if the serpent's fangs of envy and jealousy rend your poor heart, while all the time you are conscious of your own innocence, then strive, I beseech you, to possess your soul in patience, however great may be the struggle it costs you, and cease not to extol the goodness and wise providence of God. Say, not with your lips alone, but from your heart: "Whatever God does, or leaves undone, is just and right." Try to adopt as your own the words of holy Job, that most patient of sufferers: "*The Lord gave, and the Lord hath taken away; blessed be the name of the Lord.*"

But, in order that this may be your habitual frame of mind, you must endeavor, while the sunny days of youth still last, to see that the ivy plant of Christian hope is firmly rooted in your heart. And:

> Is not the pilgrim's toil o'erpaid
> By the clear rill and palmy shade?
> And see we not, up earth's dark glade,
> The gate of heaven unclose?

VII. The Blessed Fruits of Patience

Many grown-up persons, when they are in affliction, act like the child about whom I read the following anecdote. He wanted to pluck a beautiful flower he saw on a rose-tree, but he set about it so awkwardly that he tore his hand with the thorns. Then he burst into tears and loudly abused the rose-tree. His mother deftly took hold of the thorny stem in such a way that her fingers were not pricked, cut off three of the finest roses and held them out to the boy, saying as she did so: "Are you still angry with the rose-tree?" "No, mother, not now," he replied with a joyous smile.

Thus do we, poor, short-sighted mortals, allow ourselves to grow angry with the thorns, that is to say with the sorrows of life which pierce our hands when we wish to gather the roses of joy. We fail to understand how we ought to deal with these thorns; I mean, how we ought to bear sufferings and contradictions with patience, with resignation to the will of God, with a steadfast hope of heaven. It is both necessary and important that we should do this, and you, O Christian maiden, must not only learn the lesson, but also carry it into practise.

Therefore in all sufferings, be they great or small, remember how blessed are the fruits of patience. Never murmur nor complain, do not give way to discontent nor anger, do not say: It is not right that this should have happened to me, etc.

> Of chance or fate to speak is vain;
> God's wisdom doth man's lot ordain.

Afflictions, more than anything else, come straight from the hand of God; therefore, beware of finding fault with His providence. What would you say if your little sister, who as yet knows nothing about needlework, were to find fault with some elaborate piece of embroidery on which you happen to be employed? Should you not answer: "Hold your tongue, you silly child. What do you understand about embroidery?" We are like foolish children if we venture to judge the dealings of God. We cannot know or understand what is for our happiness or good. You perhaps think: "How nice it would be if I were rich!" But God may know that the possession of riches would prove a misfortune to you, and might even lead to your eternal perdition. Is it then not right that He should withhold them from you?

> In God's good providence confide;
> He will for all thy wants provide.

Leave all things to Him, both grief and suffering; for, if you bear your trials with patience, trusting in Him, the roses of joy will spring from them. Many a young girl longs to be smartly dressed, to be arrayed like one of the lilies of the field; instead of this she perhaps has to wear shabby old-fashioned clothes, which make her look more like a dull weed than a bright flower! Let her not give way to discontent, for God may have ordained that she is to wear this unpretending raiment because He destines her to blossom one day as a beauteous lily in the fair garden of paradise.

Another maiden is jilted by the man to whom she was engaged to be married. In her sad and lonely hours she turns to some book of spiritual reading, such as the "Following of Christ." Had God not laid this heavy cross upon her she might perhaps be reading a very different kind of book, one which would teach her to imitate the evil works of the devil.

In adversity even more than in prosperity must we say: "*Thy will be done on earth, as it is in heaven.*" It was said by a great master of the spiritual life, that one single act of submission to the will of God made in adversity is worth a thousand such acts uttered amid prosperity. We are not obliged to pray for crosses and sufferings, as some of the saints have done; but it is absolutely necessary that we should bear the trials which God sees fit to send us, with patience and loving confidence in Him.

In order to attain this patience, which bears such blessed fruit, and to preserve your confidence in God, you must glance behind and before, above and beneath. You must look *behind* in order to see what you have been and still are, namely, a sinner. Marvelous is the power contained in the thought: "I am a sinner." Who can dare to indulge in complaints and impatience on account of temporal losses and sufferings while conscience is telling him that his abode ought to be in hell, or at least in purgatory, because he has deserved such a lot over and over again by his sins!

You must also look *before* and contemplate One who is bearing His own cross, and who will help you to carry yours.

He is ready and willing to do this; the mere sight of Him will lighten your burden. He carried a very heavy cross up a steep hill; pale and exhausted though He was under the load, He yet bore it willingly. He was none other than Jesus of Nazareth, our divine Redeemer. Implore Him to grant you patience and endurance. He will not fail to answer your prayer. Meditate upon His sufferings, and you will be ready to suffer here on earth in order to attain everlasting felicity. He trod the way of the cross before you; do you follow in His footsteps.

Then look *down* to the abodes of everlasting torments, down to hell where the lost souls dwell; think also of purgatory where the suffering souls are detained. Is it not far better to suffer a little here on earth, than after death to endure those terrible tortures? Could the unhappy souls return to earth once more, how patiently would they bear the severest afflictions!

Finally, look *up* to heaven. Behold the eternal beauty and blessedness of paradise. If, for a brief period, you suffer here with courage and patience, you will after death be released from all suffering and enjoy unspeakable bliss for evermore. Such are the blessed fruits of patience.

Visit the churchyard, my dear daughter, where so many crosses and gravestones remind you of the life to come; pause beside the tomb of a Christian maiden who led an innocent and pious life but who was misunderstood and despised by those around her, and who had much to suffer while on earth. If you could ask her whether she were willing to return to this world, in order to begin a new but happier existence, what would she reply? "No," she would answer, "not for anything the world could give! For what could be a better lot for me than that which gained for me eternal bliss in heaven?"

If you too, my dear young friend, have already much to suffer, rejoice! Endure all things with patience, in the sure conviction that patience bears blessed fruits, the fruits of endless joy. Do as you are bidden to do in the following lines:

> If God should send thee grief or pain—
> Seek thou His purpose wise to know;
> Eternal love will not in vain
> Cause thy bitter tears to flow.

VIII. WEEP NOT!

"WEEP NOT!" Such were the words addressed by the gracious Saviour to the widow of Naim, who, filled with unutterable grief, was following the bier of her only son to the gate of the city. And I now say to you, my daughter, *"weep not!"* It is difficult, nay more, it is impossible, for a gentle, tender-hearted woman never to indulge in tears, but do not weep for every trifle, every contradiction, every unfriendly look, every hasty speech. Spare your tears, for hours will come when it will appear only natural and right that you should weep, seasons when you will have to stand beside open graves. Yet even in these hours of bitter anguish I would still say to you: *"Weep not!"* I do not mean that you should not allow your tears to have free course, but do not give way to frantic and despairing grief. Strive rather to let your attitude, as you stand beneath your cross, resemble that of the Mother of Jesus when she stood beneath the cross of her beloved Son. You cannot but weep, yet bear yourself with dignity and courage, supported and sustained by the glorious hope of a resurrection, of a blissful meeting with those whom you mourn.

Is this hope, however, well founded? Can it ever deceive us? Never! A desolate mother knelt beside the grave of her darling, her only child, a boy ten years old. She knelt thus for hours, until she was almost blinded by her tears and her voice was choked with sobs, yet, as the poet tells us:

> Although we part, with tears and pain,
> From those who hold our love;
> We know we'll find them all again,
> In the fields of light above.

Assuredly, that is not dead which the grave enfolds! An interior voice tells us this, and the same voice makes itself heard by all nations, causing them to hold in honor and to reverence the last resting places of the departed. Even the most uncultured nations entertain the hope that the sleep of death is not eternal sleep, but that an awakening will come some day.

But we who are Christians have no mere vague presentiment, but a full and perfect certainty. For Jesus Christ, who is Himself eternal Truth, has solemnly declared: "*I am the resurrection and the life: he that believeth in me although he be dead, shall live: And every one that liveth, and believeth in me, shall not die forever.*"

Yes, "weep not!" There will assuredly be a resurrection; there will be an eternal retribution; the holiness and the justice of God incontestably require it. He sees how frequently upon earth crime and injustice either walk abroad in the face of day, or else flourish in secret. But where is the richly deserved punishment, where the merited chastisement? Religion has its champions, virtue its heroes, faith its martyrs—where is their reward? Are the virtues and crimes of men, their innocence and guilt, to be of equal value in the eyes of God? In that case virtue and crime, guilt and merit, would be mere empty names, and we must perforce cease to believe in the existence of a supreme Being who is at once holy and just. Is it possible that the robber and the robbed, the traitor and the patriot, the martyr and his tormentor, the wicked son and the model daughter, should all meet the same fate, and be alike consigned simply to annihilation?

Let us draw near in imagination to a deathbed on which there lies a dying girl. She is about twenty years old, the age when life is most enjoyable, when youth is in its fairest bloom. She grew up like a lily in the garden of the Lord, modest and pure, pious and good, a pleasing spectacle to men and angels. Death is drawing near; the bystanders are weeping, but she alone sheds not a tear; rather does she smile, and looking up with a glance which seems to pierce the skies, she exclaims with her expiring breath: *"Father, into Thy hands I commend my spirit!"*

Now, tell me if it is possible that God could say to this angelic maiden: "I have doomed thee to annihilation!" Could a life dedicated to Him, spent in His service, have as its reward so awful a disenchantment? Could God be less just in His judgment of good and evil than a fallible mortal? Who would dare to utter such blasphemous words as these?

Let us draw near to another death-bed. The young girl who is stretched upon it is very close to her end. She has been a grief to her family, a disgrace to her relations, a reproach to her sex! Even the last words she utters are an additional offence against the Most High!

Tell me now whether it were possible to write upon the bier of the chaste maiden, the child of God, such words as these: "Her whole life was based on deception?" And upon the bier of the shameless other being, whom we prefer not to describe more explicitly, could we inscribe these words: "She did nothing wrong?" Could God consign alike to annihilation two beings so radically different? Could there be no other fate in store for them both except to molder in the grave? Is it possible that any sensible person can entertain so monstrous an idea as this?

Let your eyes rest in the bright springtime on field and forest. How beautiful, how gladsome, how consoling is the sight! See how awakening nature is putting forth her blossoms, how every blade of grass is arising from its winter slumber, how thousands and thousands of flowers are perfuming the air with their delicious fragrance, how fields and meadows, orchards and fruit-gardens, are arraying themselves in bridal garments, and smiling as they greet the rising sun. Even the grassy mounds in the churchyard, which rise above the last resting places of the beloved dead, proclaim the same encouraging truth of an ultimate resurrection. The pinks, roses and forget-me-nots with which the graves are adorned begin to unfold their charming blossoms and shed forth their delicate perfume.

Each spring the lovely flowers arise after their apparent decay; can it be possible that the human form, that fairest of flowers, that wondrous fabric, that marvelous microcosm, is doomed to lie forever in the grave, to remain forever what death has made it, namely, a decaying and repulsive corpse, a mere heap of dust and ashes? No, thus it *cannot*, thus it *will* not be; there must assuredly be a resurrection!

Therefore, my daughter, I say to you once more: "*Weep not!*" Weep not despairingly if your dear ones are taken from your side, weep not disconsolately when at length the fiat goes forth that you too must die! Never give way to frantic grief, but weep as a Christian ought to do, and remember that:

> When the heart's most poignant grief
> In bitter tears has found relief,
> Then the mourner first most truly feels
> He is not dead, whom now the grave conceals.

Act of Hope

O MY GOD! relying on Thy infinite goodness and promises, I hope to obtain pardon of my sins, the help of Thy grace, and life everlasting, through the merits of Jesus Christ, my Lord and Redeemer.

Memorare

REMEMBER, O most gracious Virgin Mary, that never was it known that anyone who fled to thy protection, implored thy help, or sought thy intercession was left unaided.

Inspired by this confidence, I fly unto thee, O Virgin of virgins, my mother; to thee I come, before thee I stand, sinful and sorrowful. O Mother of the Word Incarnate, despise not my petitions, but in thy mercy hear and answer me. Amen.

Te Deum

THEE, O God, we praise; Thee, O Lord, we proclaim.
Thee, O Eternal Father, all the earth doth worship.
To Thee all the angels, to Thee the Heavens and all the Powers:
To Thee the Cherubim and Seraphim cry out without ceasing:
Holy, Holy, Holy, Lord God of Hosts.
Heaven and Earth are full of the majesty of Thy glory.
Thee the glorious choir of the Apostles,
Thee the admirable company of the Prophets,
Thee the white-robed army of Martyrs doth praise.
Thee the holy Church throughout the world doth confess,
The Father of infinite Majesty;
Thy adorable, true and only Son;
Also the Holy Ghost, the Comforter.
Thou, O Christ, are the King of glory!
Thou art the everlasting Son of the Father.
Thou, having taken it upon Thyself to deliver man,
    didst not disdain the Virgin's womb.
Thou, having overcome the sting of death,
    hast opened to believers the Kingdom of Heaven.
Thou sittest at the right hand of God, in the glory of the Father.
Thou, we believe, art the Judge to come.
   (*The following verse is said kneeling:*)
Thee we beseech, therefore, to help thy servants,
whom Thou hast redeemed with Thy Precious Blood.
Make them to be numbered with Thy Saints in everlasting glory.
O Lord, save Thy people, and bless Thine inheritance!
And govern them, and exalt them forever.
Day by day we bless Thee
And we praise Thy Name forever: yea, forever and ever.
Vouchsafe, O Lord, this day to keep us without sin.
Have mercy on us, O Lord, have mercy on us.
Let Thy mercy, O Lord, be upon us, for we have trusted in Thee.
In Thee, O Lord, have I placed my hope;
    let me not be counfounded forever.

V. Blessed art Thou, O Lord, the God of our fathers.

R. And worthy to be praised and glorified for ever.

V. Let us bless the Father and the Son, with the Holy Ghost.

R. Let us praise and magnify Him for ever.

Pæonia polyanthos flore rubro.

‹ 3 ›

The Peony

Love of God

IX. *Sursum Corda!*--Lift Up Your Hearts!

Shortly after the beginning of the last century, Napoleon the Great was sent as a captive to the lonely island of St. Helena. On one occasion he is said to have endeavored to while away some of the weary hours of his exile by passing in mental review the great men who accomplished the most heroic deeds in the world's history. While he was considering Christ, he is said to have exclaimed: "Behold, He has drawn all mankind to Himself!"

And thus indeed it is. The name of Jesus Christ sounds beside the cradle of the new-born infant and the grave of the aged man, in the hovel and the palace, among the powerful and the weak, in the depths and on the heights, on sea and on land, by day and by night. Jesus alone is the hope and consolation of the unhappy, the pledge of pardon for the guilty. For the love of Jesus how many have renounced, and still renounce, the pleasures of the world!

Thus have His own words been fulfilled: *"And I, if I be lifted up from the earth, will draw all things to myself."*

With the gentle cords of love He has drawn all things to Himself. He has done all that it was possible to do, in order to win for Himself the love of the whole human race, and to hold it fast as long as time shall endure. He has given to us, miserable mortals though we are, the most signal proofs of His divine and ever-abiding love. Let these proofs encourage us; therefore "*lift up your heart!*" Lift it up to the sacred mountains, up to the cross, up to heaven!

To Mount Olivet, to Gethsemane! There, amid the shades of night illumined by the Paschal moon, under the boughs of the olive-trees, you will see a Man prostrate on the ground, bowed down, crushed as it were by some heavy load, convulsively wringing His hands, His countenance pale as death. He breathes heavily, deep sighs escape His tortured breast, a sweat of blood exudes from His pores, and trickles down His pallid face. And His dearest friends, the friends whom He loved as no friend ever loved his most beloved friend, no mother her darling child—they leave Him alone in His agony; they have no word of comfort for Him; they are asleep; they could not watch with Him one hour, although only one brief hour had elapsed since they assured Him of their willingness to follow Him to prison and to death!

But all is not yet told! His foes are approaching, like bloodthirsty wolves; one steps forward who was formerly a friend, a disciple, and imprints the hideous kiss of betrayal on the colorless lips of the Sufferer—the patient Sufferer, whose pale face wears an expression of gentleness and of loving admonition, even while He gazes on this shameless man.

They lead the innocent Lamb, the incarnate Son of God, to Jerusalem; they treat Him, the sinless One, more barbarously than the vilest criminal; they mock Him and blaspheme Him; they scourge Him, and place a crown of sharp thorns upon His head.

Now begins the ascent of Mount Golgotha. Tottering and exhausted, His bleeding and lacerated shoulders laden with a heavy cross, the Man of Sorrows climbs the steep and stony mountain! Three times He sinks upon the ground and each time He is rudely lifted up and dragged forward by His brutal executioners. When the summit is reached, they strip the garments from His sacred body, and thus tear open His wounds afresh. They stretch Him upon the cross, drive large nails through His hands and feet, in order to fasten Him to it, and elevate the infamous gibbet.

My dear child, *"lift up your heart!"* Lift it up to Mount Olivet, to Golgotha! Behold the love of your God!

But you must raise it higher still, you must raise it to the cross! There you see the Lamb of God, hanging on the tree of shame, suspended between heaven and earth, His sole support being the large, rude nails of iron, which pierce His hands and feet, so that the slightest movement aggravates His unspeakable sufferings. The blood is trickling down upon the cross from innumerable wounds, His tongue is parched by feverish thirst, and from His lips proceeds the piteous cry: *"I thirst."* Add to this the anguish which fills His soul at the sight of His beloved Mother, whom to behold thus standing at the foot of the cross causes His tender heart to well-nigh break with compassion. To this add the mockery and blasphemy of the impious men by whom He was surrounded, whose obduracy all His Passion, all His cruel sufferings, did not avail to subdue; yet on whose behalf He breathed forth the touching petition: *"Father, forgive them, for they know not what they do."*

The chalice of His Passion was filled to overflowing; then deprived of all consolation, He utters the heart-rending cry: *"My God! My God! why hast Thou forsaken Me!"* Sum up all this; raise your heart to the cross; *"attend and see if there be any sorrow like to His sorrow"*; see if there be any love which can compare with His love!

But look higher still; lift your heart up to heaven itself! Though no mortal eye is able to gaze upon the glories of that celestial abode which is the dwelling-place of the blessed, though you cannot approach the eternal God for He "*inhabiteth light inaccessible*," be not disheartened on this account; lift up your heart to heaven, for the gleam of light which God will shed upon your soul may perchance enable you to form some faint conception of its splendors.

There the Son of God, not as yet incarnate, sat from all eternity at the right hand of the Father, who "*when the fulness of time was come*" sent Him down to earth, in order that He might suffer, and die upon the cross. But what was His object in doing this? He called Him His beloved Son in whom He was well pleased. Why then send Him to endure the death of the cross?

The crucified One Himself gives the solution of the problem in the words He addressed to Nicodemus: "*For God so loved the world as to give His only-begotten Son; that whosoever believeth in Him, may not perish, but may have life everlasting.*" Thus again do we see that it was love—O sweetest, fairest, greatest and most heavenly word—yes, it was love that moved our gracious God to perform an act which neither earth nor heaven could have deemed possible, an act which alone would suffice to justify the exclamation of the Apostle of Charity: "God is charity!"

Therefore let not your heart, O Christian maiden, be enslaved by any mere earthly, still less by any sinful, affections. Lift up your heart to heaven! There alone is an object truly worthy of your love.

> Love, all other love transcending,
> Love from God's own throne descending,
> Blessings free that love unending
> From the cross is ever sending.

X. Let the Love of God Dwell in Your Heart

Love is an indispensable necessity for every human heart. But it is of paramount importance to every young person especially to have in her heart a true, genuine, and abiding love of God. It is in youth that the severest and most decisive battles with the threefold enemy—the devil, the world, and evil concupiscence—have to be fought.

If you do not now, in the golden days of youth, obtain the mastery over the devil, the world, and the flesh, you will find it difficult, if not impossible, later on, to gain the victor's crown.

But how are you to conquer, and by what means? Wholly and solely by the power of love. It is, however, only true love, the love of God, which, is able to conquer the devil, the world, and the flesh. Therefore, let a true, heartfelt, practical love of God be your guiding star, the centre of your being; let it dwell constantly in your heart!

The Apostle St. Paul says: "*And now there remain faith, hope, charity: these three; but the greatest of these is charity.*" St. Augustine thus explains the passage above quoted: "Faith lays the foundation of the house of God, hope erects the building, but it is love which completes it." Therefore charity is the greatest, the most important thing.

To take another illustration. Every flower has a root, a stem, a blossom; this last is the fairest of the three. And it is just the same with the glorious flower which the three theological virtues combine to form. From the root, which is faith, springs the stem, which is hope, and the lovely flower of charity crowns them both. Wherefore St. Paul writes in another place: "*If I should have all faith, so that I could remove mountains, and have not charity, I am nothing.*"

Therefore, Christian maiden, it is only when an ardent love of God dwells in your heart that you may hope to speak of victories. The history of the world, the pages of sacred history, the history of each individual alike teach us that without love there can be no victory.

Love, taken in a general sense, conquers both in good and in evil things. What, for instance, inflamed and inspired heroes in all ages, leading them to achieve immortal deeds of glory? It was love—love of their fatherland.

What inflamed the breast of Napoleon the Great, inducing him to push forward without rest and to drive his triumphal chariot through so many of the countries of Europe? It was love—love of fame.

What causes the miser to suppress the strongest impulse of nature, the desire for food and drink, and literally to die of hunger beside his stores of gold? It is love—love of money.

What frequently impels so-called "lovers" to commit the terrible crime of suicide, conquering even the love of life? Again it is love—sensual, earthly love, which has been rejected.

What gives a poor invalid courage to set aside fear and apprehension, and to submit to a most painful and critical operation? It is love—love of his own life which renders him ready to face every risk in the hope of preserving it.

What is the motive which makes many a mother overcome her desire for ease and comfort, sacrificing money, time, sleep, health, all and everything? Is it not love—ardent love for her child?

What enables good Christian married people to practice self-control, to overcome selfishness and to set aside their own wishes and tastes? It is love—conjugal affection, which causes them to dread giving pain to one another.

What led St. Vincent of Paul to attain so heroic a degree of self-sacrifice, as to share the prisons of the most miserable outcasts, of the unfortunate galley-slaves? It was love—love of their immortal souls.

What made it possible for millions of martyrs—tender maidens and even young children—to renounce not merely freedom, power, wealth, health, the joys of the domestic hearth, but even life itself, and to endure joyfully even unto death the most excruciating tortures? It was rendered possible only through the power of love—love for the Saviour; they exclaimed with the Apostle: "*The charity of Christ presseth us.*"

Finally, how was the greatest, the most glorious victory the world has ever seen, the victory over sin, death and hell, the victory won by the Redeemer dying on Golgotha—how, we ask, was this victory won? More than any other was this victory a victory of love—of the infinite love of God for the poor children of men.

Such is the all-conquering might of love. And, knowing as you do that it is your bounden duty to conquer the world and sin, the concupiscence of the eyes, the concupiscence of the flesh, and the pride of life, if you wish to wear in heaven the victor's unfading crown, how full of comfort for you is the thought that you can achieve all this by means of love—love for God.

And our gracious God has made it so easy for us to love Him: "*Because God first hath loved us.*" I have shown in the preceding chapter how God the Father so loved the world as to give His only-begotten Son to die for men, and how God the Son offered Himself to die once upon the cross, and now offers Himself up continually in the sacrifice of the Mass, and in holy communion. Why then should it be so difficult for the human heart to return the love of this divine Saviour, who has done so much for us? Ought it not rather to be far more difficult to refrain from loving Him?

Wherefore bestir yourself, Christian maiden! Open the door of your heart that a true love for God may enter in and dwell there. His love flows forth from the altar in the Sacrament of love—it abides in the tabernacle. At this moment the Saviour is standing at the door of your heart! Open to Him, I beseech you; give Him admittance, that He may kindle your heart with the fire of His love.

Thus will you conquer by the power of love, thus will you vanquish all evil and impure desires; for these unhallowed flames will be subdued by the sacred fire of divine love. Fan this sacred fire in order that you may be prepared to struggle with the dangers which threaten your innocence and virtue, and carefully to shun the occasions of sin.

Your future is shrouded in mystery; who can lift the veil? It may perchance conceal storms and conflicts; but if a true love of God dwells in your heart, you will walk with sure steps through the dark nights of life, and amid the gloomy shades of death. Repeat, therefore, frequently and fervently, words such as the following:

>Grant me, while here on earth I stay,
> Thy love to feel and know;
>And when from hence I pass away
> To me Thy glory show.

Or the following hymn:

My God, I Love Thee
(Hymn of St. Francis Xavier)

>1. My God, I love Thee, not because
>   I hope for heav'n thereby;
>Nor yet that they who love Thee not
>   Must burn eternally.
>Thou, O my Jesus, Thou didst me
>   Upon the Cross embrace;
>For me didst bear the nails and spear,
>   And manifold disgrace;
>And griefs and torments numberless
>   And sweat of agony;
>Even death itself; and all for one
>   Who was Thine enemy.

> 2. Then why, O blessed Jesus Christ,
>   Should I not love Thee well!—
> Not for the sake of winning heaven,
>   Nor of escaping hell:
> Not with the hope of gaining aught,
>   Not seeking a reward;
> But as Thyself hast loved me,
>   O ever-loving Lord,
> Ev'n so I love Thee, and will love,
>   And in Thy praise will sing—
> Because Thou art my Lord and God
>   And my eternal King.

XI. THE MIRACLE OF LOVE

"*Let us therefore love God, because God first hath loved us.*" Such is the exhortation addressed to us by St. John, the Apostle of love. He first hath loved us, and what proof has He given of this love? "*God so loved the world that He sent His only-begotten Son into the world.*" And in how wonderful a manner did the Son manifest His love to us! Gethsemane, Calvary, and the cross, which stands upon Calvary's summit, stained as it is with His precious blood, are silent yet eloquent witnesses of His love for us poor, sinful mortals. Yet this is not the full measure, the perpetual miracle of this love. What then is it? O Christian maiden, attend well to what I am about to say, contemplate this miracle with all the fervor, all the recollection of which your heart is capable.

St. John the Evangelist writes: "*Jesus knowing that His hour was come that He should pass out of this world to the Father: having loved His own who were in the world, He loved them unto the end.*" The other evangelists relate the manner in which Jesus instituted the Most Holy Sacrament of the Altar. This, then, was the sign that Jesus loved His own unto the end; the Most Holy Sacrament was, and indeed is, the miracle of love. It is assuredly out of pure and never ceasing love for us poor children of men, that Jesus Christ dwells, truly and substantially, in the Most Holy Sacrament of the Altar and thus bestows upon us all graces and blessings, as when He talked on earth among men *"doing good to all."* His gracious call is ever sounding in our ears, *"Come to Me, all you that labor, and are burdened, and I will refresh you."*

This miracle of love is especially shown by the fact that Jesus gives Himself entirely to us in the Most Holy Sacrament. Great indeed, as the Scripture testifies, was the love of David for Jonathan: *"The soul of Jonathan was knit with the soul of David, and Jonathan loved him as his own soul."* But who can describe the love of Jesus in the Holy Eucharist? St. John Chrysostom beautifully says: "How many desire to behold the form, the countenance, the robe of the Redeemer. Here you can see the Lord Himself, O Christian soul! You can touch Him, you can feed upon Him; is not this proof that He loves us more than His own life?" Thus does Jesus become entirely ours, because He gives Himself wholly to us.

He also abides with us *continually*. The mystery of the Incarnation is renewed in the Most Holy Sacrament of the Altar, as often as the priest pronounces the words of consecration over the species of bread and wine. Through many centuries the patriarchs and prophets of the old covenant longed for the promised *Messias*. David, the Royal Psalmist, breathed forth this longing in touching melodies, and the prophet Isaias petitions heaven in the following words: *"Drop down dew, ye heavens, from above, and let the clouds rain the just: let the earth be opened, and bud forth a Saviour."* And now we are privileged to possess this miracle of love; we have this Saviour upon our altars, in our midst; He is ours, ours forever.

Since we possess this love of Jesus, we have together with it all the riches and treasures, all the good things, we could possibly desire. We might say in regard to the love which Jesus has for us something similar to what Seneca, the heathen sage, said to one of the Roman emperors. This emperor caused a carpet of the most skilful workmanship to be manufactured at an immense expense, splendid jewels being interwoven into the fabric. When Seneca saw this magnificent and costly piece of work, he said: "Sire, hereby you have evidently impoverished yourself." I might use the same expression in regard to God, for, if the impossible could happen and God could become poor, in like manner, He would have impoverished Himself by weaving the infinitely precious jewel of the Holy Eucharist into the checkered web of human existence.

After this brief glance at the miracle of love, I would ask you, *do* you know Him, who thus dwells in our midst,—do you know how great is His love? Perhaps you will answer "yes." Why then, my daughter, have you so little confidence in Him? Why do you turn, when you meet with trials and contradictions, to anyone rather than to Him? Why do you seek for help and consolation from every friend but Him? Why do you not turn to Jesus whatever may be your need, since He is almighty and truly loves you with an infinite love? Did you but thoroughly realize the great truth that Jesus Christ dwells in the tabernacle and that His love and goodness are as infinite as they were when, during His sojourn on earth, He healed the sick, comforted the sorrowful, raised the dead, dispensed mercy and pardon to penitent sinners, and became all things to all men, how different would be your conduct!

Therefore renew your faith, your love, your confidence, and betake yourself to Jesus. There, upon the altar, our dearest Lord abides in person, in both His human and divine nature. There is no form of suffering for which He has not promised to give us a healing balm. *"Come to me,"* He says, *"and I will refresh you."* Doubt not that you will find in Him comfort in hours of gloom, light where you can see no escape, good counsel amid doubts, a blessing on your undertakings, alleviations in your sorrows, strength in temptation, joy amid humiliations, help in every time of need. All this is contained in the words: "*I will refresh you.*" Do not seek to weaken the force of that promise; take it in its full import and trust in it entirely.

Imitate in this respect the example set by a parishioner of Vianney, the well-known and saintly curé of Ars, a village in France. It was no small consolation for this holy priest to see how frequently an elderly man who was one of his parishioners paid a visit to the church, and how long a time he spent in adoration of the Blessed Sacrament. The pastor noticed that however long this pious man remained upon his knees, and however often he entered the church, his lips never appeared to move in prayer. "My good man," he asked him one day, "what do you say to our dear Lord when you are kneeling in His presence?" "You ask me what I say?" was the reply; "I just say nothing at all! I know He is there, and He knows I am here; I just look at Him and He looks upon me."

What a touching and beautiful answer! The pious man remained silent because he was so fully persuaded that it was not necessary to speak to Our Lord, since He knew everything already. He gazed upon the Saviour in the same manner as the blessed in heaven gaze upon the vision of God.

> Nor voice can sing, nor heart can frame,
> Nor can the memory find,
> A sweeter sound than Thy blest name,
> O Saviour of mankind!

XII. Love upon the Altar

Once upon a time two Religious were preaching a Mission in a certain parish. They preached with zeal and eloquence, but it was of little use; the people listened to their discourses but gave no sign of conversion or amendment. Before the close of the Mission, one of the priests determined to make a last effort to overcome their indifference and soften their hard hearts. From the pulpit he spoke with such energy, such fire, such earnestness that the exertion was too much for him; he broke a blood-vessel and a flow of blood from his lips arrested his fervid eloquence. He was carried out of the church in a dying condition. Then the other missioner, taking the bloodstained habit of his colleague, went into the pulpit and held it up to the sight of the congregation, exclaiming: "Look, this blood was shed for you, it was you who cost him his life." All his hearers were struck with horror; it led them to look into their own hearts; the confessionals were crowded, and many permanent conversions were the result.

See now how this spectacle is in a certain sense renewed day by day upon our altars. The priest holds up to view, not merely the bloodstained garment of the Saviour, but His real and actual body, the selfsame body which for our sakes was torn with scourges and pierced with nails; he elevates the blood which was shed for us upon the cross amid excruciating agonies. Holy Mass is, in very deed, the love of Jesus upon the altar. In order that you, my dear child, may rightly appreciate the value of the holy sacrifice, and may repay the love of Jesus with the love of your own heart, you must constantly seek to strengthen and confirm yourself in lively faith: you must steadfastly believe that in the Mass the God-Man, Jesus Christ, is really, truly, and substantially, present upon the altar. Lay to heart the principal grounds of this belief.

The first reason is founded upon the promise of Him who is eternal Truth. When Jesus Christ, the God-Man, promises anything, He will most assuredly not depart from that promise. He solemnly promised to institute the Most Holy Sacrament of the Altar. Upon one occasion great multitudes followed

Him, in order to hear His words; the people, having brought no provisions with them, became very hungry. Jesus had compassion on them and worked a marvelous miracle; He multiplied five loaves and two fishes to so great a quantity that 5000 men were amply satisfied, and five basketfuls of the food remained over. All present were greatly astonished; on account of what they had witnessed, they wished to make Jesus a king, for they thought that He would always supply them with food and there would be no necessity for them to work. But Jesus told them of a different kind of food, which He would give them. And to what food did He refer?

He said: "*The bread that I will give, is my flesh for the life of the world,*" meaning the same flesh which He shall offer up upon the cross for the life of the world, in order that all men may have life, the life of grace here on earth and the life of glory hereafter, in heaven. Thus, clearly and definitely, did Jesus promise that He would really give us His flesh, His body.

Holy Scripture says further: "*The Jews therefore strove among themselves.*" Why did they thus strive? Because they considered it to be impossible that Jesus should give them His flesh to eat. They said: "*How can this man give us His flesh to eat?*" Now reflect for a moment, if Our Lord had not intended to give us His flesh, His body, but only bread as an emblem of His body, what think you would He most assuredly have answered the Jews? On one occasion when I was giving instruction in my parish school, I told the children to learn the catechism well before I came again. Thereupon one of the children rejoined: "But Father, we can't learn the whole catechism before your next visit!" Of course I explained to the child that I did not mean the whole catechism, but only those answers which I had desired should be learned by heart.

In like manner would Jesus Christ have given the necessary explanation, if He had not really referred to His flesh, He would have said: "You have misunderstood Me; I will give you only an emblem of my body, I will give you only bread to eat." But did Our Lord thus speak? Certainly not; on the contrary, He reiterated His assertion and confirmed His words in the most solemn and emphatic manner: "*Amen, amen, I say unto you: Except you eat the flesh of the Son of man, and drink His blood, you shall not have life in you.*" And He adds yet another asseveration: "*For my flesh is meat indeed: and my blood is drink indeed.*" Could our dear Lord have spoken more plainly, or expressed Himself more explicitly? These words appeared so clear and plain to the disciples, that, as we read in the gospel: "*After this many of His disciples went back; and walked no more with Him*"; for, as the Evangelist continues, they remarked: "*This saying is hard, and who can hear it?*" Jesus permitted them to depart; He told the apostles and His other disciples that, if they all forsook Him, His words must remain the same, and He would in very deed give them His flesh and blood.

And what Jesus so definitely promised He has assuredly fulfilled. At the last supper He truly changed bread and wine into His most sacred body and blood. In regard to the bread which He took into His hands, He clearly and definitely declared: "*This is My body.*" He did not say "this signifies my body" or "this will become my body." At the same time He commanded His apostles: "*Do this for a commemoration of Me.*" And this command is fulfilled in the present day by bishops and priests, who are the successors of the apostles, whenever they say Mass, at the moment of consecration; the true God-Man, Jesus Christ, is present in His entire being.

Now consider a third proof that so indeed it is. Ever since the time of the apostles, our holy mother, the Catholic Church, has interpreted the words of Our Lord, "*This is My body,*" in one and the same literal sense. St. Justin, a disciple of the apostles, who died in the year 166 after Christ, expresses the belief of the Church in the following words: "We are taught that this sacred food is the body and blood of the incarnate Son of God." And St. Cyril of Jerusalem, who died in 386, speaks just as plainly: "That which appears to be bread is not bread, though it seems to be such to our palate, and what appears to be wine, though it has the taste of wine, is not such in reality, but it is the blood of Jesus Christ." The same Doctor of the Church writes in another place: "As Christ Himself says of the bread, *This is My body,* who can doubt the fact? And if He expressly says, *This is My blood,* ought any one to raise objections, and assert that it is not His blood? He turned water into wine, and can we not believe that He is able to turn wine into His precious blood?"

Whenever you hear Mass, do so with lively faith, and contemplate upon the altar the love of Jesus. Do not remain cold and insensible like the stones of the pavement, but adore Our Lord with holy recollection and the deepest reverence. Pierce with the eye of faith the veil of the sacred Host, and repeat with heart and voice:

> Jesus, ever-loving Saviour,
> Thou didst live and die for me;
> Living, I will live to love Thee,
> Dying, I will die for Thee.

XIII. IN THE BRIGHT DAYS OF YOUTH

You may perhaps know from your own experience what homesickness is—that vague, indefinite longing for home, for the beloved members of your family circle. The saints also knew what homesickness is, but in their case this feeling was of a widely different nature. They did not long for earthly things, for creatures, or for some special country; they longed for the heavenly country, for the land of bliss and pure delight, where those things are to be found of which the Apostle writes: *"Eye hath not seen, nor ear heard, neither hath it entered into the heart of man, what things God hath prepared for them that love Him."* So eagerly did the saints long for heaven that they awaited the coming of death with holy impatience.

God does not require of us that we should feel as they did, but He does require that we should love Him, and seek to serve Him faithfully. He requires this more especially, of the young, according to the exhortation of Holy Scripture: *"Remember thy Creator in the days of thy youth."* Therefore do you, my daughter, love God and serve Him faithfully in the bright days of youth.

The first reason why you ought to do this is because God requires special service at the hands of the young, since such service is more acceptable to Him than that rendered later in life. We read in the Old Testament that He commanded the Israelites to offer all first fruits to Him: the first flowers in spring, the first fruits in autumn, the first born of man and beast. The earliest period of man's life is in like manner the most pleasing to Him, and therefore does He desire to be faithfully served by you.

Therefore do not think and say, as too many foolish, thoughtless young people do: "When I am old it will surely be time enough to think about God, to love and serve Him and work for Him. At present I really have not time to occupy myself with such serious matters; I must enjoy the pleasures suitable to my age as long as I can, for they vanish like a flash of lightning and the sunny days of youth and light-hearted happiness can never return."

Do not think and talk in this manner; it is a presumptuous and dangerous way of speaking, and one which may entail bitter repentance in after life. Many an elderly woman have I known to lament that she had been so reckless when young, had not sought to avoid dangerous occasions, nor striven to love and serve God. The following anecdote was recently related to me. A woman was lying on her deathbed. She received a visit from a friend who was much attached to her, and who inquired whether there was anything she could do for her? "Alas! my darling," exclaimed the poor invalid, "if only you could give me back my youth, that I might make better use of it!"

You, dear daughter, still have your bright, joyous youth. Employ it in such a manner as you will wish you had done when you are stretched upon your deathbed; employ it in the love and service of God.

Meditate upon your past life. You will perceive how the gracious and fatherly hand of God has ordered all things with loving care. He gave you—so, at least, I confidently hope—pious parents, who led you to take delight even in your earliest years in all that is good and true. He chose you from among a thousand others; His gentle voice spoke to your heart, inviting you to love Him. He guided your every step, He enabled you to preserve your innocence, that fairest of all fair flowers.

Yet more has He done for you! He bestowed on you the inestimable benefit of a thoroughly good training. Under the parental roof the inexhaustible love of a tender mother, the wholesome severity of a judicious father, worked together, with the blessing of God, to educate you wisely and well. Perhaps you have also been fortunate enough to finish your studies in some excellent Catholic academy or college. Thus has God given proof of His special love and care for you. Be grateful to Him, love and serve Him!

But you may ask why and how you are to love Him? After all that I have said about the goodness of God in your regard, about the graces and benefits He has bestowed upon you, is it necessary that I should entreat and urge you to love Him? Will you not obey the injunction of Holy Scripture: "*Remember thy Creator in the days of thy youth.*" Will you scorn the love and goodness of your heavenly Father, will you despise His benefits and blessings? I am sure you are not capable of acting in such a manner: your heart is not a heart of stone; on the contrary, young girls are, as a rule, especially open to affection. If you were at any time obliged to live at a distance from your father and mother, did you not long for them and keenly feel the separation from them? How painful must be the feelings of an orphan girl, for whom no kind father cares any longer, on whom no affectionate mother can any more gaze with a loving eye, for whom there exists no fond maternal heart into which the sad tale of every sorrow and anxiety can be poured.

But if you had lost not only your parents, but all who loved you, there would always remain One to love you; for then would the fatherly heart of God still feel for you, then would His ever-watchful eye keep guard over you, His gracious hand protect and lead and guide you aright! Seek therefore to love this heavenly Father as you ought.

You may perhaps say: "It is my great desire to love God, but how can I do this, as I cannot see Him, nor feel His love for me?" Now tell me whether, if you were on some distant island of the ocean without any hope of ever seeing your beloved mother again, should you on this account cease to love her? Would not the love you feel for her be rather doubled in proportion to the distance which separated you from her?

Well then, remember that though you cannot see God, who is better than any earthly father can ever be, and though as yet you have never seen Him, nevertheless you experience His love and goodness day by day. Love God with your whole heart, because He is infinitely good,

At the same time you must bear in mind the exhortation of St. John: "*My little children, let us not love in word, nor in* tongue, but in deed, and in truth." Thus you perceive that you must prove your love to God by your actions, by your whole manner of life, in a word, by doing His holy will. Sermons, religious instructions, and pious books, will teach you what His will is. Ignorance of the will of God is not so frequently to be met with as the disinclination to observe it. Arouse yourself to fresh zeal in the service of God. May His grace strengthen you, and may His love abide with you forever.

I Love Thee, O Thou Lord Most High
(Hymn of St. Ignatius)

1. I love Thee, O Thou Lord most high,
    Because Thou first hast loved me;
   I seek no other liberty
    But that of being bound to Thee.

2. May memory no thought suggest
    But shall to Thy pure glory tend;
   My understanding find no rest
    Except in Thee, its only end.

3. My God, I here protest to Thee
    No other will I have than Thine;
   Whatever Thou hast giv'n to me
    I here again to Thee resign.

4. All mine is Thine; say but the word,
    Whate'er Thou willest shall be done;
   I know Thy love, all-gracious Lord—
    I know it seeks my good alone.

5. Apart from Thee all things are nought;
    Then grant, O my supremest Bliss,
   Grant me to love Thee as I ought—
    Thou givest all in giving this.

Act of Love

O MY GOD! I love Thee above all things, with my whole heart and soul, because Thou art all-good and worthy of all love. I love my neighbor as myself for the love of Thee. I forgive all who have injured me, and ask pardon of all whom I have injured.

Jesus, my Lord, my God, my All

Jesus, my Lord, my God, my all,
How can I love Thee as I ought?
And how revere this wond'rous gift,
So far surpassing hope or thought.
Sweet Sacrament, we Thee adore.
O make us love Thee more and more!

Had I but Mary's sinless heart,
To love Thee with, my dearest King;
O with what bursts of fervent praise,
Thy goodness, Jesus, would I sing!
Sweet Sacrament, we Thee adore.
O make us love Thee more and more!

O, see, within a creature's hand,
The vast Creator deigns to be,
Reposing infant-like, as though
On Joseph's arm, on Mary's knee.
Sweet Sacrament, we Thee adore.
O make us love Thee more and more!

Thy body, soul, and Godhead, all—
O mystery of love divine!
I cannot compass all I have,
For all Thou hast and art are mine.
Sweet Sacrament, we Thee adore.
O make us love Thee more and more!

Sound, sound His praises higher still,
And come ye Angels to our aid;
'Tis God, 'tis God, the very God,
Whose power both man and angels made.
Sweet Sacrament, we Thee adore.
O make us love Thee more and more!

—*Father Frederick William Faber*

◂ 4 ▸

The Rose

Love of Our Neighbor

XIV. Kindheartedness

K INDHEARTEDNESS—a beautiful, delightful word, a word which expresses one of the most pleasing qualities that anybody; and especially a young girl, can possess. You ought therefore to be kindhearted, and this signifies nothing else than that the fair rose of a real love of your neighbor should find a place in the wreath of flowers which adorns your youthful brow; this again means that you ought to practise as perfectly as possible the second great commandment of the law: "Thou shalt love thy neighbor as thyself." All men are comprised in the word "neighbor," but it refers more especially to your parents, your confessor, your friends, all the poor and afflicted, and also your enemies. You should show yourself to be kindhearted in regard to them all. I shall proceed to give you some practical suggestions upon this subject.

Shortly before He left the earth Our Lord said to His disciples: *"By this shall all men know that you are my disciples, if you have love one for another."* Thus we see that brotherly love and kindness of heart are characteristics of the followers of Christ. You must therefore be kindhearted if you wish to be reckoned among His followers; and if you possess this essential qualification, you will rejoice with the joyful, weep with the sorrowful, soothe miseries, relieve distresses, bear wrongs patiently and repay ingratitude with love. Thus will you most nearly resemble God, who is love and whose actions are always beneficent, and you will be universally beloved and regarded as an angel of peace. But, my daughter, you must be careful to expel from your heart all passion and selfishness, since only by so doing can you attain real kindness of heart.

Kindness of heart will render you courteous and polite in your intercourse with others, yet necessary prudence and circumspection must not be lost sight of.

The feminine heart is naturally tender and sympathetic, easily moved to take part in the sorrows and joys of others. In accordance with this natural disposition, and also as a disciple of Jesus Christ, the truly pious maiden is always gentle and loving. Tears fill her eyes at the mere recital of the afflictions of others, and when she perceives that those around are weeping, she mingles her tears with theirs. She is ever ready to console, to succor, to infuse sweetness into the bitter cup of life as far, at least, as it lies in her power to do all this. She reconciles those who are at enmity, she bears with the eccentric and faultfinding, and should all her kind efforts fail, she prefers to put up with everything rather than to indulge in wrangling and bitter complaints.

If you, being filled with this kindness of heart, engage in works of mercy, how rich a harvest will you reap one day! The recollection of the charitable actions you have performed will fill you with interior happiness, and thus you will have a reward more precious than all the riches and pleasures of this world. How delightful will it be to say to yourself: "I have dried the tears of many who were in affliction; by means of the small sums I was able to contribute, I have been instrumental in bringing many souls to the knowledge of the true faith and therefore to eternal salvation, and in delivering many a suffering soul from the flames of purgatory." Therefore is it written in the pages of Holy Scripture: "*It is a more blessed thing to give, rather than to receive.*"

The kindness you show to your neighbor will, moreover, encourage him to place more implicit confidence in God and to feel greater gratitude toward Him. It not unfrequently happens that when anyone is visited with a succession of trials he becomes discouraged, and begins to lose his faith and his trust in divine providence. It is only the hand of a truly kind person, who has already succored him in his hour of need, that has power to draw him back from the abyss of despair; it is only the belief in kindness and sympathy that can avail to console him. The thought of all this kindness seems to whisper in his ear: "Take courage, God has not forsaken you. He has moved your friend to take pity on you and come to your assistance. He will find a way to succor you still further."

The good effect of this kindness of heart is strikingly shown in the following instance. A Protestant paid a visit upon a certain occasion to a large Paris hospital. Among the many unfortunate beings whom the institution always shelters within its walls there happened just then to be a sick man whose wretched plight was indescribably sad. Almost an idiot, ailing from his birth, a terrible and protracted disease had deprived him of both arms and legs. This pitiable object appeared scarcely human. Mental deficiency and physical pain had rendered him so irritable that the slightest provocation caused him to break out into screams of rage.

The visitor was shocked at the spectacle, but his horror gave way speedily to amazement. He saw a Sister of Charity kneel down by the bed of the miserable creature and pay him every thoughtful attention. "Sister," exclaimed the stranger, "how can you be so cheerful while waiting on this repulsive object, the mere sight of whom fills me with horror?" "He is the one we love best in all the house," replied the Sister, "and because he is so dreadfully afflicted and naturally so repulsive, we all love him better than our other invalids." This extreme charity and tenderness deeply impressed the Protestant. He entered into himself, and shortly afterward he became a child of that Church which alone possesses power to inspire such unselfish devotion, such heroic sacrifice.

Strive therefore to be truly kindhearted. Help others in their necessities, for if you do you may confidently expect that God will not forget you in your time of need. The Royal Psalmist has said: "*Blessed is he that understandeth concerning the needy and the poor: the Lord will deliver him in the evil day.*" And Solomon teaches us in the Book of Proverbs: "*He who confers benefits upon others will himself receive many, and he who gives much, to him shall much be given.*"

But what are all earthly gifts in comparison with the sweet celestial peace, the abundant grace, the eternal reward which will assuredly be the portion of the maiden who exercises this kindness of heart in its truest, highest sense! Listen to the Saviour's words: "*Blessed are the merciful: for they shall obtain mercy.*" And again: "*Amen, I say to you, as long as you did it to one of these my least brethren, you did it to Me.*"

> He only acts a Christian part
>   Whose breast with love doth glow;
> Rejoicing with the glad of heart,
>   Feeling with others' woe.

Once again, my child, I exhort you to strive after the attainment of this kindness of heart, and in the exercise of it you will become ever more and more like unto Him, who is infinitely merciful, who is eternal charity. Strive to be like unto Jesus, who went about doing good to all.

XV. Honor thy Father and thy Mother

FATHER! MOTHER! What names sound more sweetly in our ears! On hearing these names the heart of every dutiful child, of every good daughter, thrills with joy and happiness. But these beloved names should not merely awaken such sentiment of the heart. They ought also to influence your will, leading you to fulfil your duty to your parents with scrupulous exactness. Your catechism has already taught you the nature of these duties. I desire, however, to impress them upon you somewhat more in detail.

Father! Mother! What a world of tenderness and anxious care, of joy and sorrow, do these words imply! Parental affection is faithful and tender, full of the purest and most unselfish devotion. If you seek for two other human hearts to love you in a manner as disinterested and sincere, you will not find them under the sun. All that a young girl dreams, and sings, and says about love in friendship and courtship, indicates, in too many instances, but a fire of straw, which blazes brightly for a brief space and then as quickly dies down again, leaving nothing but ashes behind. The love of a father, or a mother, is most genuine and enduring, independent of all conditions of time and distance.

Of what constant self-sacrifice is not this love capable! What is it that often causes the hair of the father of a family to turn prematurely gray? What is it that impresses furrows upon his brow and causes his once strong and stalwart form to appear bent and broken? It is his wearing toil and anxiety, his efforts to promote the temporal happiness and well-being of his children. Ask your mother to tell of the mortal anguish she has endured on your account, the hours she has spent in watching beside your bed, the cares and anxieties she has experienced through you. Truly a mother's love never dies. It is renewed with each day.

How can you ever repay such affection, how ought you to repay it? By filial love, respect, devotedness, and obedience; by honoring your father and mother; by speaking of them in terms of respect at all times and in all places; by never allowing them to hear from your lips a rude or insolent expression; by never making merry over their natural defects or moral deficiencies. Let your whole behavior to your father and mother be respectful. Even if clouds obscure the sun—I mean even if real and grave faults detract from the dignity appertaining to their position—strive to see the sun shining behind the clouds, and in spite of your parents' failings, remember the respect which is due from you. For in the fourth commandment God does not say that you are to honor a *good* father and a *good* mother. He says: "Honor thy father and thy mother." The Blessed Thomas More, who was Lord Chancellor of England, and on this account second in rank only to the king himself, constantly had his aged father with him in his own house and always assigned to him the place of honor. This dutiful son never left home to attend to business of state without asking upon his knees for his father's blessing and reverently kissing his hand. You ought to model your conduct to your parents after the example of this holy man, and to show yourself as affectionate and amiable as he was.

Love your father and mother, love them from the depth of your heart, with true, filial affection. Always take delight in the society of your parents, and thus give external proof of the love you bear them. It is scarcely necessary to remind you of this in a special manner while you are still so very young. But later on—for instance, when married or in a distinguished position—the matter may assume a widely different aspect. In that case you must be on your guard, and never cease to show the customary regard for your father and mother, and continued pleasure in their society.

Give further proof of your love by never occasioning them sorrow. Imitate the youthful Tobias, whose parents called him the light of their eyes, the staff of their old age, their hope, the solace of their days.

Give a further proof of your love for your father and mother by tending and cherishing them with special and unselfish devotion in their weakness and old age. You can never repay the whole sum, that is to say, the entire capital of the affection they have lavished upon you, but you may at least return the interest of it by contributing to their support as far as lies in your power. See that you give proof of your love for your parents by never allowing a day to pass without praying earnestly for them. It has been said that the prayer which a mother utters on behalf of her child is the sweetest music in the world, a sound which reaches to the highest heaven; and the same words apply to the petitions which a pious child breathes forth for its parents.

Finally, see that you obey your father and mother. Look into the lowly dwelling at Nazareth. There you will find Jesus Christ, your Saviour and your Lord, your Exemplar, at the same age as you now are. What did He do, what did He teach during the whole of the thirty years He spent under that humble roof? The evangelist St. Luke expresses it in one word where he says: "*He was **subject** to them*" (His parents). Thus we see that Jesus was submissive and obedient until He was thirty years old! How disgraceful it is to hear a young girl who is only sixteen, eighteen, or perhaps, twenty, say: "I am no child to be dragged about in leading-strings. I want my liberty." Alas for the girl who speaks in this way! Her language is all the more shocking the older she is, for then she cannot be excused on the score of mere childish folly. She is perfectly right in asserting that she is no longer a child. She is indeed no longer a child of God, a child according to the Sacred

Heart of Jesus, but she is a child of pride. "Do you, dear child, remain always a docile, obedient daughter of your father and mother. Your fulfilment of the fourth commandment will be as a sweet odor before the Lord, and will make you one day a partaker in the bliss of heaven.

7. And when sooner or later the heart of your kind father or of your loving mother will have ceased to beat, or in case you have already lost your parents, beware lest they should descry any stain upon the surface of your soul, now open to their sight. Such conduct will be the best monument you can raise to their memory. For, as it has been well said: "he mourns the dead, who lives as they desire." And if sorrow or suffering overtake you, causing you to feel more bitterly than ever the loss of your beloved parents and to sigh for the days now forever past, when you could lean your weary head on a tender, maternal bosom, when a mother's hand was always ready to wipe away your tears, then remember that you are not altogether forsaken, for

> Each child of man one God alone
> Hath; yet he hath parents twain:
> And when those parents both are gone
> His God doth still remain.

XVI. An Earnest of Future Blessings

To the eyes of a young, light-hearted girl the future appears dressed in roseate hues. What you eagerly hope and desire for yourself, what your parents and your confessor earnestly desire for you, is temporal and spiritual welfare, every blessing and happiness. But will these wishes be fulfilled, will the sun of prosperity always shine on you, will the fatherly blessing of God accompany you through your whole life? What happiness would be yours could these questions be answered with certainty in the affirmative, could you receive a warrant, a pledge, that such indeed shall be your lot! Rest assured that this happiness may be yours to enjoy, for God has given you a sure earnest of blessing to come, in the fourth commandment, which runs thus: "*Honor thy father and thy mother that thou mayest live a long time, and it may be well with thee in the land, which the Lord thy God will give thee.*" In these words you see how clearly and definitely God has pledged His word. And how has He kept His promise? And how does He continue to keep it?

God is infinitely faithful and true. He can never fail to perform what He has promised. Our fellow creatures too often do not intend their promises to be taken seriously, or they forget them almost as soon as they are uttered, or else they are unable to carry them out, but in regard to God we have nothing of this kind to dread.

Numerous and striking are the instances which might be adduced to prove how abundantly the promise given in the fourth commandment has been fulfilled. Remember Sem and Japheth, the dutiful sons of Noe, who received the blessing of God by the mouth of their father. Remember Tobias, who was so exemplary a son that his parents called him the staff of their old age, the light of their eyes, the comfort of their life. How rich was his reward! He lived ninety-nine years in the fear of the Lord, and saw his children's children to the fifth generation. Remember Joseph, who was so good a son and the darling of his father. In how special and marvelous a manner did Providence watch over him, and how innumerable were the blessings showered down upon him? His children and grandchildren rejoiced his heart, and when he had reached the ripe old age of one hundred and ten years, his life was closed by a calm and peaceful death. It was well with him, and he lived long on the earth.

Since all these facts combine to prove that God has indeed fulfilled His promise, we can not doubt that He will continue to fulfil it in the course of events in our own lives. Anyone who has learned to take even a comparatively superficial view of men and things will perceive children who, like Tobias and Joseph, have been specially guided and blessed throughout their whole careers. We find daughters who, when they are grown up, are esteemed and valued by all who know them. They may perhaps not be very rich, but they enjoy all the more contentment and peace of mind. Such daughters as these never fail to experience the guidance and blessing of God in their choice of a vocation which is to decide the happiness of their whole after-life. Such daughters, moreover, are often privileged to become spouses of Jesus Christ, and to spend their days in a cloister, where they enjoy a foretaste of paradise. Others again are fortunate enough to be married to good and kind husbands. They are happy in their children and grandchildren, who pay them love, obedience, and respect like that which they themselves formerly showed to their own parents. Over and over again have I heard it remarked about daughters such as I have just described that it was no wonder they got on well—they were good and dutiful children to their parents.

Let me relate a few particulars concerning just such a daughter, with whom I happen to be intimately acquainted, as she is a relative of mine. She was an only daughter. I know with what unselfish devotion she nursed her father and mother in their last illnesses, refusing attractive offers of marriage even when she was close upon thirty years of age, solely because she would not relinquish her affectionate care of her aged and beloved father. Almighty God has richly rewarded her. For the last fifteen years she has been most happily married, and, as she herself told me, never for one single instant has she had reason to regret the step she took, never for a moment has she found the wedded state to be anything but happy. Her four girls and two boys are all very good and amiable, strong in body and highly gifted intellectually, the delight of their parents, and give bright promise for the future. Thus are fulfilled the words of Holy Scripture: "*The father's blessing establisheth the houses of the children.*"

Thus do dutiful children enjoy the blessing and protection of God here on earth. And what will be their portion in eternity! When after a long and happy life, these obedient children, these good daughters, who have so faithfully kept the fourth commandment, come to die, they may, when reviewing the past, perceive many a dark spot, many faults and omissions, even perhaps many grave errors. But the thought that they always honored their father and mother, never caused them vexation, but ever tried to please them, will be as a bright star amid the gloom, giving them comfort and inspiring them with confidence.

And now they stand before the eternal Judge. He surveys them with a benignant eye, for He perceives in them a likeness to Himself. Did not He, too, when on earth, honor His parents? No further testimony is needed, yet He summons the rejoicing father and mother, addressing them in some such words as these: "Can you affirm that these your children always behaved honorably to you?" With beaming countenances they make reply: "We can, O Lord Jesus Christ! Our dear children were indeed not without faults and foibles, but they faithfully kept the fourth commandment; they in very deed loved, honored and obeyed us; they tended us with affectionate devotion in our old age and did not forsake us after our deaths, but, by means of their prayers, procured for us a more speedy admission to the abode of everlasting felicity. Therefore do Thou, O Lord, be to them a merciful Judge."

Then will the just Judge turn to those children and say: "I know that so it was, and what you did to your parents, you did to Me. Therefore come, ye blessed, of My Father, possess you the kingdom prepared for you from the foundation of the world." But who can describe the infinite glory and blessedness of the heavenly kingdom!

My daughter, see that you honor your father and mother, so that you may one day be made a partaker of that blessedness. For this reason I would say to you:

> O love as long as thou canst love,
> O love as long as life doth last;
> The hour comes, the hour comes,
> When at the grave thy tears flow fast.

Love your father and your mother, in order that you may have no cause for self-reproach when you stand beside their graves, but may experience the fulfilment of the fourth commandment to be at once an earnest of blessing here upon earth and of endless happiness in heaven.

XVII. The Ambassadors of Christ

In view of the wickedness and impiety of the days in which our lot is cast, what is it that causes the vengeance of the Almighty to tarry, and not to punish a great number of the dwellers upon earth by letting loose upon them the waters of a second deluge? It is the blood of the just Abel, of the incarnate Son of God, which is offered up every day many thousands of times upon our globe in the sacrifice of the Mass; and which ascends to the throne of God, calling down, not vengeance, but infinite grace and mercy, upon the sinful sons of Adam. How dark and how dreary would the earth appear were this mystical sun to withdraw its beams, were the daily sacrifice of the Mass to be no longer offered, were we entirely deprived of priests. This shows how very important is the office of the priest and how much respect and gratitude he merits on this account. Priests are indeed the ambassadors of God; they are the representatives of Christ.

Therefore be careful to observe the command of Holy Scripture: *"Reverence his priests."* Consider well and lay to heart all that the priest does for you. At the commencement of your life he purified you from sin in the waters of holy Baptism. He instructed you in the doctrines of the Catholic faith; he is your support in life, your comforter in affliction, your helper in the hour of death, your surety for heaven. He feeds you with the bread of angels in holy communion. When sorrow and anxieties oppress your heart, and you are ready to sink into despair, if you betake yourself to the priest in the confessional, the oil and wine of sound advice and soothing words are poured into the wounds of your soul, and you are healed by means of the Sacrament of Penance.

When at last, sick and suffering, you are stretched upon your deathbed, when no earthly friend can aid or comfort you, the priest approaches and consoles you, even if he has to do this at the risk of his own life. He stands by your side in the last awful conflict, brings you pardon and peace in the holy Sacrament of Penance, strengthens you with heavenly food in the holy viaticum, imparts to you strength and courage by means of Extreme Unction. Even after death he does not abandon you: he prays for you and offers the holy sacrifice on your behalf in order that your soul may be delivered as speedily as possible from the flames of purgatory. Now what are you to offer to the priest in return for all these benefits? You should offer three special gifts: gratitude, confidence, and prayers.

Gratitude is a charming virtue, one which it is indispensable that a young girl should possess. A grateful daughter will be also a good and dutiful daughter. And who has the chief claim on your gratitude? In the first place God and your parents, in the next the priest, by whose means God has enriched your soul with so great and so many benefits. He it was who prepared you with much pain and fatherly tenderness for your first confession and communion. Be grateful therefore to him as long as you live. Show your gratitude to him by rejoicing his heart with the sight of your blameless, truly pious life, by lightening for him the heavy burden of his office, by obeying him implicitly, and by always seconding him in all his efforts for the good of souls. I trust that you will never so far forget yourself as to cause your anxious pastor to utter the reproach: "My child, I should never have expected this of you!"

Treat your confessor with confidence. He merits your confidence, since he has been appointed by God to be the guide and guardian of your soul, your spiritual father. You may perhaps have to go out into the world, and, unacquainted as you are with its seductions and temptations, you may be led astray by them and fall grievously. On this account unspeakable anguish may enter into your soul. If you think that among the strangers by whom you are surrounded there is no one to whom you can speak of the heavy burden which is weighing you down, no one from whom you can receive counsel and comfort, or who can show you how to regain your lost footing, remember that such a friend is always to be found in the person of every good and faithful priest filled with zeal for souls.

Seek him therefore in the confessional; tell him what is troubling you; tell it in a simple, childlike spirit; confide in him and be not afraid. Never say to yourself: "But what will he think, if I tell him all this?" Believe me, my child, when I tell you that a priest, in the discharge of his duties as a confessor, for a length of time, cannot fail to become well acquainted with every kind of grief and suffering, every phase of danger, sin and temptation, every condition of the soul; so that you can tell him scarcely anything which he does not already know. As the result of study and much careful observation, he knows only too well the snares of the devil, the force of temptations, the power of evil occasions and habits of sin, the weakness of human nature, the attractions of the world,—he knows all this, I repeat, so very well that it is not probable he will be surprised at anything you may say to him.

Be particularly careful to seek his advice when it is a question of choosing a state of life, for this is the most important point you can have to decide. If you make the acquaintance of some young man whom you wish to marry, lay the matter before your director and confide in him.

A third way in which you can evince your gratitude to the ambassador of Christ, is by praying earnestly for him; therefore bestow upon him the alms of your prayers. The same may be said in regard to the prayers of a grateful, faithful, spiritual child for her confessor as has been already remarked concerning the prayers offered by a dutiful daughter on behalf of her parents. Such petitions pierce the clouds, and if we may so speak, exercise upon God Himself a sort of holy compulsion. I am speaking from my own experience when I say, that it is the sweetest consolation to a priest, when one of his spiritual children, whom he has perhaps not seen for years, and whose truthfulness he has no reason to doubt, assures him that she has not allowed a single day to pass without saying for him at least one *Hail Mary*. The confessor who is thus sustained by the prayers of his spiritual children will be all the better able to sanctify his own soul, and to do much to promote the salvation of the souls under his care

When he reflects upon the great dignity with which he is invested, the immense importance of the office he has

A similar experience may very probably be yours. You will more easily escape the perils of the world, you will more readily save your soul, if you are united to others in the bonds of pious and holy friendship, that so you may mutually warn, encourage and sustain one another, and stimulate one another to practise all good works. True friends seek to promote the good and happiness of each other.

It is certainly right and proper to entertain true friendship. This may be learned from the example of the saints, and of the Saint of saints, our Pattern and Model, our great Exemplar, Jesus Christ Himself. How deep and tender was his affection for St. John, the Apostle of Charity, for the little family of Bethania, for Mary and Martha, and their brother Lazarus! Moreover, history tells us how devotedly St. Peter loved St. Mark, and St. Paul cherished no less an affection for his disciple, St. Timothy. St. Gregory of Nazianzen was united in the closest bonds of friendship with St. Basil. St. Augustine with St. Ambrose, and so on. Thus we see that perfection does not consist in having no friends at all, but in having only those who are truly pious and good.

Therefore Christian maiden, love all mankind in truth and sincerity, as God has commanded you, but make friends only with girls who are likely to further, rather than hinder, your progress in piety and virtue. If you can converse about the love of God, about devotion and Christian perfection, then will your friendship be precious indeed! It will be truly exalted because it comes from God, because it leads to God, because in God it will remain forever. Well indeed is it to love here on earth with the same affection which the blessed in heaven feel for one another; while still in the world to be united in mutual charity in the same manner as it is our hope to be one day when it shall be our happy lot to have reached the bright abode of eternal felicity. To those who are fortunate enough to be thus united in the bonds of holy friendship, we may fitly apply the words of the Royal Psalmist: *"Behold how good and how pleasant it is for brethren (sisters) to dwell together in unity."* Certainly so it is, for the precious balm of sympathy flows from one heart into another, and God pours forth rich blessings upon a friendship such as this!

Beware of intimacies with a member of the opposite sex, for such a friendship is nearly always dangerous; still less ought you to entertain friendships which are unworthy of the name. I refer to sinful connections, or keeping company, that are the occasion of sin. This subject I shall treat at greater length in another place. In the mean time I will make only one remark, namely this, that until you are at least eighteen years of age you should not keep regular company or cultivate familiar friendship with a person of the opposite sex.

I wish most earnestly to impress upon you the necessity for watchfulness and prayer in order that your understanding may not be perverted by the indulgence of your senses and your passions. Do not say, as so many do, that the heart, i.e., the power of love, cannot be restrained. How greatly were you to be pitied if you were so weak of character as to surrender yourself to the sway of sensual affection! Be not hasty in forming close friendships. "But when you have found a friend," says a certain writer, "let neither life nor death, nor misunderstanding, nor distance, nor doubt, nor anything else interrupt this friendship and vex your peace."

You must exercise self-control in friendship. Be patient, be kind, be thoughtful, unselfish and loyal under all circumstances. Be true to your friends. Let their joys be your joys, and their sorrows your sorrows.

A friend is one of the sweetest things that life can bring. A true friend is not only our comfort in sorrow, our help in adversity; he also recalls us to a sense of duty, when we have forgotten ourselves, he inspires and encourages us to aim at high ideals, he takes loving heed of our health, our work, our plans and all that concerns us; he wants to make us good and happy.

> Sweeter than the breath of spring,
> Is the joy a friend can bring,
> Who rejoices in our gladness
> And gives solace in our sadness.

XIX. IT IS DIFFICULT YET NOT IMPOSSIBLE

WHAT is it which renders a child so sweet and lovable? Its innocence, it is true, but also its simplicity and its inability to keep up feelings of anger. A child may be angry, excessively angry, with other children and anxious to revenge itself, but in a brief space of time all is past and forgotten; it once more laughs, jests, and plays with the very children upon whom it longed to revenge itself a few minutes before. It is on account of this characteristic that the Saviour said: "*Unless you be converted, and become as little children, you shall not enter into the kingdom of heaven.*"

It is to be hoped that you, my daughter, are still a child in the best sense of the word—that your heart is pure, and that you as yet know nothing of hatred, enmities, and permanent feelings of aversion. But times will change, and you will change also. You must therefore arm yourself to resist the attacks of the strongest and most destructive of passions, those of anger, hatred and revenge. For if these passions are allowed to dwell in the heart of a woman, they remain there more permanently, and burn with a fiercer flame than in the heart of a man. Lay well to heart the truth that "it is difficult, yet not impossible," to love your enemies.

How difficult, how terribly difficult it is to love an enemy, to love one who has injured you most grievously, most shamefully! Yet, difficult as it is, it must be done. For God Himself has commanded you in these solemn words: "*But I say to you, love your enemies.*" In another place He commands you to forgive, not only once, not seven times, but seventy times seven times. Again He says: "*I say to you not to resist evil: but if one strike thee on thy right cheek, turn to him also the other.*" And if passion whispers to you that you can be consoled only by inflicting pain on your enemy, you must stifle the unworthy feeling, and forgive him. If you imagine that you must needs revenge yourself that your enemy may not repeat his offence, still you must forgive in obedience to the divine command.

If the world represents to you that your honor calls to be avenged, still you must forgive, for God will have it so. If your heart bleeds, and you feel quite bewildered, and are conscious that you have neither strength nor courage to forgive, you must make the effort, great as it may be, for God has said: "*Love your enemies.*"

Difficult it may be, but it can and must be done. For instance, some one may have grievously injured you, causing your honor and good name to suffer. Then will a craving for revenge arise in your heart, like some fierce, wild animal, and cry to you that in a case like this you cannot, ought not to forgive. Is it really true that it is out of your power to pardon your foe? Certainly it is not; thousands and thousands have been more grievously wronged, yet have been able to forgive; you can imitate their example if only you exert your will. God does not require you to perform an impossibility. He will give you the needful grace; if you pray earnestly for it, you will assuredly receive it, and find yourself able to accomplish what appeared to be an impossibility. You must forgive; otherwise the portals of heaven will remain closed against you, and damnation and despair will be your portion forevermore. But God created you for a very different end. He has said: "*I desire not the death of the sinner, but that he be converted and live."* Only pray, and you will be enabled to practise forgiveness in this life, and thus be happy forever in the next.

Should anger be firmly rooted in your heart you may perhaps say that you are ready and willing to forgive your enemy, but that you cannot love him. It is of course by no means necessary that you should love him in the ordinary acceptation of the word; but you must feel charitably toward him, return his greetings, be ready to render him any assistance in your power, whenever he may stand in need of your help, and pray for him. That attitude is quite sufficient, and it is by no means impossible for you to live accordingly.

Let us suppose you take up another line, and say: "I have a great deal to put up with, and have borne it all in uncomplaining silence, but they have really gone too far; I cannot forgive them!" Now answer me one question. Has your enemy, let me ask you, struck you, scourged you, crowned you with thorns, dragged you away to a cruel death? Yet was all this done to Jesus Christ, Our Lord and God. Are you as innocent as He was? Have you given your enemies no cause for offence? Have you not, on the contrary, frequently and grievously offended your God, and has He not repeatedly pardoned you? Do you therefore in like manner pardon your enemies, and abuse not His long-suffering.

To take one more instance. You may say: "I will certainly forgive my enemies, but I can never forget what they have done; I will avoid them as far as I can; I will ignore them; I want to hear nothing more about them." My dear child, that would not be a real heartfelt forgiveness, such as Our Lord requires of you. Suppose God were to address you in like manner! Remember the fifth petition in the Lord's Prayer. Should you like to pray in such words as these: "Forgive me, as I forgive my enemies; forgive me but do not forget my offences; pay no more heed to me; ignore me altogether." Could you bring yourself to utter such a petition as this?

As I remarked in the first part of this chapter, these serious exhortations do not so much apply to you at the present time as they will at a later period of your life; when anger and hatred may seek to gain a footing in your heart. At present it is enough for you to seek to play the part of an angel of peace, in regard to any dissensions that may chance to arise among your nearest relatives. The following anecdote is related of the celebrated Italian preacher, Saint Leonard of Port Maurice, when he was lying on his deathbed. His father loved him tenderly, but lived in the bitterest enmity with his own brother. The dying man called them both to the side of his bed, and, stretching out his arms, joined the hands of the two enemies, saying as he did so: "Father, uncle, listen to my last request! Love one another, as I love you, as you love me, as God loves us all! I cannot die until I have reconciled you." Both burst into tears, and their enmity vanished like smoke.

Do you in like manner promote peace wherever you go and reconcile those who are at variance. Above all seek, as far as in you lies, to live at peace with all men.

> "Peace be with you!" Blessed word!
> Farewell spoken by Our Lord;
> Pledge of our eternal rest
> In the mansions of the blest.

Alma Redemptoris Mater

This is one of four Marian antiphons, with concluding versicles and prayers, traditionally said or sung after night prayer, immediately before going to sleep. It is said from the beginning of Advent through February 1, the eve of Candlemas. See page 170 for the other three of these Antiphons.

Mother of Christ, hear thou thy people's cry
Star of the deep and Portal of the sky!
Mother of Him who thee from nothing made.
Sinking we strive and call to thee for aid:
Oh, by that joy which Gabriel brought to thee,
Pure Virgin first and last, look on our misery.

Up through the day before Christmas Eve:

V. The Angel of the Lord declared unto Mary.
R. And she conceived by the Holy Spirit.

Let us pray: Pour forth, we beseech Thee, O Lord, Thy grace into our hearts, that we, to whom the incarnation of Christ, Thy Son, was made known by the message of an angel, may by His passion and cross be brought to the glory of His resurrection, through the same Christ our Lord. Amen.

From Christmas Eve on:

V. Thou gavest birth without loss of thy virginity:
R. Intercede for us, O holy Mother of God.

Let us pray: O God, Who by the fruitful virginity of blessed Mary hast given to mankind the rewards of eternal salvation, grant, we beseech thee, that we may experience her intercession for us, through whom we have deserved to receive the Author of life, our Lord Jesus Christ, Thy Son. Amen.

Veni Creator Spiritus

Come, Holy Spirit, Creator blest,
and in our souls take up Thy rest;
come with Thy grace and heavenly aid
to fill the hearts which Thou hast made.

O comforter, to Thee we cry,
O heavenly gift of God Most High,
O fount of life and fire of love,
and sweet anointing from above.

Thou in Thy sevenfold gifts are known;
Thou, finger of God's hand we own;
Thou, promise of the Father,
Thou Who dost the tongue
    with pow'r imbue.

Kindle our sense from above,
and make our hearts o'erflow with love;
with patience firm and virtue high
the weakness of our flesh supply.

Far from us drive the foe we dread,
and grant us Thy peace instead;
so shall we not, with Thee for guide,
turn from the path of life aside.

Oh, may Thy grace on us bestow
the Father and the Son to know;
and Thee, through endless times confessed,
of both the eternal Spirit blest.

Now to the Father and the Son,
Who rose from death, be glory given,
with Thou, O Holy Comforter,
henceforth by all in earth and heaven.
Amen.

Veni, Creator Spiritus,
mentes tuorum visita,
imple superna gratia
quae tu creasti pectora.

Qui diceris Paraclitus,
altissimi donum Dei,
fons vivus, ignis, caritas,
et spiritalis unctio.

Tu, septiformis munere,
digitus paternae dexterae,
Tu rite promissum Patris,
sermone ditans guttura.

Accende lumen sensibus:
infunde amorem cordibus:
infirma nostri corporis
virtute firmans perpeti.

Hostem repellas longius,
pacemque dones protinus:
ductore sic te praevio
vitemus omne noxium.

Per te sciamus da Patrem,
noscamus atque Filium;
Teque utriusque Spiritum
credamus omni tempore.

Deo Patri sit gloria,
et Filio, qui a mortuis surrexit,
ac Paraclito,
in saeculorum saecula.
Amen.

Caryophyllus multiplex flo re carneo.

Caryophyllus multiplex fo lijs Flor tum ex rubro & albo dimidiatim diuisiset pun ctatis.

Caryophyllus purpureus multiplici profunde laci niato

‹ 5 ›

The Carnation

Obedience

XX. Our Great Exemplar

How sublime is the example set by the Redeemer to young people especially! Concerning Him, the incarnate Son of God, we read in Holy Scripture: "*Jesus was subject to them (His parents) and advanced in wisdom, and age, and grace with God and man.*" It is not difficult to understand that He "*advanced in age*," for in this respect He was like all other children. On the other hand, the words: "*He advanced in wisdom and grace,*" must not be taken in their ordinary acceptation. The God-Man was always full of wisdom and grace, and could not therefore advance in them, but He permitted it to be increasingly perceived that He was full of wisdom and grace.

I wish to impress very strongly upon your heart and memory these words: "*He was **subject**.*" Thus did Jesus make Himself our example in the virtue of obedience, that virtue which, like a brilliant carnation, should find a place in the garland which adorns your youthful brow, and diffuse sweet fragrance all around.

What is obedience? It consists in subjecting our own will to the will of another. This most precious virtue is termed by St. Augustine "the mother and root of all virtues." St. Bonaventure calls it, "a ship, in which one sails to heaven." Hence we learn that obedience is a virtue, indispensably necessary for everyone, but especially for children and young people; for obedience is order, and order must prevail in every place where God is and where He reigns. Disobedience, the offspring of pride, kindled the flames of hell, and peoples its dread abode. In regard to this St. Bernard says: "Abolish disobedience, and you will abolish hell." Obedience is, according to St. Francis of Sales, a sweet virtue. He says: "He who rightly obeys will live aright; he will live sweetly, as does the child in the arms of its mother, free from anxiety and care."

But obedience appears very unattractive to the eyes of young people; they want to cast off the yoke, and enjoy their liberty. Yet God has ordained that young girls should especially practice obedience. You must be conscious how weak and inexperienced you are, and how strong are your evil inclinations. Therefore is it most necessary that you should be wisely counseled, and prudently guided, in order that you may learn to know and to walk in the way of virtue and perfection. How sincerely is a young girl to be pitied if she is given her own way in everything. She will have no self-control; yet she will have to learn from bitter experience that we are all servants in one way or another. St. Thomas Aquinas says: "That wherein one man excels another man is given him of God, that therewith he may serve other men." "Servant of the servants of God" has been the Pope's title ever since the days of Gregory the Great. And Jesus said of Himself: "*The Son of Man came not to be ministered unto, but to minister.*"

Be careful to be always truly obedient. You will find it very difficult at times, when pride, or obstinacy, or bad temper, strives for the mastery. But on this account it is doubly necessary that you should learn to bow beneath the yoke; for should you fail to do so now, you will perhaps be unable to conform at a later period. Yet you must live in subjection all your life long, whether you like it or not, for such has been the lot of every woman who has lived upon this earth. Thus you see that if you thoroughly learn how to obey, while you are still young, you will have done a great deal to promote the happiness of your future life; and a large majority of the sorrows and miseries so many of Eve's daughters suffer will be spared you.

But mark this well: do not regard obedience as a painful necessity; consider it rather to be a Christian virtue. Obedience of this nature has its root in humility; faith sanctifies it, and love renders it sweet. For it is only Christian obedience, the obedience which springs from love for God, that will remain with you through life, whatever may be your circumstances. On the other hand, obedience which arises from compulsion, human respect, or a desire to please, is merely external, and therefore of no value. Obedience of this nature will never last long, and will not bring you true peace of mind.

To whom do you owe obedience? To your parents before everyone else, according to His example of whom we read: "*He was subject to them.*" Your parents are for you the representatives of God on earth. Therefore always pay heed to their exhortations, never grumble or make a pert answer. I have already said a great deal as to what your conduct to your parents should be, when I spoke about the fourth commandment.

Mark one thing more: never be ashamed of your parents. Do not imitate a servant girl who procured a situation in Prague. She had spent all her life in the country, and was speedily led astray by the seductions of town life. She procured a place in a very good family. Once her old mother, who was very shabbily dressed, came to see her. The vain creature was quite ashamed of her, and ordered her to say that she was only a distant relation. No sooner did her mistress hear of the deception than she gave the servant notice to leave; for she said that so bad a daughter could never serve her properly. And she was perfectly right!

But I think it is unnecessary to caution you against acting in such a manner, for I am sure you are too generous and right-minded ever to be ashamed of your kind parents.

However, you may not be fortunate enough to enjoy the happiness of living under the roof of your dear, good parents. You may be obliged to earn your bread by serving strangers. In this case your primary duty is to obey. Strive to practice, faithfully and conscientiously, the precepts which St. Paul laid down more than nineteen hundred years ago; which hold good just as much in the present day as they did when he uttered them: "*Servants, be obedient to them that are your lords according to the flesh, with fear and trembling, in the simplicity of your heart, as to Christ: not serving to the eye, as it were pleasing men, but as the servants of Christ, doing the will of God from the heart, with a good will serving, as to the Lord, and not to men. Knowing that whatsoever good thing any man shall do, the same shall he receive from the Lord.*" In this spirit seek to be docile and obedient to your masters and mistresses, obeying them in all things which are not sinful. Study their interests in every way, be truthful, honest, industrious and trustworthy, and you will certainly be treated with kindness and confidence.

In conclusion I would remark that it does not speak well for a girl, if she is fond of standing too long before her looking-glass. But I know of another mirror, into which you may gaze with profit, not indeed for your body, but for your soul. I refer to the holy Child Jesus at Nazareth, of whom it is said: "*He was subject to them.*" That is your mirror; He is your great Exemplar; learn of Him how to obey.

> At Nazareth a mirror bright
> Stands before the Christian's sight;
> Look therein and you will see
> How obedient you should be.

XXI. A Careful Mother

THAT which is most striking and commendable in a good young girl is her respect, obedience and dutiful affection toward her mother. I hope, my daughter, that you possess all these characteristics. You have in reality three mothers: your mother on earth; Mary, your sweet mother in heaven; and your spiritual mother, the holy Catholic Church. And how kind, how watchful, how careful is our holy mother, the Church! Meditate upon this point, lay it well to heart, in order that you may be increasingly filled with respect for this careful mother, and may obey her more readily and more exactly.

The Catholic Church is indeed a mother to you, a most gracious and watchful mother. After you had received from your earthly mother your physical existence, she bestowed upon you a supernatural, a spiritual life; she stood beside you at the outset of your career. In virtue of the power bequeathed to her by Christ, she commissioned her priest to cleanse you from the leprosy of sin, to awaken you to a new life in Christ, and to unclose for you the gate of heaven.

If your earthly mother can never cease to love you, and to be tenderly solicitous for your welfare, as long as she lives, holy Church will certainly not act in a different manner. She will love you and watch over you until the end of your life, and even beyond the grave. Was it not the Church who sent her priests to speak to you of God, to teach you His love and fear, to instruct you how to pray to Him aright? And when you have fallen into sin, does not the Church, like a tender mother, exhort you to return to your merciful Father and seek forgiveness in the Sacrament of Penance? Does she not help you to obtain that forgiveness, and to persevere in the grace of God?

Again, is it not the Church who feeds your soul with the Bread of angels, in holy communion, in order that you may not faint and fall on the steep and rocky road of life?

The time may come when you will have to go forth into the world, far from the shelter of home, far from your beloved parents. But if no one can accompany you, if you sorely miss your friends and acquaintances, there is one friend who will never forsake you. I mean your watchful mother, the Catholic Church. Wherever you may be, she proclaims to you the word of God by the mouth of her priests; she cleanses your soul in the Sacrament of Penance, and nourishes you with the supersubstantial Bread; she supplies you with consolation and strength amid struggles, trials, and temptations.

And when you stand in the greatest need of help and comfort—when, weak and powerless, you are stretched upon a bed of sickness, and among the strangers who surround you there is no one to take an interest in you—then does your tender mother, the Church, not forget nor forsake you; she has provided hospitals, and sends an angel in human shape, a Sister of Charity, to nurse and tend you; she empowers a priest, her representative, to minister to the needs of your soul, to reconcile you with God, and feed you with the Bread of eternal life.

And when at last, death, the king of terrors, draws near, when he lays his icy hand upon you, when nothing on earth can help you, and no one is of any avail—then does the Church once more befriend you, remaining beside you until the end. She, the careful mother, stands by your bed in the person of her priest, anointing you with holy oil, strengthening you for your final combat; her prayers accompany your departing soul, and conduct it to the judgment seat of Christ.

Even when your body is moldering in the grave, and your soul is expiating your transgressions amid the purgatorial flames, your watchful mother, the Church, comes to your aid by means of the holy sacrifice of the Mass, her prayers and indulgences; she ceases not to intercede for you until you are received in the abode of never-ending felicity.

O my dear child, how kind, how loving, how thoughtful a mother you have in the holy Catholic Church! How tenderly ought you therefore to love her, how grateful should you be to her! And in what way can you give proof of your gratitude?

Your duty in regard to the Church is identical with that which you owe to your earthly mother. You must honor her, love and obey her. You must honor her by never showing her any disrespect, by never mocking at her doctrines, her services, her ceremonies, and her priests. Neither ought you to listen with complacency to those who ridicule her, and speak of her in a depreciating manner; you ought rather to try to put a stop to conversation of this nature, as far as it may lie in your power to do so. Would you listen with indifference if your earthly mother were slandered, ridiculed, dragged, so to speak, through the mire? Were you capable of thus acting, you would not deserve the name of daughter!

You ought, therefore, not to read newspapers or pamphlets which treat of Catholic matters, ecclesiastical ordinances, ceremonies, and priests, in a more or less contemptuous tone. A true child of the Church should resolve to read only edifying books and newspapers; she should also subscribe for Catholic journals and magazines, according to her circumstances.

You ought also to listen in a spirit of reverence to all which the Church proclaims and teaches, guided as she is by the holy Spirit of God, and you ought to assist, whenever you can, at High Mass, Benediction, the Forty Hours' Adoration, and at all solemn services. You must be especially careful to honor the Church, your watchful mother, in the persons of priests, who are her ministers. Never treat them with contempt, as did a certain person who kept an inn somewhere in the Tyrol. When upon one occasion the parish priest felt it to be his duty to rebuke from the pulpit the drunkenness and dancing which went on in the tavern, the hostess, who was a widow, flew into a violent rage, and exclaimed: "I will set about building another drinking-saloon, and also a dancing-hall, under the very eyes of his Reverence!" She owned a plot of ground close to the pastor's residence and began to build a tavern upon it, intending that her eldest son should manage the house. Before it was finished, the young man died, and his wife fell out with her mother-in-law. The quarrel resulted in a lawsuit; the building had to be discontinued; and five of the hostess' seven strong, healthy sons died in the course of the next few years. Respect the priest and hear his word, for God has said: "*He that despiseth you despiseth me.*"

We may be quite sure that God will never own as His child anyone who does not love, honor and obey the Church, as every dutiful child loves, honors and obeys an earthly mother. This was expressly stated by the holy martyr, bishop, and Doctor of the Church, St. Cyprian, eighteen hundred years ago, in the following words: "He who has not the Church for his mother, can not have God for his Father." See that you remain a faithful daughter of this watchful and dutiful mother.

> Faith of our fathers, living still,
> In spite of dungeon, fire, and sword;
> O, how our hearts beat high with joy
> Whene'er we hear that glorious word!
> Faith of our fathers, holy Faith,
> We will be true to thee till death.

> Faith of our fathers, we will love
> Both friend and foe in all our strife,
> And preach thee too, as love knows how,
> By kindly words and virtuous life.
> Faith of our fathers, holy Faith,
> We will be true to thee till death.

XXII. Obedience: the Christian's Ornament

In the previous chapter you have seen that the Church is the best and kindest of mothers; that you owe her a deep debt of gratitude for the innumerable spiritual benefits she has bestowed upon you. And I trust that your actions will always be in accordance with the serious advice I have given you, and that you will show yourself to be her loving and obedient child. Obedience is the ornament of the true Christian, and as a Catholic girl it ought to be your brightest ornament, to obey your loving mother, the Catholic Church, at all times and in every respect. I desire to impress this upon you earnestly and forcibly, while I have the opportunity, in the hope that my words may continue to sound in your ears in your later life.

You may deem it unnecessary thus to exhort you to obey the Church. Perhaps you think that this goes without speaking, and that it is very easy and quite a matter of course. It is true that for girls who are naturally docile, and have been religiously brought up, it may be a matter of course, and no great difficulty to sanctify Sunday, to hear Mass on all Sundays and holydays of obligation, to go to confession and communion more than once a year, to keep the fasts as far as they are bound to do so, and not to marry at forbidden seasons.

But picture to yourself the position of a girl who, possessing no fortune, would gladly be provided for by means of an advantageous marriage. Suppose she gets no suitable offer until she is verging upon middle age, and then a non-Catholic, a Protestant, comes forward with a highly desirable proposal, but says from the outset that he will not comply with the conditions the Church makes in such cases. If in addition to this the strong, alluring flame of passion suddenly blazes up in her heart, you must understand, in some measure at least, how difficult, how terribly difficult, it would be for anyone thus circumstanced not to set aside the prohibition of the Church, which forbids mixed marriages without a dispensation; how hard it would be to refuse the offer.

Alas! Alas! how many girls, some even of a religious turn of mind, whose conduct is irreproachable in every other respect, who have been educated in Catholic schools and instructed in the doctrines of the faith—how many, I say, can not stand when a trial of this nature overtakes them. They become disobedient, rebel against God and the Church, finish by apostatizing, and thus perhaps are ruined both for time and for eternity.

The welfare of your immortal soul is so dear to me, and the interest I take in your future happiness is so deep, that I can leave no stone unturned, I can spare no effort in order to preserve you from taking so fatal, so unfortunate a step as to contract a union forbidden by God and by the Church. Therefore I earnestly beseech you, I entreat you as forcibly as I can, to listen at all times, and more especially when there is a question of your marriage, to the voice of your loving mother, the Church—to listen, and also to obey.

I will not now explain the reasons why holy Church forbids marriage with a non-Catholic unless a dispensation is previously obtained. I shall treat this subject more fully in another place, and I shall also show why the Church grants dispensations in particular cases. At present I wish merely to enlarge upon the strict nature of the prohibition.

A Catholic girl who marries a non-Catholic and permits the children of the marriage to be baptized and brought up in their father's religion, rather than in her own, commits a most grievous sin. For she robs her children of the priceless treasure of the Catholic faith with all its innumerable graces and blessings; she makes them strangers to the true Church. Through her disobedience she excludes herself also from the Church; she can be absolved from the grievous sin she has committed only through sincere repentance for her fault, and a resolution to remedy the evil consequences of it, as far as may lie in her power.

The Church does indeed intend her prohibition to be taken very seriously. Obey her voice; do not keep company with a non-Catholic, in order that your faith may not be exposed to danger; in order that your happiness may not be jeopardized.

Some years ago, a young German girl was sent to school in Switzerland. After her education was finished, she stayed for several months in that country, and received before long several most advantageous offers of marriage. She possessed a not inconsiderable fortune for one in her position, about 12,500 dollars. I may here remark in passing, that if you are not rich you ought to thank almighty God for that, for in marriage a wealthy girl is often sought after not for herself, but for her bank notes and securities.

So at least it was in the case to which I am now referring. The young lady refused honorable proposals which were made to her by Catholics, and gave her affections to a Protestant who had flattered her to her heart's content. She married him, without troubling herself about the prohibition of the Church. But how long did her happiness last? Before two years had elapsed, the greater part of her fortune had been squandered, the demon of poverty and discontent entered the home of the unhappy wife, and a separation soon followed. Her husband even sought her life, in order that he might become possessed of the remainder of the property.

While she was in this miserable plight, she happened one day to meet with a former schoolfellow, to whom, amid tears and sobs, she told her pitiful story. Striking her forehead she exclaimed; "O what a fool I was! I had several good offers, yet I was blind enough to marry this brute, and to disregard the command of the Church. Stupid fool that I was; would that I had listened to the voice of the Catholic Church!"

Do you, my child, always listen to, and obey the voice of the Church, your watchful mother. Obedience is the Christian's ornament. Pray for grace and strength from above, in order that if it should please God to put your obedience to so severe a test, you may be able to remain steadfast. Mistrust your own strength and insight; be very humble, for it is to the humble that God gives His grace.

> Great God, whatever through Thy Church
> Thou teachest to be true,
> I firmly do believe it all—
> And will confess it too.

XXIII. Some Objections Which May Be Urged

It is no easy task, but a burdensome and difficult matter, for fallen man to obey, to submit to the will of another. For this reason many persons, and there are many young girls among the number, strive to shake off the yoke of obedience. Often does it appear to them extremely difficult, if not impossible, to obey the precepts and commands of the Church. As I have shown in the foregoing chapter, this case most frequently occurs when it is a question of making a marriage contract. Self-love searches out all manner of pretexts and objections which may serve as excuses for disobedience, and the evil world, with its fatal maxims, invariably takes the wrong side. Let us examine a few of these objections.

For instance, the objector may say that the precepts and exhortations of the Church are too numerous to be remembered and practiced. Don't worry about that. Your conscience is a sentinel ever standing at the door of your heart. Hearken to the voice of conscience. Follow when it calls; then everything will go right, for all depends upon following its lead. Yet, is it so impossible to obey the Church in all respects? Clear and uncompromising indeed are the words of Our Lord: *"He that will not hear the Church, let him be to thee as the heathen and publican."* If we are thus compelled to hear and obey the Church, it must be possible for us to do so, since God never requires of us an impossibility. He renders that possible which would be impossible to our own strength; His grace, indeed, renders it easy. In regard to this, St. Paul says: *"I can do all things in Him who strengtheneth me."*

Another objection frequently urged against the laws of the Church concerning marriage, is that mixed marriages are often very happy and that therefore the Church is unduly severe when she warns her children against them. I answer, in the first place: If mixed marriages in which the directions of the Church are complied with, and the children are brought up as Catholics, turn out happily, so much the better. But if this so-called happiness is purchased at the price of a Protestant education for the children, it is only a hollow sort of happiness, however real and durable it may appear in the eyes of the world. Sooner or later, perhaps only when the brief span of earthly existence is ended, it will be exchanged for terrible misery.

I answer, in the second place: Experience teaches very clearly that the number of mixed marriages which are really happy is exceedingly small.

If a Catholic wife, not having been married according to the precepts of the Church, derives unalloyed happiness or good fortune from the union, how difficult must it not be for her to repent sincerely of the step she has taken, to repent in such a manner as not to be excluded from eternal happiness!

Perhaps another young girl, who has made the acquaintance of a non-Catholic, may say to me: "But the Protestant who wishes to marry me is such a good steady young fellow, no bad Christian nor unbeliever, a far better man, in fact, than many of my Catholic acquaintances." To this girl I would reply: I am very glad to hear all this, and I hope the young man in question will always remain what he is at present. But because a Protestant is religious and holds to his own beliefs, you must be all the more careful not to form a closer intimacy with him, for, if he marries you, he will certainly not allow his children to be brought up as Catholics. On this account your acquaintance with him will expose you to the risk of disobeying the Church.

A third objector may remark: "My Protestant suitor has solemnly assured me that if only I will accept him we shall be married in a church, and our children shall be brought up as Catholics. Indeed, he is prepared to embrace my creed, for there is nothing he is not willing to sacrifice for my sake. What more could be wished for?" What more could I desire for you, dear child? I could wish that you should have a little more insight into the future, and a little less blind confidence. Beware of allowing yourself to be dazzled by fine words and fair promises, or led about in leading-strings! Do not imitate so many young girls, who have to pay so terribly high a price for their foolish credulity. Imagine the feelings of a Catholic mother, who has been promised that her children shall be educated in her own faith, and has married on this condition—imagine, I say, what her feelings must be if her Protestant husband breaks his word. And how many such cases occur in mixed marriages!

Another girl, who has been married by a Protestant minister, or has contracted a purely civil marriage, deludes herself with the idea that everything can be set right later on. What extreme carelessness is this! It is like the conduct of a child who throws himself into the water in spite of all his mother's warnings, saying as he does so, that his mother can easily get him out. Your loving mother, the Catholic Church, is indeed ready to save you from eternal death in spite of your disobedience, and she offers you every means of rescue. But suppose her aid should come too late, when the floods had already engulfed you; suppose, wilful and unrepentant, you had withdrawn yourself from her protecting hands, and were to die in this frame of mind!

How widely different was the conduct of St. Frances of Chantal! During a visit she paid to her sister, a nobleman who owned large estates offered her his hand in marriage. No sooner did she learn that her wealthy and distinguished suitor was a Calvinist than she refused him without an instant's hesitation; although, in the eyes of the world, the connection would have been a highly desirable one.

Such are some of the objections which are urged against the obedience we owe to our mother the holy Catholic Church. These objections are put forward by those who have imbibed the principles of an evil world. It is very possible that you, my dear child, if obedience should require a sacrifice at your hands, may be tempted to cloak your disobedience under some such objections as we have just been considering. But for the sake of your temporal and eternal happiness beware of yielding to the temptation! You perceive how futile and unstable are all these objections. Be faithful and obedient to your holy, loving mother, the Church!

> In sorrow or joy, she stands at my side,
> My light and my refuge, my guard and my guide.

The Angelus

*This prayer is traditionally said at 6AM, Noon, and 6PM with at least one person leading (V) and at least one person responding (R). All should be kneeling and a bell should be rung. During Paschaltide, it is replaced by the **Regina Coeli**.*

V. The Angel of the Lord declared unto Mary.

R. And she conceived of the Holy Ghost.

Hail Mary...

V. Behold the handmaid of the Lord.

R. Be it done unto me according to thy word.

Hail Mary...

V. And the Word was made Flesh.

R. And dwelt among us.

Hail Mary...

V. Pray for us, O Holy Mother of God.

R. That we may be made worthy of the promises of Christ.

Let us pray: Pour forth, we beseech Thee, O Lord, Thy grace into our hearts; that, we to whom the Incarnation of Christ, Thy Son, was made known by the message of an Angel, may by His Passion and Cross, be brought to the glory of His Resurrection. Through the same Christ our Lord. Amen.

Suscipe
The Prayer of St. Ignatius of Loyola

Take, O Lord, and receive my entire liberty, my memory, my understanding and my whole will. All that I am and all that I possess Thou hast given me: I surrender it all to Thee to be disposed of according to Thy will. Give me only Thy love and Thy grace; with these I will be rich enough, and will desire nothing more.

Anima Christi

Soul of Christ, sanctify me.
Body of Christ, save me.
Blood of Christ, inebriate me.
Water from the side of Christ, wash me.
Passion of Christ, strengthen me.
O good Jesus, hear me.
Within Thy wounds, hide me.
Permit me not to be separated from Thee.
From the malignant enemy, defend me.
At the hour of death, call me.
And bid me come to Thee,
That with thy Saints I may praise Thee
For ever and ever. Amen.

◀ 6 ▶

THE FORGET-ME-NOT

PIETY

XXIV. THE REAL FLOWER

IF YOU, Christian maiden, on leaving school or other institution where you have been brought up, do not at once throw yourself into the vortex of worldly amusements, if you dress neatly and quietly and do not neglect your religious observances, prayer, and the frequenting of the sacraments, it may happen that worldly-minded persons will term you a *dévote*. Do not allow this to lead you astray! For in a way this term is applied to every truly pious person. However, a wide difference will be found to exist between various kinds of piety. Just as among flowers there are real and natural blossoms and others which are unreal, being fashioned by art, so can the forget-me-not of piety be true or false. When applied to the truly pious the term *dévote* is a calumny and a reproach; it is better suited to those who are pious in appearance alone. You must be very careful that your piety is of the right kind; if such it is the name of *dévote* need not alarm you—you ought rather to be proud of it.

But is it necessary to be pious? When addressed to a young girl this question can be answered only in the affirmative. The Creator has so formed the heart of woman that it is specially disposed to piety. But if your piety is to be real and true, you must have a right understanding of false piety, so that you may avoid it carefully. Wherein does this false piety consist?

I will point out to you a few examples of and describe some persons who, while they fancy themselves to be pious, are not so in reality. For instance, one may be willing enough to fast, but have a heart full of bitterness and dislike. Another loads herself with a multitude of religious exercises, and at the same time neglects the duties of her calling. Another repeats endless vocal prayers, but is much addicted to slander and detraction; or she may appear truly pious, while her face is always as sour as vinegar. Another gives alms very freely, but is still more free with her biting criticisms and uncharitable judgments. Another is seen to shed many tears when engaged in prayer, but frequently causes her inferiors and the members of her family to weep, on account of her haughty or impertinent behavior. Again, we find a young person eager for admission into every kind of confraternity and pious association, while all the time she carefully inscribes on her mental tablets a record of every slight she receives, every occasion on which she is not treated according to her supposed merits. Another young girl goes to holy communion every week, or perhaps even more frequently, and for this reason fancies herself a saint, being by no means unwilling that others should term her such; yet she makes no serious and determined effort to get rid of her numerous faults. You perceive that all these, and such as these, can lay no claims to the possession of genuine piety.

Their conduct—to borrow the illustration employed by St. Francis of Sales—resembles that of Michol, the wife of David. The servants of Saul came to seek for David in his house; Michol took an image, laid it in the bed, and covered it with her husband's clothes. Thus she induced them to believe that he was sick and sleeping there. In a similar manner many cover themselves with external works of piety, which are in reality mere images and shadows, destitute of all true life.

The genuine flower of piety is no mere sentimentalism, and does not consist in a multitude of pious practices. If you would be truly pious, do everything you have to do as service done to God, bearing in mind the exhortation of the Apostle, *"Therefore whether you eat or drink, or whatsoever else you do, do all to the glory of God."* Act in the spirit shown by your Immaculate Mother when she said: *"Behold the handmaid of the Lord."* Regard yourself as the servant of God; as such, hallow all your actions by referring them to Him, acquitting yourself faithfully and conscientiously of your smallest and most ordinary duties. Without making a show of piety, every occupation in which you engage, every hour which passes over your head, will thus be made to exhale a sweet fragrance of sanctity.

We see true piety to be an interior frame of mind or disposition, a love which comes from within and gives life to everything which is without. Or it is that active love of God which makes men eschew evil, do good, and endure suffering. Again, as St. Francis of Sales expresses it: "That man may be said to be truly pious who does, out of heartfelt love to God, everything which He commands, which holy Church requires, and which is incumbent on him in his particular calling and state of life."

The words of Fénelon may be quoted here, in reference to external practices of piety: "Outward forms are good, if they express the feelings of the heart. Thy worship, O God! is love, and Thy kingdom is within us; let us therefore beware of attaching too much value to externals."

An unmistakable mark of true piety is that it makes its possessor cheerful and merry. Attentively notice your companions and you will find that she who is really pious will always be cheerful. How indeed could it be otherwise? Who has more reason to be cheerful than a truly pious young girl? Who can look up to heaven with more confidence, who can trust more entirely in God, who can contemplate herself with more content, who can behold the future more hopefully, than such a one? Who takes more pure delight than she does in the benefits God bestows upon her? Whom does conscience reward with greater peace? Hence her eyes are always bright, her appearance friendly, her conversation attractive. Hence you must clearly perceive that when I urge you to be pious, I am as far as possible from wishing you to hang your head and wear a sour and gloomy aspect. To look as though you were a lamb being dragged to the slaughter-house is not only a sheer affectation, but an odious and hateful thing. It appears to me, our dear, good God loves particularly cheerful people, if only they are good and pious. Sadness is a consequence of sin, and does not come from heaven or from God.

How blessed are the fruits of true piety! It imparts to the soul that sweet, interior consolation of which those who have never experienced it cannot have the faintest idea. St. Paschal Baylon found that the consolation which is imparted to pious souls infinitely surpasses all the pleasures of the world, even if it were possible to enjoy all those pleasures at one and the same time. Weave, therefore, the forget-me-not of true piety in the garland of your virtues.

> Sweet piety! the brightest flower
> That blossoms in the maiden's bower:
> Without thee, skill, however rare,
> Shall fail to weave a garland fair;
> Led by thy light on life's dark way,
> Our steps from virtue will not stray.

XXV. "Remember Thy Last End"

CHRISTIAN maiden, you have to erect a lofty building, a building which shall reach to heaven. I refer to the edifice of your own piety and perfection. And in regard to this building, as to every other, the first and most necessary thing is to see that it has a firm and solid foundation. For, unless such a foundation is laid, the builder's toil will be only labor lost; sooner or later his work will fall to pieces and bury the occupant under its ruins. What, then, is the first and most necessary thing, the sure and firm foundation indispensable to the edifice of piety?

Holy Scripture informs us in the following words: "*The fear of the Lord is the beginning of wisdom*"; i.e., of virtue and piety. Now, by what means is this firm foundation to be laid, how are you to be most strongly established in the fear of the Lord? By remembering your last end, according to the warning of the Holy Spirit: "*In all thy works remember thy last end, and thou shalt never sin.*"

A certain young girl who lived in one of the German towns had assuredly disregarded this admonition, as was proved only too plainly when she was stricken by a mortal disease. In her days of health she had cared only about dress, flirtation, and her own good looks. When death was drawing near, she caused all her prettiest gowns to be spread upon her bed, and after gazing on them with fond longing, though her eyes were already growing dim, she exclaimed in piercing, heartrending accents: "Alas! how very sad it is! I am so young and so fair; I love life so dearly; and yet I must leave everything, yes, everything!" Having uttered these words, she sank back upon the pillows and breathed her last.

Do you, dear child, always remember your last end in order that you may not sin, but may always have a salutary fear of God, and may strive to be truly pious. Ponder well the four last things and especially—death.

Since death spares no one, you must be fully convinced that it will not spare you: you fear it because you are just as fully convinced that death is not the end of everything, but that a strict judgment and a never-ending existence will come after. Yet the most terrible thing connected with it is not its certainty, but its uncertainty. For sure and certain as it is that we must die, it is equally doubtful and uncertain when, where, and how we shall die. When shall you die? You are alive to-day, but you cannot be sure whether you shall still be alive to-morrow, the day after, in a week, a month, or a year. As you read these lines you are full of health and strength, but who can guarantee you will not fall down dead this evening, to-night, or the very next moment. Once more I ask you: can any one assure you a moment of your life?

Some years ago a few peasants were drinking together in the inn of a village situated somewhere in Bavaria. They were chatting over their beer, when the conversation happened to turn upon the uncertainty of the hour of death. "It is quite true," said one of their number, a stalwart peasant in the prime of life, "that no one can tell when he shall die; but of this I am quite sure, that I shall not die to-day." Shortly afterward he took his leave, saying that he must return home; he bade every one good-night, confident of meeting his friends again in the morning. He left the room; shortly afterward the party broke up. At the foot of a steep flight of stone steps which led to the house door, they picked up their comrade—dead. He had missed his footing in the dark, and falling down the steps, had broken his neck.

Who thinks less about death, who feels more certain of prolonged life, than a merry young girl on the dance-floor? Yet it has happened on more than one occasion that exertion and excitement caused young girls to drop down dead, owing to a stroke or heart-failure. I remember reading of just such a case which occurred in Switzerland. A girl who was only eighteen went home from a dance very late at night, and in the morning was found dead in her bed!

And there is no more certainty as to the place than as to the time of your death. Endless are the questions which might be asked on this head, but neither man nor angel could answer them. It must remain a matter of uncertainty whether you shall die in your bed, after much suffering, fortified with the last rites of holy Church; or whether death shall overtake you while you are asleep, when you are out walking, in your own room, at home or among strangers, at work or in conversation with others, by sea or on land, on foot or in a railroad car, and so on. For instance, a priest, who was taking the holy viaticum to a sick man whose life was despaired of, fell down dead as he was walking along, whereas the invalid, on the contrary, entirely recovered.

If you think seriously about this terrible uncertainty, you cannot possibly go on living in a careless spirit; you will feel constrained earnestly to strive after the attainment of solid piety.

A salutary fear must perforce take possession of you, when you remember that you cannot tell *when* or *where* you shall die. Most important, however, is the question: "*How* shall I die?" For upon the answer depends your eternal state; that is, whether you are to be happy or miserable forever and ever. It is of no consequence whether you shall die to-day or after a long series of years, while you are young or when you are old, suddenly or after a long illness, in your bed or in the public street; the one all-important point is whether you shall die in the grace of God, or in a state of mortal sin. You do not know, I do not know, and no one can tell you how you shall die. One thing only is certain: as long as a breath of life, or a spark of consciousness is left to you, you can, with the aid of divine grace, make a good end.

Let it not be displeasing to you, my dear child, that I have spoken so seriously to you about death. I have not done so with the intention of causing you to feel anxious and sad, but solely in the hope of inspiring you to strive more earnestly after the attainment of virtue and piety, in order that you may one day die well and in a happy frame of mind. Yes! for thus I saw one of my spiritual children die. She was twenty-one years of age, and had always been merry and cheerful, this disposition being the outgrowth of her true, unostentatious piety. She had been afflicted with consumption for a long time and had suffered much. Feeling that her last hour was approaching, she asked to see the wreath soon to be placed upon her bier; when it was shown her she took pleasure in looking at it and admiring its beauty. Here was a living embodiment of the truth of the lines:

> Fear God, my child, and nothing more
> On earth you have to fear;
> Solace and strength this fear imparts,
> And peace when death draws near.

XXVI. "One Thing is Necessary"

ST. PHILIP NERI was, as every one knows, very fond of young persons. There came to him on a certain occasion a youth whose face was wreathed with smiles. "Your Reverence," he began, "knew me when I was a poor orphan lad, keeping sheep in our village. I have made such progress in my studies that I am quite ready to go to the University of Bologna." "Very good, my young friend," replied the saint with a genial smile, "and then?" "I shall prosecute my studies with the utmost diligence, until I am able to take a Doctor's degree." "And then?" "My learning, eloquence and integrity will make my name famous far and near." "And then?" "I shall make my fortune, marry a rich wife, and be held in great consideration by my fellow citizens." "And then?" "Then I shall look forward to a very happy old age." "And then?" inquired the saint in a graver tone. "Then? Then?" repeated the young man, "then I shall have nothing more to do, then—then—I shall die." St. Philip Neri fixed his serious eyes upon him, and said once again, "And then?" The young man remained mute, as if struck by lightning; the solemn words "And then?" sounded continually in his ears.

In your ears also, my dear child, let these words resound. They will serve to strengthen you in the fear of God, they will make you strive more earnestly after true piety, and will constantly remind you of the one thing necessary. And what is this?

"But one thing is necessary. Mary hath chosen the best part, which shall not be taken away from her." Thus spoke Our Lord to Martha. And how had Mary, the sister of Martha, chosen the best part? She sat at Jesus' feet, and heard His words; that is, she cared more for her soul than for anything else. This, therefore, is the one thing necessary of which the Saviour speaks.

Do you take care of your soul, and see that it suffers no injury, i.e., that it may not be defiled by sin. For, as Our Lord says: "What shall it profit a man, if he gain the whole world, and suffer the loss of his soul?" Care for your soul earnestly and constantly, with holy fear and humble trust.

Care for your soul with zeal and prudence. On account of its likeness to God it is the most precious, the only really precious thing which you possess. Therefore you must take at least the same care of it which men generally take of rare and costly things. If you had a good likeness of your beloved father, or of your tender mother, and if, moreover, there were only one copy of this portrait in existence, with what care would you not preserve this treasure, how you would value and prize it!

How great then ought to be the care you take of your precious, your immortal soul, a masterpiece from the Creator's hand; the image of our heavenly Father Himself! Above all avoid sin, grievous sin, which will deface and destroy the image of God in your soul.

But you must not only strive to preserve the image of God within you with the utmost care; you must also do this without any intermission. To save one's soul is the work of a whole lifetime, not of a few days or hours. You began this work in your childhood days, when for the first time you cleansed your soul of its faults and failings by means of confession. You carried on this work in a very special manner on that happy day, the happiest day of your life—I mean the day of your First Communion. And you must prosecute this work with unwearied and unceasing diligence until your last breath.

Alas! there are too many unhappy young persons, who instead of making it their constant endeavor to preserve their soul from every spot and stain, deprive it of its most beautiful ornament. I mean chastity. With incredible recklessness they plunge their soul into the quagmire of vice, at the same time indulging the presumptuous hope that they will be able to cleanse it from its defilement at some later period, and thus render it fit for heaven.

Poor, blind creatures! They will probably discover, when it is too late, that he who does not constantly aim at the salvation of his soul too often ends by plunging it into eternal ruin. Guard your soul constantly! Save your soul!

St. Paul says: "*With fear and trembling work out your salvation.*" And, indeed, who should not fear and tremble where a matter of such infinite importance is concerned, in regard to an undertaking so momentous and so difficult? The fall of the rebel angels, of our first parents, of David, of St. Peter, ought to teach you now easily you may fall, perhaps fall forever. If lofty cedars have been overthrown, what is to become of a feeble reed! St. Peter says: "*If the just man shall scarcely be saved, where shall the ungodly and the sinner appear?*" And if you think of so many young persons, who in childhood were pious and good, but now have given themselves up to sin, and may lose their souls forever, you must surely be filled with fear and trembling!

It is right that you should feel thus; but at the same time you must have a childlike confidence in God, remembering His fatherly love, His infinite goodness. For has He not said that He wills not the death of the sinner, but rather that he should be converted from his ways, and live?

Finally, behold how God Himself has proved, in the person of the Holiest of the holy, how great is His solicitude for your soul, for the souls of all men. Gaze upon Mount Olivet, and you will perceive a Man lying prone upon the ground while a sweat of blood exudes from His pores; follow Him to the court of Pilate; see how He is scourged, spit upon, insulted, and crowned with cruel thorns; accompany Him through the streets of Jerusalem, which He dyes with His blood, until He reaches the summit of Calvary, where He is fastened with nails to the cross; listen to His heartrending cry: "*My God, my God, why hast Thou forsaken Me?*"—see Him bow His head, and give up the ghost. For what end did Our Lord suffer all this? It was in order that our souls might be saved, in order that we might gain heaven.

Your God did all this in order that you might save your soul! Ought you not therefore to strive more earnestly to work out your salvation? Adopt as your own the words of St. Augustine: "Ever since I became aware that my soul was purchased at no less a price than the blood of the Saviour, I resolved to keep it with all care, and never to sell it to the devil by means of one single sin."

> To save my soul, be this the end
> To which my hopes, my efforts tend;
> My time on earth may I employ
> So as to gain eternal joy.

XXVII Do Not Imitate Eve

THE forget-me-not of piety must not be wanting in your garland, Christian maiden; you ought to gladden heaven and earth by a truly pious life. But observe the words of St. Paul: "*All that will live godly in Christ Jesus, shall suffer persecution.*" And indeed, you must be prepared to suffer attacks, to meet with temptations. Just as in paradise the devil did not attack the man in the first place, but the woman, Eve—in a similar manner does the evil enemy act in the present day, and his myrmidons follow his example. It is the woman primarily, the maiden, whom they endeavor to destroy. For it is the maiden who can do the most for the salvation or destruction of the world.

And of what do they first of all seek to deprive her? Of that which is her dignity, her happiness, and her strength—her innocence of heart. Thousandfold are the snares which Satan, the enemy of all good, knows how to spread. Cunningly does the wicked world approach, in the guise of a well-meaning friend, and attract with its deceitful charms. The evil desires which lurk within the heart hearken only too readily to the whispers of Satan and the world, forcibly impelling us to follow where they lead.

Thus is the mournful story of the first temptation acted over and over again. Thank God, my child, if hitherto your experience in this respect has been a very limited one; but if it has been otherwise with you, be neither astonished nor discouraged. When, in my capacity of spiritual director, I witness the devout behavior of the young girls entrusted to my care; when I behold the fervor with which they join in the hymns and prayers; when I dispense to them the Bread of Life in holy communion, or when I see their innocent enjoyment during their hours of recreation, it rejoices my heart; yet a feeling of sadness steals upon me when I ask myself whether they shall always be what they are now. In five, ten, or twenty years, shall they all be merry and happy, pious and good, as they are at present?

I hope it shall be so, but I cannot be certain; this hope and this uncertainty I feel in regard to you. But of one thing I am quite sure—sooner or later you will be assailed by temptations more or less severe.

One thing is absolutely certain: you cannot pass through life, attain true piety, or reach heaven, without a struggle—without, like Eve, encountering temptations. But everything depends on your not acting like Eve. Let us therefore consider the manner in which she acted when the serpent tempted her.

In the first place, the extraordinary apparition of a serpent which spoke to her, instead of putting her on her guard, left her heedless and thoughtless. This was her first great fault—do not imitate her! But in all your intercourse with the world and especially with persons of the opposite sex, be always watchful, and mistrustful of yourself. For not without reason did Our Lord say: "*Watch ye, and pray, that you enter not into temptation.*" Yes, pray! If as soon as the serpent began to speak to Eve, she had reflected for a moment, and then said: "I will have nothing to do with thee; I desire to hold converse with God alone, and I am certain that the voice of God does not speak from thy mouth"—had she thus spoken the temptation would have been overcome.

Unite, therefore, watchfulness and prayer; hold converse with God; speak to Him with filial confidence, as a child speaks to a beloved father.

Eve committed a second fault by parleying with the tempter, instead of resolutely refusing to have anything to do with him. Again I say, beware of imitating her! Resist the temptation as soon as you become aware of it, and resist it with the utmost determination and steadfastness. Do not pause and wait until the tempters draw nearer; that is, until persons begin to treat you with a familiarity which may not be actually sinful, but which is nevertheless extremely dangerous; which may expose you to grievous temptations—nay more, will assuredly do so, if not resisted with promptitude and decision. Remember the words of the *Imitation*: "The longer any one hath been slothful in resisting, so much the weaker he becometh in himself, and the enemy so much the stronger against him."

Show courage and determination in the presence of temptation. "A resolute will conquers everything," says St. Alphonsus Liguori. A good, pious girl had made the acquaintance of a young man. She happened one day to find herself for a short time alone with him. He at once took the opportunity of making improper advances to her. Without an instant's delay she got up and left the room, saying as she did so: "You are badly mistaken in me! I am not what you take me for, and I will have nothing at all to do with you!" Under similar circumstances do you act as she did.

However violent and prolonged a temptation may be, do not lose heart. Above all, do not be discouraged if you have repeatedly yielded to temptation, and fallen into sin. Your merciful Father knows your weakness and is ready to hold out to you a sustaining hand. Grasp it without delay, rise up quickly, repent, and struggle on.

The third fault of Eve was that she did not at once betake herself to Adam, whom God had set over her, and acquaint him with the portentous language of the serpent, but preferred to manage the affair by herself. Again I repeat, beware of imitating her!

Always acquaint your confessor, who is your spiritual superior, with dangerous temptations which may overtake you. The devil dreads nothing so much as this. Acquaintance with members of the other sex, if innocent in itself, is constantly connected with perils and temptations. Therefore in these cases speak with great candor and truthfulness in the confessional. Your confessor will help and advise you, and tell you how to avoid these perils and temptations as far as it may be possible to do so. It is a very serious thing when a young girl does not speak in confession of her struggles and temptations, or when she conceals from her parents and confessor the knowledge of any acquaintance she has made.

To mention a fourth fault: Eve gave place in her heart to thoughts of pride. She listened with pleasure to the words: "*You shall be as gods.*" To be a goddess, a ruler, would have delighted her above everything! Beware of following her example! Guard your heart with the utmost care; do not indulge thoughts of pride and self-esteem; for "*Pride goeth before destruction,*" and "*He hath put down the mighty from their seat, and hath exalted the humble.*" But never despise those who have fallen, rather tremble for yourself.

When the intellect is blinded by pride and passion, it breaks through all restraints; like a runaway horse it rushes headlong to destruction. It is only humility and a holy fear of God which can ensure your safety.

Yet with all your dread of danger and mistrust of yourself, ever cherish an implicit, childlike reliance on the help of God. When beset by temptations, faithfully follow the wise counsel of a holy Doctor of the Church: "Do all that lies in your power, and God will take care of the rest. He will do all which you cannot accomplish. In every danger and temptation we must make use of all the means within our reach, just as if God did not exist and we were entirely depended upon our own exertions, at the same time calling upon God just as earnestly as if we were entirely unable to help ourselves."

> O Christian maid, I bid thee rise!
> With courage arm thee for the fight;
> A heavenly crown the victor's prize
> Who conquers sin and passion's might.
> Look up to heaven, watch and pray,
> And God will be thy shield and stay.

Make this your first and last prayer: "*O Lord, in Thee have I hoped; let me not be confounded forever.*"

XXVIII. Imitate Mary

A LITTLE child, sitting on its mother's lap, was being taught to say its prayers. Having repeated after her mother the words: "In the name of the Father, and of the Son, and of the Holy Ghost," the child suddenly interrupted her by asking: "Mother, it says the Father in heaven, and the Son in heaven. Why is there not a mother in heaven?" That inquiry comes from the depths of the human heart. The heart of man feels the need of a mother to plead for him before the throne of God; and He who created that heart, and knows its needs, has given us a mother in the person of Mary, the blessed Virgin and Mother of God.

If you, dear child, desire to be truly pious, begin by taking this mother as your pattern; earnestly seek to imitate her, and to be her faithful child. Therefore I exhort you to direct your attention more particularly to her at present.

We salute Mary with the Latin word *Ave*. If we reverse this word, we have the name of the first woman, our first mother, *Eva*. What misery and misfortune did not the sin of this first woman bring upon the world! She is no longer the mother of the living, as her name denotes, but of the dead, of those who are spiritually dead. But it is right that we should salute Mary with the word *Ave*, for she is in truth the opposite to *Eva*. By becoming the Mother of the Redeemer she won salvation, deliverance, and true spiritual life for the whole human race. As far as her example goes, she is also a direct contrast to Eve. In the preceding pages I have warned you to beware of imitating Eve; I now desire most earnestly to entreat you to endeavor to imitate the virtues of Mary. Behold her at the hallowed moment when the angel brought to her the message from on high, and the mystery of inexpressible magnitude, the mystery of the Incarnation of the Son of God, was accomplished. What cannot a virgin learn from this "*Virgin of virgins!*"

Scripture tells us in the first place: "*The angel being come in said unto her.*" Mary was not found out of doors, amid the tumult of the world, but in the sacred seclusion of her own room; she loved retirement.

Christian, maiden, love retirement and recollection. Of course, I do not mean that you ought to remain always at home, in your own room, or that you ought to hold aloof from other persons, or enter a convent and become a nun. This is certainly not my meaning, unless, indeed, God were to call you to embrace such a state of life.

Yet it still holds good, that if you wish to persevere in the path of piety, to be happy both in this world and also in the next, you must imitate Mary; you must love retirement; and though you live amid the bustle and turmoil of the world, you must not be of the world.

Especially must you endeavor to suppress the restless craving for the approbation of your fellow men. A desire to please, to attract the notice of others, and more particularly of men, is inherent in every young woman in a greater or lesser degree. But this very desire, so seldom resisted, so freely indulged, has effected the temporal and eternal ruin of many young girls and of many older women also. Struggle with all your might against this inordinate desire to please; like Mary, cultivate a love of seclusion. Remember the violet. Every one loves and values this modest little flower which thrives and blossoms most beautifully in the shade.

Prove your love of retirement by avoiding dangerous occasions and amusements as far as you possibly can. Such are clandestine meetings with men, balls, and plays of an immoral tendency. A young girl who desires to preserve her innocence and virtue must exercise the greatest caution and prudence in regard to these and similar matters.

Give further proof of your love for retirement by remembering the presence of God at all times, and in all places, and by keeping Him before your eyes whatever you may be doing; whether you are at work or amusing yourself, partaking of your meals, or conversing pleasantly with those around you.

In the second place, Holy Scripture says concerning Mary: "*Who having heard, was troubled at his saying, and thought with herself what manner of salutation this should be.*" She shrank from the praise which was bestowed upon her. Far from giving her pleasure, it caused her to fear that the apparition might not come from God. Again I repeat, do you, my dear daughter, act in a like spirit. Do you fear, when men approach you with flattering words, when they extol, in honeyed accents, your physical beauty or mental gifts, when they assure you that your society makes them happy beyond expression. Trust them not too readily! How many girls have paid for their foolish confidence, their love of praise and flattery, with the loss of their innocence! Wherefore be warned in time.

In the third place, to the proposal which would confer upon her the highest possible honor—that of becoming the Mother of God—Mary replied, with childlike humility: "*How shall this be done?*" She did not immediately grasp at the honor, she did not answer at once in the affirmative, but she desired first of all to receive an assurance that she would be able to preserve her virginity, which she had consecrated to God.

If Mary exercised such extreme caution in regard to the proposal made to her by a heavenly messenger, how careful and conscientious ought not you to be in regard to the temptations of the world and of the enemy of souls! When some tempter approaches you, and tries to induce you to join in some dangerous diversion, to remain alone with him, or to listen to improper proposals, then answer as Mary did: "'*How shall this be done?*' For, whatever be the cost, I am resolved to avoid the least stain of impurity." And you must not only speak thus, but act in accordance with your words; you must fly from the tempter, fly without delay!

If, at a later period, a non-Catholic should make your acquaintance and wish to marry you, you must imitate Mary by asking: "'*How shall this be done?*' How can I consent to a mixed marriage, since my mother, the holy Catholic Church, disapproves of such unions, and since they so seldom turn out happy?"

Finally, in the fourth place, when Mary had once perceived what the holy will of God was, she replied in a spirit of humble submission: "*Behold the handmaid of the Lord; be it done to me according to thy word.*" If you desire to be truly pious, you must be perfectly resigned to the will of God. In this respect also you must imitate Mary. This remark especially applies to the choice of a state of life. When once you perceive what is the will of God, when you have heard His voice speaking to you in clear and definite accents—then obey that voice, however great a sacrifice it may cost you to do so. Pray earnestly for grace to follow the call, and to say from your heart as well as with your lips, in imitation of Mary: "*Behold the handmaid of the Lord; be it done to me according to thy word.*"

In the manner I have described, take Mary for your model, and beseech her to intercede on your behalf.

> Hail, blessed Mother, Virgin pure.
> From every stain of sin secure;
> Hail, morning star that gilds the sky!
> Hail, Daughter of the Lord most high!
> Fairer than aught on earth beside,
> My joy and hope, my youth's sure guide!

XXIX. A Ladder to Heaven

In the course of my experience as a director, one deathbed scene remains imprinted on my memory—that of a young girl, fifteen years of age. She was good, pious and very intelligent. I had prepared her for her first confession and holy communion; and on both these occasions her seriousness and fervor had afforded me no little pleasure and edification. She must have been indeed an obedient and docile child; for she had had two stepmothers in succession, and each had loved her tenderly and prized her highly.

After an illness of a few days it became my painful duty to open the girl's eyes to the danger in which she was, and to prepare her for death. What I then witnessed showed what living faith can effect in the heart of a child. The sufferer was in no way bewildered; she remained calm and resigned to the will of God, and received the last sacraments in such a manner as to edify all who were present.

About three hours later it became evident that relentless death was approaching. When I had united with her relatives in praying for the soul so soon to depart, I said to the dying girl: "My child, you will pray for us in heaven, will you not?" "Yes, yes," she replied. Then taking my hand with a look of entreaty, she added, "but you must first pray for me, in order that I may get to heaven!" After saying farewell to all around, she repeated, "Pray! pray!" This was her legacy to the by standers.

Over and over again I would repeat to you these last words of hers, and say: "My dear child, pray! pray! Pray, because prayer is absolutely necessary for every Christian and, more especially, for every young girl." Prayer is indeed the ladder which leads to heaven, and without it we can never hope to reach that blessed place. I have spoken before of the importance of prayer, but now, when I am treating of the exercises of piety in a more lengthy and detailed manner, I wish to explain more fully to you how necessary a thing prayer is.

Nothing is more emphasized, nothing is more earnestly enjoined upon us, in Holy Scripture, than the duty of prayer. Very numerous are the exhortations we meet with to the same effect: "*Ask and it shall be given you; seek, and you shall find; knock, and it shall be opened to you.*" Again the Saviour says: "*Watch ye and pray.*" St. Paul says: "*Pray without ceasing.*"

What do we find in the writings of the saints? They declare prayer to be the breath of the soul; they pronounce a man who does not pray a lamp without oil, a body without nourishment, a plant without water, a soldier without arms.

St. Alphonsus Liguori writes as follows: "All the blessed in heaven have been saved by means of prayer. All the reprobate were lost because they did not pray; had they prayed, they would not have been lost forever."

St. Teresa frequently said: "A man who does not pray will become either a beast or a fiend."

St. Augustine asserts: "He who prays aright, will live aright."

St. Francis of Sales thus expresses himself: "One can expect nothing that is good from a man who does not pray."

We gather from all this that without prayer there can be no real virtue, no strength to resist evil, no holy death, no salvation. Alas, for the man who ceases to pray! He is lost.

Prayer is necessary for sinners. St. Augustine, that great Doctor of the Church, states that, in the ordinary course of things, God imparts the graces necessary for salvation only to those who ask Him for them. Can anything be more calculated than these words to arouse us from tepidity in prayer? It is an awful truth that God generally forsakes those sinners who do not seek refuge in prayer. Which of us would remain during a thunderstorm in a place exposed to lightning? Who would saunter along a road on which murderers lurked? or drink a poison which usually proves to be fatal? How then can the sinner dare to despise and neglect prayer, since those who do not pray run the risk of being abandoned by God?

But not sinners alone, the just also, have need of prayer. No tongue of man can describe the happiness of the Christian who is in a state of grace. Hell is closed for him, heaven is opened, the angels and saints are his brethren, God is his loving Father. But his happiness is not complete as yet, it is not as yet assured to him. The soldier cannot sing the song of victory until the battle is ended. Even though a man be in the state of grace, he is still upon the battlefield as long as he lives. The crown of everlasting felicity is promised to him, but he must fight in order to win it. In one unhappy moment he may forfeit it. Prayer is the means which will preserve him from so terrible a misfortune; which will enable him to conquer in the strife and obtain the promised reward, the crown of everlasting life.

Have you not often seen a fruit-tree in spring, covered with thousands of fair blossoms? Look at it a few months later—what has become of all this rich promise? Comparatively few are the blossoms which have ripened into fruit; or perhaps wind, frost, and rain have altogether denuded the tree of its fruit.

Just such a bright spring morning is the day on which a soul is reconciled with God by means of the Sacrament of Penance. But do all those who have thus made their peace with Him remain hereafter free from sin? What becomes of the numerous blossoms of good resolutions? Very few, or possibly none at all, are the fruits into which they develop. Whence arises this deplorable state of things? The storms of temptation have swept over the Christian and he has been foolish enough to disregard the Saviour's warning: "*Watch ye, and pray!*"

With what sorrow and concern does one behold those worldly-minded girls who have an aversion to prayer and blush to be thought pious! How can they save their souls? Not one single saint has failed to pray, and thus to draw down upon himself the grace and mercy of God. All have made use of prayer, that unconquerable weapon; all have reached heaven by no other way than the road of the cross and the ladder of prayer.

Christian maiden, see that you never let go of this ladder to heaven. Mount upward by it. If at times indifference and disgust steal over you in regard to prayer, shake off your slothfulness; say to yourself: I am not as yet in heaven; in some unhappy moment I may lose my soul; therefore I must pray. If you are duly impressed with this truth, you will be more careful in saying your morning prayers; you will more frequently raise your heart to God in the course of the day. Never fail to attend public worship whenever it is possible for you to do so; and never lie down to rest without repenting upon your knees of all the faults you may have committed and praying for the grace of a happy death. Constantly beseech God to bestow upon you the gift of prayer.

> Accept, divine Redeemer,
>   The homage of my praise;
> Take my heart and keep it, Lord,
>   Through all my earthly days;
>
> Be Thou my consolation
>   When death is drawing nigh;
> Be Thou my only treasure
>   Through all eternity.

XXX. A Fount of Healing

In ancient fairy tales one may read of a stream in which any one who bathes is instantly cured of whatever disease may afflict him; any one who is old and ugly becomes young and beautiful once more, and even he who is already dead awakes to renewed life. If there were in reality such a stream, if such healing waters did indeed exist, with what alacrity sick, old, or homely persons would hasten thither from all parts of our globe; how the dead would be carried there from far and near.

We know that for the body there exists no such stream, no healing resort of this kind, but I know that for the soul such a place does exist. Every one who makes use in a proper manner of this fount of healing is at once cured of his diseases; I mean set free from his sins. His soul is once more rendered young and fair, pure and clean, endowed with strength from above; he regains the life of grace if, unhappily, he has lost it, and with this life the hope of eternal happiness.

You have already divined my meaning. The cleansing stream, the fount of healing for souls, which derives its efficacy from the precious blood of Jesus Christ, is the holy Sacrament of Penance. The value of this sacrament is shown by its marvelous effects, which we have already indicated. Ponder these effects, lay them carefully to heart, in order that you may feel an ever increasing reverence, a holy enthusiasm, for this fount of healing.

The first effect of a good confession is the remission of sin and its eternal punishment. Think for a moment what sin is! St. Catharine of Siena once beheld in a vision all the hideousness of a venial sin. The sight was so appalling that the saint declared her readiness to walk all her life barefoot upon red-hot coals, rather than to behold such a thing again.

Now picture to yourself a man who has not only committed innumerable venial sins, but many mortal sins as well. What can be the aspect of his soul? Could such a sinner become aware of his true condition, he would prefer to die the most terrible death ten times over rather than to perceive his misery and continue enduring it. What a happiness for him to be freed from his sins! It must be as if a tremendous burden were lifted from his heart.

Such once was the experience of a young girl as she lay upon her deathbed. In earlier days she had been somewhat giddy and thoughtless. However, she had attended the sermons preached by an excellent priest in a mission and had made to him with due contrition a general confession of her whole life. When, a few weeks later, the girl was attacked by a fatal malady, she was quite resigned, and even cheerful. She exhorted every one who visited her to be diligent in going to confession, and added: "Three weeks ago death would have seemed most terrible to me, but now I am quite ready and willing to die."

Let us imagine a man who, having committed a mortal sin, knew nothing of the Sacrament of Penance. Were he to enter into himself and recognize the enormity of his guilt and the awful state into which he had plunged himself, how would he not sigh and lament! "Alas!" he would exclaim, "how happy I was in the paradise of innocence! My soul was pure; the fatherly eyes of God rested lovingly upon me; I could pray to Him with gladness and confidence! How peacefully my days went by; what joy I felt when in the house of God; when I was resting on the Sacred Heart of Jesus, under the protection of my sweet Mother Mary; how brightly shone the crown of everlasting felicity, and how hopefully I looked upward to it. Now everything is lost; my soul is as hideous as a decaying corpse; and I see hell yawning before my eyes, ready to swallow me up! Alas! can any one help me? Is deliverance still possible for me?"

If an angel from heaven were to appear to this miserable man, and tell him that God was willing to pardon his sins, to preserve him from hell, to admit him to heaven, to regard him again as His child, on the sole condition that he should sincerely and heartily repent of his sins, confessing them with real penitence to His representative on earth in the Sacrament of Penance,—with what gratitude and joy would such a sinner hail the heavenly messenger, how he would make every effort to render himself worthy of forgiveness!

You have long known that God has instituted the holy Sacrament of Penance for the remission of sins. But because you know this so well, ought the immense benefit which God has been pleased to confer upon you appear the less great and precious? Ought you on that account to hold in less esteem His condescension, His infinite mercy and loving kindness? By forgiving your sins in the Sacrament of Penance, God bestows upon you an immeasurably greater benefit than if He were to deliver you from the most dreadful bodily disease, to restore you when dead to life, or to free you from the most noisome dungeon. Great indeed are the graces and benefits which He gives to us anew in the Sacrament of Penance.

Howsoever defiled by sin, however great the distance which separates him from God, every man while he yet lives upon this earth continues to receive great benefits at His hand. In a way, the sinner can never be said to have lost everything; some graces are his portion still. He can pray, and thus storm the gates of heaven; he is permitted, nay, commanded, to hope. Not until he is summoned to appear before the awful judgment-seat, and to hear the terrible words, "*Depart from Me!*" can we say of him in the fullest, most appalling sense that all is lost.

On the other hand, all is gained, all is saved, for the repentant sinner, who by confessing his sins is restored to the friendship of God. When the priest has pronounced the absolution, the soul becomes once more the child of God, a member of His family, a coheir of the inheritance of Jesus Christ. The portals of heaven stand open to the sinner; he can confidently hope to be one day a partaker of its glory and joy, if he only persevere in the path upon which he has entered by means of the Sacrament. Hence arises the pure and lively joy which true penitents experience when they have made use of this fount of healing.

Listen to what was said on this point by no great saint, nor highly gifted soul, but by a soldier, an officer who had attended a mission preached by Father Brydaine in Paris and afterwards had made his confession to him. He followed the good missioner into the sacristy, and spoke in these words before all present: "With all his treasures and riches and enjoyments, the king of France cannot feel so peaceful and happy as I do now. In the course of my whole life I have never experienced such pure and sweet satisfaction as that which is now my portion."

If after confession you never, or at least very seldom, experience the sensible consolations of which I have spoken, do not be concerned on that account, nor imagine you have not made a good confession. If your compunction and your resolutions of amendment were really sincere, be assured that

God will give you abundant grace to lead a pious life; that you will enjoy tranquillity of mind, the consolation of the Holy Ghost, and the peace of a good conscience.

How great and wonderful a thing is the Sacrament of Penance! It is in very deed the source of life, the medicine of salvation, the death of sin, the fount of healing, the beginning of all that is good. O happy Penance, which works so marvelous a transformation! It regains what was lost, it renews what was destroyed, it awakens to new life that which was dead.

> O Christian maid, obey thy Saviour's call—
> Before His mercy-seat He bids thee fall;
> And ere the grave close o'er thee He would fain
> Have thee confess thy sins and pardon gain;
> For from His sacred wounds a stream doth flow
> To cleanse thy soul and peace of mind bestow.

XXXI. Is Confession Difficult?

Christian maiden, it is possible that you may belong to the number of those who would give an affirmative answer to the question I have just asked. You may perhaps consider confession to be a heavy burden. Then listen to me while I tell you about a Protestant who was of a very different opinion. The poet, Clement Brentano, noble-minded and gifted, had in his earlier life forsaken the path of religion and virtue; he was on this account restless, discontented, and altogether miserable. He spoke of his unhappy state of mind to the pious poetess, Louisa Hensel. She was a Protestant at that time, and was not received into the Church until two years later. Yet even then she felt the Catholic ordinance of confession to be a happiness and a blessing. To Brentano she voiced her conviction in the following words: "Why do you complain of the state of your soul to me, who am a Protestant? You are a Catholic and enjoy the privilege of confession. Therefore speak to your confessor of what is weighing on your mind."

Though not a Catholic as yet, she did not consider confession to be a burden, rather a great privilege and one which she ardently desired. Such, indeed, it is. Confession is felt to be difficult only by those who half understand it, or who do not understand it at all. In order that you may learn how to make a good confession, and may not find confession to be a difficult matter, I will proceed to make a few suggestions.

First of all, take the utmost pains to make your confession with a humble and penitent heart. Therefore always prepare yourself carefully for the reception of this sacrament. In order to achieve this end, place yourself with great reverence in the presence of God. Implore God the Father to give you strength to do penance and make satisfaction for the dishonor you have shown Him. Beseech God the Son to give you light to perceive your faults. Entreat God the Holy Ghost to kindle in your heart the fire of His love, that by means of it your sins may be consumed and destroyed. Then quietly examine your conscience. You will find this task less difficult; it will occupy but little time if you go frequently to confession—every four weeks at least—and if every evening you think over the faults of the closing day, as every pious Christian ought to do. For this purpose it is not necessary to have any special form of examination of conscience. You will find one which will answer every purpose at the end of this little volume.

Take all possible pains to awaken sincere feelings of contrition. The chief thing consists in arousing contrition; upon that feeling all else depends. This ought to be no difficult matter with the aid of divine grace, which God is at such times ever ready to bestow. And surely it cannot be difficult for young people, whom the Saviour loves in a very special manner, to awaken this sincere and heartfelt contrition. Think of the incidents in the Gospel in which Our Lord gave such striking evidence of His love for the young. Remember that He said: "*Suffer the little children to come to Me.*" Remember how He raised the young man at Naim, Lazarus, and the twelve-year-old daughter of Jarius. Imitate the latter when you go to confession—hearken to the Saviour's voice, for to you also He calls in accents of love, "*Maid, I say to thee arise!*"

He shows the same fatherly loving-kindness to you also, my dear child. How deeply ought it to pain you to reflect that you have repaid His love with black ingratitude, with indifference, and unfaithfulness!

A firm resolution of amendment must always accompany contrition. But take care never to content yourself with a merely general resolution to avoid all sins. On each occasion direct your attention to some definite and special fault into which you frequently fall.

In regard to self-accusation, you must guard yourself against a mistake into which many pious persons are apt to fall. It is by no means *necessary*, it is on the contrary often not advisable, anxiously to mention in confession *all* the little negligences and imperfections into which you have fallen. If you accuse yourself of some failings of this nature, and make a general act of contrition in regard to the rest, repenting of them as sincerely as you do of those which you have specified, then be assured that the absolution pronounced by the priest applies just as much to the latter as it does to the former.

Ought one to regard lesser sins and imperfections with indifference? Certainly not; for he who pays no heed to small faults is certain to fall before long into more serious errors. When, however, you examine your conscience previous to confession, strive to remember these lesser sins as far as you can and repent truly of them. Then do not fancy that it is absolutely necessary to recount each several item in the long list of your failings and imperfections, since we learn from Holy Scripture that even the just man falls frequently.

If you earnestly and sincerely strive after true piety and go frequently to confession, do not indulge the idea that your confession is good in proportion to the lengthy and scrupulous manner in which you accuse yourself. Nor is it so, in proportion to the length and instructive nature of the priest's exhortation. Embrace and hold fast the following maxims. Should you be fortunate enough never, or scarcely ever, to fall into mortal sin, your confession will be all the better in proportion, not to the minuteness with which you recount all your imperfections, but to the depth and sincerity of your contrition and the firmness and earnestness with which you resolve to avoid most carefully this or that particular fault. To make your confession in this, the proper manner, can surely be not so difficult a matter, so grievous a burden.

Be particular in observing the following rules: (1) Never go to confession from habit or without previous recollection; before you go always repeat some prayer, however short. (2) Do not make your confession in a vague manner, but be definite in what you say; do not mistake temptations and evil inclinations for failings and sins. (3) Do not accustom yourself to enumerate anxiously and in detail very slight faults, which are often involuntary; you would do better to dwell upon those faults against which the voice of your conscience more particularly warns you. (4) After confession do not hurry back to your ordinary occupations, and do not be anxious to engage in frivolous conversation. Is it not right and fitting that you should express your gratitude to God for the great benefit He has vouchsafed to bestow upon you?

After perusing these brief considerations, you may perchance feel compelled to acknowledge that hitherto you have been negligent in availing yourself of this fount of healing; and that, when you have availed yourself of it, your preparation has not been thorough, and the profit you have derived has been in consequence scanty and meagre. Yet do not be discouraged; say to God with childlike simplicity and heartfelt sincerity: "Thy grace, O my God, shall not have spoken this day in vain to the heart of Thy unworthy servant. From henceforth I will frequently make use of the remedy which in Thy great mercy Thou hast provided for me in the Sacrament of Penance, and I will strive to do this in a suitable manner. Grant me the assistance of Thy grace in order that what now appears to my weakness to be difficult, if not impossible, may be rendered easy and light."

> When I reflect, O Lord most high:
> Who art Thou and what am I,
> Thy mercy and Thy love I bless
> And my own sinfulness confess.

XXXII. The Table of the Lord

Progress is the watchword of modern times. No one, for instance, any longer works by the feeble light of an oil-lamp; he employs gas or the electric light. No one journeys to distant cities on foot; he travels by rail. Progress ought likewise to be found in the domain of religion—progress in making use of the means of salvation. For in these modern times the opportunities for sin are so innumerable, the dangers to morals so terribly menacing, the attractions and pleasures of the world so enticing, evil examples so seducing, that it is extremely difficult for a young girl to stand her ground if she makes use only of those means of salvation strictly and absolutely enjoined upon her. Rather should progress be your watchword. I refer to progress in one direction more particularly—that is, in a more frequent approach to the table of the Lord. Therefore I would say, go often to the sacraments, that you may learn to know yourself, may receive grace to overcome your passions and persevere to the end.

There is undoubtedly no more effectual means of preservation from the dangers and temptations which beset your age than frequent union with Our Lord in the Most Holy Sacrament of the Altar. If, impelled by holy longing, you often repair to His table, how your soul soars at such times above the world, above all that is in the world! How poor and mean do earthly pleasures appear to you, how ignoble desires are hushed and put to rest, how your courage and loyalty to God are increased, how much more fervent your prayers become! I am free to confess that I am always peculiarly impressed, and deeply touched, when I see young persons come often, and in large numbers, to holy communion with hearts full of love for Jesus. I rejoice with all my heart, for I am fully persuaded that no enemy can any more have power to harm them; because they are one with the Almighty; because He dwells in them, and they in Him. I know that they will make progress in all that is good, since they have been fortified with the Bread of heaven, the Wine of immortality.

Do you, therefore, frequently approach the table of the Lord. But do not imagine that I am advising you to do anything new or exaggerated. My advice is founded upon an intimate conviction that I can in no way better advance the interests of your soul than by committing it to the keeping of Jesus Christ, by leading it to the Fount of every good, the Source of life everlasting.

The Catholic Church has always recommended frequent communion. It has expressed a definite wish that the faithful should receive holy communion whenever they assist at Mass on Sundays; and that they should do this in an actual manner as well as spiritually. The Council of Trent declares it to be "the way of salvation, the health of the soul, a safe guide through the dangers of the earthly pilgrimage to eternal rest."

But how often ought you to approach the table of the Lord? In 1840 Peter Perboix suffered a martyr's death in China for the sake of Jesus Christ. He had faithfully adhered to the resolution he had formed on the occasion of his first communion, namely, that he would partake of this heavenly Food every month, and also on the principal festivals. His devotion at these times was so fervent that he seemed to be an angel. This frequent reception of holy communion imparted to him strength to become a missionary, and to win the palm of martyrdom.

Though you, Christian maiden, are not called to do and suffer any extraordinary things, you need help and strength from on high if you are to wage a successful warfare with the devil, the world, and evil concupiscence. And this battle you needs must fight whatever be your state of life; whether you enter the cloister, marry, or live unmarried in the world. Seek this strength in holy communion as did the saintly missionary, Peter Perboix. Make it a fixed rule to approach the Lord's table at least once a month. If you sometimes find this to be impossible do not postpone your confession and communion more than eight weeks. Under certain circumstances I would advise you to communicate *every fortnight*, or even *every week*, particularly if you should find yourself unavoidably placed in a perilous position, or exposed to grievous temptations. Frequent communion is one of the best means to advancement and perseverance in the way of perfection and salvation.

But many objections are urged against the practice of frequent communion. In the first place, it is said that this practice did not prevail in former times, yet people saved their souls; why should it be necessary now? I reply, that in the first centuries of the Church daily communion was the universal custom; many paid for it with their lives. And in our own day there are thousands of young men in every land who go to communion once a month, at least. Young girls should not be outdone in piety.

In the second place, you may possibly assert that you are not pious enough to go to communion once or twice a month. But monthly or fortnightly communion is nothing extraordinary. You are not thereby ranked with very pious persons any more than the dove is classed with feathered songsters. Besides, holy communion was not appointed for the pious alone, but for sinners, since those who are in health do not need the physician, but those who are sick.

Again, you may perhaps say that if you go so often to communion you must wear a grave face and never be merry. What an absurdity! I have already shown you that true piety renders its possessor cheerful and merry. And nothing can be plainer than this. For those who frequently partake of holy communion live in a state of grace. The children of God do not enjoy happiness in heaven only; they are happy on earth also. In heaven every one is happy; in hell, on the other hand, every one is desperately wretched and miserable. You may object, in the fourth place, that if you go to communion every month, or twice a month, or even more frequently, you will have nothing to confess. Very well! That is just what the fruit of frequent communion ought to be. You perceive that this habit would preserve you from falling into grievous sins; on this account you ought to persevere in it. You will be made better able to detect lesser faults, and will thus always find matter for confession.

Again, you may say that no matter how often you go to confession you never make any progress! How long, I would ask you, have you made the experiment, and have you made it in the right manner? For a year? Then it is not possible that you can have remained the same. You may not be conscious of the progress you have made, but it is just as certain that you have improved as it is that you cannot fail to warm yourself by standing in front of a blazing fire.

In the sixth place, you may say that you do not like going to confession. Then go without liking it; every one feels alike in this respect; there is no one who takes special pleasure in the act. But you do not work only as much as you feel inclined to do. Many young girls, and you may perhaps be among the number, work for the sake of gain the whole day long; sometimes in close rooms that are ill-ventilated and overheated. Ought you not, therefore, be willing to accept a little trouble for the sake of your immortal soul and your eternal happiness?

Wherefore put aside your petty objections; shake off your love of ease and comfort; betake yourself gladly and frequently to the Fount of grace, which flows forth in ever abounding fulness from the Sacred Heart of Jesus, in the Sacrament of His love. And on each occasion pray that with the frequenting of the Sacred Mystery, your devotion may increase and your life become more pleasing to God.

> O blessed Jesus, in this Angel's Bread,
> A pledge of life to come Thou givest me;
> Grant that to earthly things I may be dead,
> And strengthened by this Food may live in Thee.

XXXIII. The Robe of Piety

MAN consists of two parts, a body and a soul; these two parts are most intimately connected. Hence it follows that the interior feelings and emotions of the soul must of necessity find an exterior expression. Tears are the outward sign of inward grief; smiles and a bright expression of countenance betoken inward gladness. Although true piety and devotion are altogether interior—a disposition of the heart—it is quite impossible that, if they really exist, they should remain concealed, and not manifest themselves by means of corresponding acts and exercises. These acts and exercises constitute the variegated colors in the robe of piety. It is by means of this robe, and these colors, that we are able to distinguish between true and false piety. If these colors are pure and bright, if they form a harmonious whole without one jarring note, one may reasonably conclude that the piety is genuine in its nature. I am now about to direct your attention to the practices of piety, and I beg you to look closely at this brilliantly colored robe.

That which first strikes the eye is the celestial blue of fervor in prayer. The truly pious maiden recites her morning prayer devoutly and as soon as possible after rising. She is convinced that upon it the day chiefly depends, and on no account therefore does she omit it. Moreover, it is of the utmost importance that she should every morning direct her intention, for this is a spiritual alchemy which turns ordinary actions into gold. A good intention resembles the figures placed before a cipher; by it, actions indifferent in themselves, which, when they stand alone, are as worthless as ciphers, receive an infinite, an eternal value.

She is equally careful to perform her evening devotions in a proper manner. She strives to awaken heartfelt contrition for the sins and negligences into which she has fallen during the past day. She seeks to discover them by means of serious reflection, and always pays special attention to any particular fault she is trying to uproot. She also makes it a rule always to say grace both before and after meals.

Rosy red is another striking color in the robe of piety; it is zeal in hearing Mass. I do not refer to the obligation of hearing it on Sundays and festivals but the voluntary attendance on week-days. A short time ago I read of a young girl who in winter and summer walked nearly three miles every day in order to hear Mass. In this way she obtained strength to resist temptation and to live virtuously during the day. Not long afterward she died a truly pious death.

My dear child, do not you need strength just as much as she did in order that you may resist the dangers and temptations which beset you day by day? Therefore go to Mass as often as you can and you will receive grace and strength to persevere in the right way. But if it is quite impossible for you to do this, God will take the will for the deed, and bestow upon you no less a measure of grace and strength. Remember the words of a celebrated master of the spiritual life: "He who hears Mass devoutly will prosper in everything during the day."

In the third place we see the bright gold color of the practice of frequently raising the heart to God. It is a devout practice to raise the heart to God in a brief prayer every time the clock strikes the hour. At all events it is advisable that you should repeat, if only to yourself, one of the ejaculations to which the Church has attached numerous indulgences, and which you will find in the latter part of this volume. Such, for instance, are the following:

> "My Jesus, mercy!" 100 days' indulgence.
> "My God and my All!" 50 days' indulgence.
> "Jesus, my God, I love Thee above all things!" 50 days' indulgence.
> "Sweet Heart of Mary, be my salvation!" 300 days' indulgence.

The robe of piety should be distinguishable also by its hue of verdant green. This green betokens the sanctification of Sunday. It is a matter of course that you should fulfil the duty strictly binding on every Catholic never to omit hearing Mass on that day without a sufficient reason, nor engage in any unnecessary servile work. It is also of great practical importance that you should be diligent in hearing the word of God by your presence at sermons and religious instruction; that you should read edifying books and join only in those amusements which are harmless and innocent; avoiding, on the other hand, sinful diversions and occasions of sin. You must be all the more determined in adhering to this resolution because, in the present day, the temptations which would lead young girls to violate Sunday are so varied and so numerous.

White should also not be missing. By it I understand the fervor with which you should discharge your obligations as a member of confraternities and pious associations. They are, it is true, not absolutely necessary, but they afford suitable and practical means for the exercise of piety. Such associations are the Apostleship of Prayer, the Sodality of the Blessed Virgin Mary, the Confraternity of the Holy Rosary, the Archconfraternity of the Perpetual Adoration, and the Confraternity of the Scapular of Mount Carmel. Should the Association of the Perpetual Adoration be established in the place Where you live, enroll yourself in it, and see that you are a zealous member of the same. Wear with devotion the scapular of our blessed Lady of Mount Carmel; it is the most ancient of scapulars and the one most recommended by the Church. You must above all be, and also remain, a faithful and zealous member of the Congregation of the Children of Mary. It will prove a sure guide and a constant incitement to a true and childlike devotion to the Blessed Virgin Mary. Read what this book says in regard to that subject.

A pious Christian maiden ought to show zeal in regard to works of charity; this is the scarlet color in the robe of piety. What great and exalted merits for all eternity can a maiden acquire if she, without in the least neglecting her external appearance, avoids all that is showy and exaggerated in the way of dress; if moreover, instead of eagerly seeking after undesirable and dangerous pleasures and diversions she devotes all that she can save to some pious purpose, some object approved by her parents and superiors. There are, thanks be to God! many such young girls in town and country, in the houses of those who possess only limited means, as well as in the palatial homes of the wealthy. Aim at belonging to their number. At any rate see that you never omit, but constantly and diligently practice, one work of charity, the easiest of all: pray for the suffering souls in purgatory; offer up your mortifications on their behalf.

Finally, the fundamental color in the robe of piety is violet—renunciation, or self-denial and self-conquest. Without constant practice of this virtue no other virtue and no real piety can be possessed. "In proportion as thou doest violence to thyself, the greater progress wilt thou make," we read in the *Imitation*. You cannot and will not form an exception to this rule. If you have no other cross, you must daily take up the cross of self-denial, in order not only to be pious, but also to be happy.

In conclusion, a word of warning: never mistake the external robe of piety for the inward reality; the former is accessory, or accidental, the latter is essential and necessary. Keep closely to external practices of piety, but be not self-willed in regard to them; observe them in the manner consistent with your calling and state of life with moderation and charity.

> Christian soul, dost thou desire
>   Days of joy and peace and truth?
> Learn to bear the yoke of Jesus
>   In the springtide of thy youth.
>
> It may seem at first a burden,
>   But thy Lord will make it light;
> He Himself will bear it with thee,
>   He will ease thee of its weight.
>
> Only bear it well, and daily;
>   Thou wilt learn that yoke to love;
> Strength and grace it here will bring thee.
>   And a bright reward above.

Sighs to Jesus
in the Blessed Sacrament

O Jesus, sweetest Love, come Thou to me;
Come down in all Thy beauty unto me;
Thou who didst die for longing love of me;
And never, never more depart from me.

Oh, melts my heart receiving Thee, my Own;
My eyes are dim for lack of Thee, my Own;
My flesh doth hunger, needing Thee, my Own;
My soul doth faint apart from Thee, my Own.

Free me, O beauteous God, from all but Thee;
Sever the chain that holds me back from Thee;
Call me, O tender Love, I cry to Thee;
Thou art my all! O bind me close to Thee.

O suffering Love, Who hast so loved me;
O patient Love, Who weariest not of me;
Alone, O Love! Thou weariest not of me;
Ah! weary not till I am lost in Thee;
Nay, weary not till I am found in Thee.

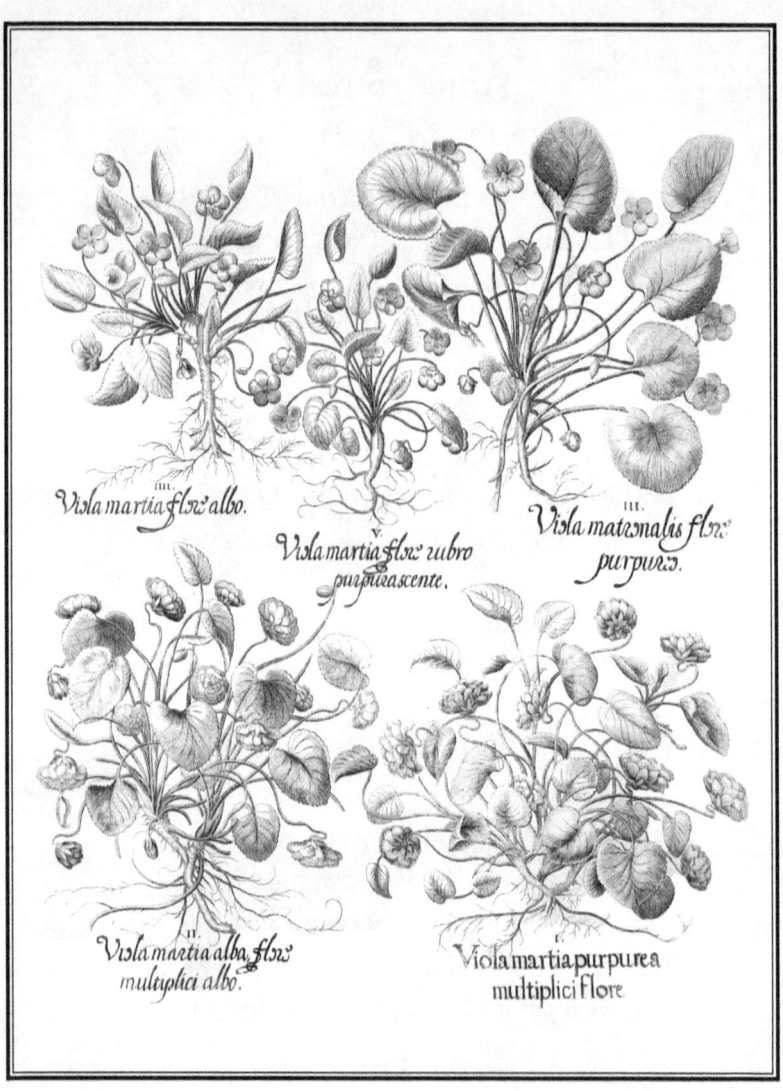

‹ 7 ›

The Violet of Humility

XXXIV. The Maiden's Ornament

From the beginning of the world God inculcated humility and lowliness of spirit upon women. Immediately after the Fall she was told that she must be in subjection, the practice of humility being thus imposed upon her as a punishment. On the other hand, the consequence of original sin—namely, the tendency of the human heart to evil—consists, in the case of the woman, precisely in a constant endeavor to rebel, in a spirit of pride, against the sentence of punishment pronounced by God.

The more firmly this tendency to pride is implanted by nature in the heart of a woman, the more edifying and meritorious it is when she, with the aid of divine grace, fights against the tendency and gradually eradicates it, planting in its stead the fragrant violet of humility, causing it to take root, to flourish and blossom. The violet of humility is indeed one of the fairest ornaments of woman, and of the young girl more especially.

In order that you may learn to value this bright ornament more highly I will relate to you an example of the fatal effect of the poisonous plant of pride. A priest had not long been stationed in a certain parish when he noticed the extremely proud and haughty demeanor of a young girl who had only shortly before left school. And her behavior must have been very noticeable, for her companions had bestowed upon her a nickname of no flattering nature. With fatherly kindness, yet with all seriousness, the priest repeatedly warned the poor foolish girl. Yet his admonitions produced no effect; he began to fear that he would have cause to grieve over this one of his parishioners, according to the true saying: "*Pride goeth before a fall.*"

Unhappily the presentiment of the good priest was only too fully verified. Before many years had elapsed the greatest misfortune which can overtake a young woman happened to this poor girl. She became a great sinner and an outcast.

Pride indeed "*goeth before a fall.*" Wherefore flee even the mere shadow of this sin; carefully practice the virtue of humility. Let us now examine more closely this bright ornament of the maiden.

God, in His infinite wisdom, endowed the maiden with beauty and power to please. He desired to teach her that, as she was externally adorned with beauty, she ought to beware lest her soul should not correspond to her physical attractiveness, but be, on the contrary, a wild and desert place. Your external charms should be a mirror in which the beauty of your soul is reflected. Remember the warning God gives to every maiden, in the book of Proverbs: "*Favor is deceitful, and beauty is vain; the woman that feareth the Lord she shall be praised.*"

Contemplate the Blessed Virgin Mary, the Mother of Jesus, and your Mother also. Her whole life was a continual practice of humility. The more highly God exalted her the more did she humble herself. The angel saluted her as the Mother of God; she called herself the handmaid of the Lord. All self-love was banished from her heart; she had renounced all the vanities and honors of the world from the moment when, as a child, she offered herself to God in the Temple. Hers was a hidden life, unheeded by men, but all the better known to God and all the more glorious in His sight. She rejected even well-deserved praise, and felt confused when she heard the angel's salutation. She ever sought to appear as a servant although she had been exalted to be the Mistress of the universe. She was in very deed the humble handmaid of the Lord, as she terms herself in the *Magnificat*.

Lay well to heart the glorious example of your Mother, and strive to imitate it. Distinguish what is really valuable from that which has only a passing and external worth. Learn to prize something more highly than the gifts of fortune—than wealth, honor, beauty, or flattering praises. Endeavor to be simple and unpretending in the eyes of men; seek before all things to please God, and to be beautiful in His sight. Employ the advantages God has bestowed upon you in such manner as to appear unconscious of possessing them.

Do not imitate the silly girls who try to attract notice by foolish airs and showy dress. Rest contented if you know that you have the approval of God; do not trouble yourself about the praise or blame of the vain world, and never torment yourself with idle fancies. Banish conceit and egotism.

Be like the violet, which blossoms unseen. This modest little flower grows in the midst of the loftier plants which surround it, being itself unheeded and unknown. Charming indeed it is in its robe of purple; delightful is the fragrance it diffuses; yet it knows not that it is so sweet and fair. Do you resemble this flower; be free from all pretension and never give yourself haughty airs, nor look with disdain upon others. Submit to advice and correction, and remember all your life long the wise counsels of your mother, teacher or confessor. Do not imagine yourself to be wise and prudent; be guided in a childlike spirit by those who are set over you; be grateful and obedient to them.

As a humble handmaid of the Lord place the most implicit confidence in God. Trust the guidance of your whole future life to Him your wise and merciful Father. Do not torment yourself with uneasy questionings about the time to come, and how you are to be provided for, Believe me, dear child, those are best provided for who place their future into the hands of their all-wise and all-powerful Father in heaven.

A young woman who is unduly anxious and troubled about her future, forgetting God and thinking only of procuring happiness in temporal advancement, often purchases what she seeks very dearly, and at the cost of many tears. For that is the fruit of pride, which despises good advice; and of vanity, which forsakes God and aims at pleasing men rather than pleasing Him. Therefore let humility be the foremost flower in your youthful garland.

Let humility be your ornament. Do not belong to the number of those thoughtless girls who do not value humility at its true worth, and do not try to practice it. Be not counted among those who fancy that humility is a virtue not suited for the young; not at least for young people in general, but only for those who have a vocation to the cloister.

Foolish and mistaken indeed is this opinion; it runs counter to all the doctrine and commands, all the example and actions of the Saviour, more especially to His weighty admonition: *"Learn of Me because I am meek and humble of heart."* Young persons should study before all things to serve and please God; they can do this only by obeying His representatives; but true obedience is possible only to the *humble* Christian.

> Let us to the violet turn,
> Wisdom's lessons from it learn;
> To lead a quiet, useful life,
> In this world of sin and strife.

XXXV. Humility is Essential to Salvation

WE read in St. Matthew's gospel: "*At that time the disciples came to Jesus, saying: Who thinkest thou is the greater in the kingdom of heaven?*" They asked this with no pure intention, but from ambition, in a proud and arrogant frame of mind. What did Jesus do? He sought, in the gentlest manner, to point out to them the perversity of their hearts, and to lead them to a better mind. He took a child, placed it in their midst, and said: "*Amen, I say to you, unless you be converted, and become as little children, you shall not enter into the kingdom of heaven.*" Thus He showed the ambitious disciples that unless they renounced their pride and haughtiness, and became humble and lowly like little children, they could never be saved, they could never hope to enjoy eternal happiness in heaven. The doctrine taught by Our Lord was intended not only for those who were at that time His disciples, but for all Christians, and for all young girls more especially. It ever has been, and ever will be true, that humility is essential to salvation. Let us consider the subject somewhat more in detail.

Without humility you can be no disciple and follower of Him who said: "*Learn of Me, because I am meek and humble of heart.*"

Again, without humility other virtues cannot last, according to the warning of St. Augustine: "If you desire to erect a spiritual edifice see that you lay the foundation in humility." Furthermore, without humility it is impossible for you to withstand the temptations and avoid the snares of the great enemy of souls.

Without humility you cannot gain the favor of God, nor obtain the pardon of your sins and a favorable hearing for your prayers. For we read in Holy Scripture: "*A contrite and humbled heart, O God, thou wilt not despise.*" And again: "*The prayer of him that humbleth himself shall pierce the clouds.*"

Without humility your mind will not be enlightened to understand the things of God, for again we can quote the words of Scripture: "*Where humility is, there also is wisdom.*" And Our Lord said: "*I confess to Thee, O Father, Lord of heaven and earth, because Thou hast hid these things from the wise and prudent, and hast revealed them to little ones.*" Without humility it is not possible that the Holy Spirit should dwell in our hearts, as Scripture testifies in the following words: "*To whom shall I have respect but to him that is poor and little, and of a contrite spirit?*" Finally, without humility we can never be exalted in heaven, as Our Lord assures us: "*Unless you be converted, and become as little children, you shall not enter into the kingdom of heaven.*" And in another place: "*He that humbleth himself shall be exalted.*"

Humility is essential to salvation! This is all the more true because where humility is wanting pride and haughtiness are certain to be found, and they lead to hell. It was pride which cast the fallen angels down to hell. It was secret pride which was the cause of the first transgression, the sin of our first parents. For we are told in Holy Writ that the devil took the form of a serpent and in this form said to Eve: "*No, you shall not die the death. In what day soever you shall eat of the forbidden fruit your eyes shall be opened, and you shall be as gods, knowing good and evil.*" (Gen. iii. 4, 5.)

In a precisely similar manner does the evil enemy act at present; more particularly in regard to those young persons who are happy enough to be living in the paradise of innocence. He attacks the obedient and promising daughter on her weak side—he flatters her vanity. He addresses her somewhat after the following fashion: "You are no child now! Do not take everything so literally that your parents and the priests see fit to tell you! Things are not what they represent them to be; they do not understand life at the present day;

they want to cut things according to the old pattern! You just let them talk, and go your own way! Then your eyes will be opened and you will see how much wiser it is to drink copious draughts of the pleasures of youth than to steer your course according to the advice of crabbed old persons. If there really is an eternity, if hell does really exist, you can turn over a new leaf later on; old age is the time to do this and it will come upon you quite soon enough."

Insinuations like these arouse and feed the vanity which lurks in the heart of every girl. She believes them, prides herself on her talent, her mental and physical endowments, begins to despise, or even to mock at and deride the affectionate warnings of her parents and confessor. She no longer seeks to avoid the dangers which threaten her soul, but, heedless of admonitions, plunges headlong into the vortex of worldly pleasures and amusements, imagining herself to be sufficiently old and experienced to know how far she can go with safety. She falls into grievous transgressions and does not avoid occasions of sin, but in her blindness regards all this as of no consequence.

When the storms of passion sweep over her, when the magic enchantments, the temptations and attractions of the world lay hold upon her heart, and she perhaps neglects prayer and the sacraments, what, alas! is to become of her? Unless the merciful hand of God interposes to arrest her downward course, pride and vanity will hurry her along the road whose end is destruction. My dear child in Jesus Christ! beware of this poisonous plant of pride; tear it up from your heart, root and branch, and plant and cultivate in its stead the violet of humility!

It must, however, be the genuine flower, true humility. A lady once said to the celebrated preacher, Father Abraham of Santa Clara, with every appearance of profound humility: "Alas, Father, I am the greatest sinner on God's earth!" Father

Abraham, being thoroughly acquainted with human nature, replied with a roguish smile: "My good lady, I am quite ready to believe that you are a sinner of the blackest dye; but do not despair, the mercy of God is infinite; He pardoned the thief upon the cross." This answer acted like a douche of cold water on the pharisaical humility of the lady. She expected some complimentary language, and, finding herself disappointed, she gave free vent to her annoyance, exclaiming: "What do you mean? What do you take me for? Who is there who can bring anything against me?"

Let not your humility be of this pharisaical nature, but let your modest little flower exhale the sweet perfume of the real violet. The Christian maiden possesses true, genuine humility if she never boasts of her talents and virtues—nor even secretly prides herself upon them; if she acquits herself faithfully of her duties without regard to any praise or recognition which may be bestowed upon her; if she does not aim at attracting notice; if, when she meets with reproofs which are undeserved, she either modestly explains herself, or, what is still better, says to herself that if the reprimand was not deserved this time it was upon other unpunished occasions; finally, if, when her parents, teachers, or confessors give her well-meant advice, she does not regard their warnings as exaggerated or too severe, but receives them in a childlike spirit, and does her utmost to carry them into practice.

Let this true, genuine humility be yours, and persevere in the exercise of it, in order that you may be happy both in this world and in that which is to come. Remember that if you desire to practice humility, or indeed any other virtue, you must deny yourself.

> Master thyself; subdue thy passion's might,
> Strive valiantly and conquer in the fight;
> And know, unless the victory thou gain,
> The bliss of heaven thou canst not obtain.

XXXVI. The Fruits of Humility

Have you ever closely observed a field of corn when it is ripe for harvest? The greater number of ears bend beneath the weight of the grains of corn which they contain. Some few stand proudly erect, but they are empty and useless, destitute of grain. Just so is it with most persons who pride themselves upon their wealth, splendid apparel, or other external advantages; they possess no true merit. They resemble a pupil of Apelles, the famous painter of ancient days. This pupil painted the figure of a woman and adorned it with rich jewels; his master said to him: "Because you are not skilful enough to paint a beautiful form, you adorn your canvas with gold and gems."

Do you, Christian maiden, avoid pride, haughtiness and self-esteem; cultivate the violet of true humility, according to the description of this virtue which I have given you in the two last instructions. It is known by its three fruits: gentleness, modesty, and decorum—purity of soul and body.

The humble maiden is distinguished by her meekness and gentleness. God has specially adapted the heart of woman for the exercise of this virtue. It is naturally soft, impressionable and sympathetic, readily moved to share in the weal or woe of others. These qualities cause the Christian maiden always to appear gentle and amiable. Bright tears glisten in her eyes at the mere recital of her neighbor's sorrows, and when she perceives that those around her are weeping she cannot restrain her own tears: she is always ready to help and comfort as far as it lies in her power to do so, and she endeavors to pour some drops of sweetness into the bitter cup of life.

Like Noe's dove, she is a messenger of peace to the quarrelsome and discontented; she reconciles those who are at enmity; she bears with the exacting and eccentric, and if her efforts to placate them are of no avail she puts up with everything in silence, never allowing herself to wrangle, or to indulge in open complaints.

Modesty is the second fruit of humility, more especially modesty in dress. See that you make this modesty your bosom friend. I do not mean that you are to cause annoyance to others by singularity in your dress. I wish only to remind you that your appearance ought to be simple and unpretending. Extravagance and ostentation in the matter of dress have reached a lamentable pitch in the present day. Many women dress far above their station. The daughter of a tradesman or a laborer is hardly to be distinguished from a lady of leisure and wealth; the servant maid can hardly be distinguished from her mistress on Sundays and holidays. Every change of fashion is followed, each one striving to outdo her neighbor.

Understand, dear child, that I am not referring to girls who dress according to their station, neatly and prettily; I am speaking of the foolish girls who try to be in the forefront of the fashion, and who spend all their thoughts on dress and finery. Girls such as these fall into almost all the deadly sins. Pride induces them to make a showy appearance. In order to obtain expensive gowns in spite of their narrow means, they become avaricious and hard-hearted in regard to the poor; unchastity and pride are closely related; vain persons allow their feelings of envy to grow into bitter hatred; their vanity is the generator of anger and family dissensions; showy girls are idle because they are afraid of disfiguring their charming persons by honest labor. A girl can preserve herself from these sins and failings by cultivating modesty and simplicity in her dress and appearance.

Let decorum, which is the third fruit of humility, accompany you throughout your life. Thus you will, according to the admonition of St. Paul, *"think on the things of the Lord, that you may be holy both in body and in spirit."* You will shrink from everything which might defile either body or soul. You will value purity of heart above all else, and rather forfeit your life than lose this precious treasure.

That is the disposition which characterizes a virgin. This sense or disposition makes its presence known by the delicate blush on the maiden's cheek, by the reticence of her glances, by the care she takes not to depart from that which becomes her sex and position in life, by her conscientious avoidance of everything in her speech, dress and demeanor which is—or might be—hurtful to modesty.

Such a maiden not only flies from what is really dangerous, but from what has the least suspicion of danger; she not only shuns what is evil, but what might lead to evil. But because she is so careful and modest she need not be melancholy, nor shrink from society. On the contrary, cheerfulness and mirth accompany the virtuous and lowly maiden in all her paths. Joyousness and innocent merriment dwell where the fear of God abides. Yes, where this holy fear protects the pure heart like an invincible shield, there does the maiden appear in her true dignity. Her dignity and gravity hold those in check who would be too familiar, and all who behold her admiringly exclaim: "How truly charming are innocence and virtue!"

You may perchance be saying to yourself that it would be delightful indeed to be such a gentle, modest, retiring maiden, but that you lack strength to make these virtues your own. You desire to possess these virtues! Well, then, be not discouraged; persevere in this desire with all sincerity, doing at the same time everything in your power to further the fulfilment of your wish.

Humility with its sweet fruits will bring peace to your soul. For this reason Our Lord so frequently exhorts us to the practice of humility. That we may more earnestly seek to acquire it He promises us peace of heart as our reward: "You shall find rest to your souls." Such are His own words. Do you not desire to have peace in your heart—peace with God and your fellow men—eternal peace one day in heaven?

In order that you may be able to gain this peace by the practice of humility, have recourse to the means which I have so often pointed out to you—be diligent and earnest in prayer. Every day strive anew to overcome vanity and pride; constantly make fresh resolutions carefully to avoid all sins against meekness and humility.

To enable you to do this, think of the eternal glory which is the reward of humility. St. Philip Neri was one day talking confidentially to Bernardine Corna, one of the lay-brothers in his community. In the course of conversation he said to him: "Bernardine, I am told that the Pope intends to offer me a cardinal's hat; what do you say to it?" The brother answered in all simplicity and sincerity: "Methinks you ought not to refuse that dignity, for the sake of the Congregation, if for no other reason." Thereupon the saint gravely lifted his biretta, and raising his eyes to heaven, with a look of holy inspiration, he said: "O, Bernardine, think not of earth, but of heaven, of paradise!" "Forgive me, Father," the brother replied, "I really did not think of it at that moment."

Alas, so it is! "I did not think of it, I did not think of heaven, I did not think of paradise," must be the confession of many Christians, of many young girls, when they give themselves to the pleasures, amusements and vanities of the world. But do you, Christian maiden, think of heaven, and then:

> Let the modest violet be
> An example unto thee;
> Love all humble, lowly ways;
> Strive not after human praise.

Sub Tuum Praesidium

We fly to thy patronage, O holy Mother of God; despise not our petitions in our necessities, but deliver us always from all dangers, O glorious and blessed Virgin. Amen.

Prayer Before A Crucifix

Behold, O good and most sweet Jesus, I fall upon my knees before Thee, and with most fervent desire of my soul, beg and beseech Thee that Thou wouldst impress upon my heart lively sentiments of faith, hope and charity, true repentance for my sins, and a firm resolve to make amends, as with deep affection and grief, I reflect upon Thy five wounds, having before my eyes that which Thy prophet David spoke about Thee, O good Jesus: *"They have pierced my hands and feet, they have counted all my bones."* Amen.

Prayer to St. Michael

St. Michael the Archangel, defend us in battle; be our safeguard against the wickedness and snares of the Devil. May God rebuke him, we humbly pray, and do Thou, O Prince of the Heavenly Host, by the power of God, cast into Hell Satan and all the other evil spirits, who wander throughout the world, seeking the ruin of souls. Amen.

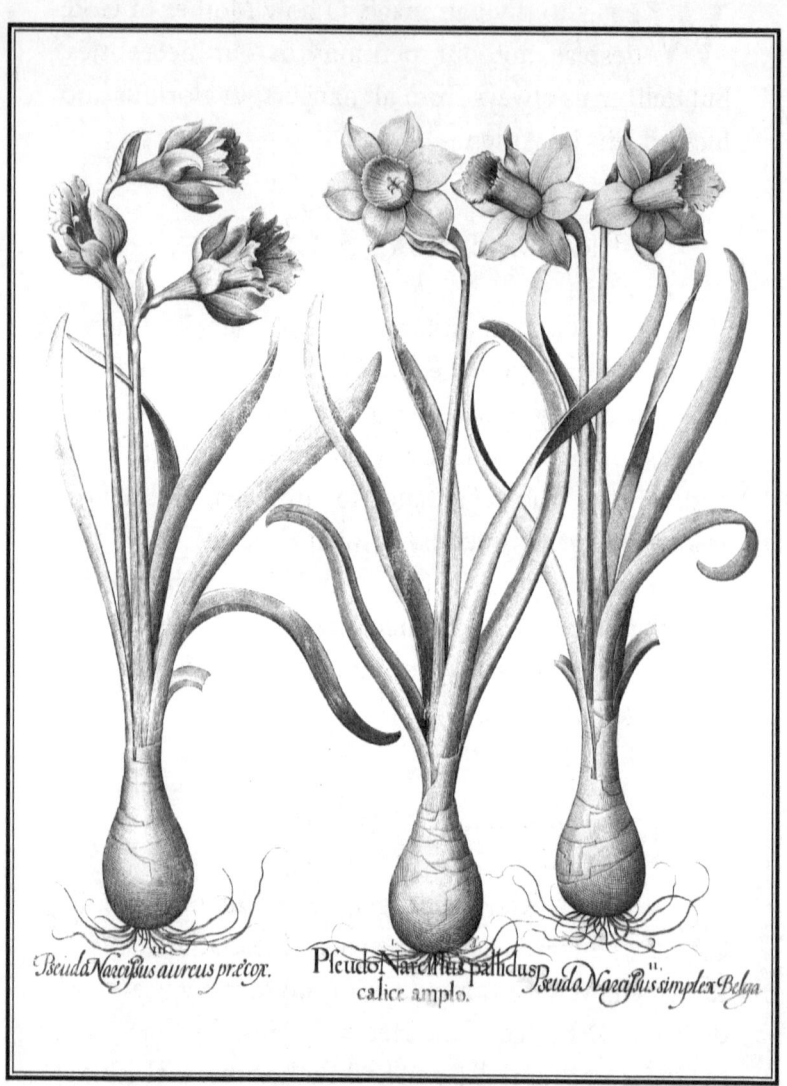

‹ 8 ›

THE DAFFODIL

INDUSTRY

XXXVII. THE VALUE OF WORK

Do not take alarm at the mention of work; the word may have a harsh sound, but the thing itself is not so harsh and bitter as it may appear at first sight. You must not, as is too often the case, immediately connect with it the idea of toil, fatigue, and degradation which pertains to a slavish occupation. For everything must, in fact, be won by work—everything which does not grow of itself, like fruit on a tree.

Work is one of the first duties of a young girl. Scarcely has the winter's snow disappeared from the sunny fields at the approach of spring when a charming, gold-colored flower makes its appearance—I mean the daffodil. I have chosen it from among its brethren and sisters, the fair children of spring and I have called it industry's flower because it hastens to blossom as soon as possible. I wish to place it before your eyes, Christian maiden, as an emblem of industry, that virtue which should find a place in the garland which decks your youthful brow.

In what light ought work to be viewed? Man, as the image of God, in a way takes part in His creative activity. Do not misunderstand me, for of course I do not mean that he can make something out of nothing; but he has power to impart to substances various forms, and by the light of his understanding to arrive at a continually increased comprehension of higher things. Now all this is achieved by means of exertion, labor, work. Work is of a twofold nature, either mental or physical. Both are indispensable to the well-being of human society; they may be termed soul and body. Direct your attention at present chiefly to the latter—namely, physical labor. It was at home in days of old, under the roof of the holy house at Nazareth.

Whom do we see at work there? None other than Jesus Christ Himself, the incarnate Son of God, together with His foster-father, St. Joseph, and His Virgin Mother, Mary. How great and exalted a thing must work therefore be!

But men have not always been accustomed to view it in this aspect. The ancient heathen, on the contrary, despised bodily labor. The so-called freeman considered it a degradation to employ himself in manual labor; even the most enlightened of the Greeks and Romans expressed, in no measured terms, the supreme contempt they felt for all work of this nature.

We find this dislike and contempt of work prevailing everywhere throughout heathendom. The North American Indians hate work and leave it to women, as did also the Teutonic races. But as manual work must be done, if men are to live and be fed, the expedient of slavery was resorted to. Matters were carried so far that men came to regard laborers of both sexes as a separate order of beings, infinitely below the rest of their fellow creatures, and scarcely above the level of the lower animals. They were considered to be mere animated machines, which their owners were free to treat in whatever fashion they might see fit. They were bought and sold like any other goods and chattels; they were thrown aside—that is, they were killed—when they were found to be no longer of any use. It was even seriously doubted whether slaves possessed a soul like other men. Such was the opinion entertained by the heathen concerning work and workmen.

Then Jesus Christ appeared, the God-Man and Our Redeemer. He did not choose for His foster-father one of the Roman emperors, a member of the senate, or a sage. No, He chose a man whose whole life was spent in hard labor, a carpenter, an artisan; and next to the temple of God, the workshop was the place where He liked best to be. What dignity this fact confers upon labor! The greatest dignity which He could bestow upon a man He bestowed upon St. Joseph, the carpenter of Nazareth. *"My ways are not your ways,"* embodies a truth which the Son of God proclaims to the whole world from His very cradle.

He Himself, the incarnate Son of God, worked in St. Joseph's shop until He was thirty years of age. Mary, His blessed Mother, was no fashionable lady caring only for society and amusements, for dress and novels. We see her, in the peaceful house of Nazareth, industriously pursuing the ordinary avocations of a poor artisan's wife. From that day forth, how different is the aspect of work when viewed by the light of the Catholic faith, by the light of the workshop at Nazareth, where the God-Man, Jesus Christ, diligently helped His foster-father, and handled the saw, axe, and plane.

Keep your gaze constantly fixed upon that workshop and thence learn to be faithful and assiduous in your work, and to regard it as honorable. Whether it be easy or difficult, servile or otherwise, consider it to be a precious remembrance, a priceless relic of the house at Nazareth. Within those walls was work also exalted and sanctified; there did it receive that patent of nobility, which, if you only know how to appreciate it aright, will win for you the favor of Jesus, Mary, and Joseph.

To this end lay to heart the description of the industry befitting a woman which Solomon gives in the book of Proverbs, and which he recommends to all. He says: "*She hath sought wool and flax, and hath wrought by the counsel of her hands. She is like the merchant's ship, she bringeth her bread from afar. She hath risen in the night and given a prey to her household and victuals to her maidens. She hath considered a field and bought it; with the fruits of her hands she hath planted a vineyard. She hath girded her loins with strength, and hath strengthened her arm. She hath tasted and seen that her traffic is good; her lamp shall not be put out in the night. She hath put out her hand to strong things, and her fingers have taken hold of the spindle. She hath looked well to the paths of her house, and hath not eaten her bread idle.*" How admirably is here set forth the value and worth which woman's work possesses in the sight of both God and men.

You may perhaps, during your school days, have learned all sorts of fine things—foreign languages, delicate embroidery, drawing, music, etc.; these are all very well, and may prove of service to you. Your best and truest vocation, however—the vocation intended for you by God—is to occupy yourself in the house. Honor these domestic duties and attend to them industriously.

Formerly, even more than now, the household was considered as essentially woman's sphere, and those who would not devote themselves to domestic avocations were looked upon askance. In the sorrows and trials of your daily life of labor recall these lines:

> If thy life seems dark and dreary,
> And thy daily toil unblest,
> Pray to Him Who bids the weary
> Go to Him and be at rest.

XXXVIII. Love of Work

CHRISTIANITY teaches us to regard work as something sacred, honorable, and exalted. Work is your duty. In a company of ladies one day the conversation happened to turn upon the ornaments most suited to women—upon gold chains, earrings, brooches, and jewels in general. Each expressed her likes and dislikes. A lady who had hitherto remained silent was appealed to at length and asked to give her opinion as to what ornament best befitted a woman. "A thimble," was the prompt reply. And she was perfectly right in attributing so much importance to this modest little thing, for the thimble is a symbol of feminine occupation.

You must not only value work very highly, you must also love it.

We are taught by daily experience that industrious, active girls who are fond of work are almost without exception virtuous and pure. Hence it follows that the highest praise which can be bestowed upon a girl is to say of her that she is industrious, never tired of work, but always usefully occupied.

Therefore a maiden who desires to please God, and to act in accordance with His will, applies herself to the exact and faithful performance of the duties which befit her age and position in life. The welfare of the household, the happiness of the entire family, is, in the majority of instances, found to depend on the prudence and conscientiousness with which women discharge their domestic duties. Though the father may toil unceasingly from morning to night, his earnings will profit him little if his wife and daughters do not practice economy.

Furthermore, without work, order and cleanliness can never be had in the house, and when disorder prevails the state of things is very uncomfortable. It is the duty of the female members of the family to see that everything is clean and well arranged, for upon this the contentment, cheerfulness, and very often the health of all depend.

To go still further, she who accustoms herself from her youth up to tolerate about her person nothing displeasing to those around will be less likely to allow blemishes to disfigure her soul. Therefore no one ought to blame a girl for laying stress upon neatness and cleanliness in the house and also in her dress. Her pleasing exterior should be an image of her soul. It does not come from pride. It costs no money. With care and pains a neat, pleasing appearance can be attained amid the poorest surroundings and in every condition of life. Carelessness, slovenliness, and want of cleanliness are bad traits in a girl.

A girl ought to learn every kind of work which she will be expected to know later in life; she ought to help her mother as much as she possibly can, and when the mother is no longer there to advise and superintend, she ought to try to manage everything in such a manner that she will not be missed. These domestic virtues are highly meritorious in the sight of God.

To do all this is no light matter. It implies that she who would accomplish it must rise early and go late to rest. It leaves no leisure for lounging, for gossip, for bad company, for useless strolling hither and thither. But its advantages cannot be too highly prized; it brings with it health, a light heart, and ignorance of evil. It wins universal respect, and causes the maiden to be the delight of her parents and the ornament of her home.

Pride yourself therefore on liking work; do it diligently, and make it your best, your inseparable friend. Whatever the nature of your work may be, do it with care and industry. If you have been away at school, take pains when you return home to show that you have learned to love work and to do it well. Attend to domestic affairs and interest yourself in all their details—not by mere words, by finding fault and making critical remarks—but by putting your hand to everything. If it happens to be just what you dislike, do it with particular earnestness. Do not incur the reproach addressed to so many girls when they finally leave school and return home—namely, that they will not work and want to play at being fine ladies. Let your industrious conduct, on the contrary, give pleasure to your parents, relations, and friends; let them see that school has not made you forget how to work, but has taught you to work well.

If your home is in the country and you have to do farm work or daily work think yourself fortunate! Do not imitate so many girls in your class who think the best thing they can do is to exchange their rural occupations for a situation in a town, or a place in a factory. Nothing could be more foolish and short-sighted. Country life and work are by far the healthiest, even if you are not very strong, and in a way most useful and necessary for society at large.

In conclusion, mark one most important particular. If your work is to be really well done, if it is to please God and gain merit for yourself, you must see that you perform it with a good intention. This must never be wanting. Each morning renew your intention, and if your words are few let them be uttered with an earnest purpose. You can at least say: "*All for the greater glory of God.*" And if in the course of the day you find some occupation very wearisome, and a feeling of impatience begins to stir within your breast, then renew your good intention and say: "*O my God: I will do everything for the love of Thee! Help me to be patient and to persevere!*"

Yes, to be patient! For without patience no labors, toils, or suffering can be meritorious in the eyes of God. Like coins that are withdrawn from circulation, which no longer form part of the currency of the realm, they have no value for heaven, and will not pass muster there. See therefore that you perform all your work with a good intention and with much patience; thus you will lay up a treasure of genuine coins by which you will gain admission into heaven.

> Swiftly time speeds on its way-
> See that thou use it well;
> Let each hour of every day
> A tale of wisdom tell.

XXXIX. Away from Home

How fortunate—how extremely fortunate—are those young girls whose family circumstances are such as to make it possible for them to remain under their parents' roof until they are married, with the exception of the comparatively short time they spend at school. However, it is but seldom that they have this good fortune now. Times are changed. Young women engage much more than formerly in business taking them away from home. It is now true of them as well as of members of the sterner sex: Man must plunge into the strenuous life; man must go forth to his daily work and confront the dangers of the world. If this should be the case with you—if you must go forth and encounter the dangers of the world—lay to heart and follow, I pray you, for God's sake, and for the sake of your own soul, the fatherly counsels which, with the kindest of intentions, I offer for your guidance.

First of all, however, be sure it is really necessary for you to leave home and to go amongst strangers, where life will be fraught with dangers for you. So many girls allow themselves to be deceived in this respect, either by their own heart or by the persuasions of other persons. There are girls who are crazy for amusements, or seem animated by a spirit of evil. They soon begin to feel themselves hampered and restrained; their own people do not allow them liberty enough; the simple pleasures to be enjoyed at home in a country town or village no longer satisfy them. However comfortably they may be situated, though they have a desirable occupation, liberal allowances and ample recreation, it all counts for nothing in their opinion.

They persuade themselves and the members of their family that life at home is not worthy of the name; that there is nothing to be learned and nothing to be earned; that, on the contrary, in large cities like New York, London, or Paris, life is really worth living, and one can literally coin money. "Besides, one can be pious in cities as well as in villages; look at our neighbor's daughter, what nice letters she writes home, and what sums of money she sends from time to time." Do you think that when girls leave home in such a spirit as this they are acting in conformity to the will of God, and can hope for His blessing? No, they are following, more or less completely, the impulse of their own perverse heart.

Others are deceived by the alluring representations of old school-fellows, or of friends, who write to them somewhat as follows: "You cannot imagine how pleasant life is here! Almost every Sunday there is something going on: an entertainment, an excursion, a concert, a play, or a dance. Certainly one is sometimes obliged to work very hard, but then there is plenty of free time, and there is nearly always something to amuse one, even when one is at work. Then again there are so many well-dressed, well-mannered boys and fashionable young men, who pay court to one, and are very lavish in spending their money. It is quite different in villages or small towns among rough country-bred lads. Do come here; I know of a most desirable place which would exactly suit you. And as to going to church and saying your prayers, you may make your mind easy; there is a Catholic church very near, with several priests."

It is not difficult to guess how a girl will go on, who is allured by highly colored pictures such as these! In the first place, it is doubtful whether she will be really happy. Therefore take care not to make up your mind too quickly to leave home, and to go forth into the wide, wide world, to seek in cities for more remunerative occupation.

But let us suppose for a moment that you really are obliged to leave home—what then? Then you must exercise the very greatest caution in taking a situation. You must not jump at the first place which offers itself through an advertisement in a newspaper. It is very sad to see how careless and thoughtless many girls are in this respect, and sometimes their parents are even more foolish. They grope about in the dark, inquire what wages are offered, and the higher these are, so much the better they consider the situation to be. They trouble themselves very little, or perhaps not at all, about innocence and morality, about faith and religion. Hence it comes to pass that young persons such as these too often wreck both their temporal and eternal happiness, having lost, when they return home at a subsequent period, both their virtue and their reputation. It is necessary to warn you that there are, especially in large cities, houses of ill-repute, into which many a young, unsuspicious, good-looking girl is decoyed by all manner of specious promises. Once there, she is detained by craft, or even by force, and she escapes only with loss of spiritual and bodily health.

Therefore, if ever you have to seek for a situation away from home, make the most thorough investigations before pledging yourself to anything. Do not enter upon a permanent engagement on the strength of newspaper advertisements. Find out whether you will be allowed to attend divine service, and learn the reputation the family bears in regard to religion and morals.

Request your spiritual director to make all needful inquiries of the priests of the place to which you think of going. You will never repent doing this; while, on the other hand, your repentance may come too late if you are careless enough to omit the necessary precautions.

Especially must extreme prudence be exercised when there is question of taking a situation abroad. Some few years back a letter appeared in a newspaper describing the perilous position in which a young woman had found herself through neglecting to make due inquiries. By means of brilliant promises, she was induced to take a situation at Nice. Scarcely had she reached her destination, when she found herself in a house of the worst possible description. For a fortnight she held out against craft and flattery, hunger, menaces, and all the various means which were employed in order to lure her to her destruction. At length a gentleman made his appearance, and literally bought her from the owners of the house, intending that she should sail in his company for Algiers on the morrow. Fortunately she got wind of the villainous design, and effected her escape by leaping from a window under cover of night. This instance is but one out of a hundred which might be adduced. Therefore be cautious, exceedingly cautious, before taking a situation abroad.

In conclusion, I must touch upon a weak side of life in the present day. Very many girls are more or less compelled to work in factories. This fact is the source of many evils. For life in a factory is fraught with numerous and grievous perils for both body and soul, in the case of young women more especially. It frequently occurs that girls who have just left school lose their virtue through working in a factory, or through going to and from their daily toil. There are—thank God!—many also who remain virtuous, but they form, I fear, a minority. Thus we see that a life so full of danger should be chosen only from urgent necessity.

> Work and pray; that alone is the way
> To gain God's blessing day by day.

*The prayers on these pages, along with the **Alma Redemptoris Mater** on p. 82, are the four great Anthems of the Blessed Virgin Mary, with their versicles and collects, which are traditionally said or sung at the conclusion of **Compline**, or Night Prayer. Each corresponds to a particular season of the church calendar, as noted at the beginning of each prayer.*

*The **Salve Regina**, or **Hail Holy Queen**, is perhaps best known as the closing prayer of the Rosary. The Collect found at the end is not part of the prayer proper, but is used in the context of Night Prayer.*

The Salve Regina is recited during that portion of the Church year known as "The Green Meadow" because of its green vestments: that is, from the Saturday after Pentecost until Advent.

SALVE REGINA

Hail holy Queen, mother of mercy, our life, our sweetness, and our hope. To thee do we cry, poor banished children of Eve. To thee do we send up our sighs, mourning and weeping in this valley of tears. Turn then, most gracious Advocate, thine eyes of mercy toward us, and after this our exile show unto us the blessed Fruit of thy womb, Jesus. O clement, O loving, O sweet Virgin Mary.

V. Pray for us, O holy mother of God.

R. That we may be made worthy of the promises of Christ. Amen.

LET US PRAY: Almighty, everlasting God, who by the cooperation of the Holy Spirit, didst prepare the body and soul of the glorious Virgin-Mother Mary to become a worthy dwelling for Thy Son; grant that we who rejoice in her commemoration may, by her loving intercession, be delivered from present evils and from the everlasting death. Amen.

Recited from Candlemas until the Easter Vigil:
Ave Regina Coelorum

Hail, O Queen of Heav'n enthron'd,
Hail, by angels Mistress own'd
Root of Jesse, Gate of morn,
Whence the world's true light was born.
Glorious Virgin, joy to thee,
Loveliest whom in Heaven they see,
Fairest thou where all are fair!
Plead with Christ our sins to spare.

V. Allow me to praise thee, holy Virgin.

R. Give me strength against thy enemies.

Let us pray: Grant, O merciful God, to our weak natures Thy protection, that we who commemorate the holy Mother of God may, by the help of her intercession, arise from our iniquities. Through the same Christ our Lord. Amen.

*Recited from the Easter Vigil until the Friday after Pentecost. During the same period, the **Regina Cæli** also takes the place of the **Angelus**.*

Regina Cæli

O Queen of heaven rejoice! alleluia:
For He whom thou wast meet to bear, alleluia,
Hath arisen as he said, alleluia.
Pray for us to God, alleluia.

V. Rejoice and be glad, O Virgin Mary, alleluia.

R. For the Lord hath risen indeed, alleluia.

Let us pray: O God, who gave joy to the world through the resurrection of Thy Son, our Lord Jesus Christ; grant, we beseech Thee, that through His Mother, the Virgin Mary, we may obtain the joys of everlasting life. Through the same Christ our Lord. Amen.

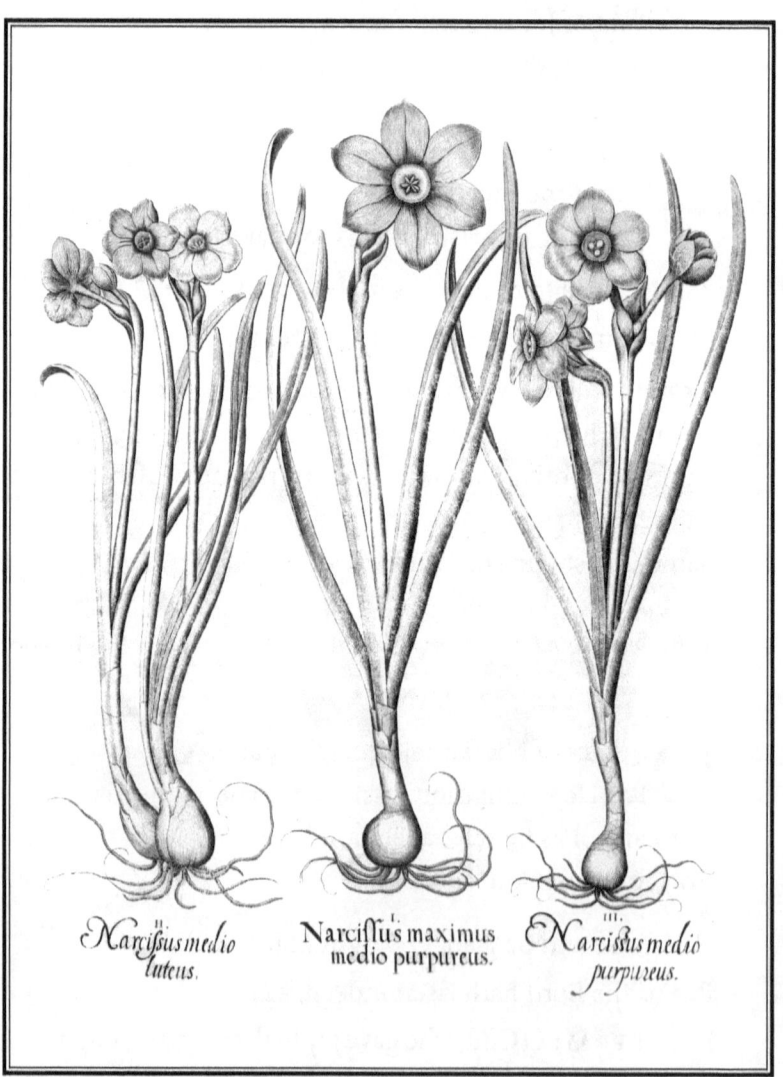

◀ 9 ▶

The Narcissus

Truthfulness

XL. False Prophets

"**B**EWARE *of false prophets*," were the words addressed by Our Lord on one occasion to His disciples. This warning is peculiarly timely in our own day and—in the first place—to unsuspicious, inexperienced girls. The number of false prophets is legion at the present time. In private and in public life, in families and communities, in church and state, everywhere false prophets seem to abound. False prophets tempt you from without: these are the numerous heretical, false opinions and maxims of worldly men. False prophets tempt you also from within: your own evil passions and unruly desires. I purpose to-day to single out one only of these false prophets and to expose it in all its hideous deceitfulness. I refer to the opinion, so widely spread, that it is not so very wrong to tell a lie, that under certain circumstances it is necessary to do so. My dear child, beware of adopting this opinion. It is a false prophet. I will tell you why.

Both reason and religion teach, that even the least, the most unimportant lie is sinful, and therefore forbidden. You know that God is infinitely truthful. He is the very Truth itself.

Therefore He hates, abhors, and positively forbids every lie. *"Lying lips are an abomination to the Lord,"* we read in Holy Scripture; this means that God abhors every one who tells a lie. Who was the first liar? The devil in paradise, and by his falsehoods he led our first parents to sin and plunged them into misery. Whose example does the liar follow, whom does he resemble? He who tells a lie, by so doing takes a step further away from God and from heaven, a step nearer to the devil and to hell.

Thus does the liar disfigure his soul and render it unsightly; it becomes unlike to God, like to the enemy. Therefore, Scripture says again: "A lie is a foul blot in a man." As a black spot of ink disfigures a beautiful white garment, so does a lie disfigure the soul of him who utters it. It rests on his soul like a black spot, a mark of shame, for he must be ashamed of it.

Every one esteems an honest, straightforward man, but he who is false and deceitful is avoided and despised. Even when he does speak the truth, he is not believed. How frequently one hears the remark: "It is impossible to trust So-and-So; he is always ready to lie and deceive." Would you like to be spoken of in this way? Then take care never to depart from the truth.

God punishes lying very severely; remember Ananias and Saphira, of whom we read in the Acts of the Apostles. The saints were always truthful and all conscientious persons carefully abstain from lying. Here is an example. A certain man was an accomplice in the commission of a crime. When examined before a magistrate, he pleaded an *alibi*, asserting that he was at home at the time the deed was done. His daughter was a good, honest girl, and he wanted her to bear witness to the fact. She was perfectly aware that by making a false deposition she could most probably save her father from prison; she was urged by threats and persuasions to do this. Yet she remained firm, saying once and again: "I will not lie; it is a sin to tell a lie."

How differently do most people speak and act? They do not scruple to tell a lie, especially if by so doing they do not injure any one. Many children are inclined to tell lies. The little creatures are always ready with a falsehood, in order to escape punishment. What is the cause of this? It is inherent in our fallen nature, the consequence of original sin, but it depends to a great extent on the parents and elder brothers and sisters of the child. They play the part of false prophets, for they think nothing of telling lies themselves, and do not, therefore, chastise a child for telling them. If it breaks a plate or a pane of glass, if it loses a few cents, its short-sighted mother beats it unmercifully; but if she catches it telling a lie, she is much too kind to dream of using the rod. Thus is the tendency to lying nourished and increased in the childish heart.

How easily do grown-up persons persuade themselves that it is an absolute impossibility always to speak the truth? The greater number of tradespeople, nearly all of them indeed, adopt the maxim of the false prophets, and assert that without telling lies they could not exist. They say: "The world is full of deceit; all who are engaged in commerce act as we do, and if we did not depart from the truth now and then, we could make no profits!" The world is changed, they say. But has God altered His command; has He given men permission to lie for the sake of gain? But every one acts in this manner! If every one tells lies and offends almighty God, is this any reason why we should follow this bad example?

Others, again, follow false prophets in holding the opinion that a lie is perfectly justifiable under certain circumstances. One or another is heard to say: "I know that I do occasionally depart from the truth, but only in order to maintain peace at home, or with my neighbors, to avoid quarrels and strife, to save some one from incurring grievous suspicion, to protect her from harm, etc., and surely in such cases as these it cannot be wrong to tell a lie, but on the contrary, it must be perfectly justifiable!" Yet in every one of these cases *lying is sinful and reprehensible*; it is impossible to imagine circumstances in which it is allowable to utter a barefaced lie. This is not my personal opinion alone; it is the doctrine and teaching of the holiest and most learned men—of St. Augustine for instance—it is the doctrine of all Christians, the view taken by all right-minded men. No sophistries, no ingenious arguments can hold good in the face of this fact; they are and remain the views of false prophets. Therefore beware of them!

Is one on this account compelled at all times and under all circumstances to utter the naked truth? Between telling the whole truth and telling an untruth there is an outlet. Let me relate a well-known anecdote which will explain my meaning. The great Bishop St. Athanasius was persecuted for the faith. He was sailing up the Nile with some trusty friends to escape from his pursuers, when a vessel containing the persecuting band met them. The soldiers on board, who did not know Athanasius by sight, hailed them, and asked the attendants of the bishop whether they had seen him. "Oh, yes," was the prompt reply, "we saw him just now; he is quite near; if you row on as fast as you can, you will easily capture him." Now this speech was not untrue, yet it was the means of saving Athanasius. In the same way it is permissible to make use of an evasion, when some great temporal or spiritual good is at stake. Be honest and truthful; thus you will please God and win the respect of men.

> O God, from falsehood and from wile
> Keep Thou my conscience pure;
> An honest heart that knows no guile
> Is of Thy mercy sure.

XLI. Truth Before All

This world is a place where truth and falsehood dwell side by side. In the beginning truth alone was to be found. But the devil, who told a lie in paradise, introduced lying into the universe. Now truth and falsehood are destined to abide together until the end of time.

Often is truth compelled to withdraw into the secret recesses of a good man's heart; falsehood, on the contrary, stalks hither and thither, lifting its insolent head with an air of triumph, spreading its hellish doctrines far and wide. How mighty is the tree of falsehood, how thick are its branches, how inviting its fruits, how refreshing the shadows it casts! How accomplished is falsehood in the art of flattering, of making itself beloved, of winning the favor of men!

My dear daughter, you are as yet young and inexperienced, but you must have noticed that a man who is proficient in the arts of falsehood, of intrigue, of flattering, lying and deceit, and who, as is usually the case, possesses a glib tongue, and knows very well how to chatter—that such a man, I say, may amass wealth, and bring his undertakings to a prosperous end. Another man who adheres strictly to the truth, and utters nothing but the truth, very often suffers failure.

Do not allow yourself to be blinded by the success which attends false men and deceivers, whether their prosperity is only brief, or whether it is more lasting. Do not be dazzled by external appearances, howsoever brilliant these may be. For though falsehood may carry on its diabolical work with triumphant success for a very long time, it cannot do so forever; sooner or later a time must come when it will be unmasked and put to shame; prostrate and humbled, it will be forced to bear witness to the truth which it hated.

Therefore, away with all falsehood from your heart; away with all duplicity from your mouth; away with all the tricks, wiles and artifices of a false and perfidious world! Away with deception, flattery, craft, and all their hellish brood! Take to your bosom this sweet and gentle daughter of heaven—Truth—and together with it, embrace all its charming companions—the virtues—that follow in its train. Suppress the fatal tendency to insincerity, which is more or less deeply rooted in every human breast.

Root out the inclination to hypocrisy and dissimulation. Strive to be always good and pious in the sight of God—not merely to appear so in the eyes of men. Be polite, amiable and friendly to every one; but be all this in reality. A young woman who behaves with great friendliness toward any person she secretly detests and talks about in an unkind manner, plays the part of a hypocrite. In the Garden of Olives, Judas greeted and kissed the Redeemer, at the very time when he was treating Him with shameful ingratitude and disgraceful treachery.

Never allow yourself to be induced to practise any kind of dissimulation. Remember the aged Eleazar, who refused to deny his faith by partaking of swine's flesh. Some of his friends, from motives of compassion, advised him to bring secretly some kind of meat that was not forbidden, and pretend to be eating the flesh of swine. But he replied: "It doth not become our age to dissemble." Truly it does not become an old man to play the hypocrite; nor does it become a young man or a child; and least of all a Christian maiden.

Be faithful to your friend, the truth. Do not be anxious to please at any cost. Every age, every rank of life, each sex, has its special and peculiar faults and foibles. Among the weaknesses belonging to the feminine sex, an excessive desire to please holds a prominent place. You must be on your guard against this desire to please, for it might easily lead you into various kinds of untruthfulness in your speech and actions. An excessive desire to please might lead you, when at home with your parents, to pray, to work, to be obedient, obliging, and friendly to every one. But you might do all this, not from a sense of duty, not from love of God, but exclusively—or almost exclusively—from the wish to win the favor and approval of those with whom you are brought into contact. In a case like this, would not the Saviour's warning be applicable to you: "*Take heed that you do not your justice before men, to be seen by them: otherwise you shall not have a reward of your Father who is in heaven.*"

> For human praise, O Christian, do not crave.
> Let not this fickle world thy foolish heart enslave;
> Seek favor from on high; though man may flatter thee,
> This will avail thee nought throughout eternity.

Let one great and holy desire enter into your heart, and there hold sway: namely, to please God in all your thoughts, words and actions. Every morning renew your intention to do all things, both great and small, for the love of God, and resolutely determine not to indulge an immoderate desire to please your fellow-creatures.

Thus will you remain faithful to your friend, the truth, and will never be betrayed into flattery. The temptation to flatter comes indeed very forcibly when you have to deal with persons whose favor might be of service to you, or whose disapproval might be injurious to you. It would be easy for you to praise them in extravagant terms, to extol their good qualities above what they really deserve, and to pay them compliments which you do not really mean.

This tendency to exaggerated politeness is one of the faults of society in the present day. Scarcely has a visitor entered a house, before he is greeted with elaborate friendliness, with apparently sincere delight, his hand is pressed, his entertainer is never tired of repeating: "How delighted I am to see you!" All the time the excessively polite person wishes the visitor at Jericho, for the time at least, since the call is paid at an inopportune hour. And when he is preparing to take leave, he is urged and besought to stay a little longer, though great would be the host's dismay were the departing guest to yield to these entreaties, and resume his seat! This is but one instance of many that might be brought forward to show the manners of society people; they practise an exaggerated politeness, which is merely external. "Outside fair, inside bare!" as the homely saying expresses it. Be careful always to observe the rules of politeness, but see that the outward form is the expression of genuine feeling and of true charity toward your neighbor. Love truth; practise sincerity; despise falsehood and dissimulations. More particularly see that your conduct toward your parents, your confessor, your teachers and friends, is free from all admixture of falseness. Prove the distich to be untrue that says:

> With a grain of love, and of faith a grain,
> A grain of deceit will always remain.

No: the truth above all, and in all things—sincerity.

XLII. Let Your Speech Be Always with Charity

Do you know what it is that overthrows and destroys concord in families, peace among neighbors, harmony among men? Do you know what sows the seed of discord in towns, villages, and communities; what lets loose the demon of hatred and envy, what leads to enmity, strife, revenge, and even murder? Do you know what plunges innumerable souls into the direst misery, into everlasting perdition? Do you know what works all this havoc? It is the insatiable, all-devouring monster, the incurable plague of mankind—*the habit of speaking evil of one's neighbor.* On this account one would fain banish this pest from every human heart, from the whole world; but the desire to do this must ever remain a pious wish, which can never be realized. But I know that the hearts of men, and your heart also, are in the hand of God; that He can guide them, as seems to Him best. Therefore do I beseech Him to come to my assistance, that what I am about to say may do something toward preventing you from contracting a habit of evil-speaking.

This pernicious habit of speaking ill of one's neighbor destroys his good name altogether, or in part at least. A good name consists in the esteem and consideration in which any person is held. He is robbed of this esteem and respect when evil is spoken of him, or when what is good in him is underrated. Since the evil which is said of any one may be either true or untrue, evil-speaking may be classed either as *detraction* or *slander.*

By detraction the faults of our fellow men which have been concealed hitherto, either wholly or in part, are disclosed without necessity. To detract from our neighbor's reputation in this way is a very common fault. The experience of every day bears witness to the truth of what I have just said. What is it that never ceases from morning till night, from one year's end to another, in society and in casual meetings, in highways and by-ways?—People's talk and gossip about one another. When two or more persons get together what do they say? How are you getting on? may be their first inquiry. What do you think of the weather? is perhaps their second question. But the conversation soon gets around to more interesting subjects—Have you heard what So-and So has said? or done? How is time spent in drinking-saloons, or more select social gatherings? It is spent in gossiping about the faults of one's neighbors.

This kind of gossip—this way of speaking—is a widespread, a universal evil. Other sins prevail only among persons of a certain state, or are peculiar to one sex. Wealthy and distinguished individuals have their special sins into which common people do not usually fall; the lower classes, on the other hand, have their own failings, which are not found among those of higher position. But backbiting and detraction are met with everywhere; these sins are committed by all sorts and conditions of men, though more frequently by the weaker sex. Indeed, persons who in all other respects are pious and virtuous are too often not free from this sin.

Attend carefully to what I say, that you may see how great a sin is this habit of evil-speaking. He who speaks evil of his neighbors is guilty of a theft; he robs his neighbor of his good name, which all upright persons regard as a most precious possession; the good name which Holy Scripture so earnestly exhorts us to preserve, because it surpasses in value all earthly riches. Riches and treasures pass from us when our life comes to an end, but a good name remains, and survives after death. Hence it follows that he who by evil-speaking deprives his neighbor of his good name, or, at least, tarnishes it, commits a greater sin than he would commit by robbing him of his property.

And in what various ways is this sin committed! In truth, they may be said to be well-nigh innumerable. You may injure your neighbor's reputation by attributing a bad motive to his most pious, most innocent actions, by perverting his words and casting suspicion upon him; by saying, for instance: Who knows what may have occurred; I do not want to speak evil about him, but it is reported, many people say, etc., etc. You may injure your neighbor's reputation by a mere gesture, an expression of countenance, or a shrug of the shoulders. You may injure your neighbor's reputation by remaining silent when you ought to speak in his praise. You may injure his reputation under the pretense that you mention his faults only in order to warn a third person against falling into them, or in order to give him good advice. You may injure his reputation under the pretense of zeal, of compassion, of charity; you may speak of his faults with an outward appearance of pity, but with a secret feeling of malicious pleasure. And there are a hundred other ways of injuring your neighbor's reputation.

Most shameful—most sinful—is *slander* or *calumny*. He who attributes to his neighbor evil actions which he has not committed, but which are a lying invention, is guilty of this sin. It is one of such magnitude as of itself to inspire horror; and we cannot but own that evil must be deeply rooted in the heart of anyone who commits it. What a horrible thing it is to impute to a fellow-creature a crime of which he is innocent!

The dissolute old men, in Jewish history, slandered the chaste Susanna and they were stoned. The Jewish people found fault with the blameless life of St. John the Baptist, and misinterpreted the marvelous acts of the Saviour. This nation was rejected by God. The same God still lives, and will visit with severe chastisement all calumniators who so shamefully wrong innocent persons.

It follows as a matter of course that the more worthy of respect the person is, against whom the calumny is uttered, so much greater is the sin. Peculiarly wicked is the conduct of those base and unprincipled Catholics whose unscrupulous tongues do not spare even the priests of God.

Do not misunderstand me! Do not imagine I have warned you so earnestly against evil-speaking and backbiting because I think you have frequently fallen into this sin. I have done so in order to inspire you for the future with a wholesome horror of this widespread vice.

But what are you to do in order never to commit the sin of evil-speaking? There is a simple method, one which may be practised without very great difficulty. St. Augustine points it out in these words: "Love, and do what you will!" Yes, real, true, honest, unselfish love of all men—or *charity*—ought to rule your heart, guide your tongue, dictate your speech. Then will no unkind word, no word injurious to your neighbor, escape your lips; then will you faithfully follow the advice contained in the following lines:

> Thy neighbor's reputation most sacred thou must hold;
> Judge not his actions rashly, with words unkind or bold.
> Another's praise, not thine, be ever heard from thee;
> And thus thy place in heaven a higher one shall be.

XLIII. There Is no Great Harm in It!

I REMEMBER once seeing an amusing cartoon. It was called "A delightful bit of news," and represented five or six feminine heads, all looking one way, and all with their mouths open. The first head was small, and the mouth proportioned to the rest of the features; the next was rather larger, with a much wider mouth; the third was larger still, and so on. This picture portrayed in a capital way what often happens, especially in small towns or villages, when some trifling incident in passing from mouth to mouth is magnified by the gossips and tattlers till it attains the proportions of quite an important event; and thus, to quote a homely proverb, a mountain is made out of a molehill.

How greatly a man may be wronged, what incalculable injury may be done him, if some trifling fault he has committed is magnified by the tongue of scandal-mongers, and spread abroad by evil-speakers who wish him ill. And yet these people will not, for the most part, allow that they are much to blame. They say with the Pharisee in the Temple:

"O God, I give Thee thanks that I am not as the rest of men," like this or that person! They allege all kinds of excuses for their conduct, and it may be well for you to hear what some of these excuses are.

Some persons say: "We had not the least intention of injuring our neighbor's reputation by what we said." But what good does that do *him?* It injures him all the same; it is detrimental to his good name. If a man were to plunge a knife into a fellow-creature's heart, what would it avail to protest loudly at the trial that the murderer had no intention of inflicting the slightest wound!

Others seek to excuse themselves by asserting that they were not the first to discover these failings, but mentioned them only because they had heard of them from others. But do such persons not know what the Holy Ghost says in the Scriptures: "*Hast thou heard a word against thy neighbor? Let it die within thee.*" And yet they imagine there is no great harm in repeating the evil they have heard about any one to those who hitherto were ignorant of it! How much evil is told which is absolutely untrue, and is merely the product of a malicious imagination! He who repeats such things is guilty of a twofold sin: in the first place, because he believed that which was utterly without foundation; in the second place, because he told it to some one who as yet did not know it.

Another will say: "These faults of my neighbor are no secret; for the person to whom I refer is notorious for his vices, and has a very bad reputation." But even if the faults which are talked about are widely known, what is the use of repeating them? And, if any one is unfortunate enough to be in bad repute, and has already lost his character, why take pleasure in talking about it? Those who act thus remind one of barbarians, who, not content with killing their victim, take a diabolical delight in stabbing and mutilating his lifeless body.

It may further be urged that the faults of one's neighbor do really exist. Are you perfectly certain of this? Does not that which appears to be simple truth often turn out to be a shameful slander? What could have seemed to be more clearly substantiated than the adultery of which the chaste Susanna was accused by the two dissolute old men? Yet it was the vilest calumny imaginable.

"But these and those faults are positively true." Granted that they are true! Let us ask ourselves whether we would like our own faults, however widely known, to be made the topic of conversation. Most assuredly we would not. Therefore you ought not to do to another what you would not like if it were done to yourself. Not only does Our Lord forbid us to act in this manner, but also natural politeness, and even our own reason, if unbiassed by prejudice. Therefore observe the golden rule. If our neighbor's faults, about which we talk, really do exist, are we ourselves faultless? Who would dare adopt the words of the Pharisee, and say: "*O God, I give Thee thanks that I am not as the rest of men*"? What man is there under the sun so pure and blameless that his conscience has nothing of which to accuse him? If there is such a one let him come forward and claim the privilege of speaking evil of his neighbor. "*He that is without sin among you,*" the Saviour exhorts us, "*let him first cast a stone at her,*" his neighbor.

Others again are found to say: "We have mentioned the unfortunate occurrence to only one or two persons whom we can entirely trust, and we have enjoined strict silence upon them." Those who talk after this fashion have perhaps lived for forty, fifty, or sixty years, and yet have never learned that out of one hundred individuals—women more especially—perhaps two are to be found who can keep a secret! If other persons are not to talk, why talk yourself? If others are to be silent, would not the best and most sensible plan be to keep silence yourself?

I will tell you an anecdote about Prince Eugene, the great Austrian general.[1] An ambitious officer wearied him with incessant requests that he tell him the plan of the forthcoming campaign. For some time the Prince only smiled at the repeated questions, but at last he seemed to have made up his mind to break the silence. With a mysterious air he led his tormentor into a room apart, and whispered into his ear: "My good sir, you want to know my plan for the next campaign?" "I should like nothing better in all the world!" was the eager reply. "But I must first ask you one question," rejoined the Prince—"can you hold your tongue?" "I can be as silent as the grave!" "That is just as it should be, I am delighted to hear it! Now listen to me: I also can hold my tongue, and therefore I prefer to keep my secret to myself!"

In conclusion, we will listen to those who say: "You are quite right; I am aware that I ought not to talk about my neighbor's faults. But though I determine never to do so, I fall into the same fault over and over again." This is not an idle excuse, but the candid confession of a humble heart. Make it your own, my dear child. However often you fail, never grow weary of renewing your resolution not to utter one single uncharitable word about your neighbor. And if sometimes you do speak unkindly, do not excuse yourself by saying there is no great harm in it, but rather remember the lines:

> The wise man will seek his own faults to amend;
> The fool to his neighbor's alone will attend

XLIV. Calumny and Contempt

My dear child, you can scarcely conceive, much less form a just idea of the bitter pain, the amount of anguish expressed in the words: *to be calumniated and held in contempt.*

---

[1] Prince Eugene of Savoy (1663–1736) was one of the most successful military commanders in modern European history.

You have as yet had nothing, or at least very little, to suffer from calumny and neglect. But what has not happened heretofore may happen at a subsequent period; hence it is well that you should be prepared to meet it, and should know what your duty would be under such circumstances.

In earlier days a singular custom prevailed in certain districts of Germany. Persons who had an evil tongue were compelled, as their punishment, to carry, suspended round their neck, a stone representing a human head. This stone was termed the clapper-stone, and such a one is still to be seen in Muehlhausen, one of the towns of Alsace. It bears the following inscription:

> Why they call me *clapper* I cannot tell,
> But the evil-speakers know me full well;
> Who does not respect his neighbor's renown,
> Perforce must carry me all through the town.

It is to be wished that stones could be hung around the necks of all who slander us and speak evil of us! But there is a better, a more effectual method of silencing evil tongues. It consists in the observance of Our Lord's command: "*Thou shalt love thy neighbor as thyself.*" We ought to conduct ourselves, in regard to those who are our enemies—those who slander us—in such a manner as is consistent with loving our neighbor.

If you are slandered—that is, if sins and misdeeds which you have never committed are laid to your charge—it is permissible to defend yourself; but you must do this with calmness and deliberation, after the example of Jesus. He, the divine Redeemer, said to the Pharisees: "*Which of you shall convince Me of sin?*" And when they hurled at Him a most horrible and unjust reproach: "*Do we not say well that Thou hast a devil?*" He defended Himself with all possible calmness and brevity: "*I have not a devil; but I honor My Father, and you have dishonored Me.*" In similar cases imitate this example;

remember that your assertion of innocence will be all the more readily believed the calmer and more self-possessed you remain.

But what are you to do if your explanation to not listened to, or if you are not allowed to defend yourself? You must stifle all desire for revenge, and bear the injustice with patience, again following the example of Jesus. St. Peter exhorts us to act in this manner, when he writes: "*That you should follow His steps: Who did no sin, neither was guile found in His mouth. Who when He was reviled did not revile: when He suffered, He threatened not; but delivered Himself to him that judged Him unjustly.*" When Jesus Christ, the Holiest of the holy, allowed Himself to be abused and slandered, to be falsely accused of stirring up the people, to be led forth to die a death of shame upon the cross—what right have poor sinners like ourselves to lament and complain, to revile those who speak of us in terms which are the reverse of laudatory? Why should we heed the foolish chatter of the world when Our Master and Lord so completely despised it? Even the heathen sages of old considered it a mark of perfection to despise the world, and when men praised them they mistrusted their praise. When Phocian, the famous Greek orator, was loudly applauded on account of a speech which he had delivered, he is said to have exclaimed: "Tell me honestly, what stupid things have I said?"

Above all, lay well to heart that, however good and pious you may be, you will sometimes be spoken against, and have to bear the wounds inflicted by evil tongues. Calumny has been the means of casting some of the most virtuous of men into prison; men whose only crime was that they were superior to their fellows; for the best and noblest are ever the most persecuted. As the magnet attracts iron so does virtue draw forth the hatred of the wicked. Remember these lines:

> If evil slander's tongue unkind
> Perchance disturb thy peace of mind—
> Courage! console thee with the thought,
> No rotten fruits by wasps are sought.

But whatever you do, do not take it into your head to try to please everybody. Almighty God Himself cannot please all. And do not expect too much gratitude in return for the benefits you confer upon your fellow creatures. Those to whom we have shown the greatest kindness often turn against us most fiercely. Socrates, the heathen sage, had found this out. Upon one occasion, when he had received and read an abusive letter, he asked: "When did I confer a benefit upon this man?"

Yet why should we speak of the ancient heathen? Let us look once again at Our Lord and Master, Jesus Christ: How He was slandered and blasphemed, declared to be a Samaritan, possessed by the devil, and addicted to various vices! In like manner were the apostles slandered, the holy martyrs, as were St. Francis of Sales and St. Ignatius Loyola; so were, in a word, all who *"lived godly in Christ Jesus."*[1] Can we compare ourselves, in even the remotest degree, with these holy persons? And if we have not committed the sins of which we are accused, must we not own that we have only too richly deserved to be blamed in other respects?

If the evil which is said of us is true, we must make every effort to amend. Such is the advice St. Peter gives us: *"Having your conversation good among the Gentiles: that whereas they speak against you as evil-doers, they may, by the good works which they shall behold in you, glorify God."* A wise man of olden days expressed himself after a similar fashion. When his disciples told him that something very bad had been said about him he replied: "Never mind; I will live in such a

---

[1] 2 Timothy 3:12 *"And all that will live godly in Christ Jesus, shall suffer persecution."*

manner as to prevent people from believing the evil which my enemies impute to me."

Therefore, the principal thing is to guard as far as possible against the fault which is imputed to us. In this way the slanders uttered against us will have the good effect of conducing to our improvement and perfection. And if the self-love innate in all men did not blind their eyes to so great an extent, they would clearly perceive that what appears to them as calumny is, at least in the majority of instances, not really such, but that they actually possess the faults which are laid to their charge.

I will give you one more piece of advice. See that you do not make mountains out of molehills! Do not allow the gossip which is circulating about you to disturb your serenity; do not be angry and annoyed by the chatter of evil tongues. On the contrary, the calmer you remain, the less you permit it to be observed that you know anything about this idle talk, the sooner will the evil-speakers be silenced.

Yet another word! If you ever receive an *anonymous* letter throw it at once, unread, into the fire. Make it an invariable rule never, under any circumstances, to read a letter to which the writer has not signed his name. In such cases never indulge your curiosity; by so refraining you will spare yourself much worry, pain and vexation, and defeat the malicious purpose and diabolical pleasure of evil-minded schemers.

Remember the words of the pious author of the *Imitation*: "Take it not to heart if some people think ill of thee, and say of thee what thou art not willing to hear. He who neither seeketh eagerly to please, nor feareth to displease, shall enjoy much peace."

XLV. SINS COMMITTED BY HEARING

You know why marshy neighborhoods and large manufacturing towns are so unhealthy. The atmosphere is tainted by the noxious exhalations, by the fumes and smoke. Something similar may be said in regard to the moral atmosphere of the countless localities in which it is the custom to talk about one's neighbors in a calumnious or uncharitable manner. He who abides there for a lengthened period gradually loses the health of his soul. Therefore it is necessary to quit this tainted air—namely, to refuse to listen to such conversation, and, as far as possible, to prevent it from being carried on. He who listens to it with pleasure falls into "the sin committed by hearing."

An old gentleman once gave a young and inexperienced man the following sage advice: "If you hear any one speak evil of another, whether justly or unjustly, say to yourself: Am I that man's judge? You know the misdeeds which, through his frailty, he has committed and you even try to find them out. How is it that you know nothing of his good deeds, of actions which are creditable to him? I know that I have deserved hell for my transgressions, and my own sins are quite enough for me without troubling myself about those of other persons."

Truly does it behoove us to follow the counsel of this good old man, and oppose every kind of lying and evil-speaking. We shall not find it so difficult to do this; if only we have a good will and a spirit of charity we shall be assisted by divine grace. If we have a real love of our neighbor, we shall imitate the crafty fox, whose cunning always enables him somehow to devise a means of protecting his young when the hounds approach his lair. In order to protect your neighbor, you must place yourself in opposition to those—be they many or few—who slander him. But you will perhaps ask: "How am I to do this? I cannot venture thus to put myself forward and offend persons whom I am bound to treat in a polite and friendly fashion." Hear how St. Chrysostom would reply to you: "A poor excuse! It brings about the damnation of many Christians. You are bound to show friendship and politeness to these slanderers? Well then, can you show them a greater kindness than by making them conscious of their sin, and exhorting them to do better in future?" Job was attached to his friends, but he knew that composedly to listen to their defamatory conversation would be wrong on his part, and therefore he rebuked them.

St. Augustine had an equal horror of slander; so great indeed was his aversion to it that he caused this inscription to be placed above his dinner table: "There is no room at this table for those who intend to speak evil of their neighbors." Upon one occasion certain guests forgot to observe this rule of the house, and began to discuss some absent persons in too free a manner. The saint promptly remarked: "Either this inscription must be taken down, or else you must put an end to such conversation; if you do not heed my admonition I shall have to leave the room!"

St. John, patriarch of Alexandria, was of the same opinion. When he heard any one indulging in evil-speaking he gently admonished him, or else he turned the conversation into a different channel. If the person thus warned persisted in talking in the same objectionable manner he remained silent, but wrote down the name of the individual. As soon as he had taken his departure St. John would give orders that the evil-speaker was never again to be allowed to enter the house.

A word of serious reproof from the mouth of a child, or of a young girl, not unfrequently puts a stop to conversation of a defamatory character.

I found this out for myself before I was ten years old. I heard a neighbor abusing our parish priest, who was much beloved and universally esteemed. I coolly reproved the old woman, telling her how wrong it is to speak in that way of priests. She was quite confused at hearing such a remark from the mouth of a mere boy, and at once held her tongue.

There are, of course, circumstances in which Christian prudence forbids us to rebuke the slanderer, and it may be equally impossible to leave the company. In such cases the best plan is skilfully to endeavor to direct the conversation into another channel. The individual aimed at will probably notice the attempt, and not feel very well pleased; but this cannot be helped. If he thinks over the matter afterward he will, if he has any sense, see that he only got what he deserved, and will guard his tongue better in the future. Often a significant silence may be observed, in accordance with the exhortation of Scripture: "*The north wind driveth away rain, as doth a sad countenance a backbiting tongue.*"

Sometimes when we wish to break off the thread of an uncharitable conversation nothing suitable to our purpose may occur to our mind. Yet it is not necessary to break it off very cleverly; if the interruption serves to divert the attention of those present from their neighbor's faults, that is quite enough.

The blessed Thomas More, Lord Chancellor of England, possessed this art in an eminent degree. When any one began to talk in an uncharitable manner in his presence he used to introduce an entirely different subject. For instance, he would say: "Have you seen the mansion which has lately been erected? Whatever your opinion may be, I think it is admirably planned, and the interior arrangements are extremely comfortable. The designer and builder must certainly be a master in his profession." In this way he prevented a great deal of unkind talk.

Another excellent plan is to mention some good quality of the person who is being blamed. Even the very worst man has a good point in his character. Among all created beings there is only one which lacks every desirable trait, and that is the devil, an embodiment of all evil. Endeavor to place the conduct of your neighbor in the most favorable light by saying that perhaps he had no bad intention in what he did, or that he had done a great deal of good in another way, etc. If you cannot avoid listening to uncharitable conversation, you must at any rate suppress any feeling of pleasure which may arise in your heart. And you must be even more careful not to show any outward sign of taking pleasure in it. Bear in mind that all those who give rise to, or encourage, evil-speaking, by asking curious questions, or evincing approval of it, are in part responsible for it, and become partakers in the sin of others. St. Bernard says that the devil sits upon the tongue of him who loves to speak against his neighbor, and in the ear of him who likes to listen to such conversation.

Would that you could behold the abode of suffering where souls are purified from the sins which as yet they have not expiated! Doubtless you would perceive that souls are, for the most part, detained there on account of sins of the tongue and of the ear for which they had not atoned. May the thought of purgatory aid you to avoid these sins.

> Hate what is evil and do what is right;
> Avoid all deceit and keep honor bright;
> Love what is good and seek what is best,
> Honest and truthful: thy life shall be blest.

XLVI. A SMALL, BUT DANGEROUS MEMBER

WOMEN are often sadly offended when it is said of them that they are very fond of talking. But they have no reason for being so sensitive in this respect. A glib tongue, which characterizes women to a greater extent than men, is a natural gift, which God has graciously seen fit to bestow upon the daughters of Eve. This fluency of speech has its good and agreeable side. It is evident that the Creator desired to place, as it were, a weapon of defence in the hands of the weaker sex. Their readiness of speech enables women to keep conversation going, and thus to brighten, to cheer, and to enhance the family circle, and this cannot but be a real, practical benefit.

But the gift of speech, like every other gift of God, can be abused and put to an evil use; too often this is the case. Hence precautions must be taken to prevent such profanation, such misuse; we must be watchful and take care lest the little school-girl should already deserve to be called a chatterbox and later on develop an evil, backbiting tongue. My dear child, I by no means wish to condemn you to silence, but I do wish most earnestly to exhort you to govern your tongue. You already know that the tongue is a small, but dangerous member.

First of all I must once more speak of the invaluable gift of speech, a most precious gift of God to man. The gift of speech places an immeasurable distance between man and the lower animals. It is not exactly because they lack the organs of speech that they have not power to speak, but because they do not possess a soul endowed with reason and capable of using these organs. We may employ the comparison of a musical instrument—let us say a guitar. It may have the necessary strings, it may even be tuned aright, yet will it either remain mute, or emit discordant notes, unless a skilful hand touches the strings.

How deeply grateful ought we to be to God for this precious gift of speech, which is the key to so many benefits and pleasures!

Yet instead of the gratitude which is His due, how often is God repaid for His gift with the blackest ingratitude! How frequently and how shamefully is this gift misused! It is misused for purposes of lying, dissimulation, hypocrisy, flattery, detraction, calumny, uncharitable conversation of every kind. It causes enmity and hatred, strife and contention. A single word from a tongue under the influence of a wicked heart may bring about the most grievous misfortunes! The diabolical work of evil tongues will often seriously disturb, if not totally destroy, union in families, affection between married couples, concord among relations and friends, peace in communities.

Therefore is the tongue rightly described as a small, but dangerous member. Thus did St. James term it when he wrote to the faithful: "*The tongue is indeed a little member, and boasteth great things. Behold how small a fire kindleth a great wood. And the tongue is a fire, a world of iniquity.*" These are hard words, but we find them in Holy Scripture; they cannot, therefore, be exaggerated. And in our daily experience we find only too many instances to prove that such expressions are neither unfounded nor extreme.

Nor can we wonder that even in the Old Testament the Holy Spirit so strictly enjoins upon men the government of the tongue, prudence in speech, the observance of silence. Solomon says in the book of Proverbs: "*In the multitude of words there shall not want sin, but he that refraineth his lip is most wise.*" And again: "*He that keepeth his mouth, and his tongue, keepeth his soul from distress.*"

St. James also says: "*If any man offend not in word, the same is a perfect man.*" In another place he exhorts us thus: "*Let every man be swift to hear, but slow to speak, and slow to anger.*" He wishes to direct the attention of all who desire to lead a pious life to the first and most essential condition of true piety, the government of the tongue. He does this in the following words: "*If any man think himself to be religious, not bridling his tongue, but deceiving his own heart, this man's religion is vain.*"

And mark well, my dear child, the great disadvantages which much talking brings in its train. A young girl who, when in the company of others, oversteps the limits which modesty prescribes, and chatters, chatters, scarcely allowing those present to put in a word, soon becomes a bore; even more tiresome still than another girl who can hardly be induced to speak at all. A girl who is too talkative will not easily gain the confidence of her friends and fellow men, because they are perfectly aware that it would not be safe to trust her with anything of importance.

A girl who is overfond of talking often disturbs her own peace of mind; her heedless words frequently cause her to feel discontented both with herself and with others. And how much valuable time is lost through this never-ending gossip—time which ought to be spent in work, or else in prayer! And amid all this constant chatter and distraction how can the improvement of the heart, and the cultivation of the mind, be duly considered!

If the words of Our Lord are true, and true they must be, since He uttered them: "*I say to you, that every idle word that men shall speak they shall render an account for it in the day of judgment,*" what shall be the fate of those who speak so many words which are not only idle, but sinful and uncharitable?

Consequently you would do well to follow the advice which a prudent director gave to a certain young man. The latter had asked permission to wear an instrument of penance round his waist in order to mortify himself. The experienced priest made the sign of the cross upon his mouth, and said: "My friend, the best instrument of penance for you is to take care that no reprehensible word may pass the threshold of your lips." Practice yourself now and then in keeping silence; check an immoderate love of talking; check it sometimes in regard to conversation which is merely indifferent, not actually sinful; in order that by so doing you may acquire greater mastery over your tongue, where weighty matters are concerned.

> You say you have two ears and one mouth;
> There is surely no cause to complain.
> That you may hear much and little may say,
> You are given one mouth and ears twain.

Petitions of St. Augustine

Oh Lord Jesus, let me know myself,
let me know Thee,
And desire nothing else but Thee.
Let me hate myself and love Thee,
And do all things for the sake of Thee.
Let me humble myself, and exalt Thee,
And think of nothing but only of Thee.
Let me die to myself, and live in Thee,
And take whatever happens as coming from Thee.
Let me forsake myself and walk after Thee,
And ever desire to follow Thee.
Let me flee from myself, and turn to Thee,
That so I may merit to be defended by Thee.
Let me fear for myself, let me fear Thee,
And be amongst those who are chosen by Thee.
Let me distrust myself, and trust in Thee,
And ever obey for the love of Thee.
Let me cleave to nothing but only to Thee,
And ever be poor for the sake of Thee.
Look upon me, that I may love Thee;
Call me, that I may see Thee,
And forever possess Thee. Amen.

Mary, Mother of Jesus the Good Shepherd,
pray for us that we may hear His voice,
love Him and follow Him.

Roses of youth with years fade away,
  Bright eyes grow dim,
    bright locks grow gray;
But there's a flower that will not fade,
A gentle flower, that loves the shade—
The graceful lily, pure and sweet,
Of innocence an emblem meet;
This be thy choice in youth's bright day:
Its charms will never pass away!

Part Second

A Wreath of Lilies

III. Centaurium minus flore albo.   I. Lilium cruentum polyanthos   II. Centaurium minus flore rubro.

‹ 1 ›

The Lily in Untarnished Splendor

XLVII. How Beautiful Is the Chaste Generation!

In the course of my instructions I have already mentioned several virtues which you ought specially to practise. There is, however, one upon which I have hitherto only occasionally touched without speaking of it in detail. And yet this virtue is the most necessary and important for you, the virtue belonging to youth, and to the young girl more particularly; a virtue without which you would indeed be a virgin no longer; a virtue to which other virtues, such as modesty, obedience, piety, serve as an escort to safeguard and protect it; a virtue which is absolutely indispensable to your temporal and eternal happiness. And what is this virtue? What is this fairest of all the flowers with which you are to adorn yourself? I am sure that your pious heart already knows full well that it is the lily of chastity.

Although I have given you many fatherly counsels and instructions, I should feel that as yet I had done but very little toward promoting your temporal and eternal happiness were I not to urge you, with all the power and earnestness which the heart of a dutiful priest is capable of feeling, to love and practise this angelic virtue; were I not to warn you, in the most forcible terms I can possibly employ, against the opposite vice; were I not to teach you how to recognize the enemies of this virtue, and tell you what weapons you must use in fighting against them.

Chastity is the lily, the pearl of virtues, the most precious of all, the most pleasing to God. It is called the angelic virtue, because it raises man almost to a level with the angels. This virtue enables man to avoid all impure, carnal, forbidden pleasures, to rise superior to temptation, to remain chaste in thoughts, words, and actions. And how utterly indispensable this virtue is for a maiden! St. Francis of Sales writes upon this subject: "Young women ought to guard their chastity with special care, to banish from their minds all reprehensible thoughts, and repel with contempt all impure desires."

And how great is the charm which innocence lends to a child, to a young girl! So magical is this charm that it often inspires even bad men and libertines with awe and veneration. For example, we find the poet Heine, whose own morals were not of the purest, writing these touching lines about an innocent child:

> How like a flower of the field,
>   Pure, fair, and sweet thou art;
> I gaze on thee, and while I gaze
>   A sigh escapes my heart.
>
> Methinks upon thy youthful head,
>   My hands I ought to lay;
> To keep thee sweet and fair and pure,
>   My God I ought to pray.

We can clearly perceive the great value which chastity possesses in the eyes of God. He has most plainly shown this in various ways. *"And the Word was made flesh and dwelt among us."* In order to atone for our sins, the Son of God subjected Himself to all human miseries; to hunger and thirst, to cold and heat, to watching and weariness. But He did not choose to come into the world in the same manner as other men: no—He did this in a manner contrary to the natural laws, by a miracle of His omnipotence: He was conceived by the Holy Ghost and born of Mary, the purest of virgins. How great was her love for virginal purity! The Doctors of the Church teach us that she was ready to decline the exalted dignity of becoming the Mother of God rather than relinquish the state of virginity.

While sojourning in the wilderness the Redeemer permitted the devil to tempt Him to ambition, to idolatry, but not to a sin against holy purity. He permitted the Jews to blaspheme and revile Him, but He did not allow them to impute to Him so much as the shadow of anything impure. Among His Apostles He tolerated one He knew would prove a traitor, but no unchaste person was to be found in the little band. Why did He do all this? In order to show us His intense abhorrence of the sin of impurity, and His great esteem for the pearl of virtues. Fire is opposed to water; therefore the flame sputters if only a few drops of moisture have fallen upon the wick of a taper. Likewise God, being purity itself, is opposed to what is impure. God loves the pure and detests the impure. He is the purest of spirits, and must therefore of necessity abhor the impure, who indulge their carnal appetites, their bestial lusts.

With whom is the chaste soul to be compared? Holy Scripture tells us that it can be compared with nothing upon earth. "What," asks St. Bernard, "is more precious than chastity, which makes an angel out of a man? A chaste man differs from an angel, not, indeed, in angelic virtue, but only in regard to the state of beatitude. The pure angels are more blessed, but chaste men are more valiant."

You, my dear child, who regard your body as the temple of the Holy Ghost, and desire to keep it pure, mark well what I am about to say. In the course of your life you may be sick and destitute and wretched, you may be despised and forsaken by men, but as long as you remain pure in soul you will never cease to be dear to God as are His holy angels. As the Saviour, whilst lying in the crib, took delight in listening to the songs of the celestial choirs, so will He not fail to listen to your petitions, for you will be an angel upon earth. Had He cared for wealth and earthly splendor, He would not have summoned poor, simple, unknown shepherds to His crib; He looks with favor upon the chaste heart adorned with angelic virtue.

The virtue of chastity has the most beneficial influence on one's whole being. A young girl who is really and truly chaste will be bright and happy, will enjoy peace of mind, will face difficulties with courage and perseverance, will pass with comparative ease through trials and sufferings. Chastity contributes not a little to the preservation of physical health, to a fresh and blooming exterior. Hence the lines:

> To keep thy soul as pure and white
> As lily thou shouldst seek;
> And then be sure that roses bright
> Will blossom on thy cheek.

If you desire to be beautiful in reality, not in appearance only, if you desire to be beautiful in the sight of God, not only before the eyes of men, be pure and chaste! If you desire to obtain everlasting happiness, immortal glory, I say again, be pure and chaste! If you desire to possess the love of God, of the saints, and of all good men, in time and throughout eternity, once more I repeat, be pure and chaste! Bear in mind the words of Holy Writ: "*How beautiful is the chaste generation with glory; for the memory of it is immortal; because it is known both with God and with men.*"

XLVIII. Blessed Are the Clean of Heart

Our Lord said to His disciples in the sermon on the mount: "*Blessed are the clean of heart, for they shall see God!*" How sweet is the solace which these words contain for the chaste maiden!

Many persons undertake journeys to distant lands, to famous spots, in order to see wonderful things. We, also, are wanderers; we are traveling along the steep and stony road of our life on earth. Our body is like luggage; we hasten on our way, our heart beats quickly, and each throb of our pulse brings us a step nearer eternity. And if this life, this journey to eternity, often appears tedious, it is for the most part because we have bad weather—I mean, because we meet with crosses and sufferings.

Whither are we going, for what are we seeking? We are striving to reach the heavenly Jerusalem—we are desirous to behold our God and Father. When we are permitted to gaze upon Him all will be well with us; care and sorrow will vanish, and we will be happy forevermore! But whose is the blessed privilege, not only to gain an entrance into heaven, but also to possess the right of citizenship, of eternal citizenship in heaven? "*Blessed are the clean of heart, for they shall see God.*"

Every Christian yearns to enter heaven. Men meet with many trials in the course of their life; God strews them like thorns along their path that their hearts may not cling to the earth, that they may not take delight in the tinsel of this world, but may seek for the true gold, for eternal happiness.

If, at a later stage of your journey through life, you meet with gloomy and inclement weather, if you long more ardently than ever for the perpetual sunshine of heaven, then open your guide book, which is your conscience, and if on not one of its pages is there recorded a sin against chastity I shall indeed rejoice in union with your guardian angel, for then will you be truly "blessed." *"Blessed are the clean of heart."*

As St. Gregory the Pope remarks, chastity by itself is not sufficient to open heaven for us. You would resemble the foolish virgins who had no oil in their lamps, and on this account were excluded from the marriage feast, if you were to observe only the sixth and ninth commandments, and violate some other commandment in an important matter; for in that case you would have no true love of God, without which no one can enter heaven. But note well the reason why *"many are called, but few chosen."* It is because so few preserve chastity according to their state of life.

A maiden who really preserves her chastity out of love to God usually keeps the other commandments. If she conquers in the difficult struggle—and in the case of many persons no struggle is more difficult than that which must be waged if chastity is to be preserved—she will not give way in less difficult encounters with the enemies of her salvation. She would be foolish indeed who, after succeeding in doing what was difficult, should fail in regard to what was comparatively easy.

O chastity, how sweet a solace thou art for all men, and for young girls more especially! *"The clean of heart shall see God!"* Must not the heart of a maiden be filled with rapture if she is conscious of spotless chastity both of soul and body? Take courage, therefore; it is after all not so very difficult to get to heaven. Tend with the utmost care the lily of chastity; for this is the token whereby God recognizes His children.

Though you are very far from being a saint, a heroine in regard to virtue, yet you perform a large number of good works every month, perhaps even every day. Doubtless you often pray, hear Mass, attend divine service, examine your conscience, confess your faults with sincere contrition, receive the body of the Lord with love and devotion, perform your daily tasks with a good intention, undertake one or other pious practice in honor of the Mother of God, etc., etc. God rewards even a cup of cold water given to a thirsty man out of love for Him; will He not therefore reward all these good works if done for love of Him? Most assuredly He will; He will give you an eternal reward in heaven, if you persevere in the grace of God and bear in your hand the lily of purity.

An ancient heathen legend relates that Hermione, the beautiful Persian princess, wore in her hair a magnificent opal of priceless value. This brilliant jewel possessed, however, a very peculiar property. A single drop of water fell upon it and dissolved it, with fatal consequences to the wearer.

Now look, my daughter; this flower of paradise, the lily of chastity, is just as beautiful, just as precious as that opal, and no less delicate and easily injured. This virtue is indeed a sublime moral force which enables the poor human heart to rise superior to its own frailties, and unite itself to God, the God of infinite purity. Hence it is said, *"Blessed are the clean of heart, for they shall see God."*

Yes, it may be said that even on earth the chaste soul enjoys a foretaste of eternal felicity. The chaste soul is in itself a paradise, a garden of delight, wherein the Holy Ghost takes pleasure; a throne of the Divinity, whence flow graces and blessings to enrich the period of its existence here below, during which it is united in sweet harmony with a body no less pure and chaste than itself.

Now tell me, Christian maiden, is it not worth sacrificing everything, surrendering everything, for the sake of this virtue, the lily of chastity, which will admit us to the beatific vision of God? Ought we to shrink from any exertion, from any struggle which it may cost us to preserve it? And ought we not every day, and many times a day, to invoke the Mother and patroness of chastity, saying to her: "O Mary, obtain for me this fair virtue. Enable me to preserve my chastity. On account of thy spotless purity thou wast exalted above the choirs of angels to a glorious throne in heaven. Help me to be clean of heart, in order that hereafter I may be privileged to enjoy the beatific vision of God forever and ever."

> Look down upon us from above,
> Mother of mercy and fair love;
> Until, bright Queen of heaven, we see
> Thy face to all eternity.

XLIX. Fight and Conquer

WHILST the holy martyr St. Perpetua was languishing in a dark dungeon she saw the following vision: She beheld a golden ladder which reached from earth to heaven. This ladder was very narrow. On each side were ranged swords, lances, knives, and sharp points of iron. At the foot of the ladder an ungainly monster kept guard to prevent any one from approaching. This vision was meant to show her that she would have to endure suffering and martyrdom for the faith.

Every maiden who is desirous of preserving her chastity intact may apply this vision to herself. For chastity is a golden ladder which reaches to heaven, but on the right hand and on the left are sharp instruments—namely, enemies, dangers and temptations proceeding from men and from her own fallen nature.

St. Paul tells us that "*all that will live godly in Christ Jesus shall suffer persecution.*" These words are particularly true in regard to chastity. The chaste maiden must be diligent in prayer, since otherwise it is impossible for her to remain pure. She must frequently approach the sacraments; she must avoid occasions of sin; she must keep her eyes, ears and tongue under due control; she must conquer herself in a thousand ways. She must no more mix with worldly-minded persons, or partake of their spirit, than Noe did with his contemporaries, or Lot with the inhabitants of Sodom.

In Rome, the chief city of Christendom, even down to the present day a room may be seen, the contents of which are of a very peculiar description. Within its walls are preserved blood-stained swords and spears with which the holy martyrs of former days were pierced: iron helmets, which were heated, then placed upon their heads; pincers, nails and darts with which they were tortured; gridirons on which they were broiled, and racks on which they were extended. Was not the battle which the martyrs so courageously fought a very painful and difficult one? But heaven is worth the price they paid for it.

In the last great day, when all the members of the human race will be gathered together, we shall behold these martyrs. What answer could we make to them, were they to address us in some such words as these: "See what tortures we endured for the faith, while you were so cowardly and pusillanimous as to shrink from the easier and painless means you had to employ to preserve your chastity!"

Let us then take courage! God does indeed require that we should undergo a martyrdom, but one of a much milder description; we have to struggle in defence of chastity. Fight and conquer! A glorious palm is promised as the reward of chastity. Do not grow weary of the endeavor to suppress evil thoughts and desires. "Just as often as you resist," St. Antony tells us for our consolation, "so often will you be crowned." If you strive to banish temptations to impurity as soon as you become aware of them, you are in nowise to blame, because they are involuntary, and if you conquer them you increase your merit.

Only fight bravely on; these unruly passions will not trouble you forever. After the conflict there will come a day of peace and victory, a day of bright, of never-ending peace and rest. If you preserve your body as a temple of the Holy Ghost it will be glorified.

What a feeling of horror, of self-loathing, must seize upon the fallen maiden when she finds herself in the presence of the relics of some saint. My body, she could not but reflect, ought to be a temple fit for the indwelling of the Deity, as was the body of this saint. It also was hallowed and sanctified by the sacraments, and was sprinkled with the precious blood of the Saviour! But now see the havoc and devastation! What joy on the contrary, what sweet consolation, must fill the heart of a girl who fully deserves the title of virgin! The body of St. Francis Xavier, who was a most ardent lover of chastity, was miraculously preserved from corruption for a long space of time. God has worked the same wonder in the case of many other saints. This reflection abounds in comfort for every chaste heart. By means of these miracles God designs to show that, even though the human frame does moulder in the grave, He has power to raise it up, and to clothe it with such brightness and glory as to make it shine like a star in the firmament.

Am I to speak only of maidens who are fortunate enough to come victorious out of the battle, and to preserve their innocence without a single stain? Are there in the world no girls to be found who have been vanquished in the hard strife, who have lost their most precious treasure, the lily of chastity? Must they on this account give everything up for lost? If I were to think that you might possibly be overtaken by this terrible misfortune should I then altogether despair about you?

Most assuredly not! It is indeed true that when the robe of innocence has once been torn there will always remain a certain blemish. The woman who has fallen may become a penitent, but after the sincerest and most complete amendment, and the severest penance, she must always bear about with her the identical body, the same soul which have made shipwreck of their innocence, and have been for a time a temple of idols, the abode of the spirit of evil.

Yet even after so grievous a fall there is some consolation left. If you should ever find yourself in this sad case (which may God forbid!) do not give way to despair! If at such moments you feel utterly wretched and cast down, if you remember with sadness the happy day of your first communion, and the innocent pleasures of your childhood, if you are filled with an intense longing for the peaceful security of the time you spent at school, I have a word of comfort for you. Your case is then like that of a soldier who upon one occasion ran away from the enemy. If you now retrace your steps, and fight bravely, you may perhaps be more pleasing to God than those who have never taken to flight because they have never been called upon to engage in severe warfare, nor have had to resist any special temptations.

Be always open and candid when you go to confession; in spite of repeated defeats never give up to the enemy; herein lies the secret of final victory. Persevere whatever may be your circumstances, persevere in the combat for the lily of innocence; then will these words be fulfilled in your case:

> Victory we will win
> Fighting against sin;
> Suffering and pain
> Heaven's bliss will gain.

L. Take Courage!

In my last instruction I exhorted you to "fight and conquer." My watchword to-day is: Take courage! I have attempted to portray the difficult nature of the struggle which must be carried on if chastity is to be preserved; and to describe how terrible a thing it is when a young girl who has hitherto been pious and virtuous falls into the snares of the evil one and is ruined. When you think of your own future, your heart is doubtless filled with dread and anxiety. Let not this dread and anxiety lead you to discouragement, or to despair. Take courage! I say for your consolation only: Take courage! For if, even after living in sin for years, it is quite possible to be truly converted, how much less difficult it is to preserve oneself from leading such a life, and to keep the robe of innocence pure and unstained!

About 400 years after Christ there lived a girl in one of the great cities of Egypt (a virgin I cannot call her, for she was a notorious sinner). Driven by an unclean spirit, she left her parents when she was only twelve years old, so as to be able to give free rein to her passions. For seventeen years she carried on her life of sin without the vengeance of Heaven falling upon her; for seventeen long years she lived in such a manner that when upon one occasion a stranger asked her who she was, she replied: "If I were to tell you the story of my life you would be filled with such loathing that you would fly from me as from a serpent." If any one had told this poor miserable sinner, in the midst of her evil life, that when she had reached the age of twenty-nine she would begin to lead the life of an angel, while yet in the same body which had been so stained and polluted by sin, and that for forty-seven years she would continue to lead this life; that she would shed floods of tears, doing ceaseless penance, mortifying herself in every way, allowing herself no pleasure or indulgence, but enduring this martyrdom for forty-seven years—if, I say, any one had told her this beforehand she would, no doubt, have laughed aloud, and imagined that a sorry jest was being made at her expense!

Yet that which appeared impossible actually took place. The notorious sinner became the renowned and holy penitent St. Mary of Egypt. Seventeen years she had been the slave of sin; but at length, touched by divine grace and aided by the

Mother of God, she was converted. From that time forth she led a life of angelic purity. After doing penance for forty-seven years in a remote and desolate wilderness she passed at length into the presence of Him who has said: "*I desire not the death of the wicked, but that the wicked turn from his way, and live.*"

Well then, my dear young friend, if it was possible for this penitent, with the help of God's grace, to burst the strong iron bonds of the worst imaginable habits, and to lead a pure life, how much easier is it for you to preserve the precious treasure of chastity, which as yet you have never lost! This is indeed a most consoling thought.

"*With God all things are possible,*" and "*I can do all things in Him who strengtheneth me.*" God gives no commands which man cannot keep. Look in winter at the dry branches of the trees. If you had not been taught by experience, you would never believe that from the boughs—which to all appearance are dead—there would spring, not a few leaves only, but hundreds of beautiful blossoms and succulent fruits. Yet so it is when the life-giving breath of spring blows over the earth. Far greater are the wonders worked by the breath of divine grace, which enlightens the understanding and inclines the will to do what is right.

Therefore never think or say, "The tendency to evil is so strong in me I am compelled to yield to it; I cannot do otherwise!" How deeply must such language grieve the fatherly heart of God, how false is the idea which it conveys in regard to Him! It is an article of faith that God desires the salvation of all men. "*It is not the will of your Father, who is in heaven, that one of these little ones should perish.*" Such are the consoling words which proceeded from the mouth of the Son of God Himself, and of all the millions of human beings inhabiting the earth there is not one who cannot say to himself that God desires his salvation more earnestly than the tenderest mother could.

Take courage! God means what He says. When a huntsman climbs one rocky peak after another, being daunted neither by thorny thickets nor yawning precipices, nobody can deny that he is in earnest, that he does really wish to capture the game he is pursuing. And who can doubt that Almighty God does seriously desire our salvation? The man who could thus think could surely never have seen the picture of an *Ecce Homo*, or gazed upon a crucifix. From the crown of His sacred head to the soles of His feet this Man of sorrows, our Redeemer, is covered with blood. Each one of His wounds cries to us with a loud voice: "O child of man, whoever thou mayest be, see how terribly in earnest thy God was in His desire to help and save thee, else would He not have done so much for thee." He gives us grace sufficient to overcome temptation; as St. Paul says: "*God is faithful, who will not suffer you to be tempted above that which you are able, but will make also with temptation issue, that you may be able to bear it.*"

Some persons assert that it is too difficult to keep the commandments, and especially to preserve chastity. To this St. Chrysostom replies as follows: "The commands of God are not difficult in themselves; they appear difficult only because of the indolence and cowardice of man." Slothful sinners say that it is difficult to avoid occasions of sin. Is it not very wearisome to lie for weeks and months in bed, in compliance with the order of a physician? Yet this is done to recover health. It is a veritable martyrdom to submit to a painful operation, yet it is undergone that life may be prolonged. And in the time of an epidemic one has to remain in seclusion to avoid contagion; though this is irksome, it is gladly done. How far more willing ought we to be to make a sacrifice in order to escape eternal death!

Therefore take courage, my dear child! However great may be the temptation, however difficult it may sometimes appear to you to avoid this or that occasion of sin—nay, though sometimes it may seem utterly impossible—though at a later period of your life you may be so unhappy as to yield to temptation, and incur disgrace, misery and want, never give way to despair, never cease to believe in the grace and mercy of God.

> If fierce temptation's waves beat high
> And threatening clouds obscure the sky,
> Let not thy sinking heart despair,
> But raise thy voice to God in prayer.
>
> Fear not lest, thus tempest-tost,
> Thou should'st be forever lost;
> God thy helper sure will be,
> Will part the clouds and calm the sea.

Prayer to St. Aloysius

O Blessed Aloysius! adorned with Angelic graces, I, thy most unworthy servant, recommend especially to thee the chastity of my soul and body, praying thee, by thy angelic purity, to plead for me with Jesus Christ the Immaculate Lamb, and His most holy Mother, Virgin of virgins, that they would vouchsafe to keep me from all grievous sin. O never let me be defiled with any stain of impurity; but when thou dost see me in temptation, or in danger of falling, then remove far from my heart all bad thoughts and unclean desires; and awaken in me the memory of eternity and of Jesus crucified. Impress deeply in my heart a sense of the holy fear of God, and thus kindling in me the fire of divine love, enable me so to follow thy footsteps here on earth, that in heaven with thee, I may be made worthy to enjoy the vision of our God forever. Amen.

Acanthus Spinosus.

‹ 2 ›

The Lily and her Enemies

LI. The Enemy in Our Own Heart

THE dangers which beset the lily of chastity are numerous and great. This is a thought upon which I have repeatedly dwelt; and it is calculated to fill even the most pious heart with fear and apprehension. What is the enemy most to be dreaded, the enemy which continually seeks to destroy the fair lily of innocence? This foe is not far from each one of us; it is to be found within; it dwells in our own heart. You are as yet chaste and pure; you regard sin with loathing and abhorrence; do not therefore be too much alarmed if I proceed to place before you the full extent of the peril to which you are exposed at the hands of this enemy. It was not without good reason that I exhorted you, in my last instruction, to take courage and have confidence in God. I shall indeed recur to this subject again and again, and point out to you what our holy religion teaches in this respect, for the consolation of all who have a good will.

    A blush of shame mantles the blooming cheek of every modest maiden if she hears even one unchaste word. We find that the ancient heathen entertained feelings of a similar kind; they sought to hide sin from the sight of their fellow men under cover of the darkness of night. They regarded the subjugation of sensual desires as something great, elevated, and meritorious. St. Jerome tells us that in olden days Roman emperors and statesmen treated maidens who had been faithful to their vow of chastity with outward marks of respect; while those who had broken their vow met with aversion and contempt, and were put to death. Not only was it engraved upon the tables of stone which God gave to Moses on Mount Sinai; it is also written on the pages of man's conscience: Thou shall not commit adultery or any impurity.

Is it not difficult to believe that, in spite of the voice of conscience, in spite of the unanimous conviction of every nation, this vice of impurity, thus universally held to be shameful and degrading, is yet indulged in so constantly? How is this fact to be reconciled with reason and conscience? St. Paul answers this question in the name of all mankind: *"I see another law in my members, fighting against the law of my mind, and captivating me in the law of sin, that is in my members. Unhappy man that I am, who shall deliver me from the body of this death? The grace of God, by Jesus Christ our Lord."*

By these words the Apostle intends us to understand that our reason—our higher self—recognizes sin, especially sins against chastity, as an evil, and regards them with abhorrence; that there is however within us a concupiscence—an inclination, a proneness to evil—which allures us, and that this tendency can be resisted and overcome through the grace of Jesus Christ. It is precisely this concupiscence, this proneness to evil, resulting from original sin, which constitutes the first and the most dangerous adversary of the lily of purity: *it is the enemy in our own heart.*

An impure thought often steals unperceived into the heart without its evil nature being recognized at once; sinful images are awakened; the imagination clothes them with form and color; sensual desires are stirred up; and the individual finds himself all at once in danger of losing God, of forfeiting heaven and eternal happiness.

Two great mistakes are made concerning this enemy in our own heart and the temptations it excites. Some persons have an exaggerated dread of evil thoughts, but most persons fear them too little. I will say a few words on both points.

For instance, if you were merely to say in confession that you have unchaste thoughts every day the priest would not be in the least able to form an opinion as to the sinfulness of these thoughts. In the midst of all these evil thoughts and imaginings your soul may be as white and pure and stainless as a fair lily, as pleasing to God as the soul of a child which has just been borne away from the baptismal font; the days and hours when you have had these evil thoughts may have been all noted down by your guardian angel, not indeed to terrify you and put you to shame when your life is drawing to a close, but, on the contrary, that he may be able to say to you: "Behold, O chaste soul, for each one of these hours and moments you shall receive a bright and unfading crown of victory."

An evil thought which is involuntary is not a sin; it is only a temptation, and affords us an opportunity to fight and conquer, to gain merit for eternity.

St. Augustine compares evil thoughts to the first sin in paradise, in which these three took part, *viz.*, the serpent, Eve and Adam. The serpent suggested to the mind of Eve the idea of breaking the command of God; Eve took pleasure in the thought, and advised Adam to carry it into action; Adam followed her advice and sinned.

The first beginning of an evil thought may be compared to the suggestions of the serpent. Eve represents the lower nature, which takes delight in the contemplation of sin; in the person of Adam we see the human will, which, agreeing to the proposal of Eve, completes the sinful act. If an impure thought enters our mind it is not a sin, so long as our free will definitely refuses its consent, and we take no pleasure in it.

There are, however, dark recesses in the heart of man. A man may not know himself, and on this account be unable to place his mental condition before his confessor in as clear a light as that in which the eye of God beholds him. Therefore remark that there are two ways in which our free will may give its consent:

1. In the first place we may sin through desire if we wish to have the opportunity of doing, seeing, or hearing that which is wrong; or we may sin in reference to the past if we reflect with satisfaction on sins into which we have fallen, and wish to commit them over again. These voluntary wishes and desires are grievous sins, as both faith and reason plainly tell us.
2. In the second place, the will may give its consent by merely finding pleasure in impure images and thoughts, even without any wish to commit sin. This conscious and voluntary satisfaction, this pleasure in scenes and ideas of such a nature is also a grievous sin.

From what I have just said you may gather an important practical lesson: Be ever on your guard against the enemy in your own heart, and, without distressing yourself too much about involuntary impure thoughts, ever be on your guard against them.

> What makes thy life on earth most fair?
> How can'st thou best for heaven prepare?
> Thy soul from sin's dark stain preserve,
> Seek God's approval to deserve.

LII. THE ENEMY IN HUMAN SHAPE

> Pure and innocent would'st thou remain,
> And keep thyself free from iniquitous stain,
> Men's society then must thou flee
> And find pleasure alone with thy God to be.

"To shun the society of men." This is a hard saying for beings created with social instincts; it is especially hard for those who are young, and who are enjoying life. Moreover did not God Himself say in paradise: "*It is not good for man to be alone; let us make him a help like unto himself.*" Most certainly it is not good for people in general, and especially for young girls, altogether to shun the society of their fellow creatures. Nor is this required of them, but only *often* or *sometimes* to shun the society of men. It therefore rests with you to know whose society you ought to shun, and under what circumstances this should be done. You must always take to flight when the enemy of your innocence, such a one as would steal your lily of purity, appears in human shape, or, to speak quite plainly, as soon as your chastity may possibly be endangered. I will mention only a few of the more important circumstances in which this may be necessary.

The most ordinary aspect in which the enemy of chastity appears in human shape is that of undesirable acquaintances. I shall take a future opportunity of speaking more at length upon this subject of "keeping company."

If you are able to spend many of the bright years of your youth under your parents' roof, give thanks to God for this great blessing. But even there you are not quite safe from the enemy in human shape. Workmen, lodgers, boarders, tradesmen's assistants, may present themselves and prove dangerous to your innocence. Young men of this class, attracted by your pleasant, obliging manner, begin to flatter you, to joke with you, at first in a way which is perfectly harmless; having gained your confidence, they try to see you alone, they take liberties with you, and if the enemy in your own heart is awake and active, if you do not avoid and fly from such dangerous companions, alas! alas! how soon is your innocence lost!

In cities and large towns girls are sometimes obliged to go to shops. In this case also be on your guard against the enemy in human shape. A clerk, or perhaps the proprietor of the shop, may look at you with lustful eyes. He will do everything he can to allure you; sometimes by offering goods at a price below their value, sometimes by attempting to give you presents, etc., etc. Never repeat your visit to a shop like this—never remain there longer than you can help—since before you are aware of it, your innocence may be undermined.

Perhaps later on you may be obliged to take a situation at a distance from home. It is possible that your employer may prove an enemy in human shape, and you may be exposed to undue familiarity on his part. Do not remain a moment in such a house; fly from it as you would do if it were on fire, even though you have to forfeit your wages. It is a thousand times better to lose your money than to part with your innocence.

The enemy in human shape most frequently attacks waitresses at hotels or restaurants, and attendants in drinking-places. There are young women, who, in spite of manifold temptations, dangerous occasions, and inducements to sin, remain pure both in body and soul, and who, by their grave and prudent demeanor, prevent much evil from being carried on. They deserve the greatest respect. It is none the less true that situations of this nature are fraught with great peril for the soul.

In rare instances, poor unfortunate girls are threatened with the greatest danger to their innocence at the hands of relatives: I mean an uncle or a cousin. I knew a girl who, having lost both parents, was adopted when she was eighteen years old by a rich uncle. Before long he made proposals to her which threatened her innocence; she sought to avoid him, but he pursued her relentlessly, and promised if she would only yield to his wishes he would make her sole heiress of his large fortune. On the other hand, he threatened if she refused, to turn her out of the house forthwith. Her answer was worthy of Joseph when in Egypt, or of the chaste Susanna: "My innocence," she replied, "is dearer to me than all the treasures of the world! Condemn me, if you will, to misery and poverty, but leave me my innocence, for then I shall still have God, and He is enough for me!" She quitted the house at once. God grant that you may never be exposed to similar temptations; if you should be, imitate the conduct of this courageous girl.

If you go out alone, be on your guard against the enemy who may approach you in the shape of a stranger—of some one with whom you are totally unacquainted. The more harmless he may appear, the more attractive his exterior, the sweeter his flatteries may sound in your ear, so much the less ought you to trust him. If he attempts to persuade you to accompany him to any particular spot, do not trust him—do not believe him, however plausible and apparently harmless may be the reasons he alleges. Under circumstances like these, many girls have, through mere thoughtlessness and good nature, been ruined both for time and for eternity!

The enemy of virginal purity is met with notably at popular amusements, where no restraint is exercised, and license reigns unchecked—such as fairs, dances, village sports, etc., or in places where soldiers are quartered, and seaports, where sailors come and go. A well-bred Christian girl, whose conscience is delicate and who is concerned for the preservation of her innocence, will, if possible, hold aloof from such amusements altogether or attend them only accompanied by her parents. Many well-principled persons are, no doubt, present at the amusements, but unprincipled men of doubtful character are also to be met with, and things are heard and seen which are objectionable.

Beware of the man who flatters you. Flatterers are always false friends; they are never to be trusted.

Do not imagine that I have said all this with any intention of making you unsociable. I have spoken thus only to make you prudent and cautious in your conduct toward persons of the other sex. Christian politeness and sociability are not incompatible with a prudent reserve.

LIII. The Enemy in Finery and External Attractions

Pythias, the accomplished daughter of Aristotle, the famous pagan sage, was annoyed with idle questions as to what color and what dress she most admired. Her answer was brief and much to the purpose: "The modest, bashful blush on the cheek of innocence." And certainly she was right; for the most beautiful dress is not the fairest ornament for a maiden, but rather innocence of heart. Very often, however, dress becomes a menace, a real danger to the lily of chastity. And I must now speak of this foe in the guise of external attractions—namely, of pride and sinful ostentation in the matter of dress. If you wish to remain pure and chaste it is absolutely necessary that you should be on your guard against this enemy. You must not be afraid that I am about to enter into particulars concerning dress and fashions—that is not my business. I have only to lay down principles, to insist upon reason and decorum in regard to these matters, and then earnestly to exhort and entreat you to shape your conduct in accordance with these principles.

First of all, listen to what I have to say in regard to beauty of person. Beauty is a gift from Heaven, bestowed more especially on the feminine sex. However, in the case of too many young girls this gift serves no good purpose, but is the means not only of causing them to lose their chastity but of leading others into sin. Therefore are we told in Scripture: *"Favor is deceitful and beauty is vain: the woman that feareth the Lord, she shall be praised."* And St. Peter writes: *"Whose adorning let it not be the outward plaiting of the hair, or the wearing of gold, or the putting on of apparel: But the hidden man of the heart in the incorruptibility of a meek and quiet spirit, which is rich in the sight of God."*

Personal beauty is fraught with danger to a young girl. The flatteries bestowed on it are so many temptations to vanity, and too often prove the first step in the downward road which finally ends in the loss of innocence.

Wherefore be on your guard against the enemy which is found in the guise of personal attractions—namely, against vanity and an over-weening desire to please. Earnestly strive to render your heart beautiful—even more beautiful than your physical form—by adorning it with virtues. Beauty is a fleeting thing, but virtue will not pass away. How painful it must be for a vain woman when the bloom of youth has departed—when lines begin to furrow her cheeks and silver threads to mingle with her abundant tresses—if, when she turns her gaze to the state of her soul, she perceives the thistles of sin where the flowers of virtue ought to be!

Take care that this lot shall never be yours; see that when, at a later period of life, your youthful beauty shall have become a thing of the past, you may be able to take delight in the beauty of a heart rich in virtues.

In regard to dress make it a first, an unalterable rule that it be suitable and decorous. It can be decorous only when it covers and conceals that which no modest, delicate-minded woman could desire to display. If, on the contrary, a vain votary of fashion by her extravagant attire seeks to attract licentious glances, and to kindle the flame of impure thoughts and desires in the breasts of those around her, or even becomes the occasion thereof, she is guilty of sin, and often grievous sin.

St. Cyprian of Carthage says: "Only maidens who have lost all sense of shame and women of depraved manners love to be overdressed, and seek to draw attention to their beauty of face and figure by means of gaudy raiment."

A second rule in regard to dress is to practice prudent moderation. It is no sin to dress in a becoming and suitable manner. You ought not, however, to aim at heightening the effect of your youthful charms only to be noticed and admired, or to attract in particular the attention of young men. Thereby you may become the occasion of sin. Beware of indulging an overweening desire to please, for this frequently proves an enemy to chastity.

The third rule I would lay down for you is: not to be a slave to fashion. I do not mean that you are to disregard fashion altogether, and pay no heed to the prevailing style of dress. It is quite permissible, and sometimes even necessary, to accommodate yourself to the customs of the day. However, it is something very different to run eagerly after and appropriate every fad and foolish fashion, and to allow your thoughts to be completely engrossed by the consideration of what you shall wear. You ought not to imitate the vain and foolish girls whose constant and anxious study seems to be to compensate, by means of cosmetics and other aids of art, for the lack of the beauty which nature has denied them. I do not allude to artificial teeth, for they are often both useful and necessary. The poet castigates some fashionable follies thus:

> False teeth and rouge and borrowed hair
> May give to age a youthful air:
> But when Death comes to call us hence
> There is an end of all pretence.

Do not allow your mind to dwell upon dress, good looks, and other like vanities. Being merely transitory and unimportant, you would be foolish to make so much of them. But as I have already indicated, an enemy to your innocence lurks in the guise of external attractions; for this reason it is all the more important that you should not allow your heart to cling to such vanities. Dress neatly and in a manner becoming to your circumstances. Moreover, seek to to conduct yourself at all times that the words of Scripture may be applicable to you: "*All the glory of the king's daughter is within.*" Keep your heart pure and fair, for it is this beauty alone which leads to the blissful contemplation of the beatific vision of God.

LIV. THE ENEMY IN OUR EYES

SIGHT is one of the greatest among the benefits we have received from God. The enjoyment which this priceless gift confers can be estimated aright only by one who has been unfortunate enough to lose it, one who is condemned to pass the rest of his days in perpetual darkness. Yet in the case of many young persons it would be the greatest benefit—it might even preserve them from eternal destruction—were they to lose the sight of their bodily eyes. To such I might repeat the words which St. Severin addressed upon one occasion to a young monk, who besought him to pray for the restoration of his sight. "My son," he said, "do not trouble yourself about the eyes of your body, but rather about those of your soul." To many young persons the saying of the prophet is applicable: "*Death is come up through our windows* (the eyes), *it is entered into our house* (the soul)." The enemy of the lily of purity enters into the human heart through the eye. In a previous instruction I have sought to portray the enemy in our own heart; to-day I shall most earnestly warn you against the enemy in our eyes.

With what did the first sin begin in paradise? With a longing look Eve gazed at the luscious fruit which hung on the forbidden tree; that look excited a wish to taste the fruit; she yielded to the wish, gathered and ate the forbidden fruit, and gave some of it to her husband; thus was the first sin committed. And if, at a period when as yet no evil concupiscence had stirred within the human breast, the eyes could work irretrievable ruin, how great—how terrible—must be the result after the fall, when the enemy in our eyes works in concert with the enemy in our heart. When we see what came of a mere love of eating, we may judge what a much stronger passion will do—unchaste, sensual desire kindled by bold, unguarded glances, and suffered to burst into fierce flames.

Experience teaches that unchaste looks very frequently lead men to a terrible end. We find examples of this in Holy Scripture. The proximate cause of David's sad fall was a bold and sinful look; with this look, the entire edifice of his virtue crumbled away—all his good resolutions were rendered null and void, and he, the man after God's own heart, became a murderer and an adulterer. Putiphar's wife cast unchaste glances upon Joseph, committed adultery in her heart, and would fain have sinned in act as well as in desire.

Yet why should we turn to olden times in order to illustrate our meaning when our own daily observation furnishes only too many melancholy examples of the truth of our assertion. Segneri relates the following incident in one of his eloquent discourses: A girl who had formed an illicit connection with a young man was attacked by a fatal disease. She sent for a priest, and amid tears of contrition made a general confession. Having done this, she caused the companion of her sin to be brought to her bedside. She thought to persuade him to repent, and be truly converted. But when her eyes fell upon him, unruly passions suddenly flared up in her soul and she exclaimed: "O my beloved! I know that I shall go to hell for your sake; yet I cannot, I will not leave you!' With these words upon her lips the unhappy girl breathed her last.

Pay heed to the warning of Holy Scripture and say: "*I have made a covenant with mine eyes that I should not look upon anything dangerous, lest death should come up through our windows and enter into the soul."* Be on your guard against the enemy in your eyes, lest it should gain power over you, and destroy both body and soul. What biting frost is to the flowers in spring, so is an impure glance to the lily of chastity.

The numerous indecent and shameless pictures and engravings to be found in the present day in the pages of certain periodicals and illustrated journals are an open grave of innocence. In cities such pictures are too often exhibited in shop windows and on bill-boards, or hawked about the streets. It is deeply sad to think how many souls, and the souls of young girls among the rest, are by this means soiled and ruined. This danger is a very great one for you, my dear daughter. Do not imitate the heedless girls who say: "We are no longer children! It is quite allowable for us to see certain things, we have reached an age when we ought to be acquainted with such subjects!" Girls who talk in this fashion are alas! no longer children of God, or at least are not to be counted among His innocent children.

Remember also that maidens who boldly fix their gaze upon persons of the opposite sex—doing this, not from mere curiosity, but with some measure of sensual desire,—are either already unchaste, or will become so before very long. St. Bernard tells us that if persons of different sexes take deliberate satisfaction in contemplating each other and yet no sinful desires arise within them, it is a more wonderful thing than if a dead man were to return to life.

One word more in conclusion. When the consort of Tigranes, the heathen monarch, was told that her husband had offered to give up his life to deliver her from captivity, she from that day forward refrained from looking at any other man.

My dear daughter, as long as you remain in the state of virginity you are indeed the bride—I might almost say the spouse—of our Lord and Saviour, Jesus Christ. And this heavenly Bridegroom was not only willing to give His life in order to deliver you from the captivity of Satan, but He did this in reality. Let your eyes be therefore fixed upon your celestial Bridegroom in everlasting gratitude and love.

> O maiden, keep thy heart serene,
> Thy soul keep pure, thy conscience clean;
> Keep careful watch o'er ear and eye
> And close them both when sin is nigh.

LV. The Enemy in What We Hear and Read

> A maiden young, and good, and pure,
> Of her own innocence secure,
> All unsuspiciously may tread
> Where Satan's fatal net is spread.
>
> And if she trust the flattering voice
> Which bids her heedlessly rejoice,
> The poison soon her heart will gain,
> With death and sorrow in its train.

WHAT kind of death is it which steals into a maiden's heart? It is the death of innocence. It is like a worm gnawing at the root of a fair lily that causes it to wither and die. And when innocence is dead, there follows terrible remorse because of the irreparable loss. The unhappy girl becomes a prey to every kind of mental torment. This death of innocence is too often brought about by the enemy in what we hear and read. Therefore, you must learn how to recognize and how to shun this enemy.

I take it for granted that you would yourself never take pleasure in immodest conversation, or improper songs. For no decent, respectable young women could possibly do so, but only girls lost to all sense of modesty and propriety.

It is, however, a deplorable fact that unchaste conversation is frequently carried on, and it may chance to reach your ears. For conversation of this nature is carried on, not only in taverns, but in private houses when young people are gathered together without any supervision on the part of their elders; likewise in streets and squares, in field and forest, at work and at recreation, on the way to church, and if the truth must be told, even in the house of God itself. Those who talk in this way are, for the most part, young unmarried men, sometimes mere boys who have just left school, and—to their shame be it spoken—young girls also. Many of these persons seem to imagine that nothing can be amusing which is not seasoned with improprieties. He who can relate the most obviously shameless and indecent anecdotes is regarded as the most entertaining companion.

In regard to such doings as these, your duty is clear and plain. Leave the company at once, if it is in any way possible for you to do so! For if those around you show so little consideration for you and your feelings of delicacy, you need no longer keep any terms with them. You are then at liberty to express your righteous anger and displeasure in no measured language and, if necessary, to administer a sharp reproof. This affords an opportunity for employing to good purpose that readiness of speech which belongs in a special manner to women, and thereby silencing unclean tongues once and forever.

The enemy in books, pamphlets, newspapers and magazines does, if possible, even more mischief than the enemy in speech. In the present day the number of books and periodicals fraught with danger to innocence is legion. Like a second deluge, they invade every class of society in villages, towns and cities, not sparing the most secluded mountain valleys. First and foremost in the foul flood are bad novels; and the greater part of novels have a more or less objectionable tendency. They treat, almost without exception, of love. By means of the glowing colors in which scenes are depicted, they heat the imagination, blind the understanding, weaken the will, and pervert the heart. Through the perusal of such novels and sentimental romances, poison is slowly, but surely, introduced into the soul; it obtains a hold there, spreads, and in the end causes death. This fatal poison is mingled with the sugar of pleasing language and fascinating narrative. Every-day experience proves how destructive are its effects. I know many instances in which girls about your age have got all sorts of wild ideas into their heads through reading bad novels, have left their parents' houses, taken up with the first man who made love to them, and thus brought about their own ruin.

It is therefore highly important for you to select your reading carefully. Do not read any book or pamphlet unless you are advised that it is harmless and good; if you are in doubt, lay it aside unread, or submit it to a competent authority for his opinion. Never keep any doubtful book, lest perchance it should happen to you as it did to Eve in regard to the forbidden fruit. Curiosity might be too much for you and in this way be fatal to your innocence. Do not be deceived by a high-sounding, harmless or apparently religious title. Do not permit yourself to be misled by the elegant binding of a book; the name of the publisher, however, may frequently serve as a guide to its contents. If there is no name given, the work is probably mere trash; toss it into the fire. Do not amuse yourself by turning over the leaves of doubtful publications, lest perchance an impure expression or objectionable picture should strike your eye and kindle within your soul, hitherto innocent and pure, the fire of lust, which might end in a fearful conflagration.

Are you therefore to abstain from reading altogether? Certainly not—you ought to read, but you must discriminate as you do in eating; it is your duty to avoid everything either injurious or excessive. Do not allow your love of reading to grow into a passion—keep it within due bounds, and do not indulge in what is termed a 'rage for reading.'

And what ought you to read? Above all, books and periodicals which have a sound Catholic tone; and these are surely to be met with in abundance. Of religious and edifying works, I would mention the *New Testament*, the *Imitation of Christ*, and *Philothea* by St. Francis of Sales. For lighter reading there are many excellent novels, interesting stories and periodicals issued by Catholic publishers.

In conclusion I will direct your attention to one book in particular—to the most sacred of all books, which contains in itself everything that is delightful, helpful and consoling; it is the divine Heart of Our Saviour Jesus Christ, which was opened upon the cross. Of this book you can never read enough; in it you can never meditate and study sufficiently. Before all else, commit to memory and seek to put into practice the injunction which stands inscribed upon it in letters of gold: "*Learn of Me, because I am meek, and humble of heart.*"

LVI. The Enemy in the Ballroom

> Pluck ye the roses while ye may—
> The fairest bloom will soon decay;
> Enjoy life while its flame burns bright—
> Ere dull age dim its flickering light.

WITH my whole heart do I agree with these lines the poet addresses to the young; but I agree with them only so long as the rose which is plucked is not the tender, celestial flower of purity and innocence. It always has been, and it still is, a great joy to me to give pleasure to young people. I have been in the habit of doing things to make young hearts happy ever since the time when, myself a mere boy, I was delighted to fetch a Christmas tree from the forest and dress it for my youngest brother. My heart truly rejoices whenever I see young people merry. It is very important that you should remember this, my dear child, while you read this chapter and also the following one. As I am now about seriously to warn you against the enemy of innocence which is found in places of amusement, you must not take my words in a wrong sense, nor imagine that I shall say anything not absolutely necessary, or paint the picture in darker hues than the reality warrants. I certainly do not grudge you any amusements which can be indulged in with impunity. We will speak in the first place of the enemy in the ballroom.

That the enemy of innocence is frequently met with in the ballroom, and that dancing is, for the most part, fraught with no little danger to chastity, are established facts which no sensible man will think of denying. I do not mean to say that dancing is in itself, and under all circumstances, a dangerous thing. On the contrary, in and by itself it is a perfectly harmless amusement; that is to say, moving about in time to the music is no more to be objected to than any other kind of gymnastic exercise. Indeed, in many excellent Catholic schools the pupils are occasionally allowed to amuse themselves by dancing. In this case no danger to innocence can possibly exist; any more than when brothers and sisters, or other near relatives, dance together. For these family gatherings the only evil is that they tend to awaken and foster a taste for what so often proves to be a dangerous amusement.

Thus we see that dancing is not, in itself, a danger to chastity; it is rendered perilous only by the circumstances attending it. A great deal depends on the person with whom one dances. If the dancers are of opposite sexes, and not very closely related to one another, if they are quite young, and therefore more likely to have their passions kindled in the intoxication of the dance, then the amusement may assume a dangerous character. An illustration will explain my meaning.

To carry a lighted candle about without any guard against the flame is assuredly not dangerous, but useful and necessary. But if you were to light a fire close to a heap of dry hay, or to take a lighted candle into a room where there had been an escape of gas, what a catastrophe might be the result!

Dancing under the circumstances which have just been mentioned is eminently calculated to arouse impure thoughts and desires, and to kindle the fire of passion: the lateness of the hour, the exciting music, the partaking of alcoholic drinks, close physical contact in the giddy mazes of the dance, words, looks, etc. Is not then the enemy of innocence very dangerous in the ballroom?

Thoughtless young persons may step forward and say: "Priests see these things in too dark a light; they can know nothing about dancing from personal experience, and are therefore unable to pronounce judgment in the matter." I thank God I know nothing from personal experience; but from what others have told me, as well as from my own common sense, I am able to form an impartial opinion as to the danger to morals occasioned by dancing. You shall hear the verdict pronounced by an old officer, a man of the world. He says:

"Both religion and common sense compel me to acknowledge that dancing is a dangerous amusement. I know that some persons can indulge in it without harm; but sometimes even the coldest temperaments are heated by it. It is usually only young persons who dance, and I refer more especially to them. They have at all times difficulty in resisting temptation; how much more then amid scenes where the universal merriment, the sound of the music, the movement of the dance, are so eminently calculated to excite their passions."

Could we question all the unfortunate girls who have lost their virtue as to the proximate cause of their fall, how startled we should be to hear so many, if not most of them, reply: "It was the enemy of my innocence in the ballroom which brought about my ruin!" The poet was quite right when he addressed the following verses to a young girl on her way to a ball:

> I question myself with sadness of heart,
> When dressed for the ball I see thee depart,
> When I see thee again can I be sure
> Thou art still innocent, simple, and pure?

Then what are you to do? Altogether to give up the pleasure of dancing? No, this would be perhaps too much to require of you, but I strongly advise you to do so; and I may suitably quote the words of the Saviour: "*He that can take, let him take it.*" At any rate, take to heart the following advice: (1) If you know nothing at all, or very little, about dancing, do not trouble yourself to learn, but think yourself just as fortunate as those who know how to dance and dance well. (2) Be watchful over yourself, and see that your pleasure in dancing does not grow into a passion; and see if now and then you cannot refrain from dancing, when it would be quite allowable for you to do so. (3) Never frequent fairs, picnics, carnivals, or public dancing-halls, where Heaven only knows what sorts of people congregate. (4) Dance only at private parties where your father or mother is present or where at least you are accompanied by some relative or trusted friend, who will go with you and see you home.

Faithfully observe the two last points, in order that the danger of frequenting balls may at least be minimized as much as possible. For the sake both of your innocence and of your eternal happiness, I earnestly entreat you to do this.

> And when youth's roses shall decay,
> Thy golden locks be turned to gray,
> Yet to thy heart a breath of spring
> Its genial warmth shall often bring.

LVII. The Enemy in the Theatre

WHEN, in the course of my last six instructions, I warned you so earnestly against the enemies of the lily of purity, you may perhaps have said to yourself: "If things have really gone so far in the world, how difficult it will be to do right and remain pure! How gladly would I fly far, far away from all this wickedness; but I cannot do this—my youth, my parents, my circumstances render it impossible." You certainly ought not to leave the world so long as it is your vocation to remain in it. I desire only to give you a thorough acquaintance with its dangers, not to estrange you from it altogether. My fatherly admonitions are not intended for nuns, but for good, Catholic girls, the great majority of whom are destined to remain in the world, and later on to become mothers, and rule a household. In the world you will be launched, as it were, upon a dangerous, wide, and storm-tossed ocean. How necessary, how important it is that you should learn to steer your course true, that you may not be shipwrecked, but may safely guide your little bark amid the rocks and quicksands which beset youth, and one day land upon the blissful shore of the celestial paradise.

I have to speak of yet one more of these various perils, to point out one more of these enemies of innocence; it is the enemy in the theatre.

What was said about dancing is true of the theatre, even to a greater degree. The theatre is not without its effect upon religion and morals; it has a powerful influence for good or evil. Good plays of a religious tendency raise the tone of morals. The histrionic art resembles the other arts—poetry, painting, rhetoric, sculpture and music—in the elevating powers they exercise. For this reason the Catholic Church has taken the fine arts one by one into her service, and thereby aided them to attain their highest perfection. The mystery plays of the Middle

Ages were employed by her as a means of religious teaching. For the same reason, Catholic educational establishments in our own day, convent schools, and colleges conducted by Religious, annually have theatrical entertainments. It is the same with Catholic guilds or societies for young men and young women, under the superintendence of priests. It is an innocent and harmless pleasure for girls to attend such plays as these.

Dramas, on the contrary, which are performed by professional actors on the stages of large cities are frequently fraught with danger for young people. There the spirit of evil, evening after evening, dwells upon its old theme: the concupiscence of the eyes, the concupiscence of the flesh and the pride of life. Immorality is not seldom, at least indirectly, inculcated. Everything combines to half intoxicate youthful spectators, to lull to deep their understanding and their will, and, on the other band, to excite their imagination to its highest pitch, and fill it with most undesirable pictures.

Therefore, you must see for yourself that you ought never to visit such theatres, unless indeed a play should chance to be acted there which obviously contains nothing injurious to young girls. Never go to a play that is performed at a theatre of doubtful reputation.

A certain French writer of plays has himself given an indubitable proof of the immoral tendency of many plays. Why did he forbid his daughters to witness the performances of the dramas which he had written? For no other reason, surely, than because he believed that their attendance at the theatre on those occasions would be injurious to their morals. What a testimony does this afford to the deleterious character of too many plays!

Therefore, do you, my dear child, stay away from all such performances of a doubtful nature! Make an exception only in cases when you have a guarantee that the play is harmless. Otherwise the saying holds good:

> Though you may take care when you go to the mill,
> Some dust of flour will cleave to you still.

Be on your guard lest your love for the theatre develop into a passion. Seek rather to take delight in simple pleasures, which are within the reach of every one. Take delight in beholding the beauteous sights which God offers to our view in the works of creation. Strive by the practice of virtue to be yourself a spectacle to angels and to men. Thus, when the toils and trials of this life are past, shall you be permitted to contemplate a glorious sight which shall never pass away—the beatific vision of God! Therefore:

> Lift, O Christian, lift thine eyes
> To thy home beyond the skies;
> Eternal bliss awaits thee there
> With which earth's joys cannot compare.

Prayer in Honor of St. Agnes

O Sweetest Lord Jesus Christ, source of all virtues, lover of virgins, most powerful conqueror of demons, most severe extirpator of vice! deign to cast Thine eyes upon my weakness, and through the intercession of Mary most blessed, Mother and Virgin, and of Thy beloved spouse St. Agnes, glorious virgin and martyr, grant me the aid of Thy heavenly grace, in order that I may learn to despise all earthly things, and to love what is heavenly; to oppose vice and to be proof against temptation; to walk firmly in the path of virtue, not to seek honors, to shun pleasures, to bewail my past offenses, to keep far from the occasions of evil, to keep free from bad habits, to seek the company of the good, and persevere in righteousness, so that, by the assistance of Thy grace, I may deserve the crown of eternal life, together with St. Agnes and all the saints, forever and ever, in Thy kingdom. Amen.

‹ 3 ›

The Faded Lily

LVIII. What a Misfortune!

In earnest exhortations I have addressed to you on the maidenly virtues, my object always has been, and always will be, to induce you to make a firm resolution to preserve your most precious treasure, the lily of chastity, in untarnished splendor, no matter what may be the cost. A glance at the faded lily will greatly tend to strengthen you in this resolution.

How great a misfortune it is when the lily has faded, and innocence is lost! Innocence is lost through any voluntary deliberate offence against chastity, in thought, word, or deed; for every voluntary transgression of this kind is a mortal sin; in other words, every sin of impurity is mortal when it receives the full consent of the will. Why then should you inquire if this or that sin be greater or less—it ought to be enough to know that *through it the soul is slain, the grace of God is forfeited, heaven is closed, and hell opened.* We can measure the terrible nature of this sin by the loss of innocence and of sanctifying grace which it entails. What a misfortune is this!

The young woman who has fallen, or perhaps even given herself over completely to vice, may be blind enough to think that she is no very great sinner after all; she may say in her heart: "I have never stolen even the smallest sum of money; I am not half so quarrelsome as this one or that one; I have never done any one an injustice; I have not deprived any one of his honor or good name. I know that I have my weakness, but where is the woman who is without frailty?" A fallen woman may talk thus to one of her class, but it is impossible for a Catholic girl, well-instructed in her religion, to adopt such language. St. Thomas Aquinas, that great Doctor of the Church, says: "Unchastity is a greater sin than any which can be committed against one's neighbor, greater than theft, calumny, or detraction; murder alone exceeds it in enormity."

We may also measure the magnitude of the misfortune occasioned by the loss of innocence by the severity of the punishments which God inflicts upon the unchaste. Even in days of yore He commanded: *"Cast them into the exterior darkness; there shall be weeping and gnashing of teeth."* How awful a sentence is this!

The fair face of the country where we now see valley and mountain, town and village, was once covered by water. Before it was submerged it was inhabited by a numerous and iniquitous population. They were happy and careless; they ate and drank, married and gave in marriage; they were given up to sensuality and pleasure. No doubt they might have been heard to say: "We are not angels, but creatures of flesh and blood. We cannot make ourselves peculiar—we must do as others do. And there can surely be no great harm in following the universal custom."

Unhappily sins of impurity everywhere prevailed. Noe alone protested against them. But his words had no effect; he was only laughed at. He built a large ship in order that he might be saved, together with the members of his family. The sinners by whom he was surrounded mocked at him, just as in the present day confessors and preachers are ridiculed when they warn sinners of their impending fate. We know how destruction came upon the sinful world; all perished in the deluge except the just Noe and his family, who had entered the ark.

To take another instance. In Asia, in the Promised Land, was a fair and fertile place, beauteous as an earthly paradise; its inhabitants were, however, given over to impurity. What has become of that fair and fertile plain? It is changed into a lake, called the Dead Sea. Nothing more desolate than this lake could possibly be imagined; no tree, no blade of grass, grows upon its shores; its waters are turbid and foul; the neighborhood is a dreary desert. Where are the unchaste inhabitants of Sodom and Gomorrha? You know the dreadful fate which overtook them—their bodies were consumed by fire from heaven. Poor sinners like these, if they die unrepentant, are "*cast into the exterior darkness; where shall be weeping and gnashing of teeth.*" We read in the Apocalypse that "*the unchaste shall have their portion in the pool burning with fire and brimstone.*"

And how sad is the condition of the conscience of a girl who has fallen! She is constantly tormented by remorse; she has no peace either by night or by day; a terrible voice sounds constantly in her ears, saying over and over again: "Where would you go if you were to die in your sins?" Yet, sad as is this state, sadder still is it if the voice of conscience has ceased to speak and the dreadful lull before the storm prevails—the false peace of hardened sinners. May such a misfortune never be your lot. Strengthen yourself anew in the firm resolution to avoid, with the assistance of divine grace, all the enemies of your lily of purity, that you may not fall into the greatest of all misfortunes—the loss of innocence!

> Heed a kindly warning, lest too late
> With tears thou should'st bewail thy cruel fate;
> If cheerful and light-hearted thou would'st be,
> Preserve with greatest care thy purity.

LIX. The Consequences of That Misfortune

Seldom has a mother loved her child as tenderly as Blanche, the saintly queen of France, loved her son Louis, who afterward ascended the throne of that country, and is known as St. Louis. On one occasion when this pious mother had been giving her son, then a mere boy, some wise counsels she concluded in these words: "O my darling child, you are the most precious thing I possess upon earth, yet I would a thousand times sooner see you lying dead at my feet than know that you had committed one single grievous sin."

In the same way would your parents speak to you, in a similar manner would I also address you. You are very dear to us, but we would rather you should die in the grace of God than fall into grievous sin and lose your innocence.

The principal care of your parents and confessor is to preserve you from that greatest of all misfortunes, the loss of your innocence. To this end will be directed the grave warning I now address to you. To inspire you with a wholesome horror of the vice which is opposed to chastity, I shall depict its deplorable consequences.

When the lily of purity has withered—when it is crushed and destroyed—what are the results? Very sad indeed. When a young girl has been weak enough to yield to temptation, and has lost her innocence, she must, after her grievous fall, immediately seek to rise up again, and *entirely* to avoid the occasion of sin. Unless she does this she will probably fall a second and a third time; she will despair of ever being able to break the fetters of sin; she will abandon herself to vice, and be led into violating nearly all the commandments. There are too many instances of this. Many a girl who was formerly innocent and good, a lily in the garden of God, the joy and hope of her parents and friends, has later on been so unfortunate as to stray from the right path, because she was not sufficiently watchful, and especially because after her first fall she did not at once rise up and resolutely turn her back upon the occasion of sin.

The first consequence always is this: The unhappy girl no longer cares to pray; she gives up her daily devotions. Then she begins to doubt whether there really is a God, an eternity; sometimes from false shame she conceals her sins when she goes to confession, thus rendering her confession and communion sacrilegious. She continues to offend God, and ends by despairing of His mercy altogether.

What terrible anxiety such a daughter causes her parents! She treats them with rudeness and impertinence, refuses to follow their advice, laughs their exhortations to scorn, embitters and shortens their lives. Sometimes unwedded mothers destroy their illicit offspring and even take their own lives. Over and over again we read in the newspapers that young persons have committed suicide as the result of "unhappy love affairs," for so they are termed.

Yet this is not all! This dreadful sin plunges its victims into poverty, misery, and the utmost degradation. The girl who is infected with this vice is, as a rule, an idle, vain, conceited, and extravagant creature. She perhaps receives large sums of money; but this money is the wages of sin—a curse rests upon it instead of a blessing. And when her beauty fades, and she can no longer make up for the loss of it by artificial means, she sinks into abject poverty, she is shunned by all, and probably ends her days in a hospital, poorhouse, penitentiary, or even in the street.

To quote one instance out of many which might be brought forward: In a certain town there lived a druggist. He was a well-educated man, and had an excellent business. His only daughter was led astray at the early age of sixteen by one who took advantage of her youth and ignorance. When the fact became only too apparent, and thus came to the knowledge of her parents, her mother fell into a state of insanity and had to be confined in an asylum for lunatics. Shortly afterward her father committed suicide. The mother died in the asylum, and the unhappy girl was left alone in the world with the offspring of her shame.

You may possibly think that I am exaggerating, that I am painting the gloomy picture in hues more sombre than the reality. It is a cause for thankfulness that such awful consequences do not invariably follow a first fall into this sin, but it is always attended by the greatest danger. Therefore, my dear child, watch and pray—make every effort to preserve yourself from such a fall. Seek to preserve the lily of purity in all its beauty to the end of your days. Suffer any loss rather than sacrifice your innocence.

> Your innocence guard with the utmost care—
> Once lost, there is nought that loss can repair.
> How sweet the fragrance it sheds around—
> No flower more fair on earth can be found.

LX. The Lily Fades! To What an End Does This Lead!

The lily fades! To what an end does this lead! It leads, in the first place, to hardness of heart. "Ask me not," says St. Bernard, "what is meant by hardness of heart; for he who does not take alarm at the mere sound of the word is probably already in the awful state which it signifies; for only the hardened heart dreads not hardness of heart." In order to walk in the way of salvation and attain eternal happiness three things are necessary: (1) We must recognize how great an evil sin is. (2) We must also hate sin and desire to avoid it.

(3) Finally, we must have a good, strong will, and strive most earnestly to carry our good intentions into practice. Well, then, what is the condition of the girl who leads an impure and vicious life? Her understanding is darkened in regard to the things of God. The word of God as preached by His ambassadors might be her salvation; but she is unwilling to hear it, and listens to sermons only when she cannot help doing so. An eloquent discourse about death, judgment, heaven and hell impresses other sinners; pious persons believe and tremble, and hasten to confess their faults. But she who is unchaste stands unmoved, like some marble statue. "What is the use," she says to herself, "of all these thunders and threatenings! These are all exaggerations. Things are not so bad."

Even when death is mentioned to her no impression is made. A young girl who had been much flattered on account of her beauty lost her innocence, abandoned herself to a life of vice, and misused her attractions to injure the souls of others. She was attacked by a fatal malady, and it soon became apparent that death was approaching. One of her companions in sin, in whose breast every spark of religious feeling was not extinguished, exhorted her to send for a priest. "A priest!" she shrieked, "what would be the use of sending for a priest? An evil spirit from hell was here already!" However, a priest was summoned; but he came too late—the miserable girl had already breathed her last!

Even should the hardened sinner become aware of her lamentable state, she is wanting in the good will which would induce her to abandon her sins; or her will is, at any rate, too weak. "Vice," as St. Augustine says, "has an iron will"—that is, the force of passion, the inclination to sin, enfeebles the will, binds it in fetters of iron.

I can never sufficiently urge you to lay to heart the fact that no sin so greatly tends to weaken the human will as the sin opposed to chastity. Water may change into solid ice; in the same way a heart that was once sensitive and soft may gradually become as hard as stone. Every fresh fall makes the tendency to sin greater, conversion more difficult, deliverance more improbable, final perdition more certain.

Yes, eternal perdition—the pool of fire in hell—is the final fate of the faded lily! God Himself tells us that *"the unchaste shall have their portion in the pool burning with fire and brimstone."* All the unchaste who die in their sins shall be thrown into an awful prison and tormented with fierce flames to all eternity. What a fearful fate is this! How the wretched captives will curse the sins which have brought them into such a plight—how they will wish they had heeded the exhortations addressed to them, for then might they have been happy in heaven forever and ever!

My daughter, you can form no idea how large is the number of those who sink into hell on account of sins of impurity. A celebrated Italian missioner said: "Unchastity fills the world with sinners, and hell with lost souls." Another master of the spiritual life went so far as to say: "Three-fourths of the wretched denizens of hell have been lost on account of impurity."

I have said enough. The considerations I have laid before you cannot have failed to fill you with dread and alarm. It is well for you that so it should be. But reflections of this nature must not deprive you of courage; and you must be careful not to allow them to have this effect in seasons when you are assailed by temptations against the holy virtue. Once more I repeat what I have so often said before: Take courage, have confidence in God! And always bear these lines in mind:

"Beware, beware, because the sun shines brightly,
  Because the flowers are fair;
Thus bright, thus gay, were bowers of Eden,
  Whilst hung that fruit in air,
And waved o'er Eve's uplifted brow
As life o'er thee is waving now."

Aubrey de Vere.

Hail, Queen of Heaven, the ocean Star
  Guide of the wand'rer here below;
Thrown on life's surge, we claim thy care.
  Save us from peril and from woe.
    Mother of Christ, Star of the sea,
    Pray for the wand'rer, pray for me.

O gentle, chaste, and spotless Maid,
  We sinners make our prayers through thee.
Remind thy Son that He has paid
  The price of our iniquity.
    Virgin most pure, Star of the sea,
    Pray for the sinner, pray for me.

An Act of Reparation
(The Divine Praises)

Blessed be God.
Blessed be his holy name.
Blessed be Jesus Christ, true God and true man.
Blessed be the name of Jesus.
Blessed be his most Sacred Heart.
Blessed be his most Precious Blood.
Blessed be Jesus in the most holy sacrament of the altar.
Blessed be the Holy Spirit, the Paraclete.
Blessed be the great Mother of God, Mary most holy.
Blessed be her holy and Immaculate Conception.
Blessed be her glorious Assumption.
Blessed be the name of Mary, virgin and Mother.
Blessed be St. Joseph, her most chaste spouse.
Blessed be God in his angels and in his saints.
Amen.

‹ 4 ›

The Lily Protected and Cared For

LXI. The Sentinels Who Guard the Lily of Chastity

Man's worst enemy is evil concupiscence—the lust of the flesh, which aims at destroying that celestial flower, the lily of purity. At no period of life is this enemy bolder and more importunate than at your present age. Then is concupiscence kindled within your breast like an unholy fire, so forcibly urging you to sin that it is necessary to make every effort, to employ every means, if you are to resist its power. Thus it comes to pass that the greater number of sins against chastity are committed by young men and young women. Therefore it is so highly important—so absolutely necessary—for you to know the means for the preservation of your chastity, and the manner in which you may best protect and cherish the fair lily of purity.

    I will proceed to direct your attention to the sentinels who guard the lily of chastity. I have already mentioned certain sentinels when I spoke of the enemies of the lily. You must resist your evil desires and inclinations, observe custody of the eyes, suppress the risings of vanity and an undue anxiety to please, be cautious in your dealings with persons of the other sex, eschew undesirable conversation and objectionable books, and seldom, if ever, go to theatres and public dances. Those habits and rules of conduct are sentinels which must be posted in the garden of your heart, untiringly to guard the lily of chastity from danger, to defend it against its foes, to ward off evil influences.

To these must sentinels of a mightier and loftier character be added. The highest and most powerful of them all is the fear of God united to humility of heart. Happy are you if you constantly feel this holy fear and never forget that you bear about you the treasure of chastity in earthly vessels. Never pride yourself upon the fact of having preserved your innocence hitherto, as if it were all your own merit. And when you hear that others have fallen into sin, and been put to shame, do not judge them harshly. Remember that we all are fallible and weak; what has happened to others may happen to us likewise. Holy Scripture thus warns us: "*Wherefore he that thinketh himself to stand let him take heed lest he fall.*" When a girl begins to pride herself on her talents and good looks, to disregard and mock at the warnings of her parents and confessor, to tell them that they do not know what they are talking about, she will, in all probability, fall into the sin of impurity when she is assailed by some strong temptation, or finds herself confronted by an occasion of sin. She even may end by following a vicious career.

It is the duty of a second sentinel to oppose a determined resistance to evil thoughts and impulses. The chief and fundamental principle in combating disease is to lose no time in employing the proper remedies. The same principle is applicable to the maladies of the soul. As soon as you become conscious of sinful thoughts, imaginations and impulses, direct your attention to something else, to the tasks you have to perform, or to anything which is free from danger, and likely to engross your mind. If you are alone seek some harmless companionship. In any case breathe forth with heartfelt earnestness some such ejaculation as the following: "*My Jesus, mercy!*" "*Sweet Heart of Jesus, be my love!*" "*Sweet Heart of Mary, be my salvation!*" Such brief prayers, if uttered with sincere devotion and childlike confidence, have a marvelous, an almost infallible power.

A third sentinel must assign to both mind and body plenty of work. "Idleness is the parent of all vice," is a proverb which is true indeed, and in reference to the sin of unchastity it is more especially true. She who has nothing—or very little—to do does not know how to while the time away; and when she is alone thoughts and imaginings of every kind come to her—the evil enemy suggests impure ideas which facilitate a fall into sin. Countless is the number of young persons who, through their own idleness, or from lack of suitable occupation, have lost their innocence. Therefore you ought to consider yourself fortunate, and give thanks to almighty God, if you have plenty to do. It is well if your parents set you one task after another, never leaving you leisure to idle about. A spring is clear and lucid because the water is in motion. How foul and turbid, on the contrary, is a stagnant pond!

A fourth sentinel ought to be kept in reserve. It has a most important and difficult duty in regard to the lily of purity. Its office is to influence the human will, and induce persons to avoid occasions of sin against the virtue of chastity.

All previously mentioned enemies of the lily lead to such occasions of sin. I will here only mention some voluntary, proximate occasions. In such a voluntary, proximate occasion is a young woman who without necessity goes to, or lingers in, any place where it is highly probable or almost certain that she will fall into sins against chastity. The same remark applies to her if she, of her own free will, seeks to be alone with any person who is very likely to lead her into sin. Such occasions must be avoided, at whatever cost, else nothing can avail to save her; even prayer and confession will be of no use.

You surmise how very difficult, how well-nigh impossible, it will at times appear to avoid such occasions. See, therefore, that you follow betimes the exhortation uttered by Our Lord: "*Watch and pray!*" Watch while you are still young—watch throughout all the years that are to come, that thus your heart may not cleave to any occasion of sin so as to refuse to be separated from it, and thus be cast into perdition.

> Keep careful watch, for who can know,
> How slight a spark wakes passion's glow;
> And should it scorch thy lily fair,
> That loss thou never could'st repair.

LXII. Sunshine

You are still in the fair springtime of life. The bright blossoms of happiness fill the garden of your heart, and we will hope that the sweet lily of innocence is to be found among them. For garden and field, and indeed for the whole face of nature, bright, warm sunshine is the most important thing in the season of spring. What marvels it effects in a short space of time in trees and flowers and each tiny plant! Under the mighty influence of its salutary beams, flowers blossom forth and fruits attain maturity.

The golden light of the sun is of the greatest importance for the lily. Were you to place the plant in a musty cellar, in a gloomy corner, it would pine and wither away. The same thing applies to the lily of chastity; to it also golden sunshine is absolutely indispensable if it is to flourish and thrive. In the case of the lily of chastity this sunshine is *prayer*.

Thus you must love prayer and be diligent in prayer. Need I exhort you to do this? In the days of early childhood no sooner did you give the first signs of awakening intelligence than you were taught to fold your hands in prayer. From the pulpit and in the confessional you are exhorted to pray; at home and in church it is your duty to pray; the sound of the church bell, the sight of the crucifix, admonishes you to raise your heart to God in prayer. My exhortations in regard to this point have been frequent and urgent, and prompted by weighty reasons. It is especially important for the young, and for young women most of all, since they are so often assailed by fierce storms of sensual desires, to heed the injunction of St. Paul to "*pray without ceasing.*" Where but in prayer can they, weak as they are, obtain grace and strength constantly to resist the attraction of the world and their own evil propensities?

Most assuredly must maidens pray; they must pray much and earnestly if they would preserve their precious lily; they must imitate the wise Solomon, who said: "*Because I knew that I could not otherwise be continent except God gave it, I went to the Lord and besought Him.*"

St. Paul indicates a special kind of prayer as calculated to aid in preserving chastity. He says: "*In all things taking the shield of faith wherewith you may be able to extinguish the fiery darts of the most wicked one.*" By this shield of faith is meant that the truths of our holy religion—more especially serious meditations upon the four last things—will enable us to conquer the fiercest temptations. If such temptations assail you, and dangers threaten you, have recourse to mental prayer. Place before you as vividly as you can death, judgment, heaven and hell. Thus will you be prevented from falling into sin, or at least from remaining in sin, and you will probably conquer and overcome. Holy Scripture reminds us of this in the following words: "*In all thy works remember thy last end, and thou shalt never sin.*"

St. Paul exhorts us to vocal prayer when he says: "*In everything by prayer and supplication with thanksgiving let your petitions be made known to God.*" Obey this injunction; pray without ceasing, that you may be kept from temptation, or at least from falling when you are tempted. Our Lord teaches us to pray thus: "*Lead us not into temptation, but deliver us from evil.*" In another place He says again: "*Ask, and it shall be given you.*" Ask, dear child, and you shall receive strength in temptation, courage in the fight, and deliverance from the bondage of sin, if you have been so unfortunate as to fall into it. As long as a young girl continues to pray all is not lost; there is certainly hope for her salvation. But if she grows careless in regard to prayer, or ceases altogether to pray, there is everything to fear, as I know by experience. To take one instance of the many which have come under my observation: A young girl who had formerly been pious and good lost her innocence, to the grief of all who knew her. Her confessor spoke to her upon the subject, and asked how her sad fall had come about. "Alas! reverend Father," she exclaimed, bursting into sobs, "this is what one comes to if one neglects prayer and at last gives it up altogether!" Fain would I say to every girl on the face of the earth: Grow not weary of praying if you would not be lost!

I will give one more reason why prayer is indispensable for the protection of the lily of purity. The most precious fruit of prayer is that it unites us to God and renders us heavenly-minded. True prayer is an elevation of the heart to God in which you hold intercourse with Him. He, the loving Father, during every moment of this sweet communion infuses more light, fresh love and strength into the heart of the child who kneels before Him in prayer. In this way the heart is more and more raised up to God and becomes increasingly like unto Him.

When Moses had communed with God for forty days, his face shone with such dazzling brightness that he was obliged to cover it when he came near to the people. We read something of a similar nature in the lives of many of the saints, who, whilst engaged in prayer and contemplation, or after they had concluded these exercises, shone with heavenly radiance.

We poor, sinful mortals cannot expect to receive from God favors such as these. One thing is certain, however: he who loves prayer, and prays frequently and devoutly, will find his soul to be illumined from on high; he will become ever more like to God, ever holier, ever purer. He will grow in the love of God, he will strive more and more to please Him, he will more and more despise all that is base, unholy, and impure. And is not this in itself chastity, or at least the best means, the right disposition of the heart, for its preservation? He, on the contrary, who does not pray at regular times, who does not raise his heart to God and to heaven, becomes of necessity more and more worldly-minded, loses all relish for higher things, and seeks only the gratification of his lower nature.

Have recourse to prayer then if you desire to protect your lily of innocence. Prayer is the sunlight which causes it to flourish—the most powerful weapon wherewith to wage war against its enemies. Like a pillar of fire, prayer will lead you unharmed through the perils of this world. Prayer will open for you the gates of everlasting blessedness. Never murmur, never despair, whatever may be the dangers and temptations that surround you! You can always pray; if not with your lips, with your heart at least, which is far better. With St. Peter cry out in these words to the Sacred Heart of Jesus: "*Lord, save us, we perish!*" But do not pray in a pusillanimous spirit; pray with firm confidence, and you will experience the truth of these simple lines:

present in our midst, and descends into our sinful hearts in all the plenitude of His grace and love.

Think you that He does not know your struggles and temptations, the manifold dangers which beset the soul He purchased with His own most precious blood? Or do you think He has not the same power which He possessed when as a man He walked among men and came so frequently and so mercifully to men's rescue and relief; or that He does not feel the same fatherly love, that He is no longer desirous to aid and deliver you? Why these foolish doubts? Go direct to Him, confidently invoke His help; say to Him: "*Jesus, Son of David, have mercy on me!*" Pray with lively faith, with childlike confidence—fight, resist, grow not weary, but persevere!

Then will you assuredly feel that strength and consolation are poured into your heart; then will you appreciate the truth of St. Paul's words: "*God is faithful who will not suffer you to be tempted above that which you are able, but will make also with temptation issue that you may be able to bear it.*" You will find that God is true to the promise He made to each one of us by the mouth of His prophet: "*Can a woman forget her infant, as not to have pity on the son of her womb? and if she should forget, yet will I not forget thee.*" How touching, how consoling is this assurance! Surely it must inspire the coldest, the most despairing heart with confidence and hope! The God of love and goodness, of mercy and long-suffering will not forget you when you are tormented by temptation, and exposed to the risk of losing your innocence. He will never, never forget you, but you must endeavor to receive Him frequently in holy communion.

For the celestial dew contained in this wondrous Sacrament imparts divine strength. How could it be otherwise? Holy communion is a union between Jesus and ourselves—a union so intimate that even His almighty love could have devised none closer. He Himself has said: *"He that eateth my flesh and drinketh my blood, abideth in me, and I in him."* This most intimate union effects a transformation by the fire of divine charity. The partaking of His most sacred body and blood weakens concupiscence and gives the feeble will strength for conflict. By partaking of this Sacrament the soul is filled with a joy compared with which the pleasures of sin appear contemptible, and bitter as gall. If Jesus, who is Purity itself, unites Himself so closely to your soul, how can the unclean spirit dare to approach you? If you frequently receive Him in this way, if He nourishes, fortifies, ennobles, and sanctifies your soul with His omnipotent grace, must not your lily of innocence ever become stronger, more flourishing, fairer and more fragrant?

Therefore adhere faithfully to this excellent practice, which you have perhaps already adopted, and endeavor in future to approach at least once every month those holy sacraments by means of which your lily is refreshed and strengthened with celestial dew. Should severe temptations assail you, and great dangers beset your path, your confessor may perhaps direct you to go to communion more often still. Ask him to counsel you, and follow his advice. Speak to him with all candor and childlike docility, especially where the lily of innocence is concerned. And amid dangers and temptations let this be your prayer:

> In life's hard conflict be Thou near,
> My God, for then no foe I fear;
> Left to myself I needs must fall;
> Strengthened by Thee, I conquer all.

LXIV. A Mother's Care

In drawing to a close my instructions concerning the fairest flower that can adorn the maiden's soul, I have kept the most pleasing and attractive subject to the last.

Whither does a child go when anything alarms or oppresses it? To its tender mother, to her gentle, loving heart. Where does it take refuge when dangers threaten, and cruel persons pursue it? It takes hold of its mother's hand, for safety and protection. To whom does it bring any treasure it may possess, anything it especially values? To its watchful mother, that she may keep and guard the treasure.

You, my dear child, have a very difficult and responsible task—you have to preserve your innocence; therefore go to your mother, to Mary, the sweet Mother of God. Dangers threaten, and hellish foes pursue you; therefore fly to your Mother and cling fast to her protecting hand. You possess a treasure of incalculable value—the tender lily of purity; therefore entreat Mary, your heavenly Mother, to watch over your flower, to protect it, to tend and cherish it.

Beseech Mary to aid you in preserving the fragrant perfume—the dazzling whiteness—of your lily. St. Bernard, who had so great a devotion to Mary, addresses you in these impressive words; "O man, whoever thou art, if thou dost not wish to be swallowed up in the abyss, turn not away thine eye from the shining star, call upon Mary. If thou art tossed hither and thither by the waves of vanity and pride, look up to this star, call upon Mary! If the billows of concupiscence and sensual desires break over thy little bark of life, look up to this star, call upon Mary!

"Keep her in thy heart; let her name be ever on thy lips. If she hold thee up, thou wilt not fall; if she guide thee, thou wilt not go astray; if she protect thee, thou hast no need to fear; if she look favorably upon thee, thou wilt escape the snares of hell, and reach the gate of eternal felicity."

Yes, dear child, in the bright days of your youth, fix your gaze upon Mary; take her for your model. She is, as the poet says, "Our tainted nature's solitary boast"; she is the pure, the immaculate, Mother of God. Look up to her, contemplate her, and you will be filled with a more eager desire to cultivate carefully, to preserve and to cherish the lily among the virtues that should adorn your soul.

Amid the dangers which threaten this fair flower, cling tightly to the hand of your Mother Mary. She has power to help, to protect, to deliver you; she will keep the poison of impurity far from you. Countless are the instances in which young persons have been delivered from the temptations of the flesh, and have received grace and strength to overcome them, because they invoked the Mother of God in a spirit of confidence. Here is one example:

A young girl had abandoned herself to a life of sin at a very early age, to the great grief of her pious mother. The latter went to Rome, and laid her burden at the feet of the celebrated Father Succhi. He requested her to bring her daughter to him. His tact and kindness speedily won the young girl's confidence. She promised every day conscientiously to repeat the following short prayer: "My Queen and my Mother! remember that I belong to thee; preserve and defend me as thy property and possession!"

This brief petition worked wonders. A few years later, Father Succhi again visited Rome. The pious mother sought him out and said, with tears of joy: "O Father, how deeply grateful I am to the Blessed Virgin and to you; my child has become an angel upon earth."

Do you likewise pray to your Blessed Mother with confidence and perseverance. Cleave closely to her maternal heart; she will guard and care for the lily of your heart, and water it from the fount of grace which flows from the Sacred Heart of Jesus.

Mark well, and imprint it deeply on your youthful heart, that if Mary loves one class of persons more than another, she regards the young with peculiar affection. She loves you, my dear child; she knows the dangers which threaten you, the battles you have to fight, the weakness which enfeebles your will. And she has the most sympathizing heart, she feels with your every need, she compassionates your soul, exposed as it is to countless perils.

Oh, what a blessed thing it is to know that there is one whose maternal heart can solace, succor, and rescue us! It is a consoling thought in all the sorrows of life, and especially when death takes your mother from you, that you have still a mother in Mary, a still more loving mother, who will never, never forsake you, unless you are so foolish and unhappy as first to forsake her.

And are you not determined never to forsake your Mother Mary? I am sure that you have already formed this resolution, and that you will frequently renew it, carrying it out into practice by piously praying to the Mother of God and by exercises of devotion in her honor. My consolation, my ground of hope on your behalf is that you are, and will remain, a faithful child of Mary.

Whilst I have been giving you these instructions upon the lily of chastity, a feeling of melancholy has sometimes stolen over me, when I have asked myself whether you will follow my exhortations and fatherly counsels. Or whether you will, at a subsequent period, wander from the right way, and finally be lost. But as I have just said, your true, childlike devotion to the Mother of God calms and consoles me. For I know that no true child of Mary can ever be lost.

Therefore often sing this sweet hymn in her honor, and pray with heart and voice to Mary in the well-known lines:

> Hail, Queen of Heaven, the ocean Star,
> Guide of the wand'rer here below!
> Thrown on life's surge, we claim thy care;
> Save us from peril and from woe.

The Canticle of the Blessed Virgin Mary

MAGNIFICAT anima mea Dominum.

Et exultavit Spiritus meus in Deo salutari meo.

Quia respexit humilitatem ancille suae; ecce enim ex hoc beatam me dicent omnes generationes.

Quia fecit mihi magna Qui potens est; et sanctum nomen Ejus.

Et misericordia Ejus a progenie in progenies, timentibus eum.

Fecit potentiam in brachio suo; dispersit superbos mente cordis sui.

Deposuit potentes de sede, et exaltavit humiles.

Esurientes implevit bonis: et divites dimisit inanes.

Suscepit Israel puerum Suum; recordatus misericordiae Suae.

Sicut locutus est ad patres nostros, Abraham, et semini ejus in saecula.

MY SOUL doth magnify the Lord;

And my spirit hath rejoiced in God my Saviour.

Because He hath regarded the humility of His handmaid, for behold from henceforth all generations shall call me blessed.

For He that is mighty hath done great things to me; and holy is His name.

And His mercy is from generation to generation, to them that fear Him.

He hath shown might in His arm; He hath scattered the proud in the conceit of their heart.

He hath put down the mighty from their seat, and hath exalted the humble.

He hath filled the hungry with good things; and the rich He hath sent away empty.

He hath received Israel His servant; being mindful of His mercy.

As He spoke to our fathers, to Abraham, and to his seed forever.

I<small>N</small> life's bright morn I see thee depart,
 I see thee go, with a trembling heart;
Farewell, sweet maid, so joyous and free,
God's blessing ever abide with thee.

When thou dost stand where the ways divide,
May the angel guardian be beside;
God grant thou may'st choose the narrow way,
And from it may thy footsteps never stray.

Part Third

AT THE PARTING OF THE WAYS

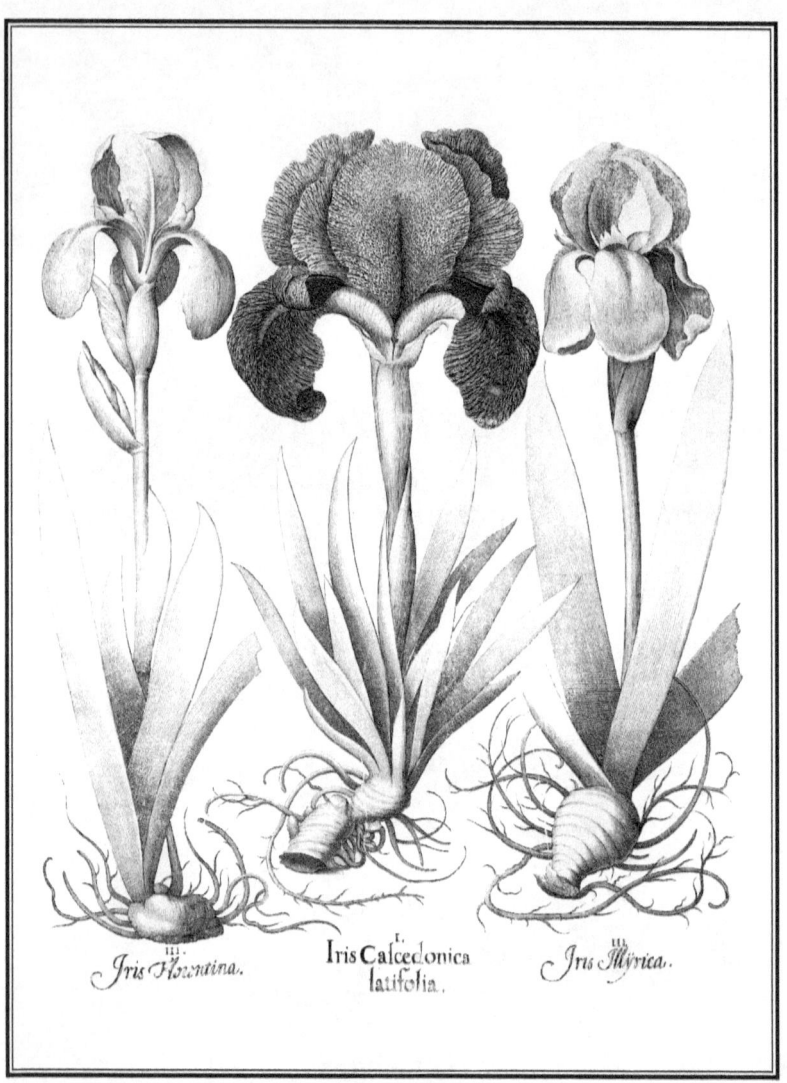

‹ 1 ›

Which is My Path?

LXV. The Decision to Be Made

Let us suppose that, while you are traveling in a foreign country, you come to a spot where one road stretches straight before you, another leads to the right, and a third to the left. It is then indeed very important for you to know which road you ought to take in order to reach your destination.

Now, you have really set out upon such a journey; your whole life is truly a journey to heaven. Perhaps you have already reached a spot where the ways part, or you may soon arrive at such a place; you will be obliged to come to a decision, and choose one of the three roads. But which are you to choose? Are you to marry, to go into religion, or to live unmarried in the world? All three roads have one and the same goal—they all lead to heaven. But each has its own special difficulties and obstacles, which every one is not equally able to surmount. Those only can do this who have the requisite qualifications, and receive the necessary graces from God. He who enters upon one of these paths without the necessary graces and qualifications, can scarcely hope to get to heaven.

Perhaps you have already reached some spot where a decision must be made, or you may soon arrive at it. You must make your choice and enter upon one of the three different paths. Consider the importance of this decision, in order that you may choose the right way.

People speak of condition or state of life, and calling; these expressions have a certain similarity, but they are not identical. By calling is understood more properly the relation in which each individual stands to society. When one inquires as to a man's calling, one does not mean to ask whether he is to marry, live single, or go into religion, but whether he is to be a shoemaker, baker, tailor, or an artisan of any description; whether he is to be a doctor, lawyer, tutor, or embrace any other learned profession. These various callings are to society what, in a manner, the different members are to the human body. Society is sound and prosperous when the various callings are properly filled and carried out, as the human body is well when all its parts are in a normal condition and regularly perform their functions. Yet in the sense we have attached to the word, it cannot be said that the salvation of the soul directly depends upon the calling of which choice may be made. Whether you become a stenographer, a dressmaker or a postmistress may be very important as far as your temporal welfare is concerned, but as far as your eternal happiness is in question, the decision is of no direct moment.

How widely different a matter is the choice of a state in life! The all-wise providence of God orders and arranges everything. His merciful eye beholds all creatures He has made, all ages and places, nations and families, from all eternity. He knows the needs of each individual and of every nation, He foresees peace and war, plenty and famine, all generations that are to come, fathers and mothers, sons and daughters. He has endowed each individual man with an immortal soul, gifted with such special capabilities as will enable him to attain his destined goal. And God permits body and soul to develop in a manner corresponding to this appointed end.

When a young person comes to the parting of the ways, the call of God makes itself heard more or less plainly, sometimes by external means, sometimes by a voice speaking within: "I have destined thee to be the father or mother of a family; upon thee I shall bestow a vocation to the religious life; I intend thee to live unmarried in the world." Thus the call of God is addressed to each one, though in widely varying ways. One hears it in his own heart from early childhood, another only when the moment of decision arrives. God calls some person suddenly by means of some unusual event; others—and these constitute by far the largest number—through the circumstances and relations of their life.

How exceedingly important it is to recognize and to follow the call of God. All men have been created in order that they may love God and keep His commandments while they are on earth, and be happy forever with Him in heaven; such is the chief end of man, his final goal. The commandments of God are the same everywhere and for all men, but all have not the same difficulty in keeping them. The same state of life is not suited for every one, nor can every one experience the same facility in reaching heaven, whatever be the state of life he may embrace.

If you are called to live unmarried, you would find it difficult to save your soul if you were to marry. If, on the other hand, it is your duty to marry, the unmarried state would prove a great hindrance in your journey to heaven. And if it is the will of God that you should become an inmate of the cloister, you could scarcely save your soul in the world. The same rule applies to the marriage state, in which the character of the husband you choose is of the utmost importance. St. Gregory of Nazianzen says: "He who errs as to his vocation will go from one mistake to another all his life long, and in the end perhaps find himself deceived in regard to his hope of reaching heaven."

It is easy to perceive the reason of this. If a young girl refuses to follow the clear call of God because to do so would cost her a considerable sacrifice, and she therefore follows her own will—for instance, if she contracts a marriage forbidden by the Church—she will not receive the graces appertaining to the state she has chosen, for the very reason that she has acted contrary to the will of God. She will be unhappy all her life, and, failing some very special intervention of Providence, be unhappy also during the countless ages of eternity.

You have as yet perhaps not reached the parting of the ways, and years may elapse before the moment for a decision arrives. You may already be filled with anxious dread lest you should make a wrong choice and wreck your prospects of happiness. But fear not, be of good courage! There is a sure and simple means of choosing aright. In the meantime be truly chaste and pious, and your choice cannot fail to be a happy one.

> By various ways God doth intend
> To bring man to his final end;
> One only way is traced for thee,
> To lead thee to eternity.

LXVI. Useful Advice

WHEN a priest contemplates the youthful members of his flock, he often asks himself, with a heavy heart, what will become of them. And I now ask myself about you who are going to read the present chapter whether you will persevere in your good resolutions; whether you will be happy in this world, and get to heaven at last. I cannot tell; I can only wish most ardently that so it may be. But one thing I do know; you will probably find happiness, and save your soul, if you choose the state of life for which you are destined by God. Therefore I am anxious to do everything which lies in my power to help you to choose wisely and well. Lay carefully to heart the useful advice I shall endeavor to give you in this chapter.

My first piece of advice is to take counsel with yourself. You must do this calmly, without prejudice. Your heart should resemble a delicately balanced pair of scales; you must weigh all things fairly. You must not try to discover where and how you can most speedily grow rich and enjoy the vanities and amusements of the world. A girl who, when choosing a state of life, should take counsel of herself in such a fashion as this, and see things from a purely material point of view, without reference to God and to her eternal salvation, would be greatly in danger of making a bad choice. Therefore I beseech you not to expose yourself to any such risk.

Take counsel with yourself in such a manner as will enable you to say to God in a spirit of resignation: "Speak, Lord, for Thy servant heareth. I desire nothing but what is Thy will. If only I can do Thy will it is a matter of indifference to me whether I am rich or poor, whether happiness or sorrow is my portion, whether my life is full of work or spent in ease and without exertion. All this is of no consequence, if only I can please Thee, O my God, and save my soul in the end."

In this resigned frame of mind examine yourself; review your characteristics, peculiarities and inclinations, good and bad; think over your past; notice what are your passions and temptations; consider the strength or weakness of your will. Then compare with all this the duties, difficulties and dangers of the state of life upon which you purpose to enter. If you feel compelled to say to yourself: "When I remember the weakness of my will and the force of the temptations which assail me, I do not think that I am capable of fulfilling the duties of that state, or of overcoming the difficulties which it presents," it becomes plain that this road to heaven is too steep for you.

Consider your case as you would that of a friend who had similar faults and the same inclinations. One is usually more unprejudiced in regard to others than one can hope to be if the matter under consideration is of a personal nature. Why should you not feel the same affection for yourself as you do for a friend? Why should you not take counsel with yourself in the same manner in which you would seek to advise her?

Act in respect to yourself as you will wish you had done when you come to lie upon your death-bed. There can be no safer rule than this. For in the presence of death matters are viewed in their true tight, and no longer seen through colored glasses. How extremely foolish it would be to embrace a state of life which would furnish cause for bitter repentance in your last hours!

My second piece of advice is: Take counsel with others. But who is to counsel you, and to whom ought you to listen? Here great caution is necessary; there are counselors who present themselves unasked, and to whom it would be wrong to listen. On no account lend your ear to bad Catholics, to persons who have no faith or who have not a good reputation. In regard to the supernatural, their understanding is either darkened or extinguished altogether; the eyes of their mind are blind as far as the eternal truths are concerned; how then could they advise others—how point out to them the right road to heaven? There are yet other counselors to whom it would be most inadvisable to listen. I mean worldly persons, who are entirely absorbed in material things. For higher interests they have no perception; their thoughts are set upon nothing else but money, honors and pleasures. Persons of this class usually deplore the entrance of a girl into religion.

Nor ought you to listen to the advice of those who have anything to gain or lose from your choice in a worldly point of view. A wealthy unmarried lady returned upon a certain occasion a very curt answer to an interested adviser who sought her hand in marriage. He implored her to make him the happiest of mortals, reminding her that marriages are made in heaven. "That is the very reason," she briefly replied, "why I wish to wait until we both get there!" Finally, do not be advised by persons who know nothing about the state of life that you may be thinking of adopting, as, for instance, the religious state. Their ignorance imbues them with the most absurd ideas and vehement prejudices, in regard to such a state of life. How could they form a correct judgment?

From whom, then, are, you to seek counsel? Holy Scripture exhorts you: *"Keep continually to a wise man, who fears the Lord."* It is very important to remember this when the choice of a state of life is under consideration. And why is it so? Because he who desires to give good advice must often offend this or that individual with regard to whose interests the results of his advice may prove to be prejudicial. For instance, there are families which, being influenced by worldly motives and advantages, insist upon the daughter choosing some particular state of life, or marrying some person they have fixed upon, though she does not feel herself called by God to coincide with their views. If counsel is sought from persons who fear man rather than God, what misery may not be the consequence of following their advice, since in giving it they view things from a purely human standpoint. Parents are, as a rule, the natural advisers of their children, and God has ordained that such they should be. But there are exceptional cases in which they rank among the evil counselors I have enumerated above; and in these instances their advice cannot be relied upon.

Under all circumstances your best adviser is plainly your confessor. You ought not only to ask his advice, but faithfully to follow it. He knows you as no one can know you, except God alone; he knows your good and bad qualities and inclinations. Therefore do not, in your youthful folly, be influenced by the fear that his advice will not coincide with your own wishes.

Rather give thanks to God that you have at least one friend whose intentions are pure, whose motives are disinterested, and who will be able to prevent you from making a fatal mistake. Consult your confessor and take his advice; that is the best way of ensuring happiness.

> When thou shalt come where the two ways part,
> Pause and consider where thou art;
> Ask counsel, seek God's will to know
> As to the path where thy steps should go.

LXVII. The Means to Make a Wise Choice

Every one desires to choose aright, but how many young persons there are who are so unfortunate as to make a wrong choice! A girl who had not long left school made the acquaintance of a young man who was not only very well off, but appeared to be all that was desirable. She married him, imagining that she had made a fortunate choice. But on the evening of her wedding-day she discovered how terribly she had been deceived. In all simplicity she showed her husband a beautiful statue of the Mother of God, which had been given her as a souvenir of the occasion. He snatched it from her roughly, and dashed it to the ground, saying as he did so: "We have done with these follies; remember that for the future!" And I regret to say this poor girl's fears were realized, for her married life proved to be most unhappy.

May you be more fortunate, not only if you should marry, but in your choice of a state in general. To this end follow the practical advice I gave you in the previous chapter and make use of the means I am about to point out to you.

In the first place, direct your heart constantly toward heaven. Have but one desire—namely, to know and to do the will of God. God will then bestow His grace upon you, and you will be certain to make a wise choice. No one must count upon an extraordinary call, such as the apostles and many great saints received. Those were very special gifts of grace, which you cannot expect. But if you keep your eye and heart constantly directed toward God, He will enlighten you with His grace, will give you prudent counselors, and so ordain external circumstances that you may, if I can thus express it, be led by the hand of your guardian angel to enter the state of life God intends for you.

Truly the ways of God are wonderful and manifold. Sometimes He impresses on the heart of a young child a desire for a particular state. Consequently, later on in life there can arise no question as to making a choice, the question having already been decided. To others He signifies His will only when a choice has to be made; and these often enter with joy of spirit into a state for which they had long experienced a rooted aversion.

In the second place, keep your soul pure. A very great deal—everything, indeed—depends upon this. The brighter and more transparent is the glass of a window, the more readily do the rays of the sun penetrate into the room; but the dimmer the glass, the darker will the apartment be. The soul may be compared to glass—to a mirror, into which the beams of divine grace shine, and in which they are reflected. If you desire to be enlightened from on high in your choice of a state of life, keep your heart clean—preserve therein the bright light of innocence. If this light is obscured or extinguished by sin, delay not to rekindle it by means of contrition and confession.

In the third place, be diligent in prayer. From what has already been said you must plainly perceive that prayer is of the utmost importance in choosing a state of life. For, on the one hand, you seek to choose the state of life which wilt best promote your eternal salvation; on the other, the world, the flesh, and the devil strive to decoy you into taking the wrong road.

There are two epochs in the life of every individual when the devil lays snares for him with particular cunning. The first is when he ceases to be a child—then comes the crisis, the critical period when the result of previous training will show in the innocence and purity of the youth or maiden, or the reverse be unhappily the case. I believe this critical period has already passed with you; I confidently hope you have successfully withstood the test and preserved your innocence.

But with yet greater cunning and force will the devil attack you either now or a few years hence, when you come to choose a state of life. Should he succeed in inducing you to take the wrong road, he will expect to emerge victorious from your final, death-bed struggle. Therefore, my dear child, pray, pray! Pray for light, that the mists may disperse and the road of life stretch clearly before you; pray for strength to resist your passions whatever sacrifices it may cost you; pray simply that you may know and do the will of God.

In the fourth place, receive frequently and worthily the Sacraments of Penance and of the Altar. These Sacraments will maintain the purity of your soul, and the Giver of grace will descend into your heart with His light and strength. After each communion entreat Our Lord, with earnestness and confidence, to teach you what are the designs of His Sacred Heart in regard to you, and to strengthen you to make any sacrifice that may be necessary. And on your communion days give some time to serious reflection. Imagine that you are stretched upon your death-bed. Ask yourself if you were in that awful hour what state of life you would wish you had chosen. Would it not be a cause of bitter regret if you had acted in accordance with your own self-will, instead of following the advice of your confessor?

I cannot refrain from mentioning one more means for arriving at a right decision—namely, a true, filial, confiding love and devotion to Mary. On the present occasion I will only make two brief remarks in regard to this devotion. If you desire wisdom and enlightenment concerning the choice of a state of life, the surest way to obtain it is through Mary, for she is "*Sedes sapientiæ*," the "Seat of wisdom." And if you wish to attain eternal salvation, the surest way to realize this is through Mary, for, as a great saint tells us, "a true servant of Mary can never be lost."

Do not imagine that thoughts like these are suited only for a young woman who is about to enter the cloister. These reflections are not intended for this one or that one, but for all who desire to choose aright so as to ensure their eternal salvation.

As you ought to beware of rashness in choosing a state of life, so ought you to guard against over-anxiety. Do not lose heart in presence of the momentous decision. Make use of the means I have pointed out to you; look constantly toward Heaven. Keep your soul pure; be diligent in prayer; frequently approach the sacraments; practise devotion to Mary; regard her as your Mother; and look with cheerful confidence into the future. Eternal peace and joy follow the earthly struggle. The way of the cross leads to the crown of immortal glory.

> 'Tis Thy good pleasure, not my own,
> In Thee, my God, I love alone;
> And nothing I desire of Thee
> But what Thy goodness wills for me.
>
> > O will of God, O will divine,
> > All, all our love be ever Thine.
>
> In love no rival canst Thou bear,
> But Thou art full of tend'rest care;
> And fire and sweetness all divine
> To hearts which once are wholly Thine.

Thou makest crosses soft and light,
And death itself seem sweet and bright:
No cross nor fear that soul dismays,
Whose will to Thee united stays.

To Thee I consecrate and give
My heart and being while I live;
Jesus, Thy heart alone shall be
My love for all eternity.

Alike in pleasure and in pain
To please Thee is my joy and gain;
That, O my Love, which pleases Thee
Shall evermore seem best to me.
May heaven and earth with love fulfil,
My God, Thy ever blessed will.

Prayer to St. Lucy

We admire, O glorious virgin and martyr, St. Lucy, that light of lively faith which it pleased the most merciful God to infuse into thy beautiful soul; enlightened by which thou didst despise the vain and trifling things of this miserable earth, keeping thine eyes fixed upon that heaven for which alone we have been created. The riches and the pleasures which the seductive world held out to thee, to the prejudice of faith and of divine grace, never clouded thy mind, nor allured thy heart. Hence, far from consenting to the proposals of thy wicked persecutor, thou didst show thyself bold and resolute to encounter even death itself, rather than be unfaithful to thy heavenly Lord. What cause of confusion for us, who, not less enlightened by faith and strengthened by grace, still do not know how to resist our guilty passions, nor to despise the evil maxims or repel the flattery of the infernal enemy. Ah! obtain for us, dear saint, from God greater light, by which we may come to know that we were not made for things here below, but for those of heaven. Amen.

Prayer for Youth to beg the Divine Direction in the Choice of a State of Life

O ALMIGHTY GOD! Whose wise and amiable providence watches over every human event, deign to be my light and my counsel in all my undertakings, particularly in the choice of a state of life. I know that on this important step my sanctification and salvation may in a great measure depend. I know that I am incapable of discerning what may be best for me; therefore I cast myself into Thy arms, beseeching Thee, my God, Who hast sent me into this world only to love and serve Thee, to direct by Thy grace every moment and action of my life to the glorious end of my creation. I renounce most sincerely every other wish, than to fulfil Thy designs on my soul, whatever they may be; and I beseech Thee to give me the grace, by imbibing the true spirit of a Christian, to qualify myself for any state of life to which Thy adorable providence may call me.

O MY GOD! whenever it may become my duty to make a choice, do Thou be my light and my counsel, and mercifully deign to *make the way known to me wherein I should walk, for I have lifted up my soul to Thee.* Preserve me from listening to the suggestions of my own self-love, or worldly prudence, in prejudice to Thy holy inspirations. Let *Thy good Spirit lead me into the right way,* and Thy adorable providence place me, not where I may be happiest, according to the world, but in that state in which I shall love and serve Thee most perfectly, and meet with most abundant means for working out my salvation. This is all that I ask and all that I desire; for what would it avail me to gain the whole world, if, in the end, I were to lose my soul? and to be so unfortunate as to prefer temporal advantages and worldly honors to the enjoyment of Thy divine presence in a happy eternity?

Most holy Virgin Mary, take me under thy protection. My good angel guardian and patron saints, pray for me. Amen.

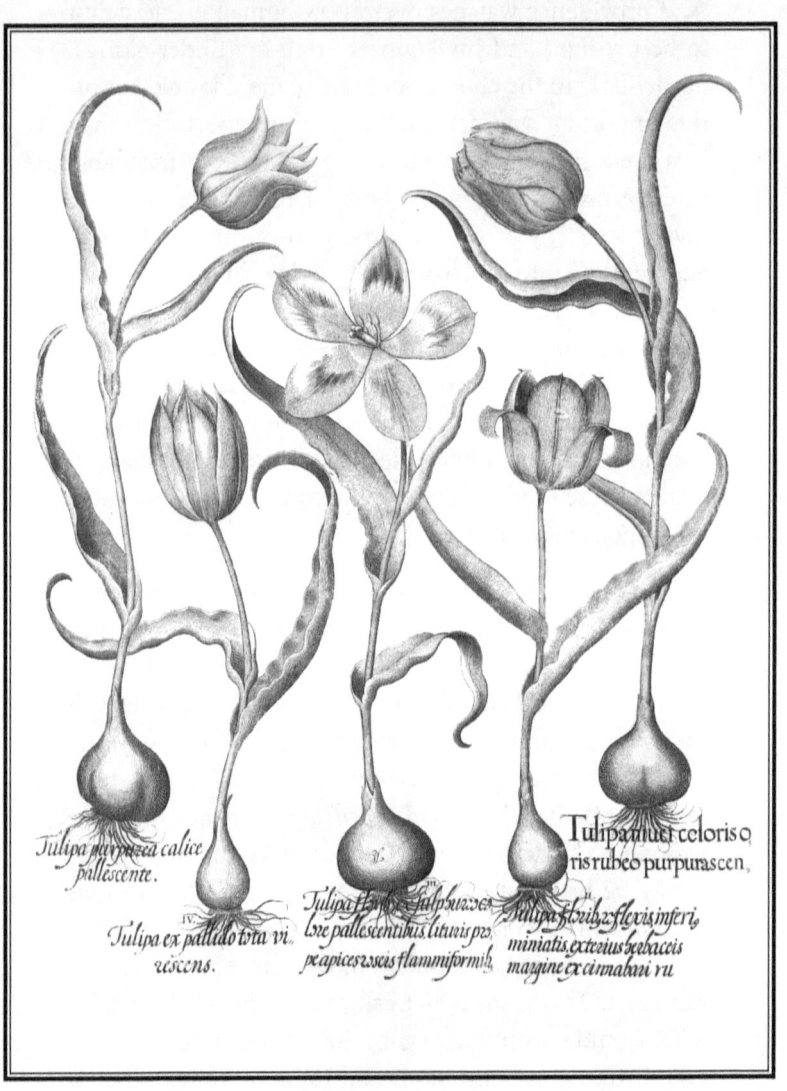

◀ 2 ▶

The Married State

LXVIII. Ought I to Marry?

O F the three paths before you when you stand at the parting of the ways one leads straight onward: it is the shortest, most direct way to heaven, and is known as the Religious life. The second trends away to the right—it also leads to the same bright, eternal goal, by a slightly circuitous route—it is the state of the unmarried in the world. The third road leads away to the left, into a hilly region—there are many pleasures and joys to be met with on that way, and also much toil and many sorrows—that is the married state. All these three states, I repeat most emphatically, are ordained by God; but any state is not fitted for any individual. Neither is it a matter of indifference to almighty God which state in life we choose for ourselves.

We will now consider each of these three states in turn, in order to aid you in making a wise choice. The reason why I speak first of the married state is simply because a great majority of mankind is called to this state, and therefore it suggests itself first to our consideration. Now, the decisive question presents itself: Are you called to the married state? Ought you to marry? Let me suggest to you a few serious thoughts.

The answer to the question, "Ought you to marry?" depends upon another question: Do you think yourself capable of fulfilling the duties of the married state? In order to answer this question you must learn what these duties really are; and I will now proceed briefly to set them before you.

One of the chief among these duties requires that husband and wife should live together in concord, love, and conjugal fidelity until death. They must remain together, since marriage is indissoluble. Only when it pleases almighty God to sever the bond by taking husband or wife out of this world may the survivor marry again.

How should married people live together? First of all in peace and harmony. They should aim at, and strive after, one and the same things; they should seek to lead a Christian life, serving God faithfully and helping each other on the way to heaven. For this end they must be united, avoiding anger, quarreling, and dissension; otherwise they will embitter their life and make it a sort of hell upon earth. Nor can they escape hell in the world to come unless they repent and amend.

The following apposite anecdote may be related here. Two married persons who lived unhappily together carried their dispute one day so far as to come to blows. A neighbor who heard what was going on suddenly shouted: "Fire! Fire!" The quarrel was forgotten; husband and wife eagerly inquired where the fire was burning. "In hell," was the unexpected reply, "and thither married people must go who persist in living in enmity, anger, and dissension."

Married people should live together in love, not in strife and in quarreling. They should endeavor to please each other, they should pray for each other, have patience and bear with each other's faults. When some grievance presents itself they should not complain to others, but mutually forgive and become reconciled.

And they should live in conjugal fidelity, keeping the promises they solemnly made at the altar. The wife must not fix her affections on any other man; the husband must not seek after any other woman; else will they be in danger of committing one of the most grievous and terrible of sins, a sin which God punishes very severely.

Another important duty is that of mutual edification. Husband and wife should set each other a good example, seeking each to sanctify the other, and walk together on the heavenward road. Such is the highest aim and object of a union which a sacrament has rendered holy. Christ loved His own unto the end, and, moreover, in such a manner that they should attain their own final salvation. So must the wife love her husband, and the husband his wife—in such a way that they may both attain their final end: eternal blessedness. They should therefore unite in prayer, attend divine worship together, and receive the sacraments at the same time. If they do this, the blessing of God will assuredly rest upon them.

Difficult and important as are those duties of married people which we have already considered, the most difficult, and at the same time the most important of all, is doubtless that of bringing up their children in the fear of God. When the Last Judgment comes, we who are priests and confessors shall not be judged in the same way as ordinary individuals; we shall not only have to answer for what we have personally done or left undone, but we shall have further to give account of the souls committed to our care. In precisely the same manner shall fathers and mothers be judged; not merely in regard to what their own lives have been, but as to the manner in which they have brought up their children. If these latter are doomed to perdition through the bad education they have received from their parents, they shall hang like millstones round the neck of their father or mother, sinking them yet deeper into the abyss of hell.

This difficult duty of the education of children, and the heavy responsibility attaching to it, is sufficient of itself to make you, Christian maiden, seriously reflect before answering the question "Ought I to marry?" in the affirmative.

If this duty of education is so difficult and burdensome for the father, it is doubly and trebly so for the mother. For the physical and spiritual training of children depends—in their earliest years at least—almost exclusively upon her. How great a load of trouble and anxiety, grief and suffering, must rest upon a mother until her four, six, eight, or even more children can feed and dress themselves—until they are, to a certain extent, independent of her! Since the day when God said to the mother of the human race: "*In sorrow shalt thou bring forth children, and thou shalt be under thy husband's power,*" the life of every wife and mother has been a life of constant sacrifice and renunciation, full of sorrows and trials.

My dear daughter, "Ought you to marry?" To sum up everything in a few words, I would say to you: If you have courage to make great sacrifices, if you are very fond of children, if you feel that you could readily submit to the will of another, if you are sound and healthy in both mind and body, if you are sufficiently versed in household matters, and have attained the proper age (I would say the age of twenty), then you may marry if you consider yourself called to the wedded state rather than to an unmarried life in the world. May God enlighten, guide, and bless you! And may the words of Solomon be exemplified in your case: "*She hath looked well to the paths of her house, and hath not eaten her bread idle. Her children rose up, and called her blessed; her husband also and he praised her.*"

LXIX. Whom Should I Marry?

IF you, Christian maiden, have attained a suitable age, feel yourself called to the married state, and receive offers of marriage, the important questions arise: Whom should I marry—or to whom ought I to become engaged—and to what ought I principally to look? I will endeavor to give practical answers to these questions.

Always look in the first place to religion, virtue and uprightness. Never make an intimate acquaintance with a man of whose antecedents you know nothing, and in regard to whom you are unable to obtain reliable information. On no account allow yourself to be lulled into security by fair speeches, solemn assurances, and brilliant promises on the part of a stranger, or of one who has lived only for a few months in the place where you live. I entreat you to believe me when I tell you that it is impossible to be too cautious in regard to strangers. Many a young wife has prepared unhappiness for both herself and her parents by carelessness in this respect, and by allowing herself to be over-persuaded by a flattering and insinuating suitor.

Therefore I once again repeat: look only to virtue, uprightness, devotedness to our holy Church and genuine religious sentiments. If you hear anything indicating the contrary from a reliable source or notice anything for yourself, act as did a young French lady. She was engaged to be married, and was spending the evening before her wedding-day in the company of her betrothed and some relatives. He began to make jocular and contemptuous remarks about religion. His intended gently rebuked him, but he jestingly replied that a man of the world could not afford to be so particular in such matters. Grieved and shocked, Elizabeth (that was the young lady's name) declared that she would not marry him. "For," she said, "he who does not love God will not love his wife truly and faithfully." Nor could the united persuasions of her parents and her lover induce her to swerve from her resolution. And I think she was perfectly right; let her maxim be yours also.

Never become engaged to a man who is careless about fulfilling his religious duties, who absents himself from Mass on days of obligation without sufficient cause, or who mocks at priests and matters connected with religion. Never keep company with a young fellow who likes to spend his time in taverns, drinking and gambling; who keeps late hours at night, neglects his work, or one who has a very violent temper. Give up at once a man who does not respect your innocence, but allows himself to take liberties and to be unduly familiar with you.

Let innocence be your greatest treasure, your only source of pride, and promptly turn away from any one who with poisonous breath or profane hand would tarnish the brightness of your purity.

You must also consider, in choosing a husband, the external circumstances of your suitor, and whether the contrast between his position and your own is not too great. Too great a disparity of age is to be avoided; a marriage rarely turns out well when the wife is much older than the husband. Never permit your marriage tie to be degraded into a mere business transaction. I chanced to read of an instance of the kind in a newspaper the other day. A very wealthy man wanted to get a son-in-law still richer than himself. He met with a young man to suit his ideas, and proposed to give him, in the event of his marrying his daughter, a very handsome sum as her dowry. The gentleman, however, who probably loved money more than he loved the girl, demanded a still larger sum. The squabble which ensued was a long one; at length the bargain was satisfactorily concluded, and the wedding took place. The young lady does not appear to have been more sensible or noble-minded than her parent; or else she would have said to him: "Father, you can do with your money what you please, but this sordid fellow shall not have me! I want a husband who wishes to marry *me*, not my *money!*"

You may perhaps ask whether you are not to pay any heed to the question of money or income in selecting a husband.

Most certainly you are; no sensible girl ought to marry a man whose calling and pecuniary circumstances do not afford a guarantee that he will be able to support a family decently without help from outside. On the other hand, no prudent and sagacious young woman would give her hand to a man *merely* because he is rich, or—this I must add—only on account of his good looks or attractive manners. But if two suitors are equally good and religious it is quite justifiable to choose the richer and more pleasing.

Another objection you may raise is this: if young girls are to be so critical and fastidious in the choice of a husband they will end by getting none at all! And in my opinion it would be a very good thing for a great many if this should prove to be the case! However, good, clever young women have nothing to fear.

For although no statistics can be obtained on this head, it may safely be asserted that among young men who are called to the married state there are quite as many—if not more—good and worthy individuals as there are among young women who likewise wish to marry. And this proceeds from the existing conditions of society. For many of the best, most intelligent and clever girls do not feel themselves called to marry, but either to enter the cloister or to live unmarried in the world. In the case of young men, almost all, with the exception of the comparatively small number of those who become priests or go into religion, are so situated as to find it desirable to enter matrimony and establish their own home. Therefore the more accomplished, pious and capable maidens are, the better prospect they have of a happy marriage.

In conclusion let me lay stress upon this point: If you are at least twenty years of age you may think of becoming engaged, but not before then. In the meantime let it be your sole effort and aim to love God, to make progress in virtue, to be pious and chaste, and to learn all you can.

> Heart with heart together meeting,
> See, they are in concord beating;
> Life is long and passion fleeting.
> —*Schiller.*

LXX. THE TIME OF COURTSHIP

YOU are aware that it behooves you at all times to watch and pray and keep strict guard over your innocence, but never is this so necessary as when you are receiving the addresses of a young man. That is by far the most dangerous time for young people. If they forget God, the period of their engagement often witnesses the ruin of their innocence, their peace of mind and the happiness of their life. This topic is consequently among the most important for one whose office it is to instruct girls and give them practical advice for their guidance in moral and spiritual matters. Let me tell you plainly what the Christian maiden should think about courtship, and how she ought to conduct herself toward her lover.

A Christian maiden ought to seek to know betimes what is allowed and what is forbidden in regard to courtship. She ought not to wait to know this until she has fallen deeply in love and yielded to improper proposals. In this case the eye of her conscience would be dimmed; it would become impossible for her to judge aright. For those who have already sinned together warnings usually come too late; persuasions, entreaties, exhortations, are equally thrown away; if such persons were to see the abyss of hell yawning before them, or if some one were to rise from the dead to warn them, they would continue to pursue their evil way, saying it was impossible for them to desist from it.

"I am determined to go on, however things may turn out," said a young girl, hitherto good and docile, to her confessor, when the latter endeavored to induce her to give up a most undesirable acquaintance. And things did turn out very badly indeed, for in a comparatively brief period the wife died in a lunatic asylum and the husband in prison.

Therefore it is important for the girl who feels that it is her vocation to be married, to have the right view in regard to courtship, before receiving the attentions of any man.

We cannot approve of any familiar and intimate social intercourse between two young persons of different sexes if the acquaintance is made and carried on without a view to marriage within a reasonable time. If a youth and maiden stand in an intimate relation to each other, and seek to be often alone together, without any idea of a speedy marriage, such a relation must be condemned. It offers, as a rule, a proximate and voluntary occasion of sins against chastity, and to seek such occasions is in itself a sin. Countless sad examples which meet us in our daily experience prove that relations of this nature are truly a proximate occasion of grievous sin.

Of course it is desirable and even necessary that two young persons who wish to marry each other should become well acquainted, and to this end courtship is quite proper. Even in this case, however, circumstances may render a continuation of the courtship undesirable, or even actually wrong. For instance, unexpected hindrances may arise that make the marriage impossible, or require it to be indefinitely postponed; and the young persons continue, in spite of this, to meet just as frequently as they did before. Or one of them may allege some frivolous pretext for delaying the marriage. How silly are many girls who allow themselves to be made fools of by young men, and do not, or rather will not, see that their admirers are thinking of anything but marriage.

Again, an acquaintance allowable in other respects becomes sinful and undesirable if the engaged parties, although determined to be married before very long, seek in the meantime to be alone together as often as possible, and at such meetings always or nearly always commit sins, if not in deed, at least in thought and desire. There is only one way of extricating themselves from so perilous a position; they must either break off the engagement altogether, or arrange never to be left alone and to hasten their marriage. The first alternative will probably appear difficult, if not impossible, but the second can be carried out if only there is a good will.

From all which has been said you must plainly perceive that the period of courtship is fraught with grave dangers for your innocence, and that it calls for the exercise of the greatest prudence. Therefore note well how you ought to conduct yourself in the time of courtship:

(a) Ask advice in regard to your engagement. A priest warned one of his parishioners not to marry a certain young man. "For," he said, "you know him to be a drunkard, and you must be aware that whenever there is a quarrel he gets mixed up in it." "All he needs is a little management," was the reply; "besides, he is a handsome fellow, and the eye wants something too." Six weeks after her marriage the wife came to the priest with her head bandaged, and said, amid many tears: "Oh Father, my husband has beaten me so dreadfully! My right eye is nearly put out!" Gravely and sadly her confessor made answer: "My poor child, the eye wants something too."

(b) Be sure to mention the fact of your engagement when you go to confession, as much evil may thereby be prevented.

(c) Do not delay your marriage too long. As far as you can, avoid being alone with your betrothed. If his visits are too frequent and too protracted, and if you seek to be alone with him when he calls, it will be nothing short of a miracle if you preserve your chastity.

(d) During the time of your engagement keep strict guard

over yourself in regard to your virginal purity, and insist that your future husband shall also respect it; for this reason avoid all undue familiarity.

Thrice happy will you be if you follow this advice, and can approach the nuptial altar in virginal purity. For this end pray frequently and fervently to the Mother of God, saying: "O Mary, purest of virgins, and my Mother, guide me, guide thy weak child, that I may pass safely through the dangers which beset my youthful steps!"

> Queen of virgins, guard and guide me:
> Let me to thine arms repair;
> In thy tender bosom hide me;
> Mary, take me to thy care.

LXXI. Marry a Catholic

ST. JEROME relates the following anecdote in regard to St. Marcella, who was left a widow while still quite young. A man of good family, Cerealis by name, wished to marry her, promising to make her sole heiress of his large fortune if she would accept his hand. Her mother urged her to close with the brilliant offer, but she replied: "If I had not determined never to marry again, I should look out for a *husband*, rather than a *fortune*."

You, Christian maiden, ought to be of the same opinion; when the time comes to choose a husband, do not think too much about riches and temporal interests. Pay all the more attention to another point, which is perhaps the most important of all: *marry only a Catholic.* On no account conclude a mixed marriage; therefore avoid engaging yourself to a non-Catholic.

In my earlier instructions I laid great stress upon this head. I shall now enter upon it more at length. For it is of the utmost importance in the present day, when Catholics and

Protestants are almost everywhere associated, and Catholic girls are more or less exposed to the danger of becoming acquainted with a non-Catholic whose object is marriage. Therefore it is absolutely necessary that you, as a Catholic, should know what you ought to think about mixed marriages and how you are to avoid them.

First of all it must be remarked that no offence to Protestants is intended when Catholics are warned against marrying them. Protestants ought to hold similar opinions, looking at the matter from their own point of view, and, indeed, they frequently do. To prove the truth of what has just been said, I will give two extracts, the first from a Protestant newspaper; they are fraught with useful lessons for Catholics. My first quotation runs thus: "A mixed marriage is always a sad mistake, and any one who forms such a union must make up his mind to experience a good deal of trouble and unhappiness. If the children are brought up as Catholics, the Protestant husband or wife must look on while they say their beads, must hear them invoking the saints, both of which things would be found very annoying, even in the case of their own children. If the children are Protestants, discontent and reproaches are sure to follow on the Catholic side; and if some are brought up as Catholics, others as Protestants, the family is divided. Parents and children ought to profess the same faith. People do not marry only to work together, but also to pray together. A Protestant artisan, who had married a Catholic, and whose only child died, expressed himself as follows: 'Standing beside the death-bed of our child, I felt how great a gulf separated my wife from me. We ought to be able, not only to live together, but also to pray together. In my opinion, mixed marriages ought to be forbidden by law.' And, indeed, no one who cares about his own salvation and that of his children ought to contract a mixed marriage."

My second illustration is taken from a pamphlet entitled, "A Word of Warning to Protestants." It runs thus: "How unhappy a wife must be who has been brought up a Catholic and remembers, every time she attends divine worship, that her children are being educated as Protestants; although she believes that her own religion is the only one which leads to heaven! And the opposite case is just as undesirable!

"Nor do I think that the religious discussions which must arise between husband and wife can be very edifying. These discussions can scarcely be avoided if each is in earnest in regard to his or her beliefs. And if religion is to be a forbidden subject, what will become of the children?"

Listen to the decision of the Catholic Church concerning mixed marriages. She has always declared her disapproval of them, and advised—nay commanded—Catholics to avoid contracting them. More than fourteen hundred years ago several Councils, among them those of Elvira, Laodicea, and Chalcedon, forbade Catholics to marry heretics unless the latter promised to become Catholics.

Two special reasons induced and compelled the Catholic Church to come to this decision. In the first place, a union between a Catholic and a Protestant can never be a perfect marriage—can never be what marriage ought to be. For marriage is a sacrament, and should be regarded and treated as such. How can this be so when the Protestant considers matrimony a merely civil contract? Married people should live in the closest union, in the most perfect harmony; they ought to have but one heart and one soul. How can this be when they hold such widely different opinions upon so many points in regard to the most sacred and most important of all subjects—namely, religion? Moreover, married people ought to help one another on the way to heaven. How can they do this when one takes the road which leads to the right, and the other treads the path which turns to the left? Finally, married people ought to give their children a religious education, and they should cooperate in carrying on the good work. Again I ask, how can they do this when their views in regard to religion differ so widely?

The second reason why holy Church looks so unfavorably upon mixed marriages is because the Catholic incurs so great a risk of losing his or her soul. When a Catholic girl marries a man who is not of her faith it is fair to surmise that she is rather lukewarm in regard to her own religion. How easy it is for her when she becomes a wife to neglect her religious duties, and gradually to cease altogether from performing them. Thence it is only a step to religious indifference—that is, to the erroneous opinion that all religions are alike good; that it does not matter what one believes; that it is of no consequence whether one is a Catholic or a Protestant, if only one leads a good life.

And how sad a prospect it is in regard to the Catholic education of the children! The Catholic wife may desire to bring the children up in her own creed, and the Protestant husband has promised that she shall be permitted do so; but how very often he fails to keep his word.

So you see the truth of the saying I quoted above: "No one who is earnestly concerned about his own salvation and that of his children ought to contract a mixed marriage." Act upon this principle, my daughter—do not listen to the addresses of a non-Catholic.

> A common faith, a common love,
> A common hope of life above—
> This only can make wedded life
> Free from discord, free from strife.

LXXII. Are Mixed Marriages Happy?

A passage from the writings of Dr. Hirscher, a pious and learned divine, may be suitably introduced here. He says:

"There is probably no single instance to be found of a mixed marriage in which (although they may in other respects have lived happily together) husband and wife did not, after the lapse of years, express the conviction that it would have been better if they had never met. There is a flaw in their mutual relations, a sore place which can never be healed."

A priest who had been in Holy Orders for a quarter of a century, and had exercised his sacred ministry in many different parishes, assured me that he had met with no mixed marriage which could be called completely happy; that many Catholics and Protestants who had contracted unions of this nature had acknowledged to him that if they could have their time over again they would not marry as they had done.

There is one case, not infrequent in occurrence, which renders the marriage of a Catholic wife with a husband who is a non-Catholic extremely unhappy. You know that the Church considers marriage to be indissoluble; she has ordained that neither of the partners in the marriage can marry again during the lifetime of the other. Protestants, on the other hand, regard marriage as a bond which can be dissolved. It is possible that the Protestant husband may institute proceedings in a divorce court for separation from his Catholic wife. Reasons for taking such a step are never far to seek. If the husband marries another woman, the discarded Catholic wife is doomed to drag on a wretched existence; she is, of course, unable to marry again, and must remain a widow as long as her husband lives. To complete her misery, her children are often taken from her and given into the custody of their father, who does not allow them to have anything to do with their mother.

I will cite one instance out of hundreds which might be brought forward. Many years ago a young girl who had lost both her parents went to reside at Neuenburg with an aunt. Before very long, a Protestant merchant began to pay her attention. At length he asked her to become his wife. The girl hesitated at first because her aunt was opposed to the marriage. Finally the girl consented, but only on the express condition that all the children should be brought up as Catholics. To this the future bridegroom readily agreed, promising to do all which might be required of him; his promise was taken down in writing, and officially legalized.

At first all went on smoothly. But in the course of a few years the husband began to grow somewhat cool toward his wife. He made fun of one and another of her pious habits. When she came home from Mass on a certain Sunday morning, she found that he had removed her crucifix, religious pictures, holy-water font, rosary-beads, and prayer-books from their customary places in the various rooms, and had made a heap of them in an attic. Shortly afterward a child was born. The father had it baptized as a Protestant, and said it was to be brought up as such. With many tears, the unhappy wife reminded him of the solemn promise he had made at the altar in regard to the education of their children. He replied abruptly: "That is my affair; it rests with me to decide what the religion of my children is to be."

Full of bitter grief, the poor mother again went to her aunt's house. While she was staying there her husband procured a divorce and married a rich Protestant widow. His discarded but lawful wife was left with a broken heart, one woman among many who have met with a similar fate. They listened to the voice of earthly affection alone, or were led solely by worldly motives, and heeded not the teaching of holy Church.

But even when matters do not reach such a pitch as this, no mixed marriage can be said to be really happy in every respect. For the husband and wife are not united in regard to the most sacred and most important of subjects—hence lesser differences are apt to arise. One disparages the other's religion and says: "I wish I had never known you!" If the children do not turn out well the Catholic mother reproaches herself with the failure, and feels how different the case would have been if she had married a pious, helpful Catholic.

Even when the wife is—and continues to be—a good Catholic, in the vicissitudes of married life a hundred reflections occur to her mind on the score of religion, tending to prevent her from enjoying true peace and real happiness. How much grief and anxiety must it cause her to know that her husband is on a wrong road; that he lacks the choicest gifts and graces of God in this life, and is in great danger of not attaining eternal happiness in the next life! And should her beloved husband die outside the Church, must not grief and anxiety on account of his soul press heavily indeed upon her heart?

Therefore in a mixed marriage a Catholic wife is always more or less to be pitied, even if she remains a good Catholic. But if she was a careless Catholic at the time of her marriage, and grows gradually more and more indifferent, consenting that her children should receive a Protestant education, she often ends by falling away from the faith altogether. Her marriage may be crowned with the highest temporal felicity, she may live happily with her husband, and they may be held in honor and esteem by their fellow men; yet in spite of all this the conscience of the wife will assail her with many a bitter reproach, and cause her to spend many a gloomy hour. Should she succeed in stifling its voice her case is still worse—it is the lull before the storm, the awful pause before she sinks into never-ending misery. To such an unhappy wife we may apply Our Lord's warning: "*What doth it profit a man if he gain the whole world and suffer the loss of his own soul?*"

In whatever light we view the matter it is obvious that a thoroughly happy mixed marriage is a thing very rarely to be found. But when this is represented to a girl who has already listened to the addresses of a non-Catholic, and perhaps fallen madly in love with him, she says that it is looking on the dark side of things; she sees a hundred ways of escaping out of the difficulty; even the most cogent arguments fail to convince her of the perilous nature of the step she is about to take; or, blinded by passion, she may merely reply: "Well, if I knew that I should go to hell I would still marry him and no one else!" Thus it is with the fire of sensual love. Once it has burst out into a blaze nothing but a miracle of grace avails to quench it— nothing else, either in heaven above or on earth below.

Therefore beware of this fire of sensual love. Carefully reflect before accepting the company of a non-Catholic, lest the fire should burst into flames which cannot be extinguished.

> Though love may clasp the nuptial band,
> Yet wedded bliss no storm will stand
> Unless the selfsame faith both share,
> And make God's service their first care.

LXXIII. THE CONDITIONS UNDER WHICH THE CHURCH TOLERATES MIXED MARRIAGES

YOU have learned in the preceding instructions how extremely rare the cases are in which mixed marriages turn out well, and what weighty reasons induce holy Church to signify her disapproval of them. She refrains, however, from prohibiting them altogether, because she is a loving and indulgent mother. It would afflict her maternal heart to witness the sad fate of those Catholics who, blinded by passion, would form mixed marriages, howsoever strictly forbidden, and would thus entirely separate themselves from her. In order to prevent the greater evil she permits the lesser; she tolerates mixed marriages under certain conditions.

These conditions are as follows: (1) The marriage must be solemnized according to the rules of the Catholic Church only. (2) Both parties must promise to have all their children baptized and brought up as Catholics. (3) The non-Catholic must also promise to leave the Catholic free to practice his religion.

This toleration or permission of mixed marriages—or, as it is usually termed, this dispensation—does not imply approval; on the contrary, the Church never ceases to protest against them in the most decided manner. As a rule, she requires of the contracting parties a written promise that the above-mentioned conditions will be faithfully carried out, especially that one which concerns the Catholic education of the children.

The Church insists so strongly upon this point because it is the chief matter to be thought of in any marriage which her children conclude. To refrain from insisting upon it would be, not love and indulgence, but treachery to the truth, which can be but one; it would virtually be placing error on a level with truth and allowing Catholics to fall away from the truth, in the persons of their children. Despite the fact that the Church ceases not to lift up her voice in protest through her bishops and priests, a considerable number of the children of mixed marriages are not brought up as Catholic. We can readily understand the feelings of grief and pain which animated a zealous German prelate when he wrote as follows to all young women who enter upon a mixed marriage without the sanction or dispensation of the Church: "The flames of a foolish passion soon die out. Conscience asserts its rights, and a weary struggle begins which prevents family life from being truly happy. The birth of the first child, which ought to be a source of joy to its mother, becomes a cause of sorrow. The child is brought up in an anti-Catholic atmosphere and thus is deprived of the true faith. What stings of conscience must pierce its mother's heart!"

The non-Catholic father, on the other hand, can certainly not find any pleasure in seeing his children taught a creed other than that which he professes. But as either husband or wife must give way on this point, it ought not to be so difficult for the non-Catholic to consent that the children be educated in the Catholic faith as it is for a Catholic to allow her children to be brought up as Protestants. For these latter hold generally that a Christian can save his soul whatever his religious beliefs may be. The Catholic wife, on the other hand, according to her faith, must look upon the Catholic Church as the one, only, true Church, founded by Christ Himself, and she ought therefore to insist that her children shall be brought up in that Church.

Do not allow yourself to be induced to depart from your determination to avoid a mixed marriage, by any plausible theories which may be put forward. For instance, you may be told that Protestants are Christians as well as Catholics, that they agree in essentials, and differ only in minor matters.

This assertion is a false one. Differences exist, not merely in minor matters, but in many most important points. That which the Catholic reveres as heavenly truth the Protestant in many cases regards as a purely human invention. For instance, the Catholic sees in the sacrifice of the Mass an actual renewal of the sacrifice Christ made upon the cross; the Protestant doctrine teaches this to be idolatry. This difference is indeed a most important one, and here unity of religious belief certainly does not exist.

Thus holy Church, as we have seen, tolerates mixed marriages if the above-mentioned three conditions are complied with, more especially if the Catholic education of the children is assured. She grants a dispensation in regard to such marriages, but does not thereby testify her approval of them. But what if the non-Catholic refuses beforehand to consent that the children shall be brought up as Catholics? In this case she refuses to give her consent to the union. How great is the blindness and how grievous the sin of those Catholics who, contrary to the command of God and of the Church, are married before a Protestant minister or the secular authorities; and, setting aside all conscientious scruples, renounce the idea of bringing up their children as Catholics.

> Each state and calling here below
> Has its own joy and its own woe;
> Yet a godless marriage, though it look fair,
> Brings little with it but sorrow and care.

The conduct of a Catholic girl as set forth in the incident I am about to relate cannot be too highly praised. She served as assistant in the store of a wealthy Protestant merchant. She so won the esteem of her employer and of his two sons that one of the latter offered to marry her, promising to leave her the free exercise of her religion. But the admirable young woman rejected this advantageous proposal simply because she was a Catholic. She preferred to remain a clerk or an employee of any kind rather than to become the wife of a rich man at the price of making a mixed marriage. This was indeed no small sacrifice! Should you ever find yourself in similar circumstances, may you be found ready to make a like sacrifice with a courage equal to hers!

To be said after the Hail Mary

My Queen! My Mother! I give myself entirely to thee; and to show my devotion to thee, I consecrate to thee this day my eyes, my ears, my mouth, my heart, my whole being, without reserve. Wherefore, good Mother, as I am thine own, keep me, guard me, as thy property and possession. Amen.

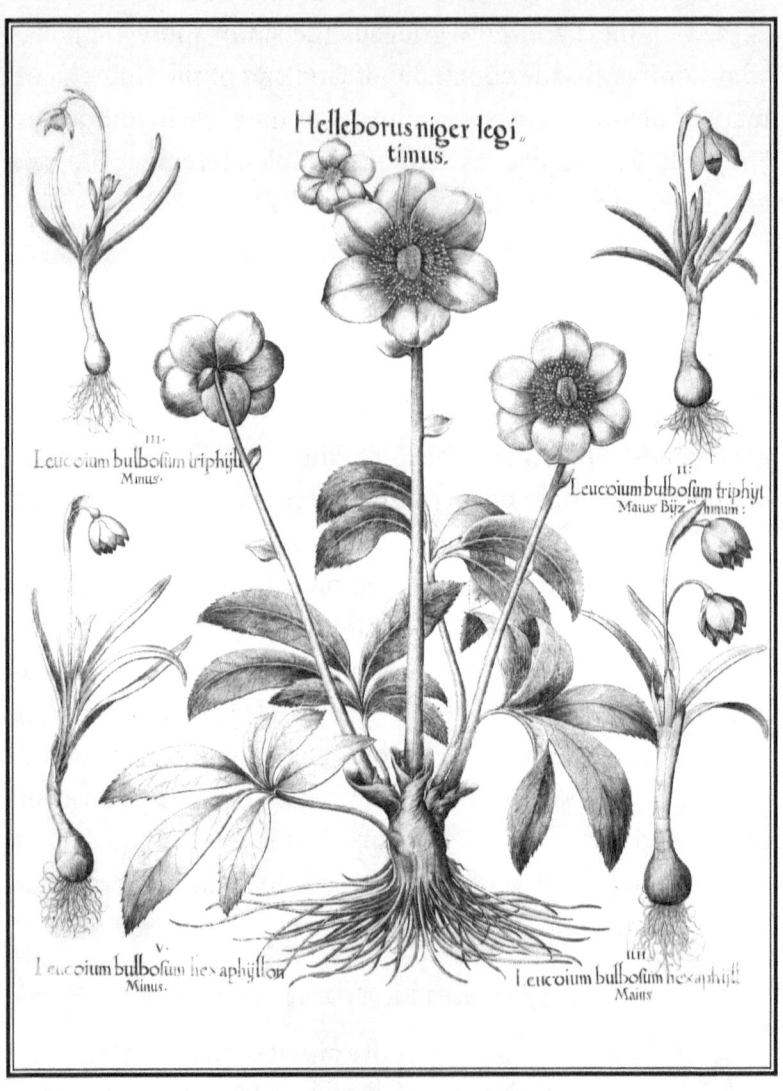

‹ 3 ›

The Religious State

LXXXIV. The Happiness of a Religious Vocation

A WONDERFUL sight is this which the Catholic Church has presented to us from the earliest times, and still presents in our own day. We see hundreds of young girls renouncing the riches, honors, and enjoyments of the world in order to shut themselves up for life within the walls and gratings of convents. Other delicate girls we see turning their backs on the comforts of civilized life to go, as Sisters of Charity, into distant lands, there to pass their days amidst strenuous exertions and severe privations, frequently exposed to the greatest perils and almost certain to meet an early death. How is such a life of sacrifice to be explained—a life which the world cannot possibly understand? I can give no other explanation than that which is contained in the Saviour's words: "*And I, if I be lifted up from the earth, will draw all things to myself.*" And again He says: "*I am come to cast fire on the earth, and what will I but that it be kindled?*"

But in what manner does the Saviour draw to Himself so many souls, more especially so many virginal souls? He draws them by the secret operation of His grace; He calls them to the Religious state. Christian maiden, give your attention to some remarks concerning this vocation, remarks which well deserve to be considered. Reflect, in the first place, upon the happiness of this vocation.

The shortsighted world is quite at fault when it pronounces the life of a nun joyless and more or less unhappy. She must, it is true, renounce much which men regard as pleasure and enjoyment, but only to be richly compensated for all she gives up by higher and purer joys. Have you ever seen the husbandman cutting the vine? The process seems to hurt it, and bitter drops, like tears, ooze from the stem; it is done for the good of the vine, to render it more valuable. It is the same with a person who has been called to the Religious state and lives in accordance with it. All the sacrifices she may have to make do but increase her happiness; they cause her to partake more abundantly of that peace of which Our Lord says: *"My peace I give unto you; not as the world giveth do I give unto you."* And she experiences the truth of His assurance when He says: *"My yoke is sweet and my burden light."*

Ponder well another utterance of the Saviour. Peter said: "Behold we have left all things and have followed thee." Jesus, answering, said: *"Amen I say to you, there is no man who hath left house, or brethren, or sisters, or father, or mother, or children, or lands for my sake and for the gospel who shall not receive an hundred times as much now in this time: houses, and brethren, and sisters, and mothers, and children, and lands and in the world to come life everlasting."* Eternal life! This promise does not occasion surprise. But the other promise is remarkable! Mark it well! Those disciples who have left all in order wholly to follow Him shall be rewarded even here on earth. And how shall they be rewarded? *"They shall receive a hundred times as much now in this time:"* freedom, peace, contentment, joy, trust in God, fraternal affection; and also, literally, houses, brethren, sisters, mothers.

Ask the Sisters who have left the world for Christ's sake if they have not truly found a mother in the convent; ask them if they have not experienced her maternal love, if they have not met with sisterly affection, with heartfelt sympathy in sorrow and in joy.

It is true that they must take human nature with them into the convent; many forms of human weakness are to be found there. But in spite of it all, one heart and one soul reign in the convent. Such is the blessing Christ bestows; such is the happiness of the Religious vocation.

Again, this happiness may be seen in the every-day life of a good Religious. By means of obedience and pious exercises each day is sanctified, and all her occupations are consecrated to God. Her first waking thoughts are of the Holy Trinity, to whom she offers up her life, her will, her heart with its inclinations. Wherever she may be, and whatever she may do in the course of the day, she remembers that she is in the house of God and is dedicated to His service. Thus a life of toil becomes a paradise in her eyes, dearer than all the passing pleasures to be found in the mansions of the great.

Her hallowed home and holy occupations bring the Religious every hour into the immediate presence of Him who is the joy of paradise, the delight of the elect. Here she worships, here she offers her sacrifices; from her Saviour—in union with whom she lives, labors and suffers—she obtains grace, strength and gladness. She can truly adopt the words of the Psalmist: "*So in the sanctuary have I come before thee, to see thy power and thy glory. For better is one day in thy courts, above thousands.*"

She likewise concludes the labors of the day in the presence of the Lord, and commends her spirit to the Sacred Heart of Jesus before she lies down to rest. And, in thought and desire at least, she ceases not to abide with Him, saying with the prophet: "*In the night I have remembered thy name, O Lord.*"

In order to make yourself acquainted to a certain extent with the happiness of the Religious state, call to mind the example of Jesus, the God-Man. He became absolutely poor for our sake; and if the Religious imitates Him and becomes poor for His sake, regarding holy poverty as her greatest riches, will not the promise be fulfilled in her case: "*Ye shall receive a hundred times as much now in this life . . . and life everlasting?*"

The life of Jesus Christ was one of more than angelic purity; it was a life of mortification and self-denial. He willed to be born only of a pure virgin, and He loved St. John, the virgin apostle, above all His other disciples. If the Religious, imitating the great love of Our Lord for virginity, treads under foot the pleasures of the world and takes refuge in a convent; if she seeks to follow in the footsteps of the pure Lamb of God and of His immaculate Mother, may she not hope to possess the sweet consolations which are unknown to the children of this world?

Finally, Jesus Christ came into the world not to do His own will, for He became obedient unto death—even to the death of the cross. If the Religious imitates this example also, placing herself for her whole life under obedience to her spiritual Superiors, will she not reap the fruit of such a sacrifice?

Thus we see how great is the happiness of a Religious vocation; and every young girl to whose lot this happiness falls ought to thank God for it. With the exception of a call to enter the Catholic Church, or a call to the priesthood, there is perhaps no greater grace than a Religious vocation.

Aspiration

Lord, enlighten me to know Your will,
And strengthen me to do it;
Prepare my heart to meet Your love,
And cling forever to it.

Two Messages

A MESSAGE from the Sacred Heart!
  What may its message be?
"My child, My child, give Me thy heart--
  My Heart has bled for thee."
This is the message Jesus sends
  To my poor heart to-day,
And eager from His throne He bends
  To hear what I shall say.

A message to the Sacred Heart!
  Oh! bear it back with speed:
"Come, Jesus, reign within my heart—
  Thy Heart is all I need."
Thus, Lord, I'll pray until I share
  That home whose joy Thou art—
No message, dearest Jesus, *there*,
  For heart will speak to heart.

LXXV. THE SACRIFICES OF A RELIGIOUS VOCATION

THE *Presentation of Mary in the Temple* is a pleasing and instructive festival for young girls. It was instituted to commemorate the day on which the Blessed Virgin, while still a child, consecrated herself to the service of God in the Temple at Jerusalem.

Virgins imitate the blessed Mother of God when, following the call of God, they enter a cloister or Religious community to dedicate their life to His service. Happy they who are thus called! But you ought not to look merely at the happiness and privileges which such a life brings with it; you must also carefully weigh the sacrifices which it demands. Let us now consider these sacrifices.

No one ought to leave the world and enter a convent with the idea of exchanging an active and arduous life for one of ease and comfort. Any one who should expect nothing but sweet tranquillity and undisturbed comfort would find herself cruelly deceived. Reflect, in the first place, upon the trials of community life. Consider one of the essential conditions of life in a convent—namely, to dwell there with many others and to be dependent upon others. Apart from contact with others, the rules of every Religious house make demands altogether opposed to the idea of sweet solitude and self-indulgence. The beloved and petted *Ego* cannot assert itself within those walls. Nor is it necessary to limit these facts to a particularly severe Order, or a convent where the discipline is remarkably strict; it suffices to consider what is implied in keeping the vows—namely, to possess nothing of one's own and to live under obedience to a Superior. This will at once make it plain that self-will must be absolutely set aside.

Thus the life of a good Religious is a life of constant self-sacrifice. For she renounces the very things which mostly bind frail mortals to this earth of ours. The Saviour Himself spoke in sublime words of these sacrifices, and invited generous souls to forsake all things for His sake. He gave the so-called evangelical counsels, which cannot be carried out except at the cost of great sacrifices.

As is well known, these counsels are: voluntary poverty, perfect virginal chastity, constant obedience to spiritual superiors. And Religious pledge themselves, when they make the vows, conscientiously to carry out these counsels under pain of mortal sin. The vows may be either for life or for a fixed period.

It is certainly no small sacrifice to take the vow of poverty, and faithfully carry it out. Can it be easy for a girl who has been surrounded by comforts, or perhaps even by luxuries, to quit all and renounce for the future the right to possess anything of her own?

Or, when she is in the convent, must she not find it difficult, her whole life long, to ask permission like a little child, in relation to every trifle which is given to her, or which she wishes to procure for herself, to exchange or to give away?

The vow of chastity is a second and a very great sacrifice; it involves the renunciation of married life, perfect purity and chastity for the Saviour's sake. This sacrifice is especially pleasing to Christ. The Saviour came into the world in a state of poverty; he gave up everything, and was cradled in a manger upon straw. One thing alone He did not give up: even in the stable He willed that His eye should rest upon virginal souls; and therefore He had Mary and Joseph at His side, near the manger. And on the eve of Our Lord's Passion, when He was about to leave the world, poor as He had entered it, at the Last Supper, it was the *virginal* John, the beloved disciple, who was privileged to lean upon the Saviour's bosom. And later, amid the gloom of Calvary, the same disciple was again privileged to stand beside the immaculate Mother at the foot of the cross.

Pure as lilies should all those virgins be who are planted in the chosen garden of God in the Religious state. This life of spotless purity is nothing less than a constant struggle, a ceaseless battle to win an angel's crown whilst dwelling in mortal flesh. But struggling and fighting involve sacrifice and renunciation.

Obedience is the third counsel. What sacrifices this word implies. St. Gregory the Great said: "It is perhaps not a very difficult thing to abandon one's possessions, but difficult indeed it is to forsake one's self." Obedience obliges us to forsake ourselves, since it requires us to give up our own will. For this reason Christ added this counsel to the two others. By it the words of St. Paul are literally verified: "*You are not your own.*"

In obedience also sacrifice is implied. These are often secret sacrifices, hidden from human ken, of which the world knows nothing, which no one praises but which pierce the inmost soul in its most sensitive part. How sublime are these sacrifices, these conquests of Self! How richly will the Father, who seeth in secret, one day repay them!

Obedience requires uninterrupted sacrifices from a Religious; she is never free from its yoke for a single instant. Obedience calls her in the morning and commands her in the evening; obedience orders everything in the house, prescribes the hours of work and the nature of that work, the time for prayer and the form of prayer, the time of recreation and the length of that recreation. Obedience guides and controls her every step, her every movement.

Little enough is the room left for the exercise of self-will. A longing for ease and comfort will certainly not be gratified in a convent. For by the practice of obedience a ceaseless war is waged against Self, and those will find themselves grievously deceived who imagine that they can shelter and tenderly humor their beloved Self in a convent cell.

Therefore if you, my daughter, think that you are called to the Religious state, examine yourself carefully to discover whether you have strength and courage to make these sacrifices with the help of divine grace. If you have the necessary dispositions, go forward! Take up the mighty weapon of obedience; with it combat the enemies of your salvation. Through disobedience man separated himself from God, his Creator and final end, through obedience he must return to Him. Even should you remain in the world you will still have to walk in the way of obedience. *Perfect* obedience to their Superiors is demanded of Religious; faithful obedience to the commands of God and of holy Church is incumbent on seculars.

All for Thee, O Heart of Jesus

How sweet it is to feel, dear Lord,
    That Thou wilt surely see
Each work, or thought, or act of mine
    That may be done for Thee!

That when I try with pure intent
    To serve, to please, to love Thee,
Thy watchful Heart each effort knows,
    Thy blessing rests above me.

Nothing unnoticed, *nothing* lost—
    Unlike to man in all things—
Grateful art Thou for all I do,
    For great as well as small things.

Empty my soul of all desire
    Man's idle praise to seek,
Hide me in Thee, for Thou dost know
    How frail I am—and weak.

Take Thou my *all*, since for so long
    Thy providence has sought me,
Make me Thine own since at such cost
    Thy precious blood has bought me.

LXXVI. The Signs of A Religious Vocation

ST. BERNARD asks: "Is it not the Religious state in which a man lives in a manner more pleasing to God, falls less frequently, rises up more speedily when he has fallen, walks more cautiously, rests more securely, dies more happily, and reaps a richer reward?" Assuredly so it is; peace and happiness are the lot of the true Religious. But she must have a real vocation. This call comes from God; no one can call himself or herself.

Therefore beware of imitating those young girls who, in spite of all their confessors urge to the contrary, obstinately persist in their predetermined opinion that they are called to embrace the Religious state. On this account it is well that you should make yourself acquainted with certain signs which show, more or less plainly, whether any one is, or is not, called to enter the cloister.

The first and most indispensable sign, or test, is a good and pure intention. You ought not to enter the convent with the object of finding there freedom from anxiety as to your means of subsistence in the future, honor and esteem, an easy, comfortable life, a provision for old age; with these and like intentions there could be no real call to enter the cloister. The Religious life must be embraced with the intention of better attaining the final end of man, of loving God more entirely, of serving Him more devotedly, and thus striving more earnestly to secure the eternal happiness of heaven. When this is not the predominant and decisive motive of any one who purposes entering the cloister, it is a case of a mistaken vocation. This pure intention and this inclination toward the Religious life must be lasting. If this desire to enter the convent has been felt from early childhood, and has grown with increasing years, that is a very satisfactory sign, but not an indispensable one. For this desire not unfrequently makes itself felt only a short time before the choice of a state. Previous to that period a disinclination for the life of a Religious may have been experienced. In any case, if the desire for the life of the cloister is strong and firm, decided and definite, the sign is a most favorable one.

The postulant must further be mentally sound and well—that is to say, it will not do for her to be afflicted with a serious affection of the mind or of the nerves, intellectually very incapable, or inclined to melancholia, and to take a morbid view of things. Weak-minded and half-witted people are certainly not made for convent life, since they can contribute nothing to the attainment of its end. Those who are of a melancholy or morbid temperament are equally unfitted for the cloister. The pious exercises and meditations, the latter often of a solemn and serious nature, may have the effect of unhinging the mind of persons who are apt to take too gloomy and severe a view of religious truths. Rejoice in the Lord: Serve the Lord joyfully! This should be the maxim for a Religious. The cloister is not a garden of weeping willows. *Physical* health is also a necessity; for to nuns are assigned difficult and important tasks, such for instance, as teaching, or nursing the sick. Only persons who enjoy good health are equal to these duties. Further, many convents have but slender sources of income, so that their inmates are compelled to work hard in order to contribute to the general support. It is plain that no one whose health is weak would be capable of doing this. If, therefore, a young woman has not received from God the requisite health, this is—according to the ordinary course of His providence—a sign that He has not seen fit to bestow upon her a Religious vocation.

The same argument applies to any hereditary diseases which may exist in the family of a postulant. If, for instance, her father or mother, or both, are consumptive, or have, perhaps, died of tuberculosis, it is to be feared that she may have inherited a tendency to consumption. Under these circumstances it would be wiser for her not to seek admission to a convent.

A gentle and docile character may also be regarded as a sign of a vocation. If the life within the walls of a convent is to be a happy one, it is a primary condition that all the Sisters should live in mutual affection and concord. They should bear patiently with one another's human imperfections and be ever cheerful, helpful and considerate. A girl whose temper is hasty and violent, or whose character is self-willed and obstinate, will find it exceedingly difficult, and well-nigh impossible, to practice the obedience and patience demanded in the cloister, unless she has a firm, determined will to overcome herself, and has already given abundant proof that she possesses the strength required to do so. Individuals whose passions and evil tendencies are unusually strong, in whose characters sensual affection, inordinate desire for pleasure, and so on, form predominant features, should pause before attempting to enter a cloister. They should wait until they have succeeded, to some extent at least, in mastering their passions.

The consent of one's parents should be obtained before entering upon the Religious state. This duty is imposed by the honor, obedience, and love which children owe their parents. It is true that some of the saints, as St. Teresa for instance, sought and found admission to an Order without the knowledge of their parents and in spite of their prohibition. But these are examples of an extraordinary guidance of Providence, and cannot, generally speaking, be imitated. In ordinary cases so important a step in life should be taken only when it is accompanied by the blessing which rests upon filial obedience. This rule is, however, of universal application if a child has special duties in regard to her parents—if, for example, she is their sole available help and support in their sickness or old age. Under such circumstances she may consider it decided that she is not to go into Religion, however other things may seem to point that way. In any case, however, seek the advice and direction of your spiritual director or confessor.

Before entering any special Order or convent it is necessary to become acquainted with the fundamental principles of that Order or convent, and to possess a decided preference, predilection and capacity for the kind of work it undertakes to accomplish. Every Order has, besides the general aim of the Religious life, its own special purpose and work; in one, it is teaching; in another, nursing the sick, and so on. Hence it may be clearly seen that all those who have a vocation to enter Religion are not equally suited for every Order.

One word in conclusion. Christian maiden, you may perhaps feel that you have long been powerfully attracted to the Religious life, although serious impediments prevent you from following out your inclination. In this case place your trust in the all-wise providence of God in a spirit of childlike confidence. Love God. Trust Him. He will lead you in the right way. Pray for light and strength that you may always do God's holy will.

The Road of Life

What is time? It has been given
That we may work and merit heaven
Though *rough* may be the path through life,
Darkened by sorrow and beset with strife,
Think of *Him* who at the distant goal
Awaits to crown the faithful soul.
Was *His* path brighter than may be
The one His love reserves for thee!
Had *He not darker* ways to tread
Than those from which we shrink in dread!
Fight the good fight, *on, onward* still,
O'er mountain pass and lonesome hill;
Let no sorrow your progress stay,
While *He*, the Saviour, leads the way.
Some future hour will heaven unfold
To thee its gates of burnished gold;
How small will then life's trials be,
Viewed in the bliss of eternity!

De Profundis (Psalm 129)

Out of the depths have I cried unto Thee, O Lord:
　　Lord hear my voice.
Let Thine ears be attentive to the voice of my supplication.
If Thou, Lord, shouldst mark iniquities, O Lord, who shall stand?
But there is forgiveness with Thee:
　　because of Thy law I wait for Thee, O Lord.
My soul waiteth on His word: my soul hopeth in the Lord.
From the morning watch even until night let Israel hope in the Lord:
For with the Lord there is mercy, and with Him is plentiful redemption.
And He shall redeem Israel, from all their iniquities.

‹ 4 ›

Unmarried Life in the World

LXXVII. The Value of Virginity

You have seen, in my last three instructions, how great is the happiness of those who have a Religious vocation. And you feel that this view of the subject is a correct one. Now let me tell you that one of the chief conditions and one of the greatest sacrifices of the Religious life can be fulfilled and accomplished without quitting the world. And that is indeed done by those girls who remain in the world and yet do not marry, but for the love of God preserve their virginity, and lead a chaste and holy life. In regard to this state some instruction is necessary. First of all, consider the true value of virginity.

The value of virginity is so great and sublime that we, poor earthly-minded mortals, are not able to esteem and honor it as it deserves to be esteemed and honored. In order that you may not think that I overestimate its worth, let us act as do those who possess some costly object—a ring perhaps, or a jewel—the value of which they do not know. What course do such persons pursue? They go to an experienced jeweller and ask for his opinion of their treasure. We will not address ourselves to the children of this world, for they are quite incompetent to give an opinion upon the subject, but we will ask God, His blessed angels and saints, His Bride the Church—we will, I say, ask them the value of virginity. And what will they reply?

I scarcely know where to begin. Our Lord Himself held virginity in the highest esteem. His whole life on earth bears witness to the fact, as has been already more than once remarked. Let us now contemplate His glorified life. Enter a Catholic church. What do the tabernacle, the altar with its daily sacrifice, the table of communion proclaim? They tell us how dearly Christ loves virginity. For there in the tabernacle, upon the altar, at the table of communion we find that which the prophet foretold: *"The corn of the elect, and wine that springeth forth virgins."* It is called the bread of angels, not because angels partake of it, but because Jesus, the Lover of virginal souls, has given it to us that through it men may be transformed into angels—angels in purity.

Now raise your eyes to heaven; look up higher and ever higher still, far above the choirs of blessed spirits. Next to the throne of the Most Holy Trinity you behold Mary, the Virgin Mother of God. In what celestial radiance does her virginal body shine! As the reward of her perfect purity, her Son, by virtue of His omnipotence, did not permit her body to molder in the grave. What rapture fills her maternal heart, on which during her lifetime no shadow of impurity ever rested! With what gladsome acclaim did the angels receive her when they saw the reward of her chastity, the honor paid to virginity in a mortal form. How joyously they greet her now with the words: *"Thou art all fair, and there is not a spot in thee!"*

St. Augustine and St. Bernard teach us the value virginity possesses in the eyes of the heavenly spirits. "The angels," they tell us, "prize virginal purity so highly that they would, if this were possible, envy men because of its glory and splendor." Virginity causes men to become like to angels—pure beings, supremely beloved of God.

Let us now inquire of the saints as to the value of virginity.

From the almost countless utterances of the Fathers on this subject I will select but one; the enthusiastic words are those of St. Athanasius: "Continency is an exalted virtue, chastity is grand and noble, virginity is praiseworthy above measure. How priceless a treasure is virginity! It renders the soul fit to be the temple of God, the dwelling-place of the Holy Ghost. How beauteous is virginity! It is an unfading crown, a precious pearl, hidden from the majority of mankind, known but by few. Continency, virtue beloved of God, held in high esteem by the saints! By mankind in general thou art little known and still less appreciated, but for all that more clearly understood, more dearly cherished by those who are worthy of thee. Death and hell have no power to molest thee, for immortality followeth in thy train.

"O Continency! delight of the prophets, glory of the apostles! Virginity! the life of angels, the brightest ornament of the saints! Happy is he who possesses this treasure; happy he who patiently, steadfastly refuses to be separated from it, for when life's brief conflict is over he will receive a rich reward. Happy is he who has learned renunciation in this life; his dwelling will be in the heavenly Jerusalem, and in the company of angels, prophets and saints he will enter jubilant upon eternal rest."

Let us in conclusion inquire of holy Church, which St. Paul thus describes: "*A glorious Church, not having spot or wrinkle, or any such thing, holy and without blemish.*" As the virginal Bride of Christ she never for one moment forgets the priceless lily which the heavenly Bridegroom planted in her garden and entrusted to her care. In the words of St. Paul she preaches to all who will hear and understand: "*Concerning virgins I have no commandment of the Lord: but I give counsel. Both he that giveth his virgin in marriage, doth well: and he that giveth her not, doth better.*"

The Church acts in accordance with this teaching. When in the sixteenth century the so-called reformation hurled its venomous shafts against holy virginity, when apostate priests and nuns impiously broke their most sacred vows, she lifted up her voice with holy zeal on behalf of the precious legacy bequeathed to her by Christ. The Council of Trent declared solemnly and publicly: "If any man shall say that the married state is higher than that of virginity, and that it is not a better and more blessed thing to remain a virgin than to bind oneself by marriage, let him be *anathema*."

Thus great and exalted is the value of virginity. Chaste virgins are indeed heroines more glorious and worthy of higher praise than those we read of in history. For the former gain not the freedom merely of a country or a city, but of their own heart; and they gain it by a successful warfare against the most formidable of enemies.

> If in obedience to thy Lord,
> Thou choose unmarried to remain,
> By purity in heart and word,
> Seek thou His favor to retain.

LXXVIII. The So-called "Old Maids"

The state of virginity is spoken of by the saints in terms of the most exalted praise. To those expressions I have already quoted in the foregoing instruction I will add one or two more. "What more pleasing," exclaims St. Chrysostom, "what more glorious than the state of virginity? It surpasses the married state in excellence as much as the heavens do the earth, as angels surpass men." And St. Thomas Aquinas remarks: "It is a privilege to be an angel, a merit to remain a virgin." I have yet to say a few words about virginity as it may be preserved by those living in the world.

A young girl may feel herself called neither to marry nor to become a Religious, but she may determine quite voluntarily to preserve her virginity while living in the world. In accordance with this resolution she may reject all offers of marriage, even the most advantageous. This case, however, is exceptional. To those for whom virginity has an attraction the all-wise Creator gives, as a rule, a desire for the Religious life, because it is in the cloister that virginity can be most easily and most surely preserved. Women who live in the world in a state of celibacy are, as a rule, those who, for some reason or other, have been prevented from either marrying or entering the cloister.

How often it happens that young girls are prevented from going into Religion! Many a one has longed from her childhood for the life of the cloister, has passed her youth in piety and innocence, has made every effort to attain the abject of her desire, knocking at the door of one convent after another, but everywhere meeting with a refusal.

Either she was found to have some mental or physical infirmity which made her unfit for the cloister; or she had duties to perform toward aged and infirm parents, or younger brothers and sisters, who were dependent upon her for support, or perhaps her character was unsuited for convent life, and so on.

It is no small trial for her, and many a secret tear does she shed because God has seen fit to refuse her the object of her ardent desires. Ought she on this account to be disconsolate? Certainly not; for God orders all things for the best. But why did He implant a longing for the cloister in her heart if this longing was never to be satisfied? It is plain that He acts thus in order to increase her merits. To find herself obliged to relinquish all hope of attaining the desired goal is the greatest and most painful of sacrifices. If she makes this sacrifice for the love of God, resigning herself to His will in a spirit of childlike submission, and striving to serve Him faithfully in the world, how great is the store of merit she lays up for herself in eternity!

And maidens like these, to whom the Religious habit was denied, seldom fail to find in the stormy ocean of the world some quiet islet which they may sow and plant, making it as a garden of the Lord, and devoting their life to Him as surely as they could have done in a convent.

A third class consists of those who had felt inclined to the marriage state. They would gladly have married, but have been compelled, by force of circumstances, to relinquish the idea. These young women are condemned, as people say, "to single blessedness," and to become "old maids." Such persons should all make a virtue of necessity, and in a Christian spirit recognize the hand of God in the arrangement of the circumstances of their life, submitting patiently to His most holy will.

Divine providence seems to have ordained that a large number of girls should remain unmarried. Statistics prove that in all nations the number of women considerably exceeds that of men; and of the latter there are many—for instance priests and Religious—who cannot marry and have a family.

Under all circumstances a Christian maiden ought to remain firmly convinced that it is no disgrace to remain unmarried, or to be what is commonly called an "old maid." Rather is it an honor and a happiness for her if she is a maid—a virgin—in the true sense of the word, and is recognized as such by the all-seeing eye of God. And indeed an unmarried woman, a true virgin like this deserves to be held in high esteem, even—and indeed particularly—when her hair has grown gray and her youthful beauty has fled. She has cheerfully renounced that which most persons regard as a great happiness, in order to choose a better part; she courageously treads the path of life alone, a path which so many do not venture to tread without the support and protection of a husband.

It truly requires courage and fortitude to pass through life in such a manner; but the Giver of all good gifts will not deny these qualities to His true servants if they keep eyes and heart fixed upon Him. Mothers and wives do much for the world, and obtain for themselves no little store of merit, by faithfully fulfilling their duties, by bringing up children to be pious and useful members of society. But many so-called "old maids" have done quite as much or even more by their advice, their help, their prayers—in a word, their benefactions.

I happened to hear the following account of just such a good and admirable "old maid": She was not beautiful, it is true, but she possessed the far more valuable gifts of a bright intelligence and an inexhaustible fund of sweetness and kindness of heart. Her mother died at a comparatively early age, and she had to undertake the task of bringing up a numerous family of younger brothers and sisters. In the course of time her eldest brother married a wife who knew very little about housekeeping. Once more the aunt came to the rescue, and instructed her sister-in-law in household matters, doing this with so much prudence and tact that her presence was never felt to be an intrusion. At a subsequent period the family of a married sister became involved in financial difficulties. Again the aunt made herself very useful; she went to live in her sister's house, paid a large sum for her board, and took charge of the children. After the death of both her brother and his wife she returned to their children, aiding them in every possible way by her wise counsel and more practical assistance. Thus this "old maid" did as much good in *three* different families as she would have been able to effect in *one* had she married.

Leave your future serenely and hopefully in the hands of God, to be disposed of as He shall see fit, and if you are to live unmarried in the world and be called an "old maid" you may say:

> Why should I blush to hear that name,
> As if a soubriquet of shame?
> For know, an old maid though I be,
> Some dames would fain change states with me,

Strive to become perfect in the following of Christ.
Ask Jesus Himself to teach you the lessons of perfection.

Jesus, Master, Teach Me

Teach me, teach me, dearest Jesus,
In Thine own sweet loving way,
All the lessons of perfection
I must practice day by day.

Teach me *Meekness*, dearest Jesus,
Of Thine own the counterpart;
Not in words and actions only,
But the meekness of the heart.

Teach *Humility*, sweet Jesus,
To this poor, proud heart of mine,
Which yet wishes, O my Jesus,
To be modelled after Thine.

Teach me *Fervor*, dearest Jesus,
To comply with every grace,
So as never to look backwards,
Never slacken in the race.

Teach me *Poverty*, sweet Jesus,
That my heart may never cling
To whate'er its love might sever
From my Saviour, Spouse, and King.

Teach me *Chastity*, sweet Jesus,
That my every day may see
Something added to the likeness
That my soul should bear to Thee.

Teach *Obedience*, dearest Jesus,
Such as was Thy daily food
In Thy toilsome earthly journey
From the cradle to the rood.

Teach *Thy Heart* to me, dear Jesus,
Is my fervent, final prayer,
For all beauties and perfections
Are in full perfection there.

A Morning Offering

I OFFER to Thee, O my God, the life and death of Thy only Son; and with them these my affections and resolutions, my thoughts, words, deeds, and sufferings of this day, and of all my life, in honor of Thy adorable Majesty, in thanksgiving for all Thy benefits, in satisfaction for my sins, and to obtain the assistance of Thy grace; that, persevering to the end in doing Thy Holy Will, I may love and enjoy Thee for ever in Thy glory.

—*The Garden of the Soul*

Night Prayer

A LMIGHTY and eternal God, I adore Thee, and I *thank* Thee for all the benefits I have received this day through Thy infinite goodness and mercy. Give me light to know my faults and grant me grace to be truly sorry for my sins.

Here examine your Conscience ; then say:

Confiteor

I CONFESS to almighty God, to blessed Mary ever Virgin, to blessed Michael the Archangel, to blessed John the Baptist, to the holy apostles Peter and Paul, and to all the saints that I have sinned exceedingly in thought, word, and deed, (*strike your breast three times:*) through my fault, through my fault, through my most grievous fault. Therefore, I beseech blessed Mary ever Virgin, blessed Michael the Archangel, blessed John the Baptist, the holy apostles Peter and Paul, and all the saints, to pray for me to the Lord our God.

V. May Almighty God have mercy on us, forgive us our sins, and bring us to everlasting life.

R. Amen.

Blessed are all they that fear the Lord: that walk in his ways.
For thou shalt eat the labours of thy hands: blessed art thou, and it shall be well with thee.
Thy wife as a fruitful vine, on the sides of thy house.
Behold, thus shall the man be blessed that feareth the Lord.
May the Lord bless thee out of Sion: and mayest thou see the good things of Jerusalem all the days of thy life.
And mayest thou see thy children's children, peace upon Israel.

Part Fourth

FAMILY LIFE

‹ 1 ›

RELIGION:
THE FOUNDATION OF FAMILY LIFE

LXXIX. THE HAPPINESS OF FAMILY LIFE

THE sphere of woman's activity, especially in the class for which I write, is preeminently the home. The object to be kept in view in a girl's education, whether she be brought up at home or in a boarding-school, is to fit her for domestic life, to give her a love of domesticity, founded on the fear of God. This you, my daughter, must seek to acquire; in order that later on, in whatever position you may find yourself, whether you live with your parents, take a situation as housekeeper, or preside over a household of your own, you may for the love of God lead a life of self-sacrificing devotion, unseen and unnoticed, working to promote the welfare of the family, the maintenance of religion and good principles. Let us consider the conditions requisite for happiness in the family. Beginning at the foundation, I wish to show in the first place that the happiness of family life is based upon religion.

A young wife who was passionately fond of reading novels said to her husband: "How tiresome it is that novels always come to a conclusion when once people are married." "My dear child," the husband replied, "that cannot be otherwise, for if the story were carried on further it would be one of disenchantment." That is true in many cases! How many young persons find themselves bitterly disappointed very soon after their marriage! Wherefore is this the case? Why do they see their brightest hopes vanish like a mirage in the desert? It is because so many newly married couples do not build their hopes of happiness on the firm basis of religion and piety.

Foolish indeed it is to say, as too many do: "One can do very well without religion." Is this true? Can one do without religion? One can accumulate money and property, indulge in sensual pleasures, and lead a riotous, dissipated life. But without religion no one can enjoy that sweet heavenly peace of which the children of this world are wholly ignorant, and that joy which is abiding even amidst sorrows and trials.

Yes—a true religious spirit must prevail. One often hears persons say: "Certainly, religion is necessary, but it is quite possible to be religious without believing everything taught from the pulpit, or being so pious or so scrupulous in matters of religion." As a rule such persons look for a cloak to hide their laxity or lukewarmness. Religion and morals, faith and practice are not to be separated. Do not allow yourself to be deceived by language such as theirs. Fathers and mothers may indeed parade their civic righteousness and virtue before the world, but unless their conduct is inspired by faith and true piety as the guide of their life, their family happiness lacks a firm footing, a sure foundation. Only too many examples of this are to be met with in daily life. Families in which no time is found for prayer, for obligatory attendance at church, for the instruction of the children; where only temporal affairs and material prosperity are considered to be of importance, where gold is eagerly sought after, and higher interests are ignored; in such families true happiness cannot be found, though riches may abound, with a superfluity of all good things; even though the palatial mansion is furnished in the most luxurious style, and its inmates are clothed in silk and satin and adorned with glittering gems and precious jewels.

There is another important point to be remarked. Even the happiest family life is and must ever be a life of sacrifice. It is difficult to realize that this is the case when one sees how young people marry nowadays, imagining themselves to be entering an earthly paradise where their days will be spent in pleasure and enjoyment, and their path will be between hedges of roses—roses without thorns! How different is the reality found to be, with its cares and crosses, labors, and sorrows! What a spirit of self-sacrifice must the various members of a family possess if peace and happiness are not to be altogether lost! Religion alone is able to impart to them this spirit of unselfishness, of self-renunciation and sacrifice. It alone will enable them to persevere in that spirit until death. Hence we see that in this case also the peace and happiness of every family must be built upon the foundation of religion.

And in yet another case this is true. If family happiness is to be complete, it is essential that the children should be well reared—without religion this is impossible. The infidel father who entrusted the education of his children to Religious because it was—as he said—a perfect hell to believe in nothing, confirmed this truth in a striking manner. An unbeliever pronounced unbelief to be a hell upon earth. This saying proclaims with a loud voice that the education of youth is a very serious thing. In regard to this subject St. John Chrysostom thus expresses himself: "What grander task can any one have than that of guiding souls, of training the young? I esteem him who understands how to mold and educate youth more highly than the painter, the sculptor, and every other artist, whoever he may be."

But where—in what family—do we find that true and wise system of education which is so important a factor in family happiness? There only where the spirit of religion and piety pervades the house, rendering it a temple in which God dwells. Only parents who possess this spirit of faith can train their children in Christian obedience, and inspire them with a horror of vice. They alone will seek assistance from God and remind their children of His presence who regard Him as the real Master of their house, and who model all their thoughts and actions, their words and works, according to the commands of His holy religion.

Now, my dear child, thank God from the bottom of your heart if He has given you parents such as these; parents who lay the greatest stress upon faith, upon religion and piety, and make every effort to bring you up or cause you to be brought up in the right way. No greater benefit could possibly be bestowed upon you! Parents who act thus lay the foundation of happiness for their family both in time and in eternity; they bear in mind the truth of these lines:

> If on Faith's firm basis founded,
> By the fear of God surrounded,
> Fast as a rock thy house shall stand,
> Dreading no storm or hostile hand.

LXXX. The Safeguard of Family Life

In the Catholic Church—in the Catholic religion—the family finds its firm support, its sure safeguard and shield. For this Church alone fearlessly preaches at all times and in all places that in which consists the sole safeguard and support of the family—namely, the sacredness of the family, the indissolubility of marriage, the sanctity of matrimony as an institution ordained by God, as a religious contract, and a holy sacrament.

The family, or matrimony, is an institution ordained by God. Human beings, like plants and the lower animals, are, according to the all-wise designs of God, intended to propagate themselves until the end of time. But man is an incomparably higher being than a plant or an animal; he is endowed with reason, free will, and immortality. God has consequently placed the manner in which the human race is to be continued on a high level. He created woman especially, and gave her to the first man as a helper, uniting the two in the closest companionship. Thus did He call the first family into existence and hallow the continuation of the human race. And thus it devolves upon human beings to educate their offspring and to perpetuate family life. In the animal world no such thing exists; there is to be found no family life, properly so called, and no education. For the family as ordained by God is the nursery of Christendom which fills the earth with true believers, one day to complete the number of the elect in heaven. Thus the family stands like a tree in the garden of God, its fruits being good children. Impress firmly upon your mind the truth that the family is no mere human invention, but an institution ordained by God. The Church has always pronounced marriage "a holy state, appointed by God," thus emphatically refuting the false teaching of certain heretics who regarded marriage as an evil thing.

In the second place the safeguard of the family consists in understanding marriage as a *religious contract*. Marriage is a *contract* because it, like every other contract, is based upon the agreement and consent of two contracting parties.

It is, however, a *religious* contract, essentially distinct from every merely civil contract. The marriage contract is *indissoluble* according to divine law—moreover, the marriage contract imparts special, supernatural graces, which no other contract does. This contract is concluded before a minister of the Church, who imparts a special blessing at the nuptial Mass.

The Christian family maintains its exalted position owing to the fact that marriage is regarded as a sacred institution— as *a holy sacrament*. We know marriage to be a sacrament, because the infallible Church teaches us that it is such, and commands us to believe this as a divinely revealed doctrine. And the following proofs may be adduced in support of this doctrine.

St. Paul expressly terms the union of a man and a woman in the marriage state a sacrament, when he says: "This is a great sacrament, but I speak in Christ and in the Church." Marriage as a sacrament is like to the mystic union which exists between Christ and the Church. As the union of Christ with the Church is a sacred bond, so is marriage between Christians.

Tradition shows us that the Catholic Church has always regarded marriage as a sacrament. The Fathers teach us that Christ was present at the marriage in Cana to show that He raised marriage to the dignity of a sacrament. St. Augustine says: "The superiority of marriage among Christians consists in the sanctity of the sacrament."

And it is easy to perceive from a purely natural point of view how useful and appropriate—nay more—how necessary it was that Jesus Christ should elevate marriage to the dignity of a sacrament. Marriage is of the greatest importance for the whole human race. This state of life has very many weighty and permanent duties and burdens. On this account married people need special graces and they receive them through Christ's raising marriage to the dignity of a sacrament.

Thus we see that the safeguard and shield of the Christian family consist in regarding marriage as an institution ordained by God, as a religious contract, a holy sacrament. The Christian religion—the Catholic Church—is the only sure foundation for this security and protection. The profanation and desecration of marriage, divorce, the disintegration of family life, and the moral deterioration of society, are the evils of the present day. Therefore, my dear child, be ever on your guard against careless, worldly views of family life.

To The Holy Family

Jesus, whose almighty bidding
  All created things fulfil,
Lived on earth in meek subjection
  To His earthly parents' will.
    Sweetest Infant, make us patient
      And obedient for Thy sake;
    Teach us to be chaste and gentle,
      All our stormy passions break.

Blessed Mary! thou wert chosen
  To be Mother of thy Lord:
Thou didst guide the early footsteps
  Of the great Incarnate Word.
    Dearest Mother! make us humble;
      For thy Son will take His rest
    In the poor and lowly dwelling
      Of a humble sinner's breast.

Joseph! thou wert called the father
  Of thy Maker and thy Lord;
Thine it was to save thy Saviour
  From the cruel Herod's sword.
    Suffer us to call thee father;
      Show to us a father's love;
    Lead us safe through every danger
      Till we meet in heaven above.

LXXXI. The Peace of Family Life

"Where there is faith, there is charity; where there is charity, there is peace." This saying applies in the first place to a family in which the true religious spirit and genuine piety prevail.

    Peace gives the young their joyous smile,
    Peace lightens manhood's daily toil;
    Peace gives the old man longed-for rest,
    Peace, the happiness of the blest!

Peace! How our heart rejoices at the sound of this word! Peace especially is the characteristic of our holy religion. Not without reason did the angels sing when Jesus was born in Bethlehem: "On earth peace, to men of good will." Can peace be wanting where Jesus dwells? And Jesus dwells where faith prevails. Let us consider this peace as it is to be found in the Christian family.

Let us begin by contemplating the bright pattern of every family presented by the holy family in the cottage at Nazareth. What deep and abiding peace is here! Whence does it spring? The holy family is poor, forsaken, despised by men. No earthly goods are there; no riches, spacious apartments, costly garments, delicate viands—nothing, in fact, which in the eyes of worldlings belongs to content and happiness. Yet Mary and Joseph with the holy Child enjoyed contentment and happiness as great as that of our first parents before the fall. The reason of this was that they had peace of heart,

This peace may be enjoyed where there is a lack of all the external gifts of fortune; it is frequently all the greater in proportion to the scantier measure in which these good things are possessed. An Eastern legend runs as follows: "A Persian monarch was once upon a time sick unto death; the magicians declared that in order to recover he must wear the shirt belonging to the only happy man in his whole realm. Messengers were dispatched to search everywhere for this fortunate individual—in the capital, in the provinces, in town and in country—but nowhere could he be found. At last one of those who had been sent forth came upon a shepherd who, in a lonely mountain valley, was lying on the grass, playing upon his pipe. The messenger entered into conversation with him, and gathered from what he said that he was indeed truly happy; but a shirt could not be obtained from this one perfectly happy man. He was too poor to own one. And so the Persian monarch died." The meaning of this anecdote is simple enough. An individual or a family may be happy and at peace without any of the gifts of fortune, if they but understand how to be so. And it will be clear to them if they ponder the words of St. Paul: *"For we brought nothing into this world: and certainly we can carry nothing out. But having food, and wherewith to be covered, with these we are content."* In order, however, constantly to enjoy this peace of mind, the members of a family must firmly establish and maintain in their home the conditions of this peace. These conditions are threefold: (1) faith in the merciful providence of God, (2) peace with God, and (3) a hope of heaven.

As Christians we believe in the goodness of God, whose overruling providence disposes all things as is best for us, with infinite wisdom and love. This belief procures for Christian parents and children—whatever be their burdens and sorrows—the consoling assurance that God has laid these trials upon them with some merciful design, and that a time will come when they will thank Him for them all. This consciousness it is which prevents peace from ever entirely forsaking them. If their desires remain unfulfilled, if they have much to suffer, they suffer in a spirit of resignation—they do not lack consolation; peace still dwells in their hearts.

The second condition of family peace is peace with God. As Christians we know God to be our holy Lawgiver and just Judge. We believe in the immortality of the soul, in heaven and hell. And as reasonable beings we know that death and judgment and the irrevocable decision as to our eternal happiness or misery may come upon us at any moment.

If Christian parents and children maintain a constant watchfulness over the state of their conscience; if they carefully avoid sin; if as soon as they become conscious of having committed any serious sin they hasten to wash it away by means of the Sacrament of Penance,—they may repose in the blissful conviction that they are children of God. For them

God is a loving Father, for them death has no terrors. It is only the gloomy portal through which they must pass in order to enter heaven. Herein lies the fulness of peace for the pious, conscientious Christian—peace with God, peace in his own soul, peace in his family.

The third condition is a hope of heaven. When all the members of a family are animated by this hope, peace dwells within the home. This hope ought to be as firm and steadfast as was that of a young girl, the closing scenes of whose life I witnessed some years ago. She was one of my parishioners and in the bloom of youth, for she was only twenty, when she was called to depart this life. She had been an intelligent child, a modest maiden, an obedient daughter, beloved by her parents, brothers and sisters. Her heart had been closed to the allurements of the world, and given to God. Death was now close at hand; her relatives stood weeping around her bed; she alone was calm and even joyous. With an expression of heartfelt piety she gazed at the crucifix which she held in her hand, exclaiming: "Help me, O my Saviour, receive me into heaven!" These were her last words. She sank back upon her pillows, and expired in the peace of the Lord.

What was it which imparted such sweet peace to the heart of this young girl at the very moment which is regarded as the most dreadful and terrifying? What but the hope that she was about to enter into the everlasting peace of heaven! If this hope is firmly rooted in the hearts of parents and children, they keep the thought of heaven constantly before their minds, and however severe may be the trials which come upon them, they never lose their peace of soul. They know that the bitterest sorrows are but transient, while the joys of heaven last forever.

Whilst you are still in the bright season of youth, see that you seek to possess the conditions of true peace. Impress deeply upon your heart a belief in divine providence. Endeavor to be at peace with God by avoiding sin. Constantly maintain and cherish within your soul the blissful hope of heaven. Then, whatever may be the circumstances in which you find yourself placed, however heavy the trials which overtake you, the misfortunes which fall to your lot, your peace of mind will be unshaken.

Prayer to St. Joseph as Patron

Blessed Joseph, faithful guardian of my Redeemer Jesus Christ, protector of thy chaste spouse the virgin Mother of God, I choose thee this day to be my especial patron and advocate, and I firmly resolve to honor thee as such from this time forth and always. Therefore I humbly beseech thee to receive me for thy client, to instruct me in every doubt, to comfort me in every affliction, and finally to defend and protect me in the hour of death. Amen.

For His Safe-Conduct Through Life

Blessed Joseph, father and guide of Jesus Christ in His childhood and youth, who didst lead Him safely in His flight through the desert, and in all the ways of His earthly pilgrimage, be also my companion and guide in this pilgrimage of life, and never permit me to turn aside from the way of God's commandments; be my refuge in adversity, my support in temptation, my solace in affliction, until at length I arrive at the land of the living, where with thee, and Mary thy most holy spouse, and all the Saints, I may rejoice forever in Jesus my Lord. Amen.

Indulgenced Prayer for a Christian Family

God of goodness and mercy, we commend to Thy all-powerful protection our home, our family, and all that we possess. Bless us all as Thou didst bless the holy family of Nazareth.

O Jesus, our most holy Redeemer, by the love with which Thou didst become man in order to save us, by the mercy through which Thou didst die for us upon the cross, we entreat Thee to bless our home, our family, our household. Preserve us from all evil and from the snares of men; preserve us from lightning and hail and fire, from flood and from the rage of the elements; preserve us from Thy wrath, from all hatred and from the evil intentions of our enemies, from plague, famine, and war. Let not one of us die without the holy sacraments. Bless us, that we may always openly confess our faith, which is to sanctify us, that we may never falter in our hope, even amid pain and affliction, and that we may ever grow in love for Thee and in charity toward our neighbor.

O Jesus, bless us, protect us.

O Mary, Mother of grace and mercy, bless us, protect us against the evil spirit; lead us by the hand through this vale of tears; reconcile us with thy divine Son; commend us to Him, that we may be made worthy of His promises.

St. Joseph, reputed father of Our Saviour, guardian of His most holy Mother, head of the holy family, intercede for us, bless and protect our home always.

St. Michael, defend us against all the wicked wiles of hell.

St. Gabriel, obtain for us that we may understand the holy will of God.

St. Raphael, preserve us from ill health and all danger to life.

Holy guardian angels, keep us day and night in the way to salvation.

Holy patrons, pray for us before the throne of God.

Bless this house, Thou, God our Father, Who didst create us; Thou, divine Son, Who didst suffer for us on the cross; Thou, Holy Spirit, Who didst sanctify us in Baptism. May God, in His three divine Persons, preserve our body, purify our soul, direct our heart, and lead us to life everlasting.

Glory be to the Father, glory be to the Son, glory be to the Holy Ghost. Amen.

◀ 2 ▶

The Religious Education of Children

LXXXII. Happiness or Misery

> How sacred is a little child,
> Simple as yet and undefiled;
> His angel, we are told, stands nigh
> To the bright throne of God on high.

IN every Christian family the greatest weight must be attached to the bringing up of the children in conjunction with the practice of religion. In relation to this matter it behooves parents to bear in mind the Saviour's exhortation; "*Seek ye first the kingdom of God and His justice.*" Parents ought not to have merely worldly aims in regard to the education of their children; they ought not only to seek to have a large fortune to leave them, or to enable them at a later period to acquire much wealth; it is their duty to take care, first of all, that their children are religiously brought up.

In the generality of cases the whole subsequent life depends upon the early training received—the happiness or misery of both parents and children. The words of Our Lord are worthy of attention: "*Do men gather grapes of thorns, or figs of thistles?*" Grapes are to be found only on vines, and figs on fig trees. In like manner one may ask: Would you look for good children with bad parents? Of course not. If you want to know whether certain children are receiving a good Christian education you have only to inquire whether the parents are good and pious.

If children see and hear only what is good, are allowed to do only what is right, and are held back with a firm hand from all that is evil, they will, as a rule, grow up good Christians. If, on the contrary, a child sees and hears scarcely anything which is not of an objectionable nature, its evil tendencies will grow stronger day by day, and we cannot wonder if it becomes both vicious and miserable.

The mother of St. Clement of Ancyra earnestly desired that her son might be a martyr. She gave him a pious, Christian education; he became a saint and eventually received the martyr's palm.

St. Blanche desired that her son might become a holy king. She imparted to him an education corresponding to her wish, and she became the mother of St. Louis, king of France. We will quote an illustration of an opposite character. There was once a godless queen of Bohemia who brought up her son Boleslaus to be as wicked as herself; he committed the crime of fratricide, and persecuted the Christians. If we wish for further examples of what has been said, we have only to look at families where the task of education is undertaken by unprincipled parents—or, more probably, neglected altogether. The character of children usually corresponds to that of their parents, as the proverb expresses it: "The apple does not fall far from the tree."

If, on the contrary, I ask you how it is that you are walking in the right way, gladly and gratefully will you answer that it is because you had good parents, who both by precept and example strove to lead you to do what is right. If we raise our eyes to heaven and ask its blessed inhabitants how they came to enjoy their present felicity, they will reply: "We had pious Christian parents." If we ask the wretched dwellers in hell how it is that they are plunged in endless misery, they will for the most part lay the blame on their education, and exclaim: "We had parents who neglected their duty and who, by their bad example, confirmed us in what is evil. Cursed be they forevermore! Our eternal misery lies at their door!"

Therefore do truly good and pious parents "*seek first the kingdom of God*" in regard to the education of their children—that is, they seek to provide for their eternal happiness before everything else. When their eyes rest upon their beloved offspring they say to themselves over and over again: "Shall even one of these dear children sink into hell through our fault? No, a thousand times no!" And then they apply themselves with renewed earnestness and increased zeal to the important work of education.

But upon education depends the happiness or misery, not of the children alone, but of their parents also. Many and manifold are the cares and anxieties, the labors and sorrows which fall to the lot of fathers and mothers of families. Surely they ought to have some pleasures, some compensations. Who can supply them with these pleasures and afford them these compensations if not their children? And it is certain that they will do this if they have been properly reared; they will be a credit to their parents wherever they may go. And when such children stand beside the death-bed of their father or mother, the gaze of these latter will rest upon them with confidence and satisfaction, and in their heart, if not with their lips, they will say: "I have no reason to be ashamed of my sons and daughters. They will not forget me; they will pray for me; they will sanctify themselves, and one day they will follow me to heaven!" That is the joy and reward of parents who have been careful to educate their children aright.

These serious thoughts and considerations will give you some idea how sublime a task is Christian education. They will urge you to do your very utmost to lighten the difficult task your parents have to perform, and to take upon yourself some portion at least of their heavy responsibility. You can and ought to do this by showing at all times and in all places how well and carefully you have been brought up; by proving yourself to be the joy and the glory of your parents. What happiness will be yours if, when their last hour shall come, they take leave of you with an expression of love and benediction.

LXXXIII. Begin the Work Early

> A child!—What mystery in this word!—
> A child was once our blessed Lord,
> Assuming our mortality,
> That thus God's children we might be.

In what does this mystery consist? In the inestimable value which the soul of a child possesses in the sight of God and of all good people. The mother of whom the following incident is related placed the right estimate on the value of a child. She had nine children, but was so poor that it was with the utmost difficulty she could contrive to feed and clothe them. One day a wealthy and charitable lady offered to adopt one of the nine little ones and give it a thoroughly good education. But the worthy woman refused to part with her child. "If you were to give me your whole fortune," she said, "I would not let you take one of my children from me; for that which is enough for eight will doubtless be enough for nine." She would not entrust the training of her child to the best woman in the world.

Considering the great value of a child in the sight of God, it follows that its education must be of the utmost importance, especially its *early* education. Every gardener who knows anything about his business is aware how much depends upon the care bestowed upon young and tender plants. If they are neglected in the early stages of their growth they soon become sickly or wither away altogether. All who labor in the garden of the Lord—all those I mean whose duty it is to educate youth—ought to lay this to heart, for education cannot begin too early.

In regard to this subject I have often heard parents say: "But what can your Reverence be thinking about! To say that a child's education ought to begin in the cradle! How can you expect a little creature like that to understand anything?" If I had uttered the retort which rose to my lips I should have replied: "You good people have not much more sense yourselves!"

The mental and—more especially—the religious education of the child should be commenced as soon as possible, and should keep pace with its physical development. For if one wishes to get the upper hand of the weeds in a garden and to keep the beds tidy, it is necessary to extirpate the germs of the weeds. And if a building is to be solid and lasting it must have a firm foundation.

Every child possesses qualities and capacities which slumber within its breast. It is easy to develop them within the tender mind; the soil is soft and receptive to all which may be planted there. The heart of a child resembles a garden, which must be properly tilled if it is to produce fruit. A garden left to itself will be overrun with weeds, and all hope of a yield must perforce be abandoned.

Parents are often heard to complain of the naughtiness and perversity of their children. As a rule we may tell such parents that they have only themselves to blame; for if they had attended to the education of their children while there was yet time, if they had cultivated the field of their heart at an early period, they would be reaping joy and consolation instead of sorrow and distress. Man must be trained from his earliest childhood to shun all that is evil and sinful.

It is the roots which keep the tender plants in the ground and supply them with sap and nourishment. The roots of the Christian life are religion and piety. These roots must be tended, and that very early; else the outlook in the field of education will be but a poor one. Priests and teachers experience the truth of this fact only too frequently. One meets with boys and girls six or seven years old who have as yet merely vegetated, growing up like little animals. About their Father in heaven, about Jesus, Mary, and their guardian angel they know nothing at all, or at best but very little. They can scarcely tell how to make the sign of the cross. The roots of religion and piety have been so neglected that they are buried deep down in the youthful hearts, or what is worse, choked by the weeds of bad habits—of idleness, greediness, lying, dissimulation, and obstinacy.

But it is a consolation to know that children who have been well and carefully trained up to their sixth and seventh year remain, as a rule, what they are at that period. It gives real pleasure to teachers when the children of truly pious parents come to their school. In the favorable atmosphere of the family circle, the spiritual life of the child—drawing its vitality from the warm heart of the mother—has been developed, religion and piety have grown and flourished. All that the child hears when he goes to school about God and about heaven, about piety and prayer, about innocence and obedience, and every virtue is not new to him. On the contrary, those virtues are dear and familiar truths. Out of the eyes of the child who has been brought up thus a new soul seems to look. The pious mother, the best of gardeners, has tilled the soil of the child's heart, so that the tender roots of good principles, of religion and piety might strike deep and not be choked by the weeds of evil habits.

It often happens that girls of your age have to occupy themselves, in one way or another, with the education of younger children. Elder brothers and sisters possess great influence over the younger ones. This influence is generally much greater than that which the parents are able to exercise. On this account, good and wise parents are extremely careful as to the training of their first child; for the eldest thus becomes no little help to them in training the others.

If you have younger brothers and sisters, or if you are placed over children in some family, be extremely careful to set the children a good example. Show them all possible patience and affection, and if you win their hearts in this way, make use of your influence to inspire them with a love of God and of virtue. What a sphere of usefulness is open to you here, and how easily you can gain the love of Him who has said: "*He that shall receive one such little child in my name, receiveth me.*"

LXXXIV. The Principal Factors and Supports in the Training of a Child

> Listen, O child, thou needs must early learn
> In this world good from evil to discern;
> Or else the useful herb thou wilt pass by
> And pluck the poisonous flower that charms the eye.

THE earliest training has this in view: to teach the child to distinguish between good and evil, between what is useful and what is poisonous, and to take delight only in the former. In order that this task may be profitably accomplished, various means are necessary. In a nursery ground the young, growing plants are fastened at an early period to stakes or supports to make them grow upright and straight; so in the training of children certain strong supports are required.

What is primarily and essentially necessary in education for the child's support is the good example of the teacher. Vain will be his words, useless his lamentations, fruitless his exhortations, if, instead of edifying his pupils by his good example, he rather gives them scandal. Children soon imitate what they see their parents do. Only too often do we experience the truth of the saying which tells us that as is the father, so is the son; as is the mother, so is the daughter. Let us take the case of parents who do not say their prayers regularly every morning and evening, or who do not say grace at meals. Children may be taught at school that they ought to say their prayers, but if they see that their parents neglect to pray they will follow this bad example.

The following incident, which was related to me, forcibly shows how great is the effect of bad example: A lady overheard a little boy about five or six years old using very bad language whilst playing in the street with other children. She stopped, and reproved him severely, threatening to complain of him to his parents. "I don't care if you do," was the unexpected rejoinder. "Father and mother curse worse than I do!" It is most deplorable that such parents should exist.

On the contrary we often find to our consolation that poor but thoroughly Christian fathers and mothers, in cities and in the country, have given their children an excellent training. The secret lies in the power of example. The children of parents who themselves practice all that religion requires of them are certain to turn out well.

The second essential in home-training consists in accustoming children to obedience from the outset. A little boy was asked; "Tell me, my child, do you obey your mother or does she obey you?" "I obey her when she is angry," he replied pertly, "but when she is not angry, she obeys me!" It was very plain that he had never been taught to obey.

Yet it is quite possible to accustom even little children to obey. This is proved by the fact that irrational animals can be trained to a certain kind of obedience. Why, for instance, do not dogs and cats jump upon the dinner table when dishes containing food are placed upon it, as their natural instincts would prompt them to do? Simply because they have learned to obey.

But there are teachers and mothers who, in their foolish fondness, themselves obey a child. The little creature has only to scream, and they hasten to do whatever the young gentleman wishes! If a child is not taught to obey from infancy, the lesson of obedience will prove very hard to implant later on and never perhaps be thoroughly grounded.

Just as it is often necessary when tying up young trees to use a certain amount of force to straighten what is crooked, so strictness is required in accustoming children to obedience; they must be reproved, and punished also. For the words of Scripture cannot but be true: "*He that spareth the rod, hateth his son.*" It is clear that this saying holds good in the present day; it can never be antiquated, even in the twentieth-century progress and vaunted humanity. It is absolutely necessary to be strict with children at certain times, and without losing one's temper.

Another main factor in the education of a child is the school. The training at school has a twofold purpose—one temporal, the other eternal. At school the child ought to be trained to be a good and useful member of society, to do the will of God, and thus to secure the reward of heaven. The supernatural part of this twofold undertaking requires that the school should not merely instruct, but educate also; educate in obedience, in truthfulness—and before all else, in the fear of God, in self-control, in purity of heart. Thus we see that the chief work the Christian school has to perform is to teach the child to be a good Christian, who will on this account be a good citizen as well.

In conclusion I will relate an anecdote from which you may learn that you ought always to listen to the wise exhortations and affectionate admonitions of your parents and teachers, and also endeavor faithfully to carry them out.

A young lady received a letter in which improper proposals were made to her, these being couched in the most alluring and flattering terms. With childlike confidence she showed the letter to her mother, who, after reading it, turned pale, and burst into tears. When the daughter saw this she exclaimed: "O my darling mother, you need not be in the least anxious about me! Your tears have entirely obliterated all the specious flatteries and fair promises which this letter contains."

The mother tenderly embraced her daughter, and gave her a diamond ring, the stones of which sparkled as brightly as do dewdrops when the sun shines upon them. Filled with gratitude, the good child said: "Dearest mother, I solemnly promise that if ever improper proposals should again be made to me I will look at these precious stones, and say to myself: These are your mother's tears." If, my dear daughter, you should ever find yourself in similar circumstances, think of Mary, your sweet Mother in heaven.

LXXXV. Studies: Higher Education.[1]

Let us now consider the study—the education which is really suited to a woman who has a house to look after—or who should be brought up and trained with a view to this. In treating the question little or no account will be taken of exceptional cases, for example, of *really* clever girls who intend to devote themselves to teaching, or to literature, or of those who have no home duties or only very light ones. In the curriculum of woman's education the first place should be given to the study of her own language, so that she may speak and write it well, and also acquire a fair knowledge of its literature and of its classical writers. This will be not only a source of improvement and

---

[1] Excerpt from "*Woman*," by the Reverend N. Walsh S.J.

pleasure to herself, but will enable her to criticise authors, to take part in conversation with husband, father, son or brother who takes an interest in and likes to discuss such topics.

The second place may be given to the study of modern languages, particularly French and German. Young men have not as a rule the time, the opportunities, perhaps the talent, for acquiring this useful branch of education, that girls have. A good knowledge of French will make them a great help—perhaps a necessity—to the other members of their family when traveling, as this delightful and educating recreation has become—owing to the railway and other causes—a matter of course, and is within the reach of all well-to-do people. I would throw in Latin, or some knowledge of it. It is the language of the Church and of the holy sacrifice, and would help those who may be called to Religion to recite more devoutly the Divine Office, or that of the Blessed Virgin. Madame de Swetchine writes to a woman friend: "Your Latin has given me at least as much pleasure as the rest; the language of our faith should never be omitted in any religious education."

The third place should be given to what are commonly called "accomplishments," and of these first of all to music, because this can be most and best utilized for the pleasure, delight, and enjoyment of home life. It is a mistake, however, to force or to allow a girl to study this or any other accomplishment for which she has neither talent nor taste, perhaps a dislike. To do this would be to lose time which could have been better employed, and would certainly end in failure. Teachers, not parents, are the best and safest persons to find out the accomplishment suited to a girl and in which she is likely to succeed, whether this be music, painting, drawing, tapestry or some other useful or ornamental handwork; for all these contribute in their own way to the happiness, brightness, and external beauty of the home.

We come now to a study of a lower kind. Fénelon recommends the woman of the house "to be well versed in housekeeping." This supposes a system of order, punctuality, everything kept in its place, cleanliness, neatness and a care of external beauty. It has been said that the cook is the most important person in the house because she can put all the others in good or bad humor. There is some truth in the saying, "God sends the meat and the devil sends the cook." A good cook can make a palatable dish out of poor material, whilst a bad cook will spoil the best. Hence the mistress should study and give attention to this important branch of "housekeeping," that she may be able to place on the table food well-cooked and well-served that she knows will please the family. God supposes all this in His description of the valiant woman, "*who hath arisen at night and given a prey to her household, and food to her maidens.*" In the words of an eminent French bishop: "A lady should diligently attend to her household affairs: it is one of her principal duties. She will never degrade herself by condescending to the smallest details, for there is a manner of doing so which compromises neither her dignity, her authority, nor her character. Manual labor of whatever nature, whether in 'the spinning of wool or flax, handling the distaff' or needle, *superintending the making of dishes* or of garments—manual labor, I repeat, is one of the best and most useful resources of woman's life; and one of the plague-spots of our present age is its being entirely laid aside, or at least rarely practised."

Fénelon says that the mistress of the house should also be well versed "in keeping accounts," and God, in His description of the valiant woman, supposes this. Men have, as a rule, the earning of the money, women the spending of it. It is, therefore, one of their duties to keep an account of monies received, of how they were spent, etc., and to keep clear of drifting into debt. It is, however, a not uncommon failing with men to think and unreasonably complain that a wife ought to do more with what is given to her than she really can.

There is no doubt that if the wife and mother is to be as the sun in her own house, she must be unselfish, act often against her natural inclination, be just yet considerate toward others, never neglect a duty through whim or because annoyed or contradicted. She must often when tired and taxed—unfairly perhaps, by others—either keep a *sweet* silence or say the right word in the right way, and conceal as best she can the interior impatience or pain which she cannot help feeling.

The example, the habitual action and ways of such a woman must—not in a moment or at once, but in the end—win the respect and admiration of all around her, and exercise a powerful influence for good in her family. Hence St. Chrysostom writes: "There is nothing more powerful than a religious and prudent woman to calm her husband and to form him to whatever she wishes." Every-day experience proves the truth of this saying of a great saint who spent his priestly and episcopal life in constant contact with seculars. All know how St. Monica illustrated this truth. She won her great son Augustine to God and His Church by her prayers and tears; but more, she won over a bad husband, who for years treated her harshly, by her sweet and patient command of temper and tongue. What has been said of wife and mother may be said, in some measure, of daughters and sisters, who, when bright and companionable with father and brothers, contribute much to the happiness of home. By way of conclusion to this point, is it too much to say that woman—the sun of the house—should do her best to make it so comfortable, cheerful, and happy that when the husband and sons—the toilers—have done their day's work, they would rather come to her and their own home than go to a queen and her palace?

It may now be asked: may not woman in her intellectual pursuits go further and higher than those subjects already referred to—subjects which are the best for making her the sun in her own house? Certainly, if three conditions be observed: (1) that no home duty be neglected or carelessly discharged on account of such study; (2) that she is capable of it; (3) that she be, as Fénelon puts it, "modest in her studies."

The intellectual cultivation of woman has always been a marked feature of the Catholic Church. "Christianity," writes Ozanam, "had scarcely appeared when already the example of Christ instructing the Samaritan woman was imitated." St. John wrote to Electa, and the Fathers of the Church, SS. Cyprian and Ambrose, and Tertullian, wrote for women. He notices the honor paid by St. Augustine to the philosophy of his mother, and how St. Jerome was surrounded by Christian matrons full of eagerness for learning, and wrote letters to Læta and Gaudentius on the education of daughters. St. Catharine of Alexandria told her judges that she had applied herself to every branch of rhetoric, philosophy, geometry and other sciences. St. Clement of Alexandria writes of some Grecian ladies who had occupied themselves in the study of literature, science and philosophy. The papal University of Bologna had on its roll learned women, and one called Maria Agnese was named professor of mathematics by a Pope. SS. Paula, Gertrude, Catharine of Siena, Teresa and others might also be named. It must, however, be borne in mind that nearly all these were exceptional cases... The practical question is, would such (higher) studies be likely to educate girls to be as the valiant woman in her house, or would they rather prevent her from becoming such?

Human respect has something to do with girls who attempt studies which are above them. Some few girls of *exceptional talents*, and others just capable of getting a smattering of higher studies, go in for them; and then parents, who do not like to think that their children are not clever, but who wish them to be on a level with those mentioned above, insist that their daughters follow their example. With what results? Well, as has been often said, with the baneful results that other more necessary and useful studies, of which they were capable, have been neglected; and that they become what may be fairly called muddle-headed by attempting a study for which they have no talent.

Fénelon dreaded, above all, women too learned in theology, and with good reason, for some such helped to get the great Archbishop of Cambrai into difficulties; besides, downright poor theologians women would make, because not intended or gifted by God for such a study. "I would much prefer," he says, "that she should be well versed in the housekeeping and accounts than in the dispute of theologians about grace." At the same time, a really solid knowledge of the catechism, philosophy and theology of a *certain kind*, ought to hold a prominent place in the education of girls. Their teachers should instruct them in the great foundation truths of Christianity; in the defined dogmas of the Church; in the principles and practices which they should esteem if they are to be good children of the Church; also in the strongest and easiest-understood arguments in favor of these; all given, however, in a manner at once interesting and suited to their capacity.

LXXXVI. The Blessing From Above

In the days of the Jewish king Ahab, the fountains of heaven were closed for the space of three years. During all this time no rain fell, so that the rivers and springs were dried, up, and men and beasts died of thirst. At length the prophet Elias ascended to the summit of Mount Carmel and earnestly besought God to send rain upon the earth. Then, as we read in Scripture, *"the heaven grew dark with clouds and wind, and there fell a great rain."*

A similar occurrence took place on the day of Pentecost; the spiritual rain of those celestial graces which are shed abroad by the Holy Ghost was poured down at Jerusalem. It refreshed and animated the hearts of the followers of Jesus, so that they at once began to blossom and bear rich and abundant fruit.

To parents and families is committed the difficult and important task of training children aright. In order to do this they need that heavenly rain, the blessing from above, the fertilizing grace of the Holy Spirit. But how are they to obtain this blessing? They must do the same as Elias did on the summit of Carmel, as the disciples of the Lord did before the feast of Pentecost.

Of these latter we read: *"They were all together in one place."* And elsewhere it is said: *"All these were persevering with one mind in prayer."* Through prayer—and through prayer alone—did Elias obtain the natural rain from above, and by the same means the disciples of Jesus obtained the supernatural blessing, the grace of the Holy Ghost. Those who have to undertake the great work of education can obtain the blessing from above—the grace of the Holy Ghost—only by means of prayer.

It is well known that what is planted in youth bears fruit in old age. Habit becomes a second nature. Those who have learned in their childhood to pray aright will not finally be lost though they may wander for a time from the right way. But suppose through the carelessness of teachers a child should not have learned how to pray—he may be lost; in this case the guilt will be laid at their door!

When the apostle St. John was upon one occasion visiting a Christian community, he saw a promising youth who as yet had not been baptized. He sought to win him over to

Christianity, and said to the bishop of the place: "Look after this young man. I commit him to thy care in the presence of Jesus Christ and of this entire community."

The bishop took the greatest pains with him, but only until he was baptized; after that his zeal grew cold. The young man got into bad company; he went so far as to join a band of highwaymen, and became their chief. Some years later St. John revisited the same community and asked the bishop to give him an account of the young man who had been confided to his care. The bishop cast down his eyes, and said: "Alas! he is dead!" "Dead, do you say?" exclaimed the apostle, "and what death did he die?" "He is dead in the sight of God," replied the bishop; "he became a scoundrel, a highwayman!" On hearing these words St. John wept aloud, crying out: "Alas! to what a keeper did I entrust the soul of my brother!"

The child is also a pledge, like this young man—a pledge which God confides to its parents in the presence of Jesus Christ and of His Church, in order that it may be cherished and cared for. In their hands He has placed it; from their hands will He require it again. When, on the great day of final account, they stand before His judgment-seat, He will address to them this question: "Parents, where are your children, where are the souls I committed to your care?" Woe to the parents if, like that bishop, they are compelled to reply; "They are dead, dead in the sight of God, lost to heaven, and all through our fault!"

Therefore must parents and teachers keep those entrusted to their care from evil, by precept and example, by watchfulness and punishment; they must lead them in the path of virtue on the road to heaven.

In so doing they must not forget the most important thing of all—they must pray with the child and for the child. They must begin and end with prayer, for without this all their efforts will avail little or nothing. Only by praying with and for the child can its heart be raised to God, can it be led on the road to heaven, to eternal blessedness. Prayer is sometimes the only means which can be employed to save a child. When, for instance, a son or a daughter has already entered upon a course of sin, no advice, no warnings can be of any more avail, and their age renders the infliction of any form of punishment entirely out of the question. In such a case what remains but prayer?

A mother had an only, darling son, who, though full of promise, was the child of many sorrows. For when the gifted boy grew to be a young man he followed in the steps of his heathen father. Before he was sixteen he lost his innocence, and sank deeper and deeper in sin. A few years later he even went so far as to boast of his wickedness. This was a bitter grief indeed for his unhappy mother! But Monica was a Christian; she was more than this—she was a saint. For sixteen long years she prayed most earnestly for the conversion of her son. So fervent were her petitions that a holy bishop said to her: "The child of so many prayers and tears can never be lost." And since she persevered with confidence in prayer, from a great sinner Augustine her son became a great saint.

But how is the blessing from above to be sought; in what way ought prayer to be made? First and foremost *family prayer* in the household is necessary. Thanks be to God that this pious custom of having daily prayers in common is observed in many families; although in numerous others it is totally neglected.

Yet it is family prayer which imparts to the household a truly Christian character, and procures for it happiness and blessings. Such prayer as this unites all hearts; it is a sight to rejoice the angels, a sweet, melodious sound in the ear of God.

A family which thus prays is a strong tower against which no hostile efforts can prevail. In the course of time the children must go forth into the world and be exposed to a thousand dangers and temptations. They can no longer hear the affectionate entreaties of their mother, the grave warnings of their father; one thing must, however, always remain with them—the impression of the pious life which was led and the prayers which were said so fervently and regularly in their parents' house.

My dear child, you will probably have to occupy yourself at a later period, in one way or another, with the training of children; this should furnish you with an additional reason for learning at the present time to love prayer and to be diligent in its practice. A great variety of oral prayers and devotional exercises is not so important as the inward spirit of prayer, the conviction of its necessity, the confidence in its power. Such is the spirit in which the training of children ought to be conducted.

> O Christian parents, my counsel heed:
> In your children's hearts implant good seed;
> God's blessing will on your household rest
> If truly you follow His behest.

Prayer of Venerable Father Olier

O Jesus, living in Mary,
Come and live in Thy servants,
In the spirit of Thy holiness,
In the fulness of Thy might,
In the truth of Thy virtues,
In the perfection of Thy ways,
In the communion of Thy mysteries.
Subdue every hostile power,
In Thy Spirit, for the glory of the Father.
Amen.

‹ 3 ›

The Housewife's Adorning

LXXXVII. Beautiful Apparel

Happiness or misery, peace or disquiet, the good or bad training of the children—all depend in the first place on the wife and mother. If the husband be ever so vicious and irreligious, the family will yet go on comparatively well if the mother is truly good, pious, and intelligent. If, on the contrary, the mother is shiftless and unfaithful to her duties, the prospects are bad for the family no matter how saintly the father may be. No better description of a model housewife can possibly be found than that which the Holy Ghost gives us in the Proverbs of Solomon. In the 31st chapter we read as follows: "*Who shall find a valiant woman? the price of her is as of things brought from afar off and from the uttermost coasts. The heart of her husband trusteth in her, and he shall have no need of spoils. She will render him good, and not evil, all the days of her life. She hath tasted and seen that her traffic is good; her lamp shall not be put out in the night. She hath opened her mouth to wisdom, and the law of clemency is on her tongue. She hath looked well to the paths of her house, and hath not eaten her bread idle. Her children rose up, and called her blessed; her husband, and he praised her. Favor is deceitful and beauty is vain: the woman that feareth the Lord, she shall be praised.*"

This description furnishes us with a lifelike portrait of the industrious housewife: occupied, as she constantly is, in keeping her house in good order, and pleasing her husband.

What a thoroughly efficient and sensible housewife can accomplish is not to be told in words. And I do not hesitate to say that the husband and children can not go wrong for any length of time when the mother understands how to strike the right chord, and to be a pattern of quiet industry and peaceful, thrifty domesticity.

Great and exalted therefore is the dignity of a mother. Of the glorious titles we give to the Blessed Virgin Mary, one of the greatest is, "Mother of the Son of God." This title shines as does the sun among the stars. And what sound is more melodious in our ears than the sweet name of mother?

What does not a mother do and suffer? Amid pain, anxiety, and care she tends her child, she watches beside it day and night, she prays for its physical and mental well-being, she thinks of it at all times. She makes the child what it is. A wise bishop went so far as to say that the education of a child begins and ends in its mother's lap. Therefore this precious garb of her dignity is the pride of every Christian housewife and mother. And for the sake of this dignity she gladly renounces the glitter and fame of public life, the strenuous joys and distracting vanities of the world.

The mother's dignity, the mother's love, have ever been respected and extolled in all ages and among all nations, civilized or uncivilized, Christian or pagan. This is proved by the numerous proverbs and quaint rhymes which are found belonging to all times and all climes, such as the following:

> "The mother is old
> But her love is not cold;
> Be he wayward and wild
> Yet she dotes on her child."

"A mother's love is new every morning."

"Better lose a rich father than a poor mother."

"Without a mother," say the Russians, "the children are lost as much as bees without their queen."

In nearly all countries one meets with some popular saying to the effect that "a poor mother will support seven children sooner than seven children will support their mother."

These examples might be multiplied indefinitely; the truths they express may well fill the maternal heart with joy and pride.

The robe of maternal dignity appears especially precious when we think of the glorious reward which is the portion of the good Christian mother. Her reward will indeed be great both on earth and in eternity.

Children, as a rule, cling to their mother and love her with grateful and abiding affection. The little child gives proof of this as soon as it begins to walk. How it clings to its mother's gown, and follows her step by step! And do not you, my dear daughter, place implicit confidence in your mother because you know that she always has your best interests at heart? Do you not confide the inmost secrets of your heart to your mother? Even grown-up sons and daughters, when they think of marrying, seek advice from their mother in preference to any one else.

This confidence is based upon an ordinance of divine providence, and only in God and the saints ought children to place greater confidence than they do in their mother.

And how glorious a reward awaits the good, faithful Christian mother on the other side of the grave. Our good God, with Mary and all the angels and saints, will welcome a soul adorned with the twofold robe of sanctifying grace and the dignity of a pious, Christian mother. Great indeed will be her reward in heaven.

My dear child, let the consideration of the dignity of a Christian mother furnish you with a fresh motive for esteeming your own mother all the more highly, for loving her all the more dearly, for striving all the more earnestly to give her pleasure. Above all, remain the faithful child of your heavenly Mother, of whom we speak in the familiar lines:

> A mother's love, how fond and true,
> Never failing, daily new;
> Mary, dearest Mother mine,
> Be gracious to this child of thine.

LXXXVIII. Gold Ornaments

In order that woman may obtain firmness of character, strength for the fulfilment of her arduous duties, endurance for her toilsome life of self-sacrifice, she needs the true religious spirit and genuine piety. "Take religion away from woman," a French writer says, "and she is deprived of morality also; in that case she is nothing but a whited sepulchre, wherein abide corruption and decay." Especially does the *housewife* need religion to accomplish her lofty task—namely, to cultivate religion in her family, to instruct her children in its truths, and thus to become the priestess of the domestic shrine. Before everything else she must be adorned with the golden ornaments of true and fervent piety.

In the cemetery attached to the Church of St. Louis at Versailles (near Paris), this epitaph may be seen inscribed in large letters on the tombstone of a married woman: "*Domi mansit.*" This epitaph may be read thus: "She did her duty in the bosom of her family." These words imply also that she was genuinely religious, that she promoted true, unfeigned piety in her household, and strove with all her might to kindle the sacred flame of faith, of devotion, and of charity, in all the members of her family.

This is the first duty of every Christian wife. She ought to be a faithful follower of the Mother of God. And where will she find the Mother of God if she wishes to tread in her footsteps? At the foot of the cross on Calvary, and in the house of Nazareth. The Catholic wife must strive to imitate Mary in that house, and if she does this her soul will not be lacking in the bright ornament of true piety. For in the house of Nazareth will the housewife learn to enter into and appreciate the inmost meaning of those words, *"Behold the handmaid of the Lord; be it done unto me according to thy word."* And there will her heart, which is destined for sacrifice and anxiety, find strength to resist its own weakness; faith and piety will render it strong and invincible.

If the soul of a housewife is truly given to God, if grace perfects all that is best in her natural character, she becomes—if I may so speak—a magnet which draws all hearts to God. She preaches without words, and the more quiet and unobtrusive her influence is, the more effectually does it work. With gentle force she draws those around her to God, just as a beautiful portrait awakens pleasing recollections of a person whom you have dearly loved.

More yet does true piety effect in the life of a housewife. It gives her a strength which overcomes all opposition, a power of endurance which shrinks from no difficulties, a sweetness which makes bitter things pleasant, and causes her heart to become a fountain of perennial gladness.

It is no wonder that a housewife such as we have just described should excite surprise in worldlings, that they should marvel to behold her cheerfulness and patience under the most trying circumstances. They are ignorant of its cause; they know nothing of the ever-flowing stream of living faith which imparts to her new power, fresh strength and courage, increased confidence in God.

I will now give you, at some length, an account of a housewife such as I have described, one who was richly adorned with the jewels of true piety. Touched by grace, and brought to a knowledge of the truth, this woman led a pious life, serving God in word and in deed. Her husband, on the contrary, was an enemy of Christianity and the slave of sin. On the occasion of a carouse with his boon companions the conversation happened to turn upon the failings and the good qualities of women. He was never tired of praising his wife and descanting upon her merits. "She possesses every excellence which can possibly be found in a woman. She is really a model wife. But you must take her pious whims into the bargain. She has her passions and emotions under perfect control. If I were to take you, my friends, to my house at midnight, and bid her get up and prepare a meal for you, I bet that she would do it at once as cheerfully and pleasantly as possible."

Those present made a bet, challenging him to put to a test what he had just said. They repaired to his house at twelve o'clock at night. "Where is your mistress," the husband inquired of the maid servant. "She went to bed a long time ago," was the reply. "Call her, and tell her to get up at once and prepare luncheon for me and my friends." The wife arose without delay, greeted the company in the most cordial manner, and told them that the meal would soon be ready. When it was placed upon the table she waited upon the guests, just as if she had invited them and they had made their appearance at a perfectly convenient time.

At length they could no longer conceal their admiration. "Madam," said one of them, "your courtesy amazes us. Our appearance at this unusual hour is the result of a wager we laid with your husband; we have lost it. But pray tell us what it is which enables you to treat us in so friendly a manner, since you certainly cannot approve of our way of going on?"

She answered pleasantly: "Gentlemen, when my husband and I were married, we were both living in sin. It pleased God to arouse me from this state. My husband is still walking in the broad path, and I tremble for his future fate. Were he to die in his present condition how sad would be his lot on the other side of the grave! Therefore it is my duty at least to make his life here below as agreeable as possible."

All present were surprised and touched by this answer, which made a great impression upon her husband. "My dear wife," he said, "are you really so concerned about my salvation? I thank you for your affectionate warning; with the help of God I will become a changed man." And he did indeed reform his manner of life; he became a true Christian and the best of husbands to the faithful wife, who, adorned with true and sincere piety, had so lovingly stood at his side.

In this instance we have exemplified the saying of St. Paul: "*Godliness is profitable to all things.*" Therefore, my daughter, in whatever state of life you may be, endeavor to cultivate true and genuine piety. God has implanted piety in your heart. Ever bear in mind that the practice of true piety will not only win for you a rich store of merit in the world to come, but will also obtain the blessing of God in the present life. By cultivating true piety you will assuredly possess peace of heart, peace with God and man.

LXXXIX. Diamonds

WOMEN, whether married or unmarried, love external ornament; they like to be well-dressed, to wear gold rings, bracelets, and necklaces set with precious stones. The housewife should indeed be decked with lovely gems, but her adorning should be inward—the adorning of the heart. By this is meant that the housewife ought to possess the virtues that are most necessary for family life—in particular, docility and patience. These housewifely virtues, her most becoming ornament, ought to be lasting and indestructible, emitting a bright and genial lustre, like two diamonds of the first water.

The first diamond in a wife's crown of virtue is *docility*. Eve was the first to commit sin and on her the sentence of punishment was passed first. The words of this sentence apply equally to all her feminine posterity: "*Thou shalt be under thy husband's power, and he shall have dominion over thee.*"

The apostle Paul speaks most explicitly of the obedience due from a wife. In his Epistle to the Ephesians he says: "*Let women be subject to their husbands, as to the Lord: Because the husband is the head of the wife; as Christ is the head of the Church.*"

In the household, therefore, the husband is lord and master; his wife, his children, the men servants and the maids are subject to him. Would that women knew how much wiser it is to rest content with the position God has assigned to them! How much dissension, how much vexation, how many disagreeable scenes in family life would thus be avoided!

Many a wife will say with more or less justice that her husband is stupid and tactless, without talent for business, and wanting in energy. In this case, the wife ought to endeavor to supply his deficiencies and in a gentle, kindly spirit, help him to manage his affairs, without any assumption of dictatorial authority.

Patience is another precious diamond in the Christian housewife's crown of virtues. A wife ought to know the character, the disposition, and the inclinations of her husband, and carefully avoid whatever excites him to anger. A misunderstanding and consequent contentions may arise, however, and lead to an outbreak of passion on the part of the husband. In that case, a good wife will not exasperate him still more by seeking to have the last word in the quarrel; a wise and discreet wife will try to restore peace and harmony as speedily as possible. She will not say: "The right is on my side."

All contentious persons persist in saying they are in the right. But the Christian housewife, who knows that self-denial is required of her, is content to lay her right on the altar of peace, and keep silence. A woman's most powerful weapon is patience, not vehemence. If she wants to rule, let her cultivate a sweet and gentle disposition. She can do nothing, gain nothing, by force—whereas with patient wisdom and wise patience she will succeed in getting her own way.

But I hear some wife or other say: "That is all very well, but how is one to keep one's patience with a man who is such a bad husband, who is addicted to drink, who squanders his money and is a regular tyrant?" Under such circumstances all a wife can do is to bear with her husband's bad ways in a spirit of penance, and earn for herself that happiness after death which is promised to the meek and to the peacemakers. Unless she views her trials in this light, she will have much to suffer here without the prospect of reward hereafter—nay more—she will have a twofold punishment, for her life will be a hell on earth, and she will not escape the torment of hell for all eternity.

There is one thing more which a good wife can do for a bad husband—she can exert herself to the utmost for his conversion and never grow weary until her end is gained, after the example of St. Monica.

I heard recently of a truly Christian wife who acted in this way. The more rude and unkind her husband was, the more meek and gentle she became. At the same time she prayed constantly to God, with tears, imploring Him to touch her husband's heart and bring him to a better mind. What was the result? One morning the man said to his long-suffering wife: "Dear wife, we cannot go on in this way. You are an angel, and I am a very devil. We are ill-matched and cannot live together any longer as we have been doing. I have determined to abandon my evil ways, and from this day forth I mean to lead a new life, as becomes a Christian." The man kept his word. Thus we see how patience and endurance conquered at last.

You must not, however, think that docility and patience are virtues wherewith it behooves you to adorn yourself only in later years; on the contrary, they must be learned and practised in your youthful days. I have told you of this repeatedly and emphatically. Obedience is the virtue which the young pre-eminently ought to possess. See that you cultivate it, and practise it conscientiously in regard to your parents and superiors.

And since you will find that the bright roses of the springtime of your life are not without thorns—the thorns of sorrows and vexations—abundant opportunity will be afforded you for the exercise of patience. Make good use of these occasions, and thus prepare to bear the sufferings of the days to come. Be patient!

> O praise thou the Lord, give thanks to His name,
> With heart and with voice His goodness proclaim;
> To Him have recourse whatever thy grief,
> He will, the mighty One, bring thee relief.

XC. Precious Stones

A LEARNED prelate has well said: "Where God has set up an altar in the heart of the wife and mother, the whole house becomes a temple dedicated to His service." Now, for that very reason the house at Nazareth where the holy family dwelt was a temple, since God had literally erected an altar, made an abode for Himself, in the heart of Joseph's holy spouse. In a certain sense this ought to be true of every mother of a family. If the household is to be a happy one it is not enough for the father to be virtuous; it is equally—

nay more—important that the mother should be so too. And to complete her set of jewel-like virtues, besides the two diamonds of which we have spoken—docility and patience—she must possess three more bright, sparkling, and precious stones.

First and foremost is the bright red ruby of *conjugal affection*—it must, however, be the true, genuine love of a wife for her husband. What is too often the experience of those who have not long been married? As soon as they find out each other's faults and failings, when the novelty has worn off, when toil and trouble and cares weigh upon them, then, as the saying is, love flies out of the window. "Would that I had never married!" many a young wife has been heard to say. But the truly Christian wife does not lose heart so easily. When the first passionate love has died out, it is replaced by a nobler, truer affection—one which death cannot destroy, and which lives beyond the grave. The virtuous wife will love her husband because God commands her to love him, because it is her duty to love him.

The early training of the children naturally falls chiefly to the wife and mother. On this account Almighty God has adorned her heart with a precious jewel, the crimson-hued jasper of *maternal love*. What the warm sunbeams are to a flower-garden, this love is to the soul of the little child. Many flowers unfold their blossoms only in the sun, and close them as soon as it ceases to shine. Children are, as it were, plants in the garden of the Lord, the Christian family. Love must, like the sun, warm their hearts, and cause their minds to open to what is good and true and beautiful. Wherefore the sun of a mother's love must never be obscured and darkened by the clouds of ill-temper or of low spirits; otherwise, the happy heart of childhood will itself be overshadowed with gloom. On the other hand, how the child delights to look into the kindly, loving eyes of its mother, and how gladly it drinks in her teaching!

Thus the precious jewel of maternal love is a powerful factor in the early training of children. An experienced Christian author says: "A child's education is almost completed in the first five years spent at his mother's knee, in the sunshine of her love. Whatever qualities or tendencies are developed in him in after years, the seed of them was sown by his mother in his early childhood. The impressions made on the soft soil of the child's heart, so sensitive to all that is good and beautiful, are never obliterated all his life long."

Children who grow up without the fostering care of a mother's love very often become selfish, secretive, morose, ready for all sorts of tricks. Therefore the jasper of maternal affection ought to shine prominently amongst the jewels that adorn the mother of a family.

The same may be said of a third precious stone—the sky-blue turquoise of *love of order*. God Himself loves order. That is why He maintains that wonderful order which is observed in the universe, in all Nature. For man, too, order has a powerful attraction; it contributes greatly to his comfort. It is to a great extent due to the strict order which prevails, even in the most minute details, in convents, that one finds more contented and cheerful individuals there than anywhere else. However small and poverty-stricken a house may appear, however simple and ordinary its inmates may be, if their family life is conducted in an orderly manner, if they are regular in their habits and everything is done at the right time and in the right place, that household will be a happy one, and one will feel himself at home there despite the plain surroundings.

But if in the household over which a young wife presides, cleanliness and order do not prevail, if everything is untidy and in confusion, there is no need to inquire what sort of person the mistress of that house is; one may take it for granted that she is quite incompetent and that but little happiness will be found in that family. For, as Chateaubriand says: "If happiness really exists here below, it is undoubtedly in an orderly, well-regulated family."

Look in imagination at the interior of the quiet house at Nazareth where the holy family dwelt. Would it not seem akin to blasphemy to suppose that the Blessed Virgin did not keep her house in perfect order? Everything in it was doubtless poor and simple, but spotlessly clean and neat. How inviting, how comfortable his home looked, when St. Joseph came back at eventide tired from his day's work. Joy filled his heart when the divine Child ran to meet him and his holy spouse stood at the door ready to welcome him. Had I a painter's skill, how much I should like to depict this charming scene in lifelike tints upon the canvas.

Only think what a sense of peace and happiness must steal over the heart of the husband when, after working hard all day, he comes home at night to be greeted with his wife's affectionate smile; when he finds his evening meal ready and everything as orderly as possible. Love of order is certainly an essential virtue in a wife.

But not only is it necessary for a wife, but for every woman—whether married or unmarried. See that you cultivate this virtue. Observation leads to the conclusion that love of order is an almost unfailing proof of the presence of other virtues, such as humility, obedience, and true charity toward one's neighbor. And at the same time, cleanliness, thrift, conscientiousness in the minutest details are inseparable from it. Love of order is generally characteristic of women, but it requires to be cultivated and brought into play in early youth if it is to stand her in good stead in after years. Therefore let me advise you to cultivate this virtue assiduously; and let your thoughts often travel to the holy house at Nazareth, that you may learn what family life ought to be.

Hymn to the Holy Family

Happy we, who thus united
  Join in cheerful melody;
Praising Jesus, Mary, Joseph,
  In the Holy Family.

> Jesus, Mary, Joseph, help us,
>   That we ever true may be
> To the promises that bind us
>   To the Holy Family.

Jesus, whose almighty bidding
  All created things fulfil,
Lives on earth in meek subjection
  To His earthly parents' will.

> Sweetest Infant, make us patient
>   And obedient for Thy sake;
> Teach us to be chaste and gentle,
>   All our stormy passions break.

Mary, thou alone wert chosen
  To be Mother of my Lord;
Thou didst guide the early footsteps
  Of the great Incarnate Word.

> Dearest Mother, make us humble,
>   For thy Son will take His rest
> In the poor and lowly dwelling
>   Of a humble sinner's breast.

Joseph, thou wert called the father
  Of thy Maker and thy Lord;
Thine it was to save thy Saviour
  From the cruel Herod's sword.

> Suffer us to call thee father,
>   Show to us a father's love;
> Lead us safe through every danger
>   Till we meet in heaven above.

Prayer to Saint Anne

Most august St. Anne! Heaven admires you, earth blesses you; God the Father loves you as the mother of His cherished daughter; the incarnate Word loves you as the parent of His well-beloved Mother; the Holy Spirit loves you as the mother of His perfect Spouse. The angels and the elect honor you as the tree producing a flower, the celestial perfume and beauty of which charms them, and whose divine fruit is their life and their joy. Repentant sinners look on you as their powerful advocate with God, the just through your intercession hope for an increase of grace, and penitents the expiation of their faults. Be propitious to us, O most merciful mother; unite with Mary, your dear and admirable Child, and by her intercession and yours, we shall confidently expect mercy from Jesus, to Whom you were so intimately allied; also the intentions of this devotion, every grace during life, and, above all, the grace of a happy death. Amen. —*A Gleaner's Sheaf.*

> Lead, kindly Light, amid the encircling gloom;
>   Lead Thou me on!
> The night is dark, and I am far from home.
>   Lead Thou me on!
> Keep Thou my feet; I do not ask to see
> The distant scene—one step enough for me.
>
> I was not ever thus, nor pray'd that Thou
>   Shouldst lead me on.
> I loved to choose and see my path, but now
>   Lead Thou me on!
> I loved the garish day, and, spite of fears,
> Pride ruled my will: remember not past years.
>
> So long Thy power hath blest me, sure it still
>   Will lead me on.
> O'er moor and fen, o'er crag and torrent, till
>   The night is gone;
> And with the morn those angel faces smile
> Which I have loved long since, and lost awhile.
>   —Cardinal Newman.

St. Aloysius, our model and patron, pray for us that we may lead a pure and holy life.

Part Fifth

A Few Concluding Words

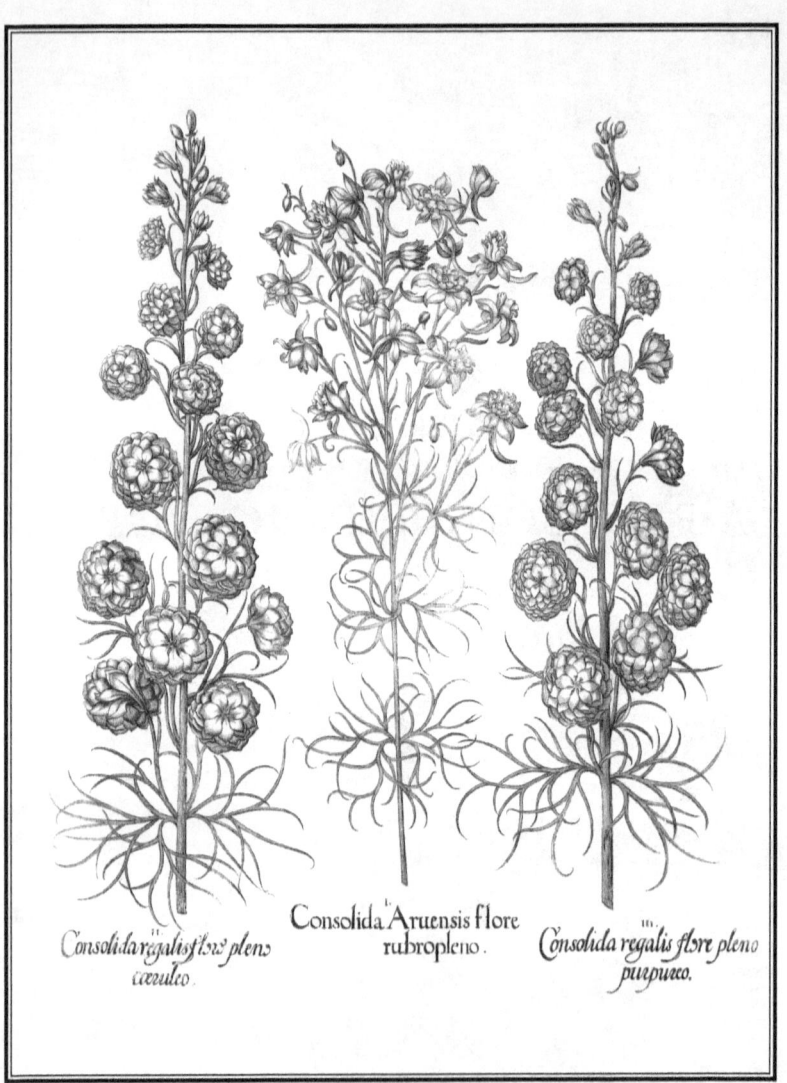

A Few Concluding Words

XCI. Farewell!

The fond father and mother have crossed the threshold of their house to accompany their daughter a few steps on her way, now that she is about to leave home and go out into the world. She is sixteen years old, and long beforehand her excellent parents have prepared her for this important and critical step; many useful instructions, good advice, and practical hints have they given her for the guidance of her daily life. Now the sorrowful moment of parting has come, they repeat with anxious hearts some of the most serious and weighty admonitions. And when the last farewell is spoken, and the hot tears can no longer be repressed, they say: "Dearest child, never forget our parting words. Remember them in the season of temptation and danger. May God bless you abundantly, and give His holy angels charge over you to keep you in all your ways."

Then the girl goes on her way. But for a long time her parents stand looking after her, their loving hearts wrung with inexpressible grief. Involuntarily they ask themselves the anxious question: Will our daughter come back to us as good and pious and innocent as she now is?

In this picture I have portrayed for you, Christian maiden, the thoughts and feelings of my own heart, now that I have come to the end of my instructions. You have followed me attentively and patiently on the long and toilsome way, over many a stone of "must" and "ought," through the regions of serious duty, so unattractive to the natural man. You have a good will, and would gladly profit by the salutary counsels and hints which I have given you in the preceding pages.

Well, then, I offer you this manual as a companion in your daily life. It rests with you to be reminded by it at any and every moment of what you ought to do and of what you ought to leave undone; you must simply turn to it for counsel by reading it carefully and repeatedly.

But in order to make it easier for you to remember what you have learned, I will now do as the parents of whom I have here spoken did on taking leave of their daughter. As my farewell word I will briefly sum up all that I have said, under eight heads. You must impress them indelibly on your memory as resolutions to be carried out and adhered to faithfully throughout your life.

Resolution the first: I will be careful to say my daily prayers regularly, and never to omit hearing Mass on Sundays and holidays without absolute necessity.

This resolution may be epitomized in one word: *Prayer*.

Prayer is the pivot on which the spiritual life of every Christian, and certainly of every Catholic girl, revolves; prayer is the very breath of the soul, its vital breath.

Resolution the second: I will make it my practice to go to the sacraments at least once every month.

Here you may impress on your mind the word: *Sacraments*.

Confession and communion constitute a never-failing source—a fount, whereby the life of the soul may be evermore renewed, maintained and strengthened. Must not every young person whose spiritual life is so often in danger feel herself impelled by a holy thirst to draw water out of the Saviour's fountains?

Resolution the third: I will scrupulously shun everything likely to prove dangerous to purity. I will be on my guard against curiosity, vanity, undue familiarity with young men, improper conversation and immoral books.

O pearl of virtues—Innocence! Purity! Let these sweet names remind you, my child, of the precious treasure you possess, and warn you to protect it, to keep it at any cost!

Resolution the fourth: In confession, I will always be conscientious and candid in regard to the sixth and ninth commandments. I will therefore tell my confessor when any suitor for my hand presents himself—as soon, in fact, as I begin "to keep company."

Yes, make it your principle to be candid and outspoken in confession, for this candor will be your safeguard.

Resolution the fifth: In regard to going to dances, or plays of a doubtful nature, I will always ask and follow the advice of my spiritual director.

This caution in the matter of dances and plays appertains to the extreme care and earnestness which is indispensable for preserving your purity.

Resolution the sixth: I will endeavor always to please my parents and superiors by prompt obedience, a cheerful demeanor, and industry at my work.

To keep the fourth commandment faithfully in regard to parents and superiors means for the Christian maiden that she is placing out at compound interest a large capital of temporal and eternal happiness, as one might say, making God Himself her debtor.

Resolution the seventh: I will be very cautious in reading novels and worldly periodicals, and content myself with a small number.

Reading anti-Christian or immoral books is as fatal to the soul as slow, deadly poison is to the body. And how widespread is this poison, how constantly we meet with it. Unfortunately the vessels that contain it have no label with a death's-head to serve as a warning—on the contrary, they bear the most attractive inscriptions. Therefore be cautious in your selection of light literature and of reading-matter in general.

Resolution the eighth: I will endeavor very earnestly to live at peace with all men, and for this end I will carefully avoid dissimulation and uncharitableness in word and action.

Charity toward our neighbor is the second great commandment, which Our Lord declares to be like unto the firsthand greatest: Thou shall love the Lord thy God. Every kind of deceit and unkindness is incompatible with true love of our neighbor.

In conclusion, let me once more impress these resolutions on your mind, with the words which Tobias the elder addressed to his son: "*All the days of thy life have God in thy mind; and take heed thou never consent to sin. Take heed to keep thyself, my son, from all fornication. Never suffer pride to reign in thy mind or in thy words; for from it all perdition took its beginning. Seek counsel always of a wise man.*" For you, this wise man will be your confessor. Finally, my last farewell shall he uttered in the words of Tobias, when his son was about to start on his journey: "*May you have a good journey and God be with you in your way, and his angel accompany you.*"

> May thy life flow, a sacred stream,
> In whose calm depths the beautiful and pure
> Alone are mirrored; which, though shapes of ill
> Should hover round its surface, glides in light,
> And takes no shadow from them.

"Our care should be not so much to live *long* as to live *well.*"
—Seneca.

"Time flies, death urges, knells call, heaven invites, hell threatens."
—Young.

"Then let us fill
This little interval, this pause of life
With all the virtues we can crowd into it."
—Addison.

"Live while you live, the epicure would say,
And seize the pleasures of the present day;
Live while you live, the sacred preacher cries,
And give to God each moment as it flies.
Lord, in my views let both united be;
I live in pleasure, when I live in Thee."
—Philip Doddridge.

A Rule of Life

"He that shall persevere to the end, he shall be saved."

1. **Daily Conduct.**—Have a fixed hour for rising in the morning; bless yourself with holy water, and as soon as possible after your toilet recite devoutly your morning prayers. During the day make at least a short meditation or a spiritual reading. It is commendable to read daily from the *Lives of the Saints*. Hear Mass; make a visit to the Most Blessed Sacrament and to Mary, the Mother of Jesus. If you cannot go to church, make your visit and adoration at home, turning toward the nearest tabernacle and receiving holy communion spiritually. Recite the *Angelus*; say the beads. In the evening, examine your conscience and recite your evening prayers.

2. **Confession and Communion.**—Receive the holy sacraments frequently—once a week or, certainly, once a month. Go as often as you can to holy communion, with the advice of your spiritual director. Choose a learned and pious confessor, and be directed always by him in all affairs of importance. When you commit any sin, make an act of contrition immediately and resolve to amend; if it is a mortal sin, confess it as soon as possible.

3. **Occasions of Sin.**—Avoid idleness, bad companions, low theatres and public balls, round dances, immoral books, sensational newspapers, salacious literature, foolish novels and romances, games of chance, and every occasion of sin. In temptations, bless yourself, invoke the most holy names of Jesus and Mary, and think of death. *"He that loveth danger shall perish in it."*

4. **Sundays.**—"Remember that thou keep holy the Sabbath-day." Be not satisfied with hearing a Low Mass on Sundays. Hear sermons as often as possible, and listen attentively to the word of God. No matter how poor an orator or preacher a priest may be, no matter how plain his language or how unattractive his delivery, remember that he is the representative of Christ, and that you can always find in every sermon sufficient matter for reflection and application to your own life and circumstances. Faithfully attend the meetings of the sodality, and never absent yourself unnecessarily from afternoon or evening services and benediction,

5. **Pious Practices.**—Keep yourself in the presence of God. Accustom yourself to saying short ejaculatory and indulgenced prayers. Keep a crucifix, holy pictures and holy water in your room. Carry your beads with you. Wear a scapular, and a medal of the Immaculate Conception. Support your parish priest and your parish church in all good works. Help the poor and the orphans according to your means. Frequently think of death and eternity.

6. **Blessed Virgin Mary.**—If you love Jesus, you will love and honor His blessed Mother. Be most devout to her and daily perform some acts of piety in her honor. A pious *Child of Mary* will erect a home-altar in honor of her heavenly Queen and Mother, before which she will recite her prayers. On Our Lady's feast-days she will place an offering of fresh flowers on this altar. Hear Mass and receive holy communion on the great feasts of the Blessed Virgin. Daily renew your act of consecration and say the *Memorare* for a happy death. Cultivate her virtues—especially purity, modesty, meekness, humility, obedience, charity, patience, resignation to the will of God and devotedness to duty.

7. **Retreat.**—Make a spiritual retreat once a year.

8. **Spiritual Communion.**—An act of spiritual communion like the following should be made frequently, and especially at Mass: "My Jesus, I believe that Thou art truly present in the Holy Sacrament of the Altar, I adore Thee. I praise Thee and thank Thee for all Thy blessings. I am sorry that I have offended Thee by my sins. By this act I wish to make reparation to Thee for all the insults and injuries committed against Thee in the Sacrament of Thy love. I love Thee with my whole heart. Come to my poor soul; unite Thyself to me...†... I thank Thee, my good Jesus. Oh! never, never leave me. Let me not be separated from thee by sin."

9. **In the Hour of Death.**—When you are dying, make acts of contrition and of love. Pronounce the sweet and holy name of "Jesus."

In life and in death, praise and be submissive to the holy will of God.

Strive to become a saint. For "*this is the will of God, your sanctification.*"

Ejaculatory prayers to obtain a good death

Jesus, Mary, and Joseph, I give you my heart and my soul.

Jesus, Mary, and Joseph, assist me in my last agony.

Jesus, Mary, and Joseph, may I breathe forth my soul in peace with you.

The Sovereign Pontiff, Pius VII, by a decree of the Sacred Congregation of Indulgences, April 28, 1807, granted to all the faithful, every time that, with at least contrite heart and devotion, they shall say these three ejaculations: an *indulgence of three hundred days;* and an *indulgence of one hundred days,* every time that, with the same dispositions, they shall say one of these ejaculations.

The Art of Being Happy[1]

I.

What must we do to be happy? The thing is not hard. Much knowledge is not necessary for this, nor much talent, but only a real good will to do one's duty. Happiness—as far as it can exist here below—consists in peace, in the joy of a good conscience. Our conscience will be joyous and peaceful if it know not remorse; it will not know remorse if we are careful not to offend God. To fly from sin is, therefore, the chief source of happiness on earth. If our conscience is pure, our life will be happy. There are none happier than saints, for there are none more innocent.

II.

What is it that secures happiness in a home? Before everything, religion: let all love well our good God, let all say their prayers morning and night, let all put their trust in divine providence. In the next place, union: let the members of the household be affectionate toward one another, having only one heart and one soul, not saying or doing anything that may pain any one of them. Then again, the spirit of sacrifice: we must be ready to do without something in order to make another member of the family enjoy it, we must give up our own personal tastes to conform to the tastes of others. Finally, pliancy of character, not to be hard to deal with, touchy, sour, proud, not to be obstinately rooted in one's ideas, not to grow impatient about mere nothings, but to have a large mind and a generous heart. A family whose members possess these qualities is a paradise on earth.

---
1 From the French by the Rev. Matthew Russell, S.J.

III.

There is a word which cannot be said too often to every Christian whom God has destined to live, converse and labor in the society of his fellow creatures: Be indulgent. Yes, be *indulgent*; it is necessary for others, and it is necessary for your own sake. Forget the little troubles that others may cause you; keep up no resentment for the inconsiderate or unfavorable words that may have been said about you; excuse the mistakes and awkward blunders of which you are the victim; always make out good intentions for those who have done you any wrong by imprudent acts or speeches; in a word, smile at everything, show a pleasant face on all occasions; maintain an inexhaustible fund of goodness, patience, and gentleness. Thus you will be at peace with all your brethren; your love for them will suffer no alteration, and their love for you will increase day by day. But above all, you will practise in an excellent manner, Christian charity, which is impossible without this toleration and indulgence at every instant.

> "I have sought for happiness in the brilliant haunts of society, in sumptuous banquets, in the glare of theatres. I have sought it again in the possession of gold, in the excitement of the gaming-table, in the illusions of romance; but all in vain—whilst an hour passed in visiting a sick person, or in consoling some afflicted one, has been enough to give me enjoyment more delightful than all delights." —*Anon.*

IV.

Flattery is never worth anything; but to give a little praise at the right moment to some one under us is an excellent way of encouraging him and giving him a pleasure as sweet as it is salutary. For this a mere "thank you" is enough, an approving smile, a kind look, or even a simple word, such as these: "I am greatly pleased"—"that has succeeded very well"—"this is precisely what I wanted," etc. Why should we always keep up an air of indifference and coldness toward workmen, servants, children, opening our mouths only when we have some rebuke to give them? Is this charitable? Is this Christian? Let us put ourselves in the place of these inferiors, and let us be happy in making them happy. Let us show ourselves satisfied with their good will and make them understand that we love them. Not only will they serve us much better and attach themselves to us with true devotedness, but we shall thus gain their hearts, and it will then be easy for us to secure their fidelity to the duties of religion and the fulfilment of the practices of Christian piety.

V.

Economy is praiseworthy; stinginess is not: it contracts the heart of a man and makes him miserable. Pious persons must be on their guard against this snare of the devil, for many are caught in it without knowing. Some persons will give several dollars to a beggar, and an hour after they will haggle about three pennies with an honest workman, or go on bargaining about some worthless object. Pious Catholics ought not to let it be said that they are harder and fonder of money than other people! They ought not to be afflicted by or bewail any little losses that they may suffer. Let us be economical when there is question of our pleasures, of our table, or of our dress; but let us be large-hearted and generous in all our relations with others.

VI.

A poet was gazing one day at a beautiful rose-tree. "What a pity," said he, "that these roses have thorns!" A man who was passing by said to him: "Let us rather thank our good God for having allowed these thorns to have roses." Ah! how ought we also to thank Him for so many joys that He grants to us in spite of our sins, instead of complaining about the slight troubles that He sends us!

VII.

Let us do good, let us avoid evil, and we shall be happy. "There is but one way," said a man of genius, "of being happy, and it is to do well all one's duties."

VIII.

How sweet and agreeable an occupation it is to give pleasure to those around us! It is quite natural amongst Christians, but it becomes almost a duty amongst the members of a family or a community, especially toward persons whom age or rank places above us. And, to give pleasure, what is necessary? Things the most insignificant, provided they be accompanied by amiable manners; what is necessary above all is to have habitually a smile on our lips. Oh! who can tell the power of a smile? For ourselves, it is the guardian of kindness, patience, tolerance—all the virtues that we have occasion to exercise in our relations with our neighbor. There is, in fact, no danger of our being rude or severe so long as a smile rests on our lips. For others, it is a source of contentment, joy, satisfaction and encouragement. Without even uttering a single word we put those around us at their ease; we inspire them with a sweet confidence, if we approach them with a smile. Perhaps you will object that you cannot smile, that you are naturally serious or even severe. Undeceive yourself: with real good will you will acquire this empire over yourself, you will soon do by custom what you at first did by constraint; and the interior joy that you taste will recompense you superabundantly for your trouble and your efforts.

IX.

A great secret for preserving peace of heart is to do nothing with overeagerness, but to act always calmly, without trouble or disquiet. We are not asked to do much, but to do well. At the Last Day God will not examine whether we have performed a multitude of works, but whether we have sanctified our souls in doing them. Now the means of sanctifying ourselves is to do everything for God and to do perfectly whatever we have to do. The works that have as their motive vanity or selfishness make us neither better nor happier, and we shall receive no reward for them.

X.

"I feel happy," said a holy person, "in proportion as I do my actions well." Let us meditate an instant on this luminous saying. To do well what one has to do—here again is the secret of being happy. Every man, then, can be happy; and, if we have not been happy hitherto, it is because we have not put this lesson into practice. But what is necessary for this? Oh, very little. To do every action with a view of pleasing God; to do every action in the manner that God commands, either through Himself or through those who hold His place in our regard; to do every action as if we had nothing else to do but this, and as if we were to die after having done it.

XI.

There are some who are affable and gracious to every one as long as things go according to their wishes; but if they meet with a contradiction—if an accident, a reproach or even less should trouble the serenity of their soul, all around them must suffer the consequences. They grow dark and cross; very far from keeping up the conversation by their good humor, they answer only in monosyllables to those who speak to them. Is this conduct reasonable? Is it Christian? Let us always be kind and good-humored so as always to make our brethren happy, and we shall merit to be always made happy by God.

XII.

Blessed are the poor in spirit, blessed are the meek, blessed are they that mourn, blessed are they that hunger and thirst after justice, blessed are the merciful, blessed are the clean of heart, blessed are the peacemakers, blessed are they that suffer persecution for justice' sake. Blessed are ye when they shall revile you and persecute you for My sake.
—St. Matthew v, 3-11.

Blessed are they that hear the word of God and keep it.
—St. Luke xi, 28.

Blessed is the man that endureth temptation.
—St. James i, 12.

Blessed are the dead who die in the Lord.
—Apocalypse xiv, 13.

Appendix

Devotions for The Month of May

THE return of May—when nature, awakened from her winter sleep, is clad in all her vernal beauty—reminds us that all should be fair and bright within us also, that our hearts ought to be adorned with fair virtues, so as to be pleasing to Jesus and Mary. Devotion to the Blessed Virgin, frequent meditation on her life and contemplation of her example, earnest endeavor to imitate her virtues—these are all excellent means of sanctifying the soul and of advancing in the love of God. And since the May devotions are intended to attain this laudable end, since they are commended to us by holy Church and enriched with indulgences, it especially behooves us, who are the adopted children of Mary and her devoted clients, to perform these exercises with a willing heart and in the spirit of piety. The following suggestions will serve as your guide.

1. If possible, receive the sacraments at the beginning of the month of May, in order that the meditations and devotions may bear more abundant fruit in your soul.

2. The chapters in the fore part and at the end of this book will furnish you with suitable matter for meditation and spiritual reading; to this you may add the Litany of Loretto and other prayers to the Blessed Virgin.

3. As your principal object propose to yourself to combat and thoroughly master some fault or bad habit, and to acquire the opposite virtue.

4. Every morning offer up your actions to Jesus and Mary, and endeavor earnestly to model your *whole conduct*

by the example of the Blessed Virgin.

5. If you can manage to hear Mass daily, see that you do so; and if the May devotions are not held in public, perform them by yourself, either in church before the shrine of Our Lady, or at home before your own little altar of the Blessed Virgin.

6. Recite the Rosary frequently.

7. Finally, do your utmost to promote devotion to our blessed Lady amongst those with whom you come into contact.

INDULGENCES FOR THE MONTH OF MAY

The Sovereign Pontiff Pius VII, by a rescript from the Office of the Secretary of Memorials, March 21, 1815, granted to all the faithful who, either in public or in private, shall honor the Blessed Virgin with some special homage and devout prayers, or the practice of other virtuous acts, an indulgence of three hundred days, every day; a plenary indulgence, once in this month, or according to the rule already established on one of the first eight days of June, on the day when, being truly penitent, after confession and communion, they shall pray for the intention of his Holiness.

By a rescript of the S. Congr. of Indulgences, June 18, 1822, the same Sovereign Pontiff confirmed forever these indulgences. —*The New Raccolta.*

PRAYER OF ST. ALPHONSUS DE LIGUORI TO THE BLESSED VIRGIN MARY

Most holy and immaculate Virgin! O my Mother! thou who art the Mother of my Lord, the Queen of the world, the advocate, hope, and refuge of sinners! I, the most wretched among them, now come to thee. I worship thee, great Queen, and give thee thanks for the many favors thou hast bestowed on me in the past; most of all do I thank thee for having saved me from hell, which I had so often deserved. I love thee, Lady most worthy of all love, and, by the love which I bear thee, I promise ever in the future to serve thee, and to do what in me lies to win others to thy love. In thee I put all my trust, all my hope of salvation. Receive me as thy servant, and cover me with the mantle of thy protection, thou who art the Mother of mercy! And since thou hast so much power with God, deliver me from all temptations, or at least obtain for me the grace ever to overcome them. From thee I ask a true love of Jesus Christ, and the grace of a happy death. O my Mother! by thy love for God I beseech thee to be at all times my helper, but above all at the last moment of my life. Leave me not until thou seest me safe in heaven, there for endless ages to bless thee and sing thy praises. Amen.

Indulgence of 300 days, each time; plenary indulgence once a month, on the usual conditions.—Pius IX., Sept. 7, 1854.

THREE OFFERINGS IN HONOR OF THE BLESSED VIRGIN MARY

I.

HOLIEST Virgin, with all my heart I worship thee above all the angels and saints in paradise as the daughter of the eternal Father, and to thee I consecrate my soul and all its powers. *Hail Mary, etc.*

II.

HOLIEST Virgin, with all my heart I worship thee above all the angels and saints in paradise as the Mother of the only-begotten Son, and to thee I consecrate my body with all its senses. *Hail Mary, etc.*

III.

HOLIEST Virgin, with all my heart I worship thee above all the angels and saints in paradise as the spouse of the Holy Ghost, and to thee I consecrate my heart and all its affections, praying thee to obtain for me from the ever-blessed Trinity all the graces which I need for my salvation. *Hail Mary, etc.*

Indulgence of 300 days, each time.—Leo XII., Oct. 21, 1823.

ST. ALOYSIUS' ACT OF CONSECRATION

Most holy Mary, my Lady, to thy faithful care and particular protection and to the bosom of thy mercy, to-day and every day, and particularly at the hour of my death, I commend my soul and my body; all my hope and consolation, all my trials and miseries, my life and the end of my life, I commit to thee, that through thy most holy intercession and by thy merits all my actions may be directed and ordered according to thy will and that of thy divine Son-Amen.

Indulgence of 200 days, once a day.—Leo XIII., March 15, 1890.

PRAYER TO OUR QUEEN
OF THE MOST HOLY ROSARY

Queen of the most holy Rosary, in these days of bold impiety show forth thy power by the tokens of thy former victories, and from die throne on which thou sittest as dispenser of pardon and of graces look down upon the Church of thy Son, upon his vicar and upon all Orders of ecclesiastics and laymen who are struggling against the fierce assaults of the enemy; hasten, powerful conqueror of heresies, hasten the hour of mercy, though the hour of justice is hurried on every day by innumerable sins. Obtain for me, the least of men, as I kneel in humble supplication before thee, the grace I need most to live among the just on earth, to reign among the just in heaven, whilst, in the meantime, together with all the faithful in the world, O Queen of the most holy Rosaiy, I salute and hail thee.

Queen of the most holy Rosary, pray for us.

His Holiness Leo XIII., by a rescript of his Eminence the Cardinal Vicar, July 3, 1886, granted to the faithful who shall recite the said prayer, an indulgence of one hundred days, once a day.

Meditations on the Life of Mary[1]

INTRODUCTION

Mary's Vocation

I.

Let your prayer at the beginning of the month of May be for a true devotion to our blessed Lady.

To speed your prayer on its way make little acts of mortification, such as denying yourself some delicacy at table, keeping silence when your feelings are hurt, checking curiosity, preserving a cheerful countenance under all circumstances, being patient when your plans are thwarted, visiting the Blessed Sacrament when doing so means sacrificing a little pleasure, striving to perform the daily little duties well and carefully in imitation of Mary. By these and similar practices we honor Mary and advance our prayer by making it more pleasing to God.

Why should we observe the month of May? For the love of Jesus, for the love of Mary, and for the good of our own souls.

True devotion comes from God and leads to God. The fundamental rule in regard to the homage which we offer to the

---

1 These short meditations are intended especially for the *Month of May* or *October*, though they may be used at any time with profit, particularly in connection with novenas and the celebration of the feasts of Our Lady. They are founded on the chief incidents in the life of the Blessed Virgin Mary as recorded in Holy Scripture, or handed down by tradition. Each of them is broken up into three heads or points, intended to furnish, directly or indirectly, some practical suggestion to the devout servant of Mary. They are taken (with the exception of the *introduction* and a few minor additions) from "The Devout Year" (*Maria Magnificata*), by Rev. R.F. Clarke, S.J.

Blessed Virgin Mary and the saints is, that it must ultimately be referred to God and our eternal salvation. Our devotion to the Blessed Virgin would be of no avail if it did not tend toward our union with God—toward possessing Him eternally.

True devotion extends itself to the saints without being separated from the eternal *Source* of all sanctity.

"*For other foundation no man can lay, but that which is laid; which is Christ Jesus*" (i Cor. iii.). Let Him be the foundation of our devotion to His holy Mother.

We are not able to honor our blessed Lady adequately, since, through her, Jesus has come to us. Oh, how great, how sublime was Mary's vocation! God predestined her before all ages to be the Mother of the Saviour of the world. And having called her to fill this most glorious office, He would not have her be a mere channel of grace, but an instrument cooperating, both by her excellent qualities and by her own free will, in the great work of our Redemption.

For thousands of years the world had been expecting the promised *Messias*. The fulness of time has now come. The eternal Father sends a heavenly messenger to Mary, to treat with her of the mystery of the Incarnation. She pronounces the word "*Fiat!*" "Be it done!" And the heavens open; the earth possesses a Saviour; *Mary has become the Mother of God.*

Years pass by. The time has arrived when the great sacrifice is to be consummated. We find Mary at the foot of the cross. With the dying breath of Jesus she receives the Church as an inheritance. *Mary becomes our Mother*.

These are the two great titles which give Mary a claim on our veneration and affection. She is like a fountain from which the waters of grace have spread themselves abundantly over the whole human race. As we have once received through her Jesus, the Source of all blessing and grace, so we also obtain through her powerful intercession the various effects and applications of this grace in all the circumstances of life. Her maternal charity, which shines forth in the mystery of the Incarnation, also causes her to take a share in the consequences of this universal principle of benediction. Thus Mary is, by her intercession, the Mother of all Christians, the Mother of all men. Her overflowing charity is an appropriate instrument for the operations of grace.

Who is better able than Mary to plead in our behalf? She can confidently speak to the Heart of her divine Son, where her wishes, her sentiments, find an echo. She fears no refusal. The love of the Son makes Him lend a favorable ear to the request of His Mother.

II.

Our blessed Lady is able and willing to help us. But in order to secure her powerful and generous assistance we must have a sincere devotion to her.

This devotion must be practical. It ought to consist not only in *words*, but also in *action*.

A person truly devout to Mary will be enrolled in her Sodality; will celebrate her feasts very piously; will wear her scapular and medal; will venerate her images and visit her shrines; will love to read books on her life and virtues, and will endeavor throughout the year—but especially in May—to imitate her example. Certainly, a girl, a woman, cannot be said to have a true devotion to the Mother of God unless she honors and invokes her by frequent and fervent prayers.

Of the various exercises in her honor, comes in the first place the *Mass of our blessed Lady*. Let us hear Mass in her honor on her feast-days, and on Saturdays. The Office of the Blessed Virgin, the Litany of Loretto, and the holy Rosary are singularly pleasing to her and enriched with indulgences.

Other indulgenced prayers, acts of consecration, one of which might easily be said every day, the *Salve Regina* and other anthems, the *Memorare* and many short invocations, are to be found in this book.

Let us not imagine, however, that, to secure the special protection of the Mother of God, our prayers must needs be very long. Much will depend upon our circumstances of life. But let us not forget the advice which Blessed John Berchmans gave to his companions at his death: "The least homage is sufficient, *provided it be constant.*" Hence, what we have once resolved to do in honor of our blessed Lady must never be put aside or neglected, but must be faithfully persevered in, *daily*, until death.

Father Bowden, of the Oratory, in his *Miniature Life of Mary*, suggests the following practices in honor of Mary. They may be drawn by lot, or otherwise chosen, at the beginning of a month.

1. Take a short time from your recreation to spend in solitude conversing with Mary, or in meditation on the mysteries of her life.
2. Rise punctually in the morning, invoking her as "the morning star."
3. Invoke her sixty-three times as "Virgin Mother" in honor of her sixty-three years.
4. Visit in spirit one of her great sanctuaries.
5. Mortify your will three times as an offering to Mary.
6. Say three *Glorias* in honor of the saints and Doctors who have explained and defended her prerogatives.
7. Gain indulgences for the soul in purgatory most devoted to the Blessed Virgin in life; offer Mass and communion for this purpose.
8. Ask Mary to be present with you during the day to drive away evil spirits.
9. Perform some act of kindness with inconvenience to yourself.

10. Say three Hail Marys in reparation for the blasphemies uttered against her.
11. Give an alms in honor of her poverty.
12. Invoke the saints who were related to her—Saints Joseph, Joachim, Anne, etc.
13. Mortify your sight, once or more, in honor of Mary's modesty.
14. Burn a candle before her image or picture.
15. Recall with devotion her words recorded in the Gospel, remembering how many of your sins are committed in speech. Bear your sufferings and sorrows silently and patiently.
16. Say the litany for the conversion of a soul for Mary to offer to God.
17. Shun idleness during the day in imitation of Mary at Nazareth.
18. Say a Hail Mary in honor of St. Gabriel, who brought it to earth.
19. Practise some little mortification at meals.
20. Before going to sleep, place yourself with the infant Jesus in Mary's arms.
21. Say seven *Glorias* with extended arms, in honor of her seven dolors.
22. Make a spiritual communion in union with her dispositions at the Annunciation.
23. Say a *Memorare* to obtain Mary's help at the hour of death.
24. Keep silence for a short time, and with Mary ponder on God's words in your heart.
25. Say a Hail Mary before going to bed, to prevent one mortal sin during the night.
26. Visit her altar or image in atonement for the desecration of her sanctuaries.
27. Say nine Hail Marys in union with the nine choirs of angels who are ever praising her.

28. Say a *Salve* for the spread of devotion to her.
29. Say fifteen *Glorias*, in honor of the last fifteen years of Mary's life, for the grace of perseverance.
30. Kiss the ground, and say three Hail Marys for the virtue of holy purity.
31. Say a Hail Mary in reparation for your neglect of Mary's service during this month.
32. Distribute leaflets in praise of Mary, scapulars, medals, pictures, and beads, to promote devotion to the blessed Mother of God.

III.

Oh, how powerful are the motives of this devotion, and how wonderful are its effects! If, therefore, you are tossed to and fro on the stormy ocean of this world, do not turn away your eyes from this resplendent star, lest you perish in the tempest. If the winds of temptation blow, if you are in danger of being dashed against the rocks of adversity, look at the star, call upon Mary. If the waves of pride, of ambition, of detraction, of anger, of avarice, or lust, threaten your soul, call upon Mary. If, troubled at the sight of your manifold sins, frightened at the thought of the just Judge, you begin to sink into the abyss of sorrow and despair, think of Mary. In all dangers, in all your trials, invoke Mary. Let her name be on your lips, let her memory be in your heart. If you follow her, you will not go astray; if you trust in her, you will not be disappointed; if she takes care of you, you need not fear; if she protects you, and intercedes for you, you will safely arrive at the haven of eternal felicity.

Hymn to the Blessed Virgin
Ave Maris Stella

Ave, maris stella,
Dei Mater alma,
Atque semper Virgo,
Felix coeli porta.

Sumens illud ave
Gabrielis ore,
Funda nos in pace,
Mutans Hevæ nomen.

Solve vincla reis,
Profer lumen caecis,
Mala nostra pelle,
Bona cuncta posce.

Monstra te esse Matrem,
Sumat per te preces,
Qui pro nobis natus,
Tulit esse tuus.

Virgo singularis,
Inter omnes mitis,
Nos culpis solutos,
Mites fac et castos.

Vitam praesta puram,
Iter para tutum,
Ut videntes Jesum
Semper collætemur.

Sit laus Deo Patri,
Summo Christo decus,
Spiritui sancto,
Tribus honor unus. Amen.

Hail, thou star of ocean!
Portal of the sky!
Ever Virgin Mother
Of the Lord most high!

Oh! by Gabriel's Ave,
Uttered long ago,
Eva's name reversing,
Grant us peace below.

Break the captives' fetters,
Light on blindness pour;
All our ills expelling,
Every bliss implore.

Show thyself a Mother;
Offer Him our sighs,
Who for us Incarnate
Did not thee despise.

Virgin of all virgins!
To thy shelter take us:
Gentlest of the gentle!
Chaste and gentle make us.

Still, as on we journey,
Help our weak endeavor,
Till with thee and Jesus
We rejoice forever.

Through the highest heaven,
To the almighty Three,
Father, Son, and Spirit,
One same glory be. Amen.

1st Day:
Mary's Immaculate Conception

The Lord God said to the serpent: I will put enmities between thee and the woman. (Gen. iii. 14, 15.)

1. In these words the Immaculate Conception of the Blessed Virgin Mary was announced to our first parents. It was to be the reversal of the friendship with the serpent contracted by Eve, when she listened to his voice and fell under his power.

The second Eve was never to be under the power of the devil; the enmity between them was to admit of no possible exception. This involved the grace of being conceived *immaculate.*

2. Mary's Immaculate Conception was the foundation of all her graces. The absence of any stain or spot of sin distinguished her from all the rest of mankind. It distinguished her from the holiest of the saints, since they, one and all, were sinners. Her perfect sinlessness was the source of all her glory and all her majesty; it was this which opened the door to the unlimited graces that she received from God; it was this that qualified her for her divine maternity, and raised her to her throne as Queen of heaven.

3. If sinlessness is so priceless a treasure, how I ought to value it! And how I ought to hate sin with a deadly hatred, and to detest and avoid even what are called little sins!

Learn from Mary immaculate the holiness which God requires in those whom He chooses as His own. Pray Him to cleanse you more and more from the least stain of sin, and add your own endeavor.

> "Simple and chaste should be those eyes which are accustomed to behold the body of Christ. —*Imitation.*

The purity of Blessed John Berchmans' soul beamed so brightly from his face that persons passing him in the streets would stop to ask his prayers. As a child he had vowed to live a virgin for Mary's sake, and thenceforth he kept his senses sealed to things of earth. During his three years in Rome he never raised his eyes to witness any spectacle, save that of Corpus Christi. He never passed Our Lady's statue without saluting it, nor left a church without visiting her altar. At every meal before tasting food, and at night before composing himself to sleep, he said a Hail Mary in honor of the Immaculate Conception; and to this practice he ascribed his exemption from all temptations of the flesh. He invented a Rosary in honor of that mystery, and made a vow, signed with his blood, ever to defend its truth. At the age of twenty-two he was already ripe for heaven, and went to his reward.

How eagerly should I cry out to the immaculate Mother of God, this day and every day, in words that she herself suggested to one of her servants:

> O Mary, conceived without sin,
> Pray for us who have recourse to thee!

2ND DAY:
MARY'S FIRST GRACES

Her foundations are in the holy mountains. (Psalm lxxxvi. 1.)

1. Mary began her journey along the road to perfection at a height to which other saints arrived only at the end of a long life of saintliness. God loved her more at the first moment of her existence than He loved the holiest among the rest of men at the time that their earthly pilgrimage was over and they were ripe for their heavenly reward. What glory must have been hers even from the beginning!

2. What was the cause of this special predilection that God had for this newly created soul? In all other children of Adam original sin prevented the divine generosity from having a free course. But Mary was created immaculate, and therefore

the grace of God streamed into her soul without check or hindrance. Oh, happy child whose sinlessness received so glorious a recompense! Like Mary, we also have been present to God from all eternity; we too have had our special place appointed for us. Are we faithful to our high calling? Are we accomplishing our life's work day by day?

3. What is it that checks in us the inflow of God's supernatural gifts? It is always sin; not so much sins in the past as sins and imperfections wilfully admitted in the present. These must be relinquished if we desire God to give us good measure of His grace. We must try to hate sin as Mary hated it, and we must cry to her:

> Hail, Mary, ever undefiled!
> Hail, Queen of purity!
> O make thy children chaste and mild,
> And turn their hearts to thee.

3RD DAY:
MARY'S EARLIEST GIFT

God said to Abraham: walk before me and be perfect. (Gen. xvii. 1.)

1. The highest praise that can be bestowed upon the saints of God during their earthly pilgrimage is that they *"walked with God."* In this consists all perfection, as we see from God's words to faithful Abraham. This was the privilege of our first parents before they sinned. This was the praise of Henoch and of Noe. It is an anticipation of the eternal happiness of heaven, where the just will walk with God forever in the glory of the beatific vision.

2. What is meant by walking with God? It means an intimate union with Him, a continual and joyful remembrance of His presence, a perfect agreement of will with God. This was the beginning of God's gifts to Mary; it was the result of her sinlessness. It rendered her life a sort of heaven on earth.

From the first moment of her existence she could cry out: "*My Beloved to me, and I to Him*" and He could answer: "*Thou art all fair, O My love, and there is not a spot in thee*" (Cant. iv. 7.)

3. God was thus always present to Mary's thoughts. Every action, every movement, was directed to His glory. This was the secret of her unapproachable holiness. How different am I from Mary! I think so little of God, and do so little for Him! I will try to do more, that I too may become more pleasing to God, more full of His graces and gifts.

Holy Mother of God, pray for me!

4TH DAY:
GOD'S DESIGN IN BEAUTIFYING MARY

Wisdom hath built herself a house. (Prov. ix. 1.)

1. God did not bestow all her gifts and graces on Mary for her own sake. She had done nothing to earn that first grace that was the foundation of all the rest. It was the free gift of God. He chose her of His own good pleasure. He fixed His love upon her simply because He willed to do so, "*that He might show the riches of His glory on the vessel of mercy, which He hath prepared to glory*" (Rom. ix. 23), and to a glory more resplendent than the combined glory of all the other saints.

2. But He had a special object in the exceeding glory conferred on His chosen daughter. It was because she was to entertain her Creator, because she was to carry in her womb the co-equal and co-eternal Son of God. It would have been unworthy of the divinity that God should take to Himself flesh from one whose flesh had ever been tainted with sin. It was to adorn a house for Himself, when He came to dwell amongst men, that Mary was adorned with such surpassing beauty.

3. Mary was also decked with these wondrous graces to prepare her for her work of intercession. If she was to be the Mother of all men, to take them all under her sacred

protection, it was right that she should be from the first far exalted above them all, their model as well as their Queen and their Mother. Oh, happy we, to have such a Mother and such a model!

> Him who gave us such a Mother,
> Let our grateful songs proclaim;
> Loving hearts and joyful voices
> Praise her great Creator's name.

5TH DAY:
THE BIRTH OF MARY

The light shineth in darkness, and the darkness did not comprehend it. (St. John i. 5.)

1. At the time of Mary's birth the whole world was plunged in darkness. The heathen nations were steeped in vice and pride. The Jews, too, had corrupted their ways and departed from God. Everywhere there was sin and gloom, scarce a bright spot on the face of the earth. But when Mary was born a light arose amid the darkness: the dawn of the glorious day that was to usher in the Redeemer. So, too, the darkness of the sinner's soul is dispersed by Mary's holy influence. Where the love of her is born in the soul, all becomes full of light, and Jesus comes to make His habitation there.

2. Before Mary's birth God sought in vain for one who would always be faithful to Him, for one soul that would always love Him as it ought. For four thousand years He had invariably been disappointed, but now at length He had found one who fulfilled all His desires, who satisfied the yearnings of His divine Heart. A worthy daughter of His omnipotent love!

3. Mary, in the first hour of her life, brought more glory to God than all the saints of the Old Testament. In her were made perfect the obedience of Abraham, the chastity of Joseph, the patience of Job, the meekness of Moses, the prudence of Josue. It is because she is the model and pattern of these and all other

virtues that she can communicate them to us. I must beg of Mary to obtain for me obedience, chastity, patience, prudence, and all else I need.

> Virgin most pure, star of the sea,
> Pray for the sinner, pray for me!

6th Day:
The Presentation of Mary in the Temple

The king shall greatly desire thy beauty: for He is the Lord thy God, and Him they shall adore. (Psalm xliv. 12.)

1. Mary from the first moment of her existence offered herself to God as an entire and an unblemished holocaust. From the instant when she was conceived immaculate the burden of her continual song was this: : "*I live; not I, but God Who lives in me.*" Oh, glorious child, who was thus from the first a participator of the divine nature!

2. But she was not content with this mere offering of her heart. She must in outward act consecrate herself to God. As soon as her tiny feet could walk she was brought to the Temple by her holy parents, Joachim and Anne. With what an ecstasy of delight she must have entered into the Temple, crying out: "*How lovely are Thy tabernacles, O Lord of hosts: my soul longeth and fainteth for the courts of the Lord*" (Psalm lxxxiii. 1, 2.) Have I any of the same desire to consecrate my life to God?

3. Mary knew that God is not to be found in the midst of the tumult and confusion of distracting cares, but that it is in silence and in solitude that He speaks to the heart (Osee ii. 14). She was teaching us to give, in some quiet retreat, now and again, our thoughts and our heart to God and God alone.

> Mary, it was thy lowliness,
>   Well pleasing to the Lord,
> That made thee worthy to become
>   The Mother of the Word.

7TH DAY:
MARY'S LIFE IN THE TEMPLE

Here will I dwell, for I have chosen it. (Psalm cxxxi. 14.)

1. Let us watch this tender little maiden in her daily life in the Temple. How exact in her obedience to all her superiors! How punctual in the performance of every duty! How full of charity for her little companions! How she delights to anticipate the wishes of those who represented almighty God to her! How she rejoices in the most menial offices! How she retires during her leisure to pray in secret! When I examine my daily life, does it at all correspond to hers?

2. What is it Mary is continually praying for? That God would hasten the coming of the *Messias*, and that, if it were God's will, she might be thought worthy to be the handmaid of His Mother. It never entered into her wildest dreams that she was the chosen one, who was to usher into the world the Saviour of the world. Thus it is that the holiest always esteem themselves as worth nothing. If I were more holy, I should be more humble.

3. What a joy it is to Mary to take part in the sacred psalmody of the Temple! As she sings the praises of God it seems to her that she is in heaven, singing with the angels. How sweet her voice sounds in the ears of God, sweeter than all the music of the heavenly choirs! What is it gives such surpassing beauty to her song? It is her heavenly purity. Blessed are the pure in heart. Their voice always sounds sweet as it rises in prayer or praise to God.

> Virgin of all virgins,
>   To thy shelter take us.
> Gentlest of the gentle,
>   Chaste and gentle make us.

8TH DAY:
MARY'S ESPOUSALS

I have put my trust in Thee, O Lord:
I said: My lots are in Thy hands. (Psalm xxx. 15.)

1. When Mary arrived at the age when it was the custom for Jewish maidens to leave the service of the Temple, the high priest told her that a husband would be chosen for her. But Mary had already made a vow of virginity to God, under the inspiration of the Holy Spirit; and now she received the command to join herself in wedlock, and God inspired her to obey. What a trial for her faith and confidence in God!

2. What a trial, too, for her humility, that she who had consecrated her virginity to the Most High should appear before the world in the ordinary state of wedlock, that she who was the Bride of the Most High should be counted as the bride of mortal man! Yet Mary rejoiced in this humiliation. She knew well that those whom God humbles He will in due time exalt.

3. Mary's confidence in God was not disappointed. He did not fail to fulfil the desires of His handmaid. She found, on being espoused, that Joseph her spouse had, like her, made a vow of chastity, and that she could therefore dwell with him in perfect security. Oh, how good God is to those who hope in Him!

> Hail, holy Joseph, hail!
> Sweet spouse of Mary, hail!
> Chaste as the lily flower
> In Eden's peaceful vale.

9TH DAY:
THE MARRIAGE OF MARY

The young man shall dwell with the virgin,
and the bridegroom shall rejoice over the bride. (Isaias lxii. 5.)

1. Mary, the unspotted spouse of Joseph, learned by degrees how her marriage was a part of God's wonderful designs

regarding her. If she had become a mother in an unmarried state, the world would naturally have regarded her as guilty of sin. The Jews, unable to understand so wonderful a mystery, would have pointed the finger of scorn at her. Thus God always guards the good name of those who are true to Him.

2. Mary, too, needed a protector. She was very young; she was to be exposed to many a hardship, to journey afar, to dwell in a strange land. How could the tender, youthful Mother have passed through all these vicissitudes without the guardianship of Joseph's love? How thoughtfully God provides for the welfare of those who commit themselves to Him!

3. Mary, moreover, needed one who would provide for her maintenance. Her wants were few, she loved poverty, but how could she have provided food and clothing for herself and her divine Son? To Joseph she was entrusted that he might by his labor earn what was necessary for their support. How generously God supplies all the wants of those who trust in Him!

Dear St. Joseph, be near us when we die!

> When the treasures of God were unsheltered on earth,
> Safe-keeping was found for them both in thy worth;
> O father of Jesus, be father to me,
> Sweet spouse of Our Lady, and I will love thee.

10th Day:
The Annunciation

Fear not, Mary, for thou hast found grace with God. (St. Luke i. 30.)

1. Mary's life as Joseph's spouse was no less one of devotion and recollection and prayer than her life in the Temple. In their little cottage her time was spent, when her household duties were done, in fervent prayer to God. Thus she is said to have been occupied when the archangel Gabriel appeared to her. Mary's prayers and Mary's longing desires had moved the Heart of God to send a Redeemer for mankind! Oh,

omnipotent efficacy of earnest desire and persevering prayer!

2. The message the angel brought bewildered the chaste and humble maiden. Her first thought was one of fear—fear lest the privilege announced to her should be purchased at the cost of her immaculate virginity: she would not sacrifice this even to be Mother of the *Messias:* anything rather than forfeit that priceless jewel!

3. But God, Who sent an angel to comfort Christ in His Passion, reassured Mary by the angel's voice: Fear not, thou hast found grace with God: Because thou dost esteem thyself the most unworthy, God will exalt thee to a dignity which seems almost beyond the power of God to confer. He will make thee the Mother of His Son. Oh, wondrous dignity of true humility!

> Mary, it was thy lowliness,
> Well pleasing to the Lord,
> That made thee worthy to become
> The Mother of the Word.

11TH DAY:
THE INCARNATION.

The Word was made flesh. (St. John i. 14.)

1. God would not take flesh in Mary's womb without her consent. The angel, after giving his message, awaited her reply. No false humility prevented Mary from obeying the mandate; no self-consciousness made her shrink back. In words which are a model of obedience and prudence and forgetfulness of self she accepted the divine maternity: "*Behold the handmaid of the Lord; be it done to me according to thy word.*"

2. One thing only was present to Mary's mind when she spoke these words: the wish to do exactly what God desired of her. This is the secret of all true virtue—to make His will the motive and the guiding principle of every action we do. If we do this we shall soon be saints. God speaks to our soul

by His *inspirations*, by the voice of our *superiors* or *spiritual directors*, and in other ways. Be attentive to the voice of God, and when you know His holy will, do it *promptly, generously,* and *perseveringly*.

3. When Mary spoke these words: "*Be it done to me according to thy word*" an event took place which seems incredible. The infinite God became of the same nature with one of His finite creatures. The union between Mary and her God became the most intimate possible to any created being. God became flesh of her flesh and bone of her bone. What must have been the more than angelic purity of her nature before her God came to dwell with her! What must have been her almost infinite dignity after He had taken flesh in her sacred womb!

> For the heaven He left He found heaven in thee;
> For He shines in thy shining, sweet star of the sea!

12TH DAY:
THE VISITATION

As soon as the voice of thy salutation sounded in my ears, the infant in my womb leaped for joy. (St. Luke 44)

1. Mary's first action after God had come to dwell in her was one of self-denying charity. She undertook a troublesome journey in order to visit her cousin Elizabeth. Thus she proclaimed charity to be the virtue which above all Christ brought with Him from heaven. "*By this shall all men know that you are My disciples, if you have love one for another.*" How can I stand this test?

2. God made Mary's visit the occasion of a wonderful miracle. On her entrance into St. Elizabeth's dwelling, St. John Baptist was cleansed from sin in his mother's womb. Mary was the channel of the exceptional privilege of the cleansing away of sin in the case of the unborn child. As then

so now: Mary is the channel of all graces, and above all, of the restoration of the sinner to friendship with God.

3. Mary's charity is not less present now than at the time of the visitation. Nay, she is far more eager now than then to promote the happiness and console the sorrows of those who fly to her for succor. Why do not I obtain more graces and blessings than I do through Mary's intercession? It is no fault of hers—it is, alas! because I am proud, self-willed, obstinate, selfish, indifferent.

> Mother of God, star of the sea,
> Pray for a wanderer, pray for me!

13TH DAY:
MARY'S TIME OF EXPECTANCY

Joseph, son of David, fear not to take unto thee Mary thy wife: for that which is conceived in her, is of the Holy Ghost. (St. Matt. i. 20.)

1. In due course of time it became evident that Mary was to be a mother. She had said not a word to St. Joseph about the angel's visit, and her holy spouse knew not what to think. Yet she was still silent. She left it to God to vindicate her in His own good time. How different her conduct from my eagerness to justify myself.

2. St. Joseph, like a faithful and prudent man, did not act without due deliberation. How miserable he must have been during those weeks of hesitation. He could not suspect Mary of evil; yet there was the clear evidence of fact. The true solution was one that no one could have supposed possible. He contemplated sending her away quietly—what an agony to lose his precious spouse! Yet patiently and prudently he waited and prayed.

3. God does not forsake His servants in their distress. An angel by night announced to Joseph that he was the spouse of the Mother of God—the foster-father of the King of heaven.

What joy must have inundated his soul! how he must have cried out in the joy and gratitude of his heart: *The Lord is indeed good to those who hope in Him!*

Jesus, Mary, and Joseph, I give you my heart and my soul.

14TH DAY:
THE NATIVITY

She brought forth her first-born Son: and called His name Jesus.
(St. Matt. i. 25.)

1. Mary brought forth her Son in poverty and humiliation. She had been slighted and scorned. No room was found for her in the inn. In the cave where the ox and ass are stabled, the Mother of God brought into the world the King of kings. Oh, blessed humiliation! Oh, happy poverty! You are the indications that God is going to do a great work—where you are absent, we cannot expect lasting and solid fruit.

2. How Mary rejoiced in this humiliation! how she welcomed such poverty as this! How could she fail to rejoice in it, with Jesus in her arms? If we are wise we shall pray for humiliation, for without it we never can have the divine infant Jesus for our own companion: we never can bring Him forth in the souls of others; we must be humbled if He is to exalt us: we must be poor in spirit if we are to be blessed in our work.

3. Mary could say of Jesus as no other mother ever said of her first-born son: He is mine and mine alone. Every other son has an earthly father who has a share in his begetting: Jesus had no father save His Father in heaven. Thus He was Mary's own child, her sole property and possession. What union could be more close (the hypostatic union alone excepted) than that of Mary and Jesus?

Holy Mother of God, pray for us!

15TH DAY:
MARY'S PURIFICATION

After the days of her purification according to the Law of Moses were accomplished, they carried Him to Jerusalem, to present Him to the Lord. (St. Luke ii. 22.)

1. Mary's purification! How strangely the phrase sounds in our ears! What purification could be needed for her, who was the pattern and model of all purity? Yet Mary remained retired for forty days after the birth of her Son; and then went up to the Temple, as if to be purified. Why was this? It was because she loved obedience to the law, even though obedience might result in her being misunderstood. She sought no exemption from its precepts.

2. But she had another reason for her purification. She was to take part in her Son's work of Redemption, and therefore had to share His reproach. He chose the road of contempt. He was circumcised, as if a sinner; baptized in the Jordan with sinners, as if a sinner; and Mary's joy was to tread the path with Him.

3. Mary presents her divine Son in the Temple, renewing on that day her consent to the sacrifice of His life for the sins of the world. She saw with agonizing presentiment all that He had to suffer—dimly at first and vaguely, but none the less painfully—yet joyfully she made the sacrifice. She spared not her own Son, but delivered Him up for us all. Live to-day a life of detachment.

> Joy, joy, the Mother comes,
>   And in her arms she brings
> The Light of all the world,
>   The Christ, the King of kings.

16TH DAY:
SIMEON'S PROPHECY TO MARY

And thy own soul a sword shall pierce. (St. Luke ii. 35.)

1. At these words of holy Simeon all Mary's joy was changed to sorrow. Her divine Son was to be a sign that would be contradicted. His life was to be one long series of disappointments, outrages, insults, ill-usage from those He had come to save. Who can describe the grief of Mary at hearing this? Her darling Son, her God, was to be persecuted even to the death.

2. From that time forth Simeon's words were ever present to her mind. There came up before her all the prophecies, the full meaning of which she had not realized before. She remembered holy David's words, "*They pierced My hands and My feet,*" and she thought as she watched the divine Infant of His eventual crucifixion. The cry of the Psalmist, "*My God, why hast Thou forsaken Me?*" reminded her of the dereliction of His human soul. From this time forward she was indeed the Mother of sorrows.

3. Yet God in thus giving Mary so large a share in the sorrow of her Son was manifesting His special love for her. "*Whom the Lord loveth He chastiseth.*" (Prov. iii. 12.) Mary's chastisement was great in proportion to His love for her. If we remembered this we should welcome suffering, not shrink from it, and say in real earnest:

> Holy Mother, pierce me through,
> In my heart each wound renew
> Of my Saviour crucified.

17TH DAY:
THE FLIGHT INTO EGYPT

Arise, and take the Child and His Mother, and fly into Egypt.
(St. Matt. ii. 13.)

1. It was not long before Mary experienced how true Simeon's prophecy was to be. In the night, as she slept with the

divine Infant by her side, she was aroused by St. Joseph, who ordered her to prepare to leave their home and to go forth into the darkness—and whither? To Egypt, the land of Israel's foes; far away across the desert, where they would be unknown and despised. What a trial for Mary's obedience!

2. The command, moreover, seemed so harsh and arbitrary; surely the omnipotent God could have provided for the safety of His own Son in a thousand ways without imposing a long and painful journey. Yet Mary murmured not. If I had received such a command, would I have yielded a willing and uncomplaining obedience?

3. Watch Mary in her preparations; how prompt, how orderly! She is thanking God for this trial as she gets ready what is necessary for the journey. How cheerful she is! how she makes the best of everything! how she consoles St. Joseph by her thoughtfulness, her charity, her never-failing good humor! What a model to us when unforeseen annoyances arise! The only way to make our crosses light is to accept them cheerfully, as Mary did.

Mary, model of resignation, pray for us!

Refuge in grief, star of the sea,
Pray for the mourner, pray for me!

18th Day:
Mary's Life at Nazareth

Besides Thee what do I desire upon earth? (Psalm lxxii. 25.)

1. When the holy family returned from Egypt, they took up their abode in a little cottage at Nazareth. Yet that cottage was the closest approximation to heaven upon earth that ever has been or ever can be found. There dwelt the omnipotent God, the Queen of heaven, the protector of the whole Church of God. This poor and humble dwelling was chosen by almighty

God as the most suitable abode for those He loved best.

2. What an unspeakable joy and consolation it must have been to Mary to dwell for those years in familiar conversation with Jesus! To carry in her arms her God, *hers* as He was none other's, flesh of her flesh, bone of her bone! to enjoy His sweet caresses! to hear Him call her Mother! to gaze on the unveiled countenance of God made flesh! What an ecstasy of happiness for Mary!

3. What happiness, too, Mary found in the company of her chaste spouse, St. Joseph! No husband was ever so thoughtful as Joseph, none so gentle, so unselfish. Such a tower of manly strength! What a pleasure it was to her to obey him! How she watches for every expression of his will! How promptly, joyfully, loyally she carries it out! Is this the way I behave to those to whom I am subject?

> Oh, nought did Jesus love on earth
> So tenderly as thee!

19TH DAY:
Mary's Loss of Jesus for Three Days

Thy father and I have sought Thee sorrowing. (St. Luke ii. 48.)

1. When Jesus was twelve years old, He went up with His parents for their annual visit to the Temple. On their return they missed Him, and for three days sought Him, and sought Him in vain. What must have been the agony of Mary's heart during those three days! Had Jesus left them never to return? Could it be that she had unconsciously, by some negligence, forfeited the privilege of the company of Jesus? Was she never to behold Him again? Such were thoughts that occurred to her in the piercing anguish of her heart. Let us compassionate the holy Mother of God in her desolation.

2. What a cruel void in Mary's heart! The light of her eyes and the joy of her heart had gone from her. What an

utter blank all else seemed without Jesus—how could she live without Him? Without Him life would be death. *"How shall I comfort thee, O Virgin daughter of Sion? for great as an ocean is thy sorrow."*

3. Mary, then, can understand our sorrow in times of darkness and desolation. No blackness of desolation in our hearts is ever like the desolation of Mary—when she had lost Jesus. In all our anguish we will cry to her. She will not be deaf to our despairing cry, but will most surely succor us and restore to us peace and joy, as to her there returned peace and joy unspeakable when she found her divine Son in the Temple.

Mother of sorrows, pray for us!

Hear, sweet Mother, hear the weary,
Borne upon life's troubled sea!

20th Day:
The Death of St. Joseph

Precious in the sight of the Lord is the death of His saints.
(Psalm cxv. 15.)

1. For nigh thirty years Joseph had been the faithful spouse of Mary, the gentle foster-father of Jesus. But now the time came for him to die. How tenderly Mary nursed him in his failing strength! How she delighted in supplying all his wants, in ministering to them during the day, in watching by his side during the night! What a model to us who often grow weary with the long sickness of some invalid whom we are tending!

2. St. Joseph's death! Model of a happy death! What joy to die in the arms of Jesus and Mary! to be consoled by the Queen of heaven! to receive the last blessing from God Incarnate! No wonder that *he* is the patron of a happy death, since from the beginning of the world there was none whose death was surrounded with such glorious privileges and blessings as his.

3. How had Joseph procured so happy a death?

(a) By waiting for God's guidance in all his actions and promptly following it.

(b) By his devotion to Mary and to Jesus.

(c) By his patience, meekness, prudence, gentleness, purity.

Imitate St. Joseph. Pray to him for a happy death.

Jesus, Mary, and Joseph, I give you my heart and my soul!
Jesus, Mary, and Joseph, assist me in my last agony!
Jesus, Mary, and Joseph, may I die in peace in your blessed company!

21st Day:
Mary at Cana

Whatsoever He shall say to you, do ye. (St. John ii. 5.)

1. Jesus' first miracle was performed at the marriage-feast at Cana. Thither Mary was invited, and from the words of the Gospel it seems as if Jesus was invited because His Mother had been already asked. Thus we learn that where Mary comes Jesus is sure to come also. He who entertains her with love and devotion will find that the love of Jesus will soon spring up in his heart.

2. During the marriage-feast the wine runs short. Our Lady notices it; it grieves her; she appeals to her Son in a model prayer. She simply states the need, and leaves all else to Him: "*They have no wine.*" Like this should be our prayers. Jesus likes us to tell Him our needs; He knows them, but He makes prayer a condition of fulfilling our desires.

3. Jesus' words at first seem a rebuke: "*Woman, what is it to Me, and to thee?*" He often pretends to turn a deaf ear to us. How does Mary behave under the seeming slight? She regards it as a sign that He will grant her request, and turning to the servants bids them obey Him in all things. "*Whatsoever He shall say to you, do ye.*" Mary knew that it is to the submissive

and obedient that Christ gives His best gifts. May the most blessed and holy will of God be done in all things! Amen.

> My Lord, my God, what willest Thou?
> Thy blessed will is mine!

22ND DAY:
MARY DURING OUR LORD'S PUBLIC LIFE

Whoever shall do the will of My Father that is in heaven; he is My brother, and sister, and mother. (St. Matt. xii. 50.)

1. When Our Lord left the cottage at Nazareth and went forth to enter on His public ministry, what an aching void must have been left in Mary's heart! How her heart must have yearned to be with Him! Earth was indeed for her a barren waste as long as He was away. Have we any of this love of the company of Jesus? any desire to seek Him out where He awaits us in the tabernacle, that we may enjoy sweet intercourse with Him?

2. Yet Mary murmured not. She was willing to sacrifice for the good of others even the solace of Jesus' presence. She knew that by her obedience she would be united to Him in bonds far more intimate than the bonds of the closest earthly union. Therefore in joy and in sorrow, in consolation and desolation, whether Christ was with her or far away, her only desire was to submit to the holy will of God.

3. Mary by her prayers and tears and intercession took part in Our Lord's work. He had decreed that His Mother thus should help Him in His public ministry. Though He could do all, He left something for her to do, as He does for all the saints. What a happiness and privilege this! I, too, can take my part in the redemption of mankind!

> Queen of sorrows, guide and guard me,
>   Let me to thine arms repair;
> In thy tender bosom hide me,
>   Mary, take me to thy care!

23RD DAY:
MARY MEETS JESUS CARRYING THE CROSS

Bearing His own cross He went forth to that place which is called Calvary. (St. John xix. 17.)

1. As the time of the Passion drew near, Mary's realization of the approaching sufferings of her Son became more vivid. The sword of Simeon pierced her heart as it had never done before. How could she endure to see her Son and her God outraged and ill-treated, insulted, and put to death? *"Weeping, she hath wept in the night: there is none to comfort her among all them that were dear to her."* (Lament, i. 2.)

2. At last the storm of anguish burst upon her. The apostles bring her the heart-breaking news: He has been seized by the Pharisees, insulted by the soldiers, dragged before Pilate, scourged, condemned to the death of the cross. What a night and morning for the Mother of Jesus! Each moment full of an agony worse than death.

3. At last she could refrain no longer. She must go and meet Him Whom her soul loved. What a meeting must that have been! Her darling Son all masked in blood, toiling under the weight of the cross. Oh, holy Mother, who would not be moved with compassion? *"Attend, and see if there be any sorrow like to my sorrow."* (Lament, i. 12.)

> O thou Mother! fount of love!
> Touch my spirit from above,
>   Make my heart with thine accord;
> Make me feel as thou hast felt;
> Make my soul to glow and melt
>   With the love of Christ my Lord.

24TH DAY:
MARY AT THE FOOT OF THE CROSS

There stood by the cross of Jesus His Mother. (St. John xix. 25.)

1. What words can ever describe the indescribable anguish that rent the sacred heart of Mary as she looked upon

her divine Son hanging on the cross! Was there ever such a spectacle? He is so torn and mangled, covered with a mantle of blood from head to foot, that one can scarcely recognize in that unsightly figure the human form. Can it be He, the fairest among the children of men? My God, what can have transformed Him into this piteous, this ghastly object?

2. Every wound in Jesus' body was also a wound in the heart of Mary: every fibre, every nerve throbbing in agony. Every pang He suffered reechoed in her heart. She endured by her *compassion* a share in all the anguish of His Passion. What was the thick darkness around compared with the black darkness that overspread her heart!

3. Why did Mary suffer all this? That she might be our Mother—the Mother of mankind. She who brought forth her divine Son without a pang suffered many a piercing pang when from the cross her dying Son commended to her the sinful sons of men. That was indeed a maternity of sorrow she suffered for our sins: for mine.

> Jesus, when the three hours were run,
> Bequeathed thee from the cross to me.
> How can I rightly love thy Son,
> Sweet Mother, if I love not thee?

25TH DAY:
Jesus is Placed in His Mother's Arms

My God, My God, why hast Thou forsaken Me? (St. Matt, xxvii. 46.)

1. These words must have echoed in Mary's heart when the body of her divine Son was placed in her arms. She was alone! Jesus was dead. She had heard His last cry of agony, and seen the spear pierce His sacred side. She was alone! Oh, Mary, what must have been thy desolation now that thy Son and thy God was no more! Listen to her words: "*Therefore do I weep, and my eyes run down with water: because the comforter of my soul is far from me.*" (Lament, i. 16.)

2. Watch the holy Mother as she washes the blood from the body of her Son! How she kisses each wound with adoring love! Amid all her desolation there is nevertheless an underlying fount of joy at knowing that those wounds have wrought the salvation of the world, that in the paradise of God they will shine like jewels to all eternity.

3. In this mingled joy and sorrow Mary is *especially* full of love for sinners, and she loves them because they cost her so much anguish and because her divine Son loved them so dearly that for them He suffered and died. Mary loves me because I am a sinner—this at least may comfort and encourage me—Jesus died for me because I am a sinner.

> Oh, give me tears to shed with thee
> Beneath the cross on Calvary.

26TH DAY:
MARY SEES JESUS LAID IN THE SEPULCHRE

Where thy treasure is, there is thy heart also. (St. Matt. vi. 21.)

1. When Mary had finished the mournful task of preparing the sacred body of her Son for burial, the disciples carried Him to the sepulchre in the garden of Joseph of Arimathea. Watch that mournful procession, and realize, if you can, the desolation of Mary's sacred heart. All her hopes, all her joys, all her affections, were buried with Jesus. He was her one and only treasure, and where her treasure was laid, there was her heart also.

2. Mary amid all her anguish had experienced a strange and melancholy pleasure in embracing the dead body of her Son and performing for it the last offices of love. She knew, too, that though the human soul was parted from it, the divinity was still there. She could adore with the highest worship that mangled form, those limbs livid and cold. But now she was

separated even from that sacred body. How empty, how blank, was all around without Jesus!

3. Yet Mary, in spite of her desolation, was never dejected, never gloomy. She was full of joy and peace. In the anguish of her separation from Jesus she was more than comforted by the knowledge that all His sufferings were past, and that He had already begun to see the fruit of His travail. Those who love God more than themselves have always a fount of consolation in every sorrow.

> By the hope thy name inspires,
> By our doom reversed through thee,
> Bring us, Queen of angel choirs,
>   To a blest eternity!

27th Day:
Jesus Appears to Mary after the Resurrection

According to the multitude of my sorrows in my heart;
Thy comforts have given joy to my soul. (Psalm xciii. 19.)

1. Holy Scripture tells us nothing of Our Lord's appearance to His blessed Mother after His Resurrection. It takes it for granted that He must have appeared first to her. He who doubts it has but a poor understanding of Mary's part in the work and life of Jesus. As she was first in sharing His sufferings, so she was of necessity first in being partaker of His joy.

2. How Mary had been longing and praying for the Resurrection! It is a pious belief that for her sake those three days were shortened. How eagerly she had been expecting the dawn of that first Easter Day! She had been saying over and over again to herself, "*I know that my Redeemer liveth.*" She knew that the darkness would in God's time usher in a glorious morning. This should be my comfort when all seems dark. I, too, must pray and wait.

3. What a meeting must that have been! All her anguish was more than compensated by the ecstasy of her joy at beholding her divine Son, radiant with heavenly beauty, conqueror over hell and death. See how she falls at His feet in a rapture of delight! See how He raises her up with words of love! Who can tell the exquisite delight of hearing such words from Jesus' lips?

> See the Mother's fond embrace,
> See her joy to view Thy face!
> When all bright in radiant bloom
> Thee she welcomed from the tomb.

28TH DAY:
MARY THE MOTHER OF THE INFANT CHURCH

Her children rose up and called her blessed. (Prov. xxxi. 28.)

1. When Our Lord ascended into heaven, we are told that the apostles went back to Jerusalem with great joy (St. Luke xxiv. 52). But there was none of them so joyful as Mary. Her sacred heart overflowed with happiness and delight. The greatest possible joy for her was thus to witness the triumph of her Son and to hear the angels welcoming the King of glory to His throne in heaven.

2. Yet Mary's life must have been one long desire after heaven, more so than ever after Jesus had ascended. Still she had no wish even for the heavenly paradise as long as it was God's will that she should remain on earth. She was quite content to wait. Am I resigned and patient when the will of God contradicts my inclinations and desires?

3. Why was Mary left on earth? To comfort and sustain, to instruct and advise the first disciples of Christ. None knew like her the secrets of His Sacred Heart; none had such an instinctive perception of what He would desire in the many doubts and difficulties that arose; none could impart such

sweet consolation to the afflicted. How often the disciples beheld in her their Mother! In heaven she is still our comforter, adviser, guide.

> The Mother sits all worshipful,
>   With her majestic mien;
> The princes of the infant Church
>   Are gathered round their Queen.

29TH DAY:
MARY'S DEATH

Precious in the sight of the Lord is the death of His saints.
(Psalm cxv. 15.)

1. During the years which succeeded Our Lord's Ascension Mary had been making a progress in holiness and perfection which surpassed all that had gone before. She had become more and more a partaker of the divine nature, more and more like to the image of her divine Son. What a contrast I am to Mary! Yet at least I can admire her and rejoice in her unspeakable perfections.

2. At length the time came when this soul, so exquisitely beautiful, was too beautiful for earth to detain longer. She had long been languishing with love—yearning after her Beloved. Her death was not like that which we call death. She had no sickness, no pain. She died simply of love, of her insatiate desire for God. Do I long for the presence of God, for the day when I shall behold Him face to face?

3. Why was Mary's death such a triumph, such a scene of peace and joy and heavenly consolation? Because she was sinless. The sting of death is sin. It was also because she had stood by her Son's deathbed of the cross, and shared by her compassion in His agony. In return for this, Jesus Himself came to receive the sacred soul of His dear Mother. All the angels of heaven were present there, singing sweet melodies.

> O happy, happy death!
> If death indeed could be,
> Blest Virgin, that sweet end
> Which God bestowed on thee.

30TH DAY:
MARY'S ASSUMPTION INTO HEAVEN

*Thou wilt not leave my soul in hell; nor wilt Thou give
Thy holy one to see corruption.* (Psalm xv. 10.)

1. On the third day after Mary's death, when the apostles gathered around her tomb, they found it empty. The sacred body had been carried up to the celestial paradise. Jesus Himself came to conduct her thither; the whole court of heaven came to welcome with songs of triumph the Mother of the divine Word. What a chorus of exultation! Hark how they cry, "*Lift up your gates, O ye princes, and be ye lifted up, O eternal gates, and the Queen of glory shall enter in.*"

2. Why was Mary's body received into heaven instead of remaining in the earth, like the rest of mankind? The grave had no power over one who was immaculate. Her flesh could not see corruption. Her body had been overshadowed by the Holy Ghost; it had been the sacred temple in which had dwelt God Incarnate, and so it had a claim to ascend whither the body of her Son had already gone before.

3. But the chief reason was that as she had shared in each detail in the sorrows and agony of her Son, so it was right that she should take part in His triumph. To her it was due that she should without delay enter into the joy of her Lord, her Son, her God. Oh, happy Mary! what were all her dolors compared with the joy of that first moment of heaven! How light are all our sorrows compared with the eternal weight of glory prepared for us!

> See the Virgin Mother rise,
> Angels bear her to the skies!

31st Day:
Mary's Coronation as Queen of Heaven

The Queen stood on Thy right hand in gilded clothing.
(Psalm xliv. 11.)

1. It was not enough that Mary should be received into heaven. She was to be no ordinary denizen of the celestial court. Mary was, by her perfect and unfailing conformity to the will of God throughout her life, raised to a pre-eminence to which none other of the saints could attain. By her cooperation in the Passion of her Son she had a dignity beyond the reach even of the highest of the archangels. Mary was to be crowned Queen of heaven by the eternal Father: she was to have a throne at her Son's right hand.

2. Mary, too, enjoyed a happiness different from that of all the other saints. All others knew that if they had been more faithful they might have been more full of happiness. Though their happiness is perfect, it is not perfect with the same perfection as Mary's. She possesses all that it was possible for God in the present order to bestow upon her. What must be her happiness now! short only of the infinite happiness of the infinite God!

3. But Mary is not Queen of heaven only for her own sake, but also for ours. Day by day, hour by hour, she is praying for us, obtaining graces for us, preserving us from danger, shielding us from temptation, showering down blessings upon us. She is our dear Mother as well as Queen of heaven. How she loves us! What a confidence we should have in her! Once more we will cry out:

> O Mary, conceived without sin!
> O Mary, Queen of heaven!
> Pray for us who have recourse to thee.

REMEMBER, O most gracious Virgin Mary! that never was it known that any one who fled to thy protection, implored thy help, and sought thy intercession, was left unaided. Inspired with this confidence, I fly unto thee, O Virgin of virgins, my Mother! To thee I come; before thee I stand, sinful and sorrowful. O Mother of the Word Incarnate! despise not my petitions, but, in thy mercy, hear and answer me. Amen.

Ejaculation

O Mary, who didst come into this world free from stain!
Obtain of God for me that I may leave it without sin.

Mary, thy Heart

Mary, thy heart for love
   Alone had ever sigh'd;
So much it loved at length,
   Of very love it died.
O happy, happy death;
   If death indeed could be,
Blest Virgin, that sweet end
   Which God bestowed on thee.

Tis in a sweet repose,
   With smile of heavenly mirth,
Thou takest joyful flight
   To paradise from earth:
And see! above the choirs
   Of saints and angels bright,
God's Mother near her Son
   Enthroned in dazzling light.

Come, then, to fetch thy child,
   O Mary, Mother dear;
And tarry by my side
   When my last hour is near.
Yes, this I hope from thee—
   Despise not my request—
To yield my soul in peace
   Upon my Mother's breast.

Devotions for Confession
(Read Instructions XXX and XXXI, pages 126-134)

Prayer before Confession

Come, Holy Ghost, enlighten my understanding that I may rightly discern the sins of which I have been guilty; touch my heart and move it to sincere contrition; strengthen my will that I may make a firm resolution of amendment; grant me Thy grace that in the Sacrament of Penance I may confess my faults to the priest with sincerity and humility, and give me such assistance as may enable me to produce worthy fruits of penance.

Mary, Mother of mercy, refuge of sinners, pray for me that I may make a good confession and be reconciled to thy divine Son. Pray for my confessor also, that he may speak to my heart, and that his words may conduce to the health of my soul. *Hail Mary, etc.*

EXAMINATION OF CONSCIENCE FOR YOUNG WOMEN

PRELIMINARY EXAMINATION ON YOUR LAST CONFESSION

1. How long is it since I last went to confession?
2. Did I take sufficient pains to awaken contrition?
3. Did I omit to confess a mortal sin, either intentionally or through forgetfulness?
4. Did I intentionally neglect to say the penance which was imposed on me, or was I so careless as to forget it?
5. Have I carried out the resolutions I then made, or have I paid no heed at all to them?

Examination on the Ten Commandments of God

The First Commandment

On our conduct in regard to God and divine things.

Sins against faith:

1. Have I entertained and yielded to doubts against the faith?
2. Have I allowed myself to listen to those who spoke with contempt or derision of our holy faith?
3. Have I ever willingly omitted my morning or night prayers?
4. Have I spoken irreverently of holy things?
5. Have I taken pleasure in hearing sacred things spoken of with disrespect?
6. How often have I read books, newspapers or periodicals of an anti-Catholic tendency?

Sins against hope:

1. Have I deliberately despaired of God's mercy?
2. Have I rashly presumed upon His forbearance in order to commit sin?
3. Have I given way to pusillanimity with full consent?
4. How often have I allowed myself to commit a venial sin under the plea that it did not amount to anything?

Sins against charity:

1. Have I willingly entertained feelings of repugnance toward religious practices, such as prayer, attendance at divine service, etc.?
2. Have I murmured against the ordinances of divine providence, the trials and sufferings sent upon me, etc.?

Sins against the reverence due to God:

1. Have I made use of superstitious practices or consulted fortune-tellers?

2. Have I omitted prayers, genuflections, the sign of the cross or other religious duties through motives of human respect?

3. Have I been guilty of voluntary distraction at my prayers?

4. Have I wilfully caused disturbance during public worship?

5. Have I spoken with levity of sacred objects and places?

6. How often have I done what is good more from a desire to please than from any better motive?

THE SECOND COMMANDMENT OF GOD

1. Have I in any important matter taken God to witness in what was untrue, or have I sworn falsely?

2. Have I voluntarily broken an oath, or failed to fulfil a vow?

3. Have I taken God's name in vain, or uttered it without respect?

4. Have I sworn rashly, or used God's holy name as an imprecation?

5. Have I called God to witness without sufficient reason?

6. Have I postponed the fulfilment of a promise without any necessity?

THE THIRD COMMANDMENT OF GOD

On the observance of Sundays and holy days.

1. Have I omitted hearing Mass on any Sunday or holy day of obligation without a good reason? How often?

2. Have I on Sundays or holidays indulged voluntary distractions during Mass?

3. Have I done any servile work without necessity on Sundays or holy days?

THE FOURTH COMMANDMENT OF GOD

On our duty toward parents and superiors.

In regard to the respect that is due parents and superiors:

1. Have I been disrespectful in my behavior toward my parents, toward priests or other superiors?
2. Have I imagined them guilty of grievous sins, or exaggerated their faults?
3. Have I offended against them by using contemptuous or injurious language toward them?
4. Have I been wanting in my duty to my parents, and judged their actions unlovingly or uncharitably?
5. Have I shown them disrespect by word or act?
6. Have I been ashamed of my parents on account of their poverty or their infirmities?

In regard to the love due to parents and superiors:

1. Have I in earnest and deliberately wished evil to my parents, my pastor, or others in authority over me?
2. Have I ever intentionally grieved them?
3. Have I neglected to succor my parents in their necessities, although it was within my power to do so?
4. Have I injured them in any manner through my own fault?
5. Have I shown impatience at the rules made by my parents and superiors, or irritability at their failings?
6. Have I neglected to pray for my parents and my pastor?

In regard to the obedience due to parents and superiors:

1. Have I been disobedient to my parents, my confessor, or my superiors, in any important matter?
2. Have I obeyed their directions or admonitions grudgingly, or neglected them altogether, in minor matters?
3. Have I shown annoyance at their advice and paid little heed to it?

THE FIFTH COMMANDMENT OF GOD

1. Have I been guilty of injuring any one's health through culpable negligence, through quarrels or unkind treatment?

2. Have I shown enmity or rancor toward my neighbor, as, for instance, by refusing to return his greeting?

3. Have I uttered imprecations and evil wishes against my neighbor?

4. Have I taken little or no pains to suppress feelings of hatred and hostility?

5. Have I been guilty of quarrelling with my neighbor, and how often?

6. Have I punished children when I was angry?

7. Have I rejoiced in my neighbor's adversity?

8. Have I neglected to give alms through avarice, or through indolence omitted any work of mercy that I ought to have performed?

9. Have I done anything in word or deed which I foresaw would cause my neighbor to sin, such as speaking improperly in the presence of children, dressing indecorously, etc.?

10. Have I actually tempted another to commit a deadly sin, and if so, what sin?

11. How often have I led my neighbor to commit a venial sin?

12. Have I ever intentionally led him to do wrong?

Sins against one's own life:

1. Have I injured my health by indulging to an excess in amusements, by intemperance, or outbursts of anger?

2. Have I, when vexed and impatient, desired my own death?

3. Have I eaten or drunk immoderately, or studied my palate too carefully?

4. Have I not sometimes injured my health through want of ordinary prudence and precaution?

5. Have I often given way to anger and impatience?

6. Have I often yielded to dejection and sadness?

THE SIXTH AND NINTH COMMANDMENTS OF GOD

On our conduct in regard to purity.

Impure thoughts:

1. Have I with pleasure allowed my thoughts to dwell on impure subjects?

2. Have I consented to unchaste suggestions and temptations instead of banishing them instantly from my mind?

3. Have I wished to look at unchaste objects, or to take improper liberties?

Impure words:

1. Have I talked in an unchaste manner?

2. Have I taken pleasure in listening to unclean conversation?

Impure actions:

1. Have I willingly, and with a sinful pleasure looked at immodest things? Committed an immodest act?

2. Have I read books of an immoral tendency?

3. Have I dressed immodestly or with excessive finery simply to attract admiration?

4. Have I sinned through undue familiarity with persons of the other sex, or allowing improper liberties to be taken with me?

5. Have I been careful to avoid persons and places which may be, or have been, occasions of sin for me?

6. Have I been to dances and plays of a dangerous nature, and how often?

THE SEVENTH AND TENTH COMMANDMENTS OF GOD

On our conduct in regard to the property of others.

1. Have I been guilty of causing any considerable damage to my neighbor in his house or property?

2. For how long have I wilfully delayed to make due satisfaction and restitution?

3. Have I, when at home, pilfered trifling sums or things to eat?

4. Have I disposed of things belonging to my employers or others without their knowledge? And if money, to what amount?

5. Have I desired my neighbor's goods, not caring whether I acquired them justly or unjustly?

6. Have I wasted my money in prodigal expenditure as, for instance, on dress and finery?

7. Have I through my negligence, indifference, or indolence caused loss, even to a slight extent, to my employers or relatives?

THE EIGHTH COMMANDMENT OF GOD

On our conduct in regard to truth.

1. Have I ever borne false witness in a court of law?

2. Have I told a falsehood in any matter of consequence?

3. Have I entertained, without sufficient ground, a bad opinion of my neighbor and taken his wrongdoings for granted through rash judgment?

4. Have I calumniated my neighbor, accusing him of wrongdoing of which I did not know him to be guilty?

5. Have I injured my neighbor's good name and lessened his reputation in any great measure by detraction?

6. Have I, for any length of time, voluntarily neglected to make good the injury done him, to the best of my ability?

7. Have I written anonymous letters in abuse of any one, or to cause misunderstanding and quarrels?

8. Have I repeated to my neighbor the ill that I heard said of him?

9. How often have I said what was not quite true to save myself from blame, or in a joke?

10. Have I entertained unfounded suspicions of my neighbor?

11. Have I judged uncharitably of the actions of others?

12. Have I published the faults and misdeeds of others without necessity?

13. Have I been guilty of deceit, insincerity, flattery, or hypocrisy? How often?

THE COMMANDMENTS OF THE CHURCH

1. Have I deliberately and without sufficient reason eaten meat on abstinence days?

2. Have I, being at least twenty-one years of age, eaten more than one full meal on the fasts of the Church?

3. Have I listened to the addresses of a non-Catholic with a view to marriage?

Act of Contrition

O MY GOD, I am heartily sorry for having offended Thee, and I detest all my sins, because I dread the loss of heaven and the pains of hell, but most of all because they offend Thee, my God, Who art all-good and deserving of all my love. I firmly resolve, with the help of Thy grace, to confess my sins, to do penance, and to amend my life.

Resolution of Amendment

I Humbly beseech Thee, my Lord and Savior, mercifully to forgive me, and to receive me once more into Thy favor. I detest and abhor all my sins, and I promise Thee, my God, to do better for the time to come. Henceforth I will love Thee above all things and will avoid all occasions of sin, so that I may not have the misfortune to fall again into my old transgressions. Jesus, mercy! Jesus, my Lord, my God, and my all!

Prayer for the Grace to Persevere

Lord, Thou knowest my frailty and weakness; my resolution is indeed firm and heartfelt, yet Thou must fortify me if I am to carry it into practice. O Thou Who hast inspired me with the determination to cast off the yoke of sin, strengthen my will, that I may perform that which I purpose. In Thee, O God of might, I can do all things. Manifest in me, therefore, omnipotent God, the abundance of Thy mercy, and arm me with the power necessary to preserve me from falling into sin. Succor me in danger, protect me from the snares of the spirits of evil, and awaken within me an implacable hatred of every kind of wickedness. Amen.

Clementissime Jesu

O Most compassionate Jesus! Thou alone art our salvation, our life, and our resurrection. We implore Thee, therefore, do not forsake us in our needs and afflictions, but, by the agony of Thy Most Sacred Heart, and by the sorrows of Thy immaculate Mother, succor Thy servants whom Thou hast redeemed by Thy most precious blood. Amen.

Additional titles available from
St. Augustine Academy Press
Books for the Traditional Catholic

Titles by Mother Mary Loyola:

Blessed are they that Mourn
Confession and Communion
Coram Sanctissimo (Before the Most Holy)
First Communion
First Confession
Forgive us our Trespasses
Hail! Full of Grace
Heavenwards
Holy Mass/How to Help the Sick and Dying
Home for Good
Jesus of Nazareth: The Story of His Life Written for Children
The Child of God: What comes of our Baptism
The Children's Charter
The Little Children's Prayer Book
The Soldier of Christ: Talks before Confirmation
Welcome! Holy Communion Before and After

Titles by Father Lasance:

The Catholic Girl's Guide
The Young Man's Guide

Tales of the Saints:

A Child's Book of Saints by William Canton
A Child's Book of Warriors by William Canton
Illustrated Life of the Blessed Virgin by Rev. B. Rohner, O.S.B.
Legends & Stories of Italy by Amy Steedman
Mary, Help of Christians by Rev. Bonaventure Hammer
The Book of Saints and Heroes by Lenora Lang
Saint Patrick: Apostle of Ireland
The Story of St. Elizabeth of Hungary by William Canton

Check our Website for more:
www.staugustineacademypress.com

www.ingramcontent.com/pod-product-compliance
Lightning Source LLC
Chambersburg PA
CBHW031559170426
43196CB00031B/78